Mathematics Content
for Elementary Teachers

DATE DUE

GAYLORD			PRINTED IN U.S.A.

Mathematics Content for Elementary Teachers

Douglas K. Brumbaugh
Peggy L. Moch
MaryE Wilkinson

LAWRENCE ERLBAUM ASSOCIATES, PUBLISHERS
2005   Mahwah, New Jersey   London

Lawrence Erlbaum Associates, Inc., Publishers
10 Industrial Avenue
Mahwah, New Jersey 07430

Cover design by Kathryn Houghtaling Lacey

Library of Congress Cataloging-in-Publication Data

Brumbaugh, Douglas K., 1939–
    Mathematics content for elementary teachers / Douglas K. Brumbaugh, Peggy L. Moch,
MaryE Wilkinson.
        p.   cm.
    Includes bibliographical references and index.
    ISBN 0-8058-4247-0 (acid-free paper)
    1. Mathematics—Study and teaching (Elementary).   I. Moch, Peggy L.   II. Wilkinson,
MaryE .   III. Title.

QA135.6.B768   2004
327.7—dc22   2004050674
                                                             CIP

Books published by Lawrence Erlbaum Associates are printed on acid-free paper,
and their bindings are chosen for strength and durability.

Printed in the United States of America
10 9 8 7 6 5 4 3 2 1

In loving memory of Pat and Web Brumbaugh
To Shawn, Mike, Jennifer, and Laura, Doug's kids
To Linda Brumbaugh, simply the best

In loving memory of Elma McGrew Moch,
Flossie Jenkins McGrew, and Mary Wheeler Jenkins,
who all cherished and encouraged their children to learn
despite being denied the opportunity for much
of a formal education of their own.
To Julie, Peggy's favorite and only child

To Grady

To all our teachers
To students: past, present, and future

Contents in Brief

Contents

7   Problem Solving   203

8   Reasoning and Proof   209

Preface

TO THE STUDENT

What is mathematics? You are probably wondering just what sort of question that is for someone who has completed the general education mathematics prerequisites. It is an important question because your own opinions and attitudes will influence your teaching of mathematics for your entire career. Whether or not you are conscious of the process, you are already defining and redefining your personal practical theories about teaching. These theories are deep-seated beliefs that may result from your nonteaching experiences as a student or parent and be influenced by your practical experiences in designing and implementing curriculum as you teach (Cornett, 1990, p. 188). You may find it difficult to articulate your personal practical theories. However, they will significantly influence your students' attitudes about the mathematics that they will learn.

The dictionary defines mathematics as "the study of quantity, form, arrangement, and magnitude; especially the methods and processes for disclosing, by rigorous concepts and self-consistent symbols, the properties and relations of quantities and magnitudes, whether in the abstract, pure mathematics, or in their practical connections, applied mathematics" (Funk & Wagnalls, 1968, p. 835). How does this formal, dictionary definition of mathematics compare with your own opinion? How will you define mathematics to others, especially children?

As an elementary educator, you will be expected to teach children in a variety of subject areas. In this text, the focus is on one content area—mathematics. To teach mathematics, you will need a significant command of the foundations of elementary school mathematics content. If a teacher is not competent and confident with the subject matter, then there may be barriers to creating a positive experience best suited for each student. We want you to understand what some of these barriers are and how you can begin to prepare yourself to avoid them by building a strong foundation in mathematics content.

As you go through this text, you will see that we present you with multiple ways of doing arithmetic operations. We do that to help you help your future students. You will find that not all students think the same way. Furthermore, you will learn that not all students will understand how you do some arithmetic. Having command of several ways to do a given arithmetic operation, combined with your knowledge of your students, enables you to select a method of doing the work that has a better chance of connecting with students.

Our main purpose is to introduce the "what" and the "why" of teaching mathematics; in other words, elementary school mathematics content. In many of the chapters, you will find hints about the "how" of teaching mathematics to children, but we do not develop instructional concepts in depth. It is expected that, later in your educational program, you will enroll in a mathematics methods course. In such a course, the groundwork we establish will be expanded and you will learn to use effective methods to teach children mathematics. The hints we provide are intended to help you with your quest to gain the content proficiency that will equip you to make the most of your mathematics methods course.

Focal Points

Teaching Mathematics to ALL Students. The National Council of Teachers of Mathematics (NCTM) has developed a document called *Principles and Standards for School Mathematics* (NCTM, 2000), which presents the position that an effective teacher of mathematics will be able to motivate all students to learn. We agree with this position. It is important for all students to develop a strong basis in elementary school mathematics because it is the key to many opportunities. Mathematics opens doors to educational opportunities and careers, enables informed decisions, and helps us compete as a nation. We want to help you develop the ability to absorb new ideas, adapt to change, cope with ambiguity, perceive patterns, and solve unconventional problems (Mathematical Sciences Education Board [MSEB], 1989). This is an important lesson because we know you will need to pass these skills along to your students in the rapidly changing world of the 21st century.

Understanding How Children Learn. Our own opinions about child development have been influenced greatly by the seminal works of visionaries such as Dewey, Piaget, Bruner, Vygotsky, and Montessori. We believe that children of all ages benefit from learning experiences at each of four developmental levels. Children at the "concrete" level need a physical object to manipulate. At the "semi-concrete" level,

they are able to understand a connection between the concrete object and a pictorial representation of that object. At the "semi-abstract" level, they might move to a visual aid, such as a tally, which is not an actual picture of a real object. At the "abstract" level, they will understand mathematics using only numbers and symbols. We will not establish ages at which you should expect children to move from one level to the next. You will find that children need a spiraling strategy, with the initial introduction of each concept at the "concrete" level. Children learn by experiencing mathematics and there are windows of teaching opportunities that must be recognized and used effectively. Finally, we believe that children must take center stage in the classroom. Teachers should give up the role of sage on the stage and concentrate on what children need to become active participants in the learning environment. Frequently, teacher telling, which has children being passive learners—like they are sponges who should be soaking up every word the teacher utters—is the model used.

Learning by Doing. In this book you will find that we introduce mathematics content concepts in ways that you may not have seen before. An effective teacher of mathematics continues to investigate new mathematical concepts and teaching strategies. Such a teacher is a lifelong learner, always ready to investigate new ideas or an alternate way of doing something familiar. Children think in different ways as they develop, so we will be presenting concepts at the four distinct developmental levels: concrete, semi-concrete, semi-abstract, and abstract. Your own elementary school teachers may have skipped one or more of these levels, teaching most often at the semi-abstract or even abstract level. If you sometimes feel as if we are treating you like the children you will someday teach, then you are right! It is not that we want to treat you like elementary schoolchildren, but we believe you must experience mathematics at each level if you are to understand how children learn and then help them master the tasks placed before them. At the same time, you will find relatively few algorithms in this text as we focus on the "what" and "why." We don't really think that you need help with algorithms. This text will mention manipulatives as learning tools. Anything that helps a person learn mathematics might be called a *manipulative*. We believe that you will be aided in your use of manipulatives in your classroom if we introduce some of them and ask you to solve problems using them. If you were not taught using manipulatives, then you may find their use not easy or natural for you—but keep in mind that children do not learn as you were taught. Use your experiences as you learn to exercise your "concrete" or "semi-concrete" brain to understand how difficult it is for children to learn an abstract concept.

We Believe That Every Child Can Learn. Children will not learn at the same rate or in the same way. We hope that you will set the following goal for yourself: I will do all I can, including learning all the mathematics content I will need, to help each child learn to value mathematics as well as how to do mathematics. This text contains many features to help you accomplish this goal. We have tried to keep the reading at an informal level and have provided a glossary for the terms with which you may not be familiar. Rather than write about general school mathematics, we have concentrated strictly on the mathematics that is taught in elementary schools. We have spaced the activities and exercises throughout each section; rather than assignments at the ends of chapters, you will find brief sets that immediately follow discussions.

TO THE INSTRUCTOR

The major objective of this text is to help the prospective teacher of elementary school mathematics learn content beyond the rote level; to stimulate your students to think beyond "getting the problem right." Our experiences have shown that if the ideas expressed in this text are used with prospective teachers of elementary school mathematics, then the likelihood of their development into thoughtful, reflective, self-motivated, lifelong learners is much greater. We encourage you to challenge your students to achieve that status.

Although there are many excellent texts available that combine mathematics content and methods in creative ways, we believe there is a need for a text that stresses the "what" and "why" of elementary school mathematics content. We provide hints about "how" elementary school mathematics should be taught, but we leave most of the methods part for later course work and a text that is dedicated to that purpose. It is important to reverse the current trend of combining elementary and middle school mathematics content. The audience for this text is preprofessional teachers in elementary education programs. We focus all of our attention on the mathematical needs of prospective teachers at this level, giving us the luxury of sufficient space to carefully develop concepts starting at the concrete level and building to the abstract level.

To gain and hold both the attention and the trust of preprofessional elementary school teachers, we write informally. Often the needs of prospective teachers at this level are better addressed when they are allowed to feel as comfortable as possible with the discussions. We provide brief activities and exercises immediately following short discussions and easy access to complete solutions. We have spaced them more frequently, so that your students will practice for shorter times but complete many activities.

The text is based on several fundamental premises. First, we, as teachers of mathematics, do not have the right to mark the work of any student "wrong," if that student does not use exactly the procedure we recommend. We believe that the focus of mathematics needs to be on the process, not the answer. Thus, the students using this text need to become proficient in understanding the foundations behind doing a problem so they can adapt their thinking to interpret the work they will see from their students. To that end, they must move beyond thinking that the way they do a problem is the only way it can be approached.

Second, we believe that teachers of mathematics should consider three axioms (Dr. Joby M. Anthony of the University of Central Florida mathematics department, personal communication, May 26, 2003):

1. Know the content being presented.
2. Know more than the content being presented.
3. Teach from the overflow of knowledge.

Third, being a teacher who is flexible enough to allow a student to use different procedures, who knows the content, and who teaches from the overflow of knowledge implies knowing how to do a given operation more than one way and being willing to examine many different ways. Thus, it is imperative for prospective teachers of elementary school mathematics to learn how to carefully cover the topics to be taught, to reflect on them, and to be able to organize them. Further, this thinking and organizing needs to be done well in advance, to al-

low time for the ideas to germinate and blend in the prospective teacher's subconscious mind so that they can connect topics from different lessons throughout the course. To help your students concentrate on the mathematics content, they will be expected to teach and begin to build the groundwork for the methods they will use, we have not included middle school concepts.

Based on these premises, in this text we do not focus solely on "pure" mathematics content, but also include hints about topics that are typically found in mathematics methods texts. We do this because we know that, in reality, mathematics content and methods of teaching are closely connected. Thus, in addition to mathematics content, you will find:

- Different approaches to present to students for doing operations and problems
- Methodology
- Suggested problems and classroom activities
- Use of technology
- References to current school theory and practices

OVERVIEW OF CONTENT

The text is built around the standards expressed by NCTM in "Principles and Standards for School Mathematics" (2000). Standards 2000 will dictate the basic sections for the text. For example, the first major section is headed "Number and Operations" (Standard 1 in *Standards,* 2000). Within each section, appropriate specific topics will be developed, intertwined with technology, problem solving, assessment, equity issues, planning, teaching skills, use of manipulatives, sequencing, and much more. The text is organized into 11 chapters:

1. Guiding Principles
2. Number and Operations
3. Algebra
4. Geometry
5. Measurement
6. Data Analysis and Probability
7. Problem Solving
8. Reasoning and Proof
9. Communication
10. Connections
11. Representations

PEDAGOGICAL FEATURES

Questions, exercises, and activities are interspersed within the sections. We believe students will progress more effectively if they are given several small and varied opportunities to practice as opposed to larger ones like those typically found at the end of a chapter.

Pedagogical features of the text:

- Informal reading with a focus on the preprofessional teacher
- Purpose: The "what" and "why" of elementary school mathematics, with brief hints about "how" to teach
- Concentration on the mathematics taught in elementary school grades
- Brief sets of activities or exercises immediately following discussions
- Complete solutions for exercises
- Discussions organized according to NCTM standards
- A focus on multiple methods of problem solving at four developmental levels

REFERENCES

Bruner, J. S. (1986). *Actual minds, possible worlds.* Cambridge, MA: Harvard University Press.

Bruner, J. S. (1996). *The culture of education.* Cambridge, MA: Harvard University Press.

Cornett, J. (1990). Utilizing action research in graduate curriculum courses. *Theory into Practice, 29*(3), 187–195.

Dewey, J. (1997). *How we think.* Mineola, NY: Dover. (Original work published 1910)

Dewey, J. (1948). *Experience and education.* New York: Macmillan. (Original work published 1938)

Funk & Wagnalls. (1968). *Standard college dictionary* (text ed.). New York: Harcourt, Brace, & World.

Mathematical Sciences Education Board. (1989). *Everybody counts.* Washington, DC: National Academy Press.

Montessori, M. (1965). *The Montessori method; scientific pedagogy as applied to child education in "the Children's Houses" with additions and revisions by the author* (A. E. George, Trans.). Cambridge, MA: R. Bentley. (Original work published 1912)

Montessori, M. (1967). *The discovery of the child* (M. J. Costelloe, Trans.). Notre Dame, IN: Fides Publishers.

National Council of Teachers of Mathematics. (2000). *Principles and Standards for School Mathematics.* Reston, VA: Author. [http://www.nctm.org/tcm/tcm.htm]

Piaget, J. (1952). *The child's conception of number* (C. Gattegno & F. M. Hodgson, Trans.). London: Routledge & Kegan Paul.

Piaget, J. (1999). *The child's conception of geometry* (E. A. Lunzer, Trans.). London : Routledge. (Original work published 1960)

Vygotsky, L. S. (1978). *Mind in society: The development of higher psychological processes.* Cambridge, MA: Harvard University Press. (Original work published 1934)

Vygotsky, L. S. (1987). The development of scientific concepts in childhood. In R. W. Rieber & A. S. Carton (Eds.), *The collected works of L. S. Vygotsky* (N. Minich, Trans., Vol. 1, pp. 167–241). New York: Plenum.

Personal Acknowledgments

Dr. Gina Gresham came into our lives near the end of this writing. Dr. Gresham left the State University of West Georgia and joined the mathematics education faculty of the University of Central Florida in August 2003. Dr. Gresham read the entire manuscript in its final stages and offered a plethora of useful suggestions. We are grateful to her for her contribution and look forward to working with her.

Dr. Michael Reynolds has provided a brief description of a very real condition called math anxiety, which hinders mathematics achievement in people of all ages. We invite you to take a careful look at this summary (see p. 7) and to review his ongoing work, as well as the work of other researchers, in this important area. We thank Dr. Reynolds for his valuable contribution to our effort.

We offer a special thanks to the following undergraduate students who read the manuscript in its formative stages: Crystal Jackowski (University of Central Florida), Wendy Lane (Valdosta State University), Michelle Backes (Valdosta State University), and Emily M. Hunter (Valdosta State University).

Naomi Silverman has again served as the supportive, cooperative, encouraging, helpful, guiding editor. Such a joy to work with! Thanx again Naomi.

We once again thank Dr. Gina Gresham. She prepared the Index section of this book. Thanks again Gina! Well done!

We are grateful to the wonderful staff at Lawrence Erlbaum Associates, particularly Lori Hawver. Lori was always available to answer our many production questions. Class act! Thanx again Lori. Eileen Meehan has provided invaluable guidance and assistance as our production supervisor. Thanx Eileen.

Last, but certainly not least, are our respective families. They sacrificed a lot so we could create this text, and it is appreciated. To some extent we have become one big blended family, which is a wonderful experience. Thanks to each of you for your support in this adventure.

About the Authors

DOUGLAS K. BRUMBAUGH

I am a teacher. I teach college, in-service, or K–12 almost daily. I received my BS from Adrian College, and went on to the University of Georgia for my master's and doctorate degrees in mathematics education. As I talk with others about teaching and learning in the K–20 environment, my immersion in teaching is beneficial. Students change, classroom environments change, the curriculum changes, I change. The thoughts and examples in this text are based on my experiences as a teacher. Classroom-tested success stories are the ideas, materials, and situations you will read about and do. This text's exercises and activities will stretch you while providing a beginning collection of classroom ideas. Learn, expand your horizons, and teach.

PEGGY L. MOCH

I had the good fortune to have wonderful teachers as I was growing up that encouraged me to be the best at whatever I was interested in at the time. I became a medical laboratory technologist in the late 1970s, but in the early 1990s I decided to go back to school to become a teacher of mathematics. I studied medical technology in Aurora, Colorado, obtained a BS

and MEd in mathematics education and a PhD in curriculum and instruction with an emphasis in mathematics education at the University of Central Florida in Orlando, Florida. I have always loved mathematics and took the opportunity afforded me by this book to share the passion my teachers ignited in me with all you in the hope that zeal will continue to spread. Mathematics is in everything, it is unavoidable. Embrace the challenge, be enthusiastic, and watch your own love for mathematics grow!

MARYE WILKINSON

I am a teacher because of the wonderful teachers I had, including Dr. Brumbaugh. My degrees were earned at the University of Central Florida. I taught mathematics to high school students for 9 years, then began work on my doctorate and my new found love for teaching mathematics and mathematics methods to preprofessional elementary school teachers. I am humbled when I realize how rich and deep the concepts of mathematics for children are! I am always delighted when a young person teaches me something new. My teaching days are spent with college students; my field days are spent with many of those same college students and the children who will be their students. Who could ask for a better job?

1
Guiding Principles

Although we hope you will be a lifelong learner, we know that your focus will soon turn from learning mathematics to the art of teaching mathematics to children. It is possible that this will be the last formal course you will take in mathematics content. Because you are enrolled in this course, we know that you have successfully learned a significant amount of mathematics content, either from your own elementary, middle school, high school, and college teachers or on your own.

Much of your study during this term will review material that is familiar to you. We want you to look at concepts from different points of view. In order to successfully help children learn mathematics, you will need more than the ability to do mathematics. You will need a profound understanding of the mathematics you will be expected to teach. You will need to know which concepts are easy to learn, which are difficult to learn, and just what makes each concept easy or hard. This means that you must accept the challenge to probe deeply into elementary school mathematics content, expanding and solidifying your knowledge into a powerful base of content knowledge from which you may draw as you help children learn and understand mathematics. We call this *pedagogical content knowledge* (Shulman, 1986) because it is a class of knowledge that is held almost exclusively by expert teachers.

In *Principles and Standards for School Mathematics*, the National Council of Teachers of Mathematics invites you to "imagine a classroom, a school, or a school district where all students have access to high-quality, engaging mathematics instruction" (NCTM, 2000, p. 3). The environment in which such a dream can come true will exist only if you, as the classroom teacher, have a deeply reflective pedagogical content knowledge so you can provide rich curricula and help your students learn and understand the important concepts of elementary school mathematics. It is on these central concepts that your future students will rely as they find their ways through their higher educations. You must prepare for a future that will require an ever greater understanding of mathematical concepts in your personal life, workplace, and scientific and technical communities. In the *Principles and Standards for School Mathematics*, NCTM identified six principles for school mathematics (pp. 10–27).

THE EQUITY PRINCIPLE

Excellence in mathematics education requires equity—high expectations and strong support for all students. (NCTM, 2000, p. 12)

We can no longer consider mathematics to be an enrichment subject for the most able students. We cannot allow mathematics to be the separator between the haves and the have-nots. Individuals who hold a limited mathematical background and understanding are severely handicapped as they select a career. Furthermore, studies now indicate that individuals entering the 21st-century workforce will change careers up to five times over their working years. Changing careers implies a revamped education with each new selection. Persons who do not possess fundamental mathematical skills and understandings will have difficulty finding options that allow for a limited mathematical background. Every elementary school teacher must be ready to help all students learn and understand mathematics. In every classroom, you will find students ranging from those with deep and abiding interests and talents in all academic subjects to those with special educational needs in some or all subjects.

Traditionally, certain groups of students have been viewed with reduced expectations. Some of these children live in poverty, aren't fluent in English, or have learning disabilities. Additionally, female and non-White students have been victims of lowered teacher expectations. Your pedagogical content knowledge must be sufficient to facilitate learning for all.

Simply being able to do arithmetic will be insufficient to the task you have set for yourself. Your goal must be to have the ability to teach mathematics as component parts and as an integrated whole, to identify each student's academic need, and to provide the exact amount of support needed by that student. You will be responsible for helping each student obtain a common elementary foundation of mathematics. To do this, you must solidify your own pedagogical content knowledge so you can maintain high expectations and provide strong support for each and every one of your future students. In your mathematics methods course, you will learn a variety of techniques for putting your pedagogical content knowledge to use in lesson planning and teaching.

THE CURRICULUM PRINCIPLE

A curriculum is more than a collection of activities; it must be coherent, focused on important mathematics, and well articulated across the grades. (NCTM, 2000, p. 14)

To say that the mathematics curriculum in elementary schools is arithmetic is insufficient because it gives the impression that you only need to be proficient in arithmetic to teach it to children. The foundations of mathematics must be formed in elementary schools, which means that children will need the underpinnings of many interwoven strands of mathematics. Arithmetic is certainly one of those strands, but it is not the only one.

Some preprofessional elementary school teachers have told us that they want to teach kindergarten, first, or second grade because the early grades require less arduous mathematics. This is simply not true. The foundations of important mathematics strands, such as algebra and geometry, are formed very early in the lessons of the elementary school mathematics curriculum. Mathematics must not be broken into discrete, disconnected bits. You may not be involved in designing the curriculum for your school or grade level, but you will most certainly be responsible for organizing lessons that teach the power of interconnected strands of mathematics. You will find that you must understand and be proficient in the elementary school mathematics of all grade levels in order to be an effective teacher. A reflective knowledge of the concepts taught in the classes before and after the grade level to which you are assigned will help you focus on the important mathematics your students already know and will need to learn before they move on. You will be one rung of their ladder of learning and you must help them deepen and extend their understanding of mathematics.

Whether you are assigned to kindergarten or sixth grade, your curriculum will include foundational concepts such as the Base 10 numbering system, place value, sets of numbers, proportionality, and functions. These foundational concepts will support your students as they work to connect and extend their ideas through mathematical reasoning, conjecturing, and problem solving. Additionally, concepts such as symmetry will help your students see life's beauty. Modeling problems on real-world phenomena will help them recognize the importance of quantitative literacy. You can see that the daily mathematics curriculum of your classroom will significantly depend on the extent of your pedagogical content knowledge.

THE TEACHING PRINCIPLE

Effective mathematics teaching requires understanding what students know and need to learn and then challenging and supporting them to learn it well. (NCTM, 2000, p. 16)

Your decisions and actions in your classroom will determine what your children learn. Consider your own elementary school experiences: Which memories are rich and satisfying and which memories are disappointing and lacking? It is very likely that each memory is linked to a teacher and that teacher's ability to challenge and support you as you learned. You may not remember whether your teachers possessed profound knowledge of the subjects they were teaching, but you learned the most from those teachers who knew the most. Your ability, confidence in that ability, and your attitudes toward mathematics were shaped by your elementary school teachers. Take a few moments to reflect on how you will shape the abilities, confidence, and attitudes of your students.

Many elementary school teachers spend a great deal of time trying to understand the mathematics they are teaching. With college courses and certification examinations completed, they find that they simply don't have knowledge that is deep enough or flexible enough to teach mathematics to children. Some take years to become confident in their understanding of and ability to teach mathematics. These teachers reach high and go far by continuing to learn and grow in their knowledge of mathematics and mathematical pedagogy. Perhaps the best gift you can give your future students is to start today to be a self-reflective lifelong learner—a person who loves to learn and loves to help others learn.

What of the children who sit in a classroom while their teacher is striving to increase personal knowledge of the subject to become a more effective teacher? We cannot afford to ignore the needs of children while their teachers study to become proficient. We invite you to work during this term to construct and solidify a base of pedagogical content knowledge on which you can build during your mathematics methods course. That way, you will become a teacher who is capable of reaching the mathematical curricular needs of each student—and a lifelong learner who will continue to grow into an even stronger teacher.

THE LEARNING PRINCIPLE

Students must learn mathematics with understanding, actively building new knowledge from experience and prior knowledge. (NCTM, 2000, p. 20)

For many decades, there have been disagreements about what concepts in mathematics are important and how they should be taught. Traditionally, elementary school teachers have guided students in how to perform operations, isolating basic skills into discrete segments, and building incrementally toward higher order skills. This reflects a behavioral or information-processing point of view in which the teacher conveys the knowledge and the students record (supposedly memorize—without understanding what is going on) the steps involved. Whereas this may lead to proficiency in each skill, it does not necessarily lead to understanding or flexibility of knowledge. Students, who can follow memorized steps with precision and accuracy, often lack the ability to connect basic skills to problem situations; they simply don't understand when or why to apply these basic skills. That is why many students find it so difficult to solve word problems in which the required operations are not explicitly defined.

The daily experiences provided by teachers influence what and how students learn. The mathematics content provided in a classroom depends on the content knowledge of the teacher. If the teacher doesn't know the concepts required by the curriculum, those concepts may be poorly taught or even ignored. Additionally, teachers who are insecure about their own knowledge of mathematics often provide activities that are teacher centered—focusing only on following a given rule to get a single right answer. Students in such a classroom may learn algorithms without applications and will certainly learn teacher-dependent behaviors. Students adopt the teacher's mathematical insecurities. In contrast, a teacher who is secure and confident of the content—not only what is being taught, but also that which precedes and follows the particular concept being addressed—encourages student independence and delivers less rule-based, more heuristically based lessons, enabling students to recreate their thinking and find connections to applications of mathematics. To create autonomous learners, a teacher must have the content knowledge and confidence to select tasks that are appropriate for encouraging students to tackle hard material, explore alternate paths, and become tenacious, independent, problem solvers.

Foundational concepts are best taught at the concrete, or hands on, level. Manipulatives are important tools for building understanding of foundational concepts. When you think about how you learn, you may realize that manipulatives are needed when learning something new, even within your university courses. In this text, manipulatives such as Base 10 blocks, algebra tiles, Cuisenaire rods, number lines, colored chips, buttons, and coins are discussed and used. Some of your study time will be spent learning to use these tools.

Anything, at any age, that helps you understand can be considered a manipulative. Concrete learning experiences are certainly not limited to elementary age children. Think about your experiences as you learned to drive a car. Of course, you learned the rules of the road first so that you would not be a danger to yourself or others. But to learn to drive you actually got into a car or a simulator, grabbed the steering wheel, put your foot on the pedals, and drove. A car as a learning tool? Sure! We hope that you will make it a point to look for learning tools whenever and wherever they might be useful.

THE ASSESSMENT PRINCIPLE

Assessment should support the learning of important mathematics and furnish useful information to both teachers and students. (NCTM, 2000, p. 22)

One might think that a discussion of assessment has no place in a content course. Indeed, the discussion of how and when you will assess the mathematics learning of your students will be left for your methods course and classroom experiences. However, an early understanding of the purposes of assessment may help as you develop a focus on this important part of a teacher's responsibility.

The assessments to which you are subjected as a college student are summative. They are designed to determine what you have attained with respect to the instructional goals of the course and may be used to establish your grade for the course. However, you can use all of the activities of the course as personally formative assessments. As you examine your progress, you can make decisions about which concepts need to become the basis of further investigations and which only need polishing efforts.

Feedback from formal and informal assessment tasks provided by your instructor is intended to assist you in setting your learning goals and becoming a more independent learner. Even if feedback from the instructor is not provided for a task, you can examine your own completed work to determine if it represents your best effort, if it completely satisfies the task requirements, and if improvements are desirable. A good strategy is to enlist the support of a critical friend who is involved in the course with you. The folks who are taking this course with you may very well become your colleagues and establishing a rapport with them now may provide a support system for you later. Critical friends encourage and challenge each other based on examinations of one another's work and behaviors. In this way, you can gain formative assessments from several points of view.

Making personal assessment a vital, productive part of your education now will provide an understanding of and practice with summative and formative assessment that will aid you as you begin to determine assessment tasks for children.

THE TECHNOLOGY PRINCIPLE

Technology is essential in teaching and learning mathematics; it influences the mathematics that is taught and enhances students' learning. (NCTM, 2000, p. 24)

While you were in elementary school, did you have daily access to calculators and computers? Even if you were lucky enough to have significant exposure to classroom technology during elementary school, it is likely that your students will have access to technology that will be much more sophisticated than the devices you used. Now is the time for you to experiment and learn about some of the tools that will become commonplace as the 21st century continues.

Calculators and computers will not eliminate the need for you to be proficient in the basic skills of elementary school arithmetic. But the use of technology can save time and effort that can then be focused on decision making, reflection, reasoning, and problem solving. Using the tools of technology alongside your review of basic concepts will help you deepen and extend your understanding of when and why to use those concepts to make important connections within elementary school mathematics. It is important for students to memorize number facts and the functions involved in operational algorithms. Those certainly are a part of the curriculum. However, they are not the only part. Technology can provide opportunities to open a variety of windows for your students. Technology should not be used just to get answers. Skillfully used, technology can stimulate student learning and inquisitiveness into the world of mathematics.

An important aspect of learning mathematics is *conjecture posing*, an activity that is supported when more examples, representative forms, and possibilities can be investigated quickly and efficiently. You and your students will no longer be limited to easy problems because calculators and computers can provide computational and graphic power to support your inquiries into number sense, measurement, geometry, algebraic thinking, and statistics. With this support, you can examine real-life problems and connections much more efficiently and effectively than using paper and pencil.

We hope that you will take the time to examine as many different calculators as possible. You should begin your investigation with the four-function calculators that are generally available in the early grades, followed by scientific calculators, and, finally, graphing calculators. If possible, you should not confine your investigation to the machines commonly used in elementary schools, but rather experiment with different models. As the level of sophistication continues to increase, the more complex and powerful models will

appear in ever-earlier grades. You may begin your inquiry by visiting various Web sites provided by the manufacturers of different calculators:

Casio: http://www.casio.com/

Hewlett Packard: http://www.hewlettpackard.com/ (handheld/calculators)

Sharp: http://www.hewlettpackard.com/ (business/calculators)

Texas Instruments: http://education.ti.com

These Web sites are commercial, but provide a great deal of information about features and activities. Many of the manufacturers are willing to loan new models for review and classroom sets for examination and experimentation.

Visiting various Web sites will also provide a great deal of information about the software that is available for elementary school mathematics. Many programs can be described as plug-and-chug, simply transferring worksheets to the computer screen. Such programs are useful only as practice or review and we question the value of using a valuable tool like a computer as a drill machine. However, there are powerful programs available that allow and, indeed, encourage experimentation and learning of important concepts in all areas of mathematics. These are the computer programs on which we hope you will focus your investigation.

THE CHALLENGE

In this chapter, we have provided brief overviews of the six principles delineated in NCTM's *Principles and Standards for School Mathematics* (2000) to provide you with important information about the features of high-quality mathematics instruction. We have focused this discussion of equity, curriculum, teaching, learning, assessment, and technology on your role as a learner of the elementary school mathematics that you will be expected to teach. You should read and study this important document as you continue your education, extending your pedagogical content knowledge of mathematics with knowledge of teaching methods.

An earlier NCTM document, *Curriculum and Evaluation Standards for School Mathematics*, published in 1989, was the basis for the standards established in many states. This document, along with two other NCTM publications, *Professional Standards for Teaching Mathematics* (1991), and *Assessments Standards for School Mathematics* (1995), represented an important and historical attempt to explicitly articulate the goals of mathematics education in America. *Principles and Standards for School Mathematics* (2000) was written to revise and update the earlier documents.

Math Anxiety

Teachers who lack adequate mathematical preparation can foster math anxiety in their students. *Math anxiety* is a term that is often used to describe feelings of helplessness and nervousness that many individuals experience when they are expected to complete a mathematical task or assignment. Math anxiety is not limited to elementary students—it can become a lifelong condition for many people. People are not born with math anxiety; indeed, many educational specialists believe that most people develop math anxiety during elementary school. It is important, therefore, that you be aware of the threat of math anxiety and take active steps to avoid its inception in your future classroom.

The consequences of math anxiety are frequently detrimental. Those with math anxiety tend to perform at lower levels in mathematics classes and many adopt the behavior of math avoidance—choosing to enroll in the fewest (and easiest) mathematics courses. A single statistics course requirement or business mathematics course can be the difference between a student selecting a major they feel drawn to and choosing a major simply because it does not require an extra mathematics course. For these and other reasons, mathematics has been labeled a critical filter into the job market (Sells, 1978).

Cognitive and external factors such as intelligence, aptitude, and the quality of one's mathematical instruction may have a greater impact on achievement than math anxiety. However, recent findings indicate that math anxiety is more detrimental to achievement than any other psychological factor, including self-concept, self-efficacy, or the value that one places on mathematics (Reynolds, 2003). Motivation may be an extremely powerful factor in mathematics learning and teaching. Given the overpowering impact that math anxiety can have on mathematical motivation, the impact of math anxiety should not be underestimated.

Some common elementary classroom practices have been shown to cause math anxiety, including excessive drill and practice, a focus on answers rather than processes, excessive criticism of minor errors, embarrassment as a means of discouraging questions or mistakes, and inadequate class time spent helping students with mathematics. Many sufferers of math anxiety are able to recall the humiliation of a single negative episode as the reason for their math anxiety.

Although math anxiety is not a learning disability, it can disable those who suffer from it. As educators, we have a responsibility to be aware of the condition, to show respect and consideration, and to realize that math anxiety is not terminal— with patience and care, it can be reversed. According to Stuart (2000), "People like to do something if they think they are good at it, and to feel good about mathematics, you have to believe that you are good at it. Therefore, as teachers, we must be the mathematics coaches— the ones to build that self-confidence while refining the skills needed to be successful" (p. 334).

Where to From Here?

The success of this continuing effort to improve mathematics education in the United States will depend on you, the pre-professional classroom teacher, who will teach mathematics to children in the future. Your ability to fulfill this dream will depend to a great extent on your pedagogical content knowledge of elementary school mathematics. Increasingly, accountability is discussed in educational circles. Many states administer high stakes tests at several levels in public schools. Many teachers across the United States are providing sound educational experiences for their students—and many of those students are doing just fine on high stakes tests. Widespread suc-

cess on these tests seems illusive. There is no definitive information on how to prepare students for mandated evaluations, even though the results have serious implications for both students and teachers. Your challenge is to take the opportunity provided by this course to deepen and extend your knowledge of this vital and wide-ranging subject.

REFERENCES

National Council of Teachers of Mathematics (NCTM). (1989). *Curriculum and evaluation standards for school mathematics*. Reston, VA: Author.

NCTM. (1991). *Professional standards for teaching mathematics*. Reston, VA: Author.

NCTM. (1995). *Assessment standards for school mathematics.* Reston, VA: Author.

NCTM. (2000). *Principles and standards for school mathematics*. Reston, VA: Author.

Reynolds, J. M. (2003). The role of mathematics anxiety in mathematical motivation: A path analysis of the CANE model (Doctoral dissertation, University of Central Florida, 2003). *Dissertation Abstracts International, 64*, 435.

Sells, L. (1978). Mathematics a crucial filter. *Science Teacher, 45*(2), 28–29.

Shulman, L. (1986). Those who understand: Knowledge growth in teaching. *Educational Researcher, 15*(2), 4–14.

Stuart, V. B. (2000). Math curse or math anxiety? *Teaching Children Mathematics, 6*, 330–335.

2
Number and Operations

SETS

A firm understanding of the concept of sets establishes a critical background for the study of mathematics. We start by looking at collections of things. From there, we focus on how many things are contained in the set. Once we have that cardinal number (total number of elements in the set), the emphasis may shift to performing different operations with the numbers associated with sets. The basics of arithmetic are established through our work with sets. Once one has arithmetic under control, the sky is the limit.

Set Definitions

You have probably already encountered the concept of sets, so you undoubtedly have some idea of what the word means in a mathematical context. We could be talking about a set in a tennis match, a set for a play, the set for a lesson you are going to teach, or a set of dishes. Actually, any set of dishes begins very naturally to establish mathematical leanings because you might ask if the "service" is for 4, 6, 8, 10, or 12. Useful considerations are given to the numbers of different types of pieces in the set, including or excluding the service pieces. This is only one example of how we use the ideas of sets in our daily lives.

Mathematically, we may speak of a set in terms of a collection, a group, a flock, a gaggle, a herd, a bunch, a pile, some things, and so on. We can use a variety of ways of saying the same thing and, as long as the people in the conversation understand the desired meaning, the discussion continues without confusion.

Mathematicians are concerned that every set be well defined. If a set is well defined, then it is easy to tell whether or not something belongs to it. If we talk about the names of the people in your family, you might wonder if you should include grandparents, first cousins, second cousins, and so on. If one person in the conversation is not sure whether second cousins should be included or excluded, then the set is not well defined. At the same time, if you were asked to list the names of the people in your immediate family, typically you would interpret the set to include only your parents and siblings. That is fairly well defined, but where should a married person with children draw the line? Perhaps the definition "your immediate family" is not completely descriptive. The set of all the stars in our solar system is a clearly defined set, isn't it? How many items are contained in that set? Is the Earth in that set? Think of the set of clothes in your closet or drawers. Is it clear which items fit and which do not?

It is not reasonable to try to define a set without discussing the items contained in the set. Whether the items in a set are concrete (e.g., plates or bowls) or abstract (e.g., numbers), they are called *elements*. An element of a set is a member of the set, something that is in the set. Most of the time it is easy to tell what is and what is not a member of a set. More than likely, the sets you've seen have been made up of things with common themes: a set of dishes, a set of silverware, a herd of sheep, a flock of birds, a gaggle of geese, and so on. Those sets lead to the impression that the elements of a set must have something in common. This conclusion may seem reasonable, but it simply is not required.

Think of a classroom. If you were asked to list everything in it, what would you include? Desks (or tables and chairs), overhead projector, books, pads, pens and pencils, chalk (or markers), boards, erasers, carpet, and who knows what else. Would you list the people too? Suppose you do include people. If that whole collection of elements makes up the set we are discussing, then what is the commonality? One answer might be, "All of those things are in this room." Although that would be a shared characteristic, it is not a typical use. You could give a unified definition for the set of desks in your room, even if several different sizes or types of desks are present. You might also talk about the group of people and the connection is made. But, putting all of the things in one big set seems strange because of the lack of any shared characteristic (except being in the same room). Still, this is technically a well-defined set. There is no need for the elements of a set to have common attributes.

In the discussion about the members of your family and immediate family, the ambiguity of wording was easily corrected so the words gave an adequate description of the set. The set was described verbally, which is an important way of communicating the required image. Effective discussions may focus on verbal descriptions of all sorts of things that are common in people's lives: pets, things in a toy box, different kinds of shoes, or a myriad of other important real-life objects. Most of the time, these discussions are clear and the desired images are projected.

Another common way of discussing the elements of a set is to list all of the elements by name. Every teacher has a list of students in a grade book. Look at that list and you quickly know who is and is not supposed to be in the class. Santa Claus frequently calls his reindeer by name. Rudolph was added later in the story, so, for a long time, he was not listed as a member of the set of Santa's reindeer.

Sometimes sets are discussed using titles or names. An example of a set defined by a title is "Students." This is useful, but sometimes the issue of whether the set is well defined creeps back in. When you think of students, do you think of your current class and the people in it, all the students who matriculate at your college, children in elementary school, or some adult who might be a student of life? Even a name as simple as "Students" might not deliver a clearly defined message. The set $A = \{1, 2, 3, 57\}$ tells you what is being described. Set A has four elements: 1, 2, 3, and 57. You know what does and does not belong to this well-defined set and you have a quick, easy way of referring to the set—just call it Set A. Braces are commonly used when naming sets this way. Customarily, the beginning capital letters of our alphabet are used for naming sets in mathematics classes, but this is not mandatory. Later, you will encounter R, C, Z, and W as the names of sets of numbers.

Sometimes we can list all the elements of a set, as with A = {1, 2, 3, 57}, but that is not always possible or even desirable. When discussing the counting numbers, we generally call the set, N. However, we cannot possibly list all of them as we did with Set A. Please do not try this at home; even professionals on closed tracks don't attempt this chore. Why not? A solution for this dilemma is to use an ellipsis and write, N = {1, 2, 3, 4, . . .}. A couple of things happen right there. First, enough of a pattern is established to clarify what set of numbers is being discussed. Furthermore, the impression that things keep on following that pattern is established by those three dots, or ellipsis. When you see those, it means that the pattern continues. The continuation could be infinite, but sometimes it terminates.

In a large, but finite, set where the pattern stops, the ellipsis is still used, as shown by: B = {2, 4, 6, 8, . . . , 50}. What do you suppose that means? Do you see the even counting numbers, starting the pattern with 2, 4, 6 and continuing until it stops at 50? Did you notice that in the set notation you see 2, 4, 6, 8 and yet in the discussion we gave only 2, 4, and 6? That is not a big deal, as long as the pattern is clear. If in doubt, then you may insert additional elements of the pattern to avoid any possible confusion.

Sets can be written in a variety of formats. Often the environment and backgrounds of the participants determine how the set is expressed. The examples we discussed have included formal set

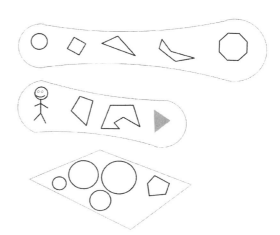

FIG. 2.1.

notation, using mathematical sentences and braces. Figure 2.1 gives ways of showing sets of things using looping. Figure 2.2 depicts things that are not examples of sets of things being looped.

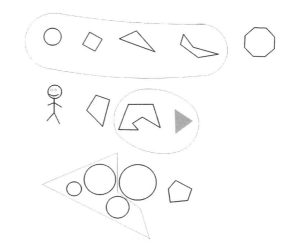

FIG. 2.2.

Your Turn

1. Based on the examples in Figs. 2.1 and 2.2, write a definition of what looping the elements of a set means.

Notice that we switched tactics on you. Initially we told you that a set was a collection, a group, a flock, a gaggle, a herd, a bunch, a pile, some things, and so on.

We told you about elements of a set and how a set would be well defined. That is a common way of doing business in the world of teaching mathematics, but it is not always the best way for you to learn things. We know that having you be an active participant in your learning is much better than if you are constantly being told. Research shows that you will retain 50% of the material if you participate within group discussions, 75% if you actually practice the skill, and 90% if you are given the opportunity to teach the material to others (National Training Laboratories, Bethel, Maine; http://www.gareal.org/learningpyramid.htm). We have provided an answer section and you could certainly look at it, which is equivalent to being told the answers. We hope you do not do that. The more you think about what is being discussed, the easier it will become, the better it will be for you, and ultimately, your future students will benefit.

Now that you know what sets and elements are and how to show things in different ways, we can deal with some of the other common terminology that accompanies sets. The following sets are finite:

A = {1, 2, 3, 57}.
B = {2, 4, 6, 8, . . . , 50}
The hairs on your head

These sets are not finite:

N = {1, 2, 3, 4, . . .}
The set of multiples of 3
The set of integers

Your Turn

2. Define the term *finite set*.
3. Define the term *infinite set*.

These last two exercises can be used to raise some interesting questions. Is the total population of the earth finite or infinite?

Most people would say finite, even though it is a very big number that changes because of births and deaths. Is the number of blades of grass on your campus finite or infinite? This gets a little more obscure, but most people would say it is finite. It might take a while to determine how many blades there are, but it is still finite. Extend that idea to all the campuses in the world, and you still have a finite number. Throw in all the yards, fields, pastures, and whatever other name you can come up with for a grassed area and the number will still be finite—huge, but finite. Well, how about the grains of sand at Daytona Beach? Finite. Put in all of the beaches in the world and the number of grains of sand is still finite—again, huge, but finite. Almost anything you name will be finite when counted. It is only when you shift to abstract ideas, like sets of numbers, that you get into the realm of the infinite.

Now that set is defined, we need to examine some other aspects of the topic. In each situation, we will give you examples and nonexamples of situations. Your task will be to extrapolate a definition from the information. Each of the following examples shows a set as a part of another set, or a subset:

{2, 7} is a part of {1, 2, 5, 7, 19}.
{Jo, Chris} is a part of {Jo, Chris, Pat}.
Dogs and cats are a part of the set of mammals.
{2, 4, 7} is a part of {7, 2, 4}.

The following are situations where the first set is not a subset of the second:

{Honda, Chevrolet} is not a part of {Historically American-made cars}.
{H, O, W} is not all part of {V, O, W, E, L}.
{2, 4, 6, 8, 11, 12} is not part of the set of even numbers.
{2, 4, 7, 8} is not part of {7, 2, 4}

Your Turn

4. Define the term *subset*.

Think about a set that has no elements in it, in other words, an empty set. Although that might sound strange, the empty set is an important part of the tools necessary to build our number system. Historically, the formalization of the idea of the empty set took a long time to develop. When a cave man looked at the cave walls of the next cave man over, it was easy to tell what the neighbor had. The pictures of three horses, four brontosauruses, and two chickens told the story. No pictures of cows on the walls made it clear that the neighbor had no cows. Before the idea of the empty set developed, nobody gave a second thought to that which was not listed. Thus, at least initially in our mathematical developmental history, the concept of an empty set was not even considered!

As times changed, there was a need to be able to say, "I do not have any cows." This was the beginning of the development of the empty set. Although you know the cave man discussion is a figment of our imaginations, you should see the major idea—the empty set depicts a set with no elements in it.

The empty set plays an important part in our lives. Have you ever passed a construction site and noticed a 55-gallon drum with "MT" written on the side in large letters. Say those letters fast, one after the other, and you get empty. The letters mean the drum is empty. That naming method is not normally seen in the school curriculum, but it accurately describes the situation for the members of the construction crew. In mathematics classes, we use either { } or ϕ to depict the empty set. A very common error is to use $\{\phi\}$ to represent the empty set. Use either

{ } or ϕ, but NEVER use the two symbols together. As soon as something is placed between the "{" and the "}", the set is not empty, even if the only element of the set is the symbol ϕ.

Another definition needed in the framework for using sets is demonstrated in the following examples of proper subsets:

{2, 7} is a part of {1, 2, 5, 7, 19}.

{Jo, Chris} is a part of {Jo, Chris, Pat}.

Dogs and cats are part of the set of mammals.

The empty set is a part of every set.

These are nonexamples of proper subsets:

{2, 4, 7} is a part of {7, 2, 4}.

{1, 2, 3, 4} is not a part of {2, 4, 6, 7}.

Your Turn

5. Define the term *proper subset*.

Improper subsets are generally discussed along with proper subsets. The following example of an improper subset coupled with your definition of proper subsets should help you create a definition for improper subsets:

{2, 4, 7} is an improper subset of {7, 2, 4}.

Your Turn

6. Define the term *improper subset*. How many improper sets may any set have?

We are now at a point in our discussion where we need to take the first steps toward developing the number system you use every day. One initial interest in a set often revolves about what is called the *cardinality*, or *cardinal number*, of a set. We would say:

The cardinality of {2, 4, *, ^} is 4.

The cardinal number of {3, ♥, ∇, ⊗, #} is 5.

The cardinality of the letters of our first names {M, a, r, y, E, P, e, g, g, y, D, o, u, g} is 11 because letters are not repeated when elements of a set are listed.

Your Turn

7. Define *cardinality*.

8. What is the cardinality of the empty set?

9. What is the cardinality of {φ}?

10. What is the cardinality of {BMW}?

A lowercase n is placed in front of the letter name of a set to express the cardinality of that set. If D = {0, 1, 2, 3, 4, 5, 6, 7, 8, 9}, then the cardinality of D is 10 and would be written n(D) = 10.

With the basic definitions established, we can investigate some interesting mathematical ideas. The set {3} has two subsets: { } and {3}. Of those two subsets, one is improper and one is proper. The set {7, $} has four subsets: { }, {7}, {$}, and {$, 7}. Of these four subsets, one is improper and three are proper. The set {13, ℘, &} has 8 subsets: { }, {13}, {℘}, {&}, {13, ℘}, {13, &}, {℘, &}, and the set itself or {13, ℘, &}. Of these, one is improper and seven are proper subsets. A set with four elements has 16 subsets. You should list them and observe the patterns that are forming:

# elements in set	# improper subsets	# proper subsets	# subsets
1	1	1	2
2	1	3	4
3	1	7	8
4	1	15	16

Your Turn

11. Generalize the pattern established by the total number of subsets as the number of elements in the set is increased one element at a time.

12. A set with 11 elements will have _____ subsets, _____ of which are improper, and _____ of which are proper.

13. Is there a case where the number of proper and improper subsets will be equal? Is there more than one case? Why or why not?

Now that cardinality of sets has been introduced, the definitions of finite and infinite sets should be revised. Finite sets have cardinality, whereas infinite sets do not have a defined cardinal number. Sometimes it is said that the cardinality of any infinite set is infinite. That may seem like saying a rose is a rose and yet, in our language, infinite is how we name never-ending situations if elements are being counted.

Two more ideas grow directly from the concepts of sets and their cardinality: equal and equivalent.

{$, 5, ♦} is equal to {$, 5, ♦}

{∃, &, ∠, } is equal to {∃, &, ∠, }

{3, BMW} is equal to {BMW, 3}

{$, 5, ♦} is equivalent to {B, M, W}

{∃, &, ∠, } is equivalent to {5, ♦, ∠, }

{3, BMW} is equivalent to {BMW, 8}

Your Turn

14. Define *equal sets* and *equivalent sets*.

15. Which tells you more about two sets: equal or equivalent? Why?

For the next few exercises, we will provide statements and ask you to formulate more definitions:

{∃, &, ∠, } and {5, ♦, ∠, } are overlapping sets.

{∃, &, ∠, } and {5, ♦, 83, 409, ∠, } are overlapping sets.

{3, BMW} and {3, 4, 5, 6} are overlapping sets.

{3, BMW} and {∃, &, ∠, } are disjoint sets.

{A, B, C, D, E, F} and {312, 409, 513} are disjoint sets.

{1, 2}, {Buckle my shoe}, {5, 6}, and {Pick up sticks} are disjoint sets.

{1, 2, 3, 4, 5, . . .} can be partitioned into {1, 3, 5, . . .} and {2, 4, 6, . . .}.

The shoes I wear can be partitioned into right or left.

Triangles can be partitioned into equilateral, isosceles, and scalene.

Your Turn

16. Define *overlapping sets*.
17. Define *disjoint sets*.
18. Define a *partitioned set*.

Another subset idea that needs to be carefully defined is when we want to talk about everything BUT the subset. Let A = {s, t, a, r}, where two subsets could be formed like B = {a} and C = {s, t, r}. The subset B is all the vowels in A and C is all of the consonants in A. Together, B and C, would form A. So far, that isn't anything new. Mathematicians look at the relation between B and C and say C is everything in A BUT the elements in B. They call a set with such a set with such a correlation the complement of B. This can be written symbolically in a variety of ways: $\overline{B}$, ~B, or B′. We will use the notation B′ to represent the complement of a subset. If C is the complement of B, or C = B′, then what is implied about B to C? The complement of C is B, or B = C′. This association will exist anytime a set is split into two disjoint parts such that all of the elements of the original set are accounted for by the subsets.

Your Turn

19. Define *complements of sets*.

Set Operations

We operate (add, subtract, multiply, divide, raise to a power, . . .) on numbers. We can also operate on sets, but the operations are different from those applied to numbers. We talk about 3 + 4, but it would be inappropriate to talk about A + B, where A and B are names of sets. With that in mind, consider the following examples of set operations where ∪, ∩, and X represent union, intersection, and set multiplication, respectively:

{1, 2, 3, 4} ∪ {5, 6, 7} =
  {1, 2, 3, 4, 5, 6, 7}

{1, 2, 3} {4} ∪ {7, 8, 15} =
  {1, 2, 3, 4, 7, 8, 15}

{1, 2, 3, 4} ∪ {5, 6, 4} = {1, 2, 3, 4, 5, 6}

{1, 2, 3, 4} ∩ {5, 6, 4} = {4}

{1, 2, 3, 4, 5} ∩ {3, 4, 5} = {3, 4, 5}

{1, 2, 3, 4} ∩ {5, 6, 7} = { }

{1, 2} X {A, B} =
  {(1, A), (1, B), (2, A), (2, B)}

{C,D} X {3,4} = {(C,3), (C,4), (D,3), (D,4)}

{A, 1, &} X {♣, ▽} =
  {(A, ▽), (1, ▽), (&, ▽), (A, ♣), (1, ♣), (&, ♣)}

The set operation of subtraction is related to the complement of a set idea and is called the *relative complement* of a set.

The relative complement of A to B is written B − A and can be read, "The complement of A relative to B" or "The set difference between B and A." This operation is used between any two sets that intersect. Revisit the two previous statements about intersection:

$$\{1, 2, 3, 4\} \cap \{5, 6, 4\} = \{4\}$$
$$\{1, 2, 3, 4, 5\} \cap \{3, 4, 5\} = \{3, 4, 5\}$$
Let A = {1, 2, 3, 4}, B = {1, 2, 3, 4, 5},
  C = {5, 6, 4}, and D = {3, 4, 5}.

Observe the following examples of relative complements:

A − C = {1, 2, 3}   the complement of C
                    relative to A is {1, 2, 3}
C − A = {5, 6}   the complement of A
                    relative to C is {5, 6}
B − D = {1, 2}   the complement of D
                    relative to B is {1, 2}
D − B = { }   the complement of B
                    relative to D is { }

Your Turn

20. Define ∪ (the union of sets).
21. Define ∩ (the intersection of sets).
22. Define X (set multiplication or set product).
23. Define *relative complement* (set subtraction).
24. State a generalization about the cardinalities of sets and their union.
25. State a generalization about the cardinalities of sets and their set product.

Special Sets

Some sets will occur often throughout this text. They are commonly used in the world of mathematics and, because the definitions are generally agreed on for these, we choose to list them for you. Please take the time to refresh your memory about the following sets because the need for lengthy reflections about what they mean as you move on will slow you down and may limit your understanding:

Digits, or D = {0, 1, 2, 3, 4, 5, 6, 7, 8, 9}
Counting numbers, or
  N = {1, 2, 3, 4, . . .}
Whole numbers, or W = {0, 1, 2, 3, . . .}
Integers, or
  Z = {. . . ⁻3, ⁻2, ⁻1, 0, ⁺1, ⁺2, ⁺3, . . .}
Rational numbers, or
  Ra = $\left\{ \dfrac{a}{b} \text{ where } b \neq 0 \right\}$ (a and b ∈Z, b ≠ 0).
  Note that some people use Q to represent the rational numbers. We will use Ra in this text.
Irrational numbers, or IRa = {numbers that cannot be written as $\dfrac{a}{b}$ (such as π or $\sqrt{2}$)}
Real numbers, or R = {Ra ∪ IRa}
Complex numbers, or C = {a + bi where a and b are real numbers, $i = \sqrt{-1}$}
Universal set, or U = contains all the elements needed to describe a situation

Venn Diagrams

You have probably heard the expression, "A picture is worth a thousand words." *Venn diagrams* are pictures that clarify some of the mathematical situations you might encounter. Figure 2.3 shows examples of disjoint sets in a Venn diagram. Do the pictures show what you believe are disjoint sets? Figure 2.4 depicts intersecting or overlapping sets. The darkened section in each example is common to all the sets involved. Both Fig. 2.3 and Fig. 2.4 are generic and although they depict the situation, they are not very helpful in determining exactly what is meant by the

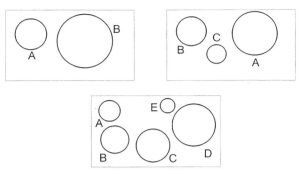

FIG. 2.3.

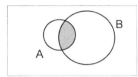

FIG. 2.4.

positive and negative numbers; counting numbers less than 100, the counting number 100, and counting numbers greater than 100; as well as many others. Notice that one of the examples (counting numbers less than 100, 100 itself, and counting numbers greater than 100) involved three disjoint sets. The only stipulation for disjoint sets is that you need at least two sets, with no common elements. Later, in statistics, you will see disjoint sets referred to as mutually exclusive sets.

Suppose you had set A = {1, 2, 3, 4, 25, 35, 57} and the digits (D). Figure 2.6 shows how these overlapping sets might appear in a Venn diagram.

two situations. Suppose you had the set of odd counting numbers, O, and the set of even counting numbers, E. Both of those sets are infinite so all the elements cannot be shown. Some elements of the disjoint sets are shown in Fig. 2.5. An ellipsis could perhaps be inserted in each set to indicate their infinite natures but that could be confusing. Some people might consider using "etc." That too could be confusing. One method that is sometimes used to indicate infinite sets in Venn diagrams is to make the loop dashed, which we have done.

Similar diagrams could be generated using the rational and irrational numbers;

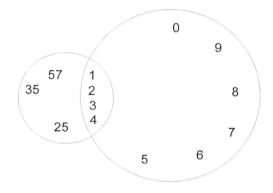

FIG. 2.6.

Venn diagrams may have more than two sets; the possibility for examples is limited only by your imagination. For example, you could use counting numbers in one set and whole numbers in another set; even counting numbers in one set and digits in another set; or counting numbers in one set, digits in a second set, and integers in a third set. The possibilities are limitless. A fine detail you should notice is that the overlapping, or common elements, appear only once in the Venn diagram. In Fig. 2.6, the numbers in the overlapping part, 1, 2, 3, and 4, are shown only in the overlapping part because they "belong" to each set.

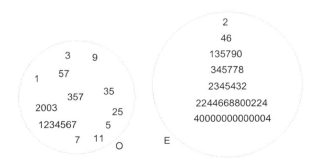

FIG. 2.5.

Your Turn

26. Describe what the universal set might be for each of these examples of unions and then construct a Venn diagram that accurately depicts each statement:

a) $\{1, 2, 3, 4\} \cup \{5, 6, 7\} = \{1, 2, 3, 4, 5, 6, 7\}$
b) $\{1, 2, 3\} \cup \{4\} \cup \{7, 8, 15\} = \{1, 2, 3, 4, 7, 8, 15\}$
c) $\{1, 2, 3, 4\} \cup \{5, 6, 4\} = \{1, 2, 3, 4, 5, 6\}$

27. Describe what the universal set might be for each of these examples of intersections and then construct a Venn diagram that accurately depicts each statement:

a) $\{1, 2, 3, 4\} \cap \{5, 6, 4\} = \{4\}$
b) $\{1, 2, 3, 4, 5\} \cap \{3, 4, 5\} = \{3, 4, 5\}$
c) $\{1, 2, 3, 4\} \cap \{5, 6, 7\} = \{\ \}$
Let $A = \{1, 2, 3, 4\}$, $B = \{1, 2, 3, 4, 5\}$, $C = \{5, 6, 4\}$, and $D = \{3, 4, 5\}$.
d) $A - C = \{1, 2, 3\}$
e) $C - A = \{5, 6\}$
f) $B - D = \{1, 2\}$
g) $D - B = \{\ \}$

28. Describe what the universal set might be for each of these examples of set multiplication and then construct a Venn diagram that accurately depicts each statement:

a) $\{1, 2\} \times \{A, B\} = \{(1, A), (1, B), (2, A), (2, B)\}$
b) $\{A, B\} \times \{1, 2\} = \{(A, 1), (B, 1), (B, 2), (A, 2)\}$
c) $\{A, 1, \&\} \times \{♣, ▽\} = \{A, ▽), (1, ▽), (\&, ▽), (A, ♣), (1, ♣), (\&, ♣)\}$

29. Let the universal set for each of these examples be the set of digits and then construct a Venn diagram that accurately depicts each statement:

Let $A = \{1, 2, 3, 4\}$, $B = \{1, 2, 3\}$, $C = \{5, 6, 7\}$, $D = \{3, 4, 5\}$, $E = \{4\}$, and $F = \{7, 8, 9\}$.
a) $A' \cup C = \{0, 5, 6, 7, 8, 9\}$
b) $A' \cap D = \{5\}$
c) $C - F' = \{7\}$
d) $(A - D) \cup B' = \{0, 1, 2, 4, 5, 6, 7, 8, 9\}$

Properties

There are properties, rules, axioms, and ideas that are consistently true as we study numbers. There is a basic collection of 11 properties, sometimes called *field axioms*, which are developed, used, and referred to throughout the mathematical curriculum. These properties are fundamental to the development of mathematical knowledge and can even save time as number facts are learned. As one progresses to the study of more advanced mathematical topics, some of the properties are removed to create groups, loops, rings, and other topics in the study of abstract algebra. So, what are these properties?

Commutative property of addition on a set

Commutative property of multiplication on a set

Associative property of addition on a set

Associative property of multiplication on a set

Identity element for addition on a set

Identity element for multiplication on a set

Inverse element for addition on a set

Inverse element for multiplication on a set

Closure property of addition on a set

Closure property of multiplication on a set

Distributive property of multiplication over addition on a set

As we discuss these important properties in detail, we will use proper terminology as opposed to slang (yet commonly accepted) terms. Any discussion of a property must begin with a set of elements and an operation.

Undoubtedly, you are aware that the order in which you add two numbers is of little consequence: 3 + 5 = 5 + 3. This is an example of the commutative property of addition on the set of counting numbers; the property is true for all the sets we will discuss (digits, wholes, integers, rationals, reals, or complex). The significant thing is that an operation (addition) and a set of elements have been identified. In our discussion of 3 + 5 = 5 + 3, we did not merely mention the commutative property. It was called the commutative property of addition on the set of counting numbers. Although you might know what is meant when someone mentions the commutative property, or commutativity, there is a need for precision of language in the world of mathematics. We must be careful to differentiate between the commutative property of addition on the set of counting numbers and the commutative property of multiplication on the set of integers.

In our example, we could have used the commutative property of multiplication on the set of whole numbers, saying that 3 × 5 = 5 × 3. You know that multiplying these two factors will always give you the same product, regardless of the order in which you choose to use the factors. The gist of the commutative property of

either addition or multiplication for the set you use is that the order of the elements can be switched and the result will be the same. You have probably seen these two properties defined together as:

a + b = b + a and a × b = b × a, where a and b are elements from the chosen set and the operation is either addition or multiplication.

Stating the properties with letters rather than specific numbers generalizes the idea. This is a convenient way of summarizing the statements for all numbers because any number could be substituted for either a or b.

There is a difference between the commutative property of addition on the set of whole numbers and the commutative property of multiplication on the set of whole numbers. This is generally not difficult to see with 2 + 3 = 3 + 2 and 2 × 3 = 3 × 2. The addition gives a sum of 5 and the multiplication gives a product of 6, so saying whether or not you are commuting 2 and 3 over addition or multiplication is important. However, you could have 2 + 2 = 2 + 2 and 2 × 2 = 2 × 2, each of which gives an answer of 4 and implies that saying commutative alone is sufficient. Generally, it does make a difference, however, as you deal with addition or multiplication.

Is there a commutative property for subtraction on the set of integers? If you said yes, then you need to revisit the thinking process that led you to that conclusion. For that statement to be true, it must be the case that 6 − 2 = 2 − 6. Notice that, with subtraction over the set of integers, 6 − 2 = 2 − 6 is not a true statement because 6 − 2 = 4 whereas 2 − 6 = ⁻4. There is a BIG difference between 4 and ⁻4. In general then, there is not a commutative property for subtraction on the set of integers. We could provide an example to show that there is not a commutative property for division on the set of integers. However, we ask you to consider it, using our subtraction example as a model, to give you a chance to exercise your reasoning skills. Can you think of any exceptions to these general rules?

The associative properties for addition and multiplication on a given set are similar to those for the commutative property of an operation with some set. The order of the elements does not change, only the placement of the parentheses, which indicates the operation to be performed first. Some examples of the associative property of addition and multiplication on the set of counting numbers are
$(2 + 4) + 7 = 2 + (4 + 7)$ and
$(2 \times 4) \times 7 = 2 \times (4 \times 7)$. The more general statement is typically given as:

> $(a + b) + c = a + (b + c)$ and $(a \times b) \times c = a \times (b \times c)$, where a, b, and c are elements from the chosen set and the operation is either addition or multiplication.

This last statement generalizes what is going on. You should be able to describe it in words as well as give specific examples or a generalized version involving letters. Why do you think our discussion revolves about addition and multiplication only? Investigating this property for subtraction and division will enhance your understanding of the associative property of addition or multiplication on a given set.

The concept of closure within a set for any operation is difficult for some to grasp. Fraternities and sororities are examples of closed groups. Although guests are welcome to attend many functions, only members are permitted to vote. In such an exclusive situation, who is and who is not a member is clearly known. The closure property is quite similar, actually. Think of any two counting numbers. Add them. Is the sum a counting number? Of course, you say. Is there any example of adding two counting numbers where the sum is not a counting number? No? It is said that the counting numbers are closed under addition (notice the set and operation are both named there). True or false—the digits are closed for multiplication? False. At first glance, you might ask, "What about $2 \times 3 = 6$?" This statement is true because the product is a digit. However, $5 \times 7 = 35$ gives a product that is not an element of the set (digits). The conclusion must be that the digits are not closed for multiplication.

The identity elements for addition and multiplication are special numbers. Zero is the identity element for addition and one is the identity element for multiplication within any set that contains these respective elements. Consider $3 + 0 = 3 = 0 + 3$. The commutative property for addition on the set of wholes is implicit in the example. We cannot generalize from a single example, but we assume that you are already familiar with the idea that zero is the additive identity (identity element for addition). You may have seen $a + 0 = a$, where a is an element of any set that contains 0. Similarly, one is the identity element for multiplication starting with the counting numbers, typically shown as $a \times 1 = a$, where a is an element of any set that contains 1.

Whereas the inverse element for an operation on some set is easy to conceptualize, it is often difficult to express. First, look at some examples where elements are the operative (either additive or multiplicative) inverse for a given element from some appropriate set:

$3 + {}^-3 = 0; \ {}^-3 + 3 = 0$

$72 + {}^-72 = 0; \ {}^-72 + 72 = 0$

$$19 \times \frac{1}{19} = 1; \frac{1}{19} \times 19 = 1$$

$$\frac{1}{47} \times 47 = 1; 47 \times \frac{1}{47} = 1.$$

Given these examples, you should have the idea that the inverse element needs to commute for the given operation in the selected set, and when the operation is completed, the result is the identity element for the respective operation.

The remaining property is unique in that it is the only one that combines two operations. You have seen it many times in your prior work and yet might not have recognized it. Perhaps you recall seeing $3 \times (4 + 5) = (3 \times 4) + (3 \times 5)$. Notice that the order of the elements is maintained, which is significant. You probably call this the distributive property even though it is properly called the left distributive property of multiplication over addition because the 3 is being distributed via multiplication from the left over the sum of $4 + 5$. Did you remember seeing this concept while learning to factor in your algebra class? Perhaps you saw it with the setup reversed. Also, because the times sign looks so much like a variable, you might have seen an expression or equation involving juxtaposition, or implicit multiplication, such as $4yz + 12z = 4z(2y + 3)$ where multiplication is indicated, but the multiplication symbol is absent, but implied or understood to be there. Still, you can recognize this as the left distributive property of multiplication over addition on the set of numbers.

We will use all of these properties throughout the text. We encourage you to become comfortable with concepts as well as the different ways of referring to them. You are invited to use the phraseology that is most comfortable for you, but be advised that other teachers or writers might express specific preferences. When you are in Rome, ...

Your Turn

30. We know $2 + 2 = 2 \times 2$, as discussed with the commutative property of addition on the set of counting numbers. Are there any other pairs of numbers for which the sum and product are equal?

31. Is there a situation where commutativity of subtraction on some set would exist?

32. Is there a situation where commutativity of division on some set would exist?

33. Generalize the idea of commutativity of operations for some set in your own words.

34. We know $2 + 2 = 2 \times 2$ as discussed with the commutative property of addition on the set of counting numbers. Are there any examples that will work like this for associativity?

35. Is there a situation where associativity of subtraction on some set would exist?

36. Is there a situation where associativity of division on some set would exist?

For each of 38 through 41, select True or False and explain the reason for your choice.

37. Generalize the idea of associativity of operations for some set in words.

38. The even counting numbers are closed for addition.

39. The odd counting numbers are closed for addition.

40. The even counting numbers are closed for multiplication.

41. The odd counting numbers are closed for multiplication.

42. Give an example of a set that is closed for addition and describe why it is so.

43. Give an example of a set that is closed for multiplication and describe why it is so.

44. Would the commutative property for addition on a given set have a negative impact on the situation if we insisted that it hold true while we discussed closure?

45. Generalize the idea of closure of operations for some set in words. Don't forget about division and subtraction.

46. Generalize the idea of the identity element for an operation for some set in words.

47. Generalize the idea of the inverse element for an operation for some set in words.

48. In general, is there a left distributive property of multiplication over subtraction in the real numbers?

49. In general, is there a right distributive property of multiplication over addition or subtraction on the set of reals?

50. In general, is there a left distributive property of division over addition in the reals?

51. In general, is there a right distributive property of division over addition in the set of real numbers?

52. Generalize the idea of the distributive property for multiplication over addition for some set in words.

Factors and Multiples

Concepts involving the properties of whole numbers, or number theory, provide the foundations for much of the study of higher mathematics. Factors and multiples of numbers appear early in the study of numbers as aspects of division and multiplication. The emphasis of multiples and factors is a central part of work in beginning algebra, but often receives too little attention in our elementary schools. Yet, two important concepts surrounding factors and multiples, often referred to as LCM (least common multiple) and GCF (greatest common factor), are confusing for many students. Usually, the definitions are known, but people struggle to know which definition goes with which concept.

Your Turn

53. Using the following examples, write a definition of multiple and a definition of factor:

Multiples of 12 are 12, 24, 36, 48, . . .

Multiples of 5 are 5, 10, 15, 20, 25, . . .

Multiples of 7 are 7, 14, 21, 28, 35, . . .

Multiples of 2 are 2, 4, 8, 16, 32, 64, 128, . . .

Factors of 12 are 1, 2, 3, 4, 6, 12

Factors of 7 are 1, 7

Factors of 100 are 1, 2, 4, 5, 10, 20, 25, 50, 100

Factors of 36 are 1, 2, 3, 4, 6, 9, 12, 18, 36

Prime and Composite Numbers

Can you state definitions for the *set of prime numbers* and the *set of composite numbers*? Traditionally, these definitions, with examples, are provided by teachers and memorized by students. An approach using patterning allows you to discover the sets of prime and composite numbers. This approach requires a basic understanding of finding areas of rectangles, but it is well worth the effort to develop.

Using only counting number dimensions, how many different rectangles are there with area 2 square units? You might wonder if the position of the rectangle matters in this discussion. Most people would say there are two rectangles that fit this requirement, as shown in Fig. 2.7.

FIG. 2.7.

It should be noted that both the 1 unit by 2 unit and the 2 unit by 1 unit rectangles in Fig. 2.7 are in standard position and that there are infinitely many rectangles that would have dimensions of 1 unit by 2 units and areas of 2 square units as indicated in Fig. 2.8.

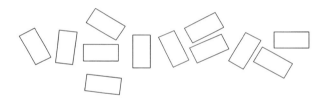

FIG. 2.8.

Although there is an infinite number of rectangles with areas of 2 square units, given counting number dimensions, the rectangles in Fig. 2.8 are all rotations of the same 1 unit by 2 unit (1 × 2) rectangle. A convenient way to organize this discussion is to give only one of the infinite set of rectangles with counting number dimensions as representative of the entire set, and list the smaller dimension first.

We talked about figures with a given area, 2 square units. Some mathematicians say that the word area implies the presence of square units whereas others feel the idea of square units should always be included in the discussion. The easy answer to the situation is to always list square units with a discussion about area.

Develop a three-column table in which you list the areas given in the following questions in the left column, the counting number dimensions of all rectangles that give each area in the middle column, and the total number of different dimension pairs in the right column. For example, for area two, you will have 2 in the left column, 1 × 2 in the middle column, and 1 in the right column. It would be helpful if you sketch your rectangles on square grid or dot paper.

Using only counting number dimensions, how many different rectangles are there with area 3 square units?

Using only counting number dimensions, how many different rectangles are there with area 4 square units? For this one, you must remember that all squares are rectangles, so you count the 2 × 2 square, in addition to the 1 × 4 rectangle, giving you two rectangles.

Using only counting number dimensions, how many different rectangles are there with area 5 square units? With area 6 square units? With area 7 square units? With area 8 square units? With area 9 square units? With area 10 square units? With area 11 square units?

Your Turn

54. What conclusions can you draw from your table?

An example like Fig. 2.9 may prove helpful in leading to the desired conclusions about your table in Exercise 51. Your table should indicate two distinct sets of numbers. Some rectangles have areas that are found only one way (2, 3, 5, 7, 11), whereas others can be found two ways (4, 6, 8, 9, 10). Do you recognize these sets? They are the prime and composite numbers. Given the information you have so far, you might define these sets as, "Prime numbers give only one rectangle" and "Composite numbers give two rectangles."

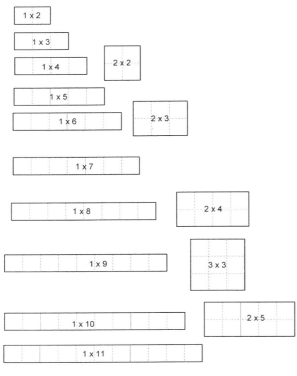

FIG. 2.9.

cific set of prime factors will give only one product, and conversely, that any composite number is generated by a unique set of primes. Without that uniqueness, we do not have the assurance that $12 = 2 \times 2 \times 3$ because there might be some other prime lurking out there somewhere that we do not see, or know about. To avoid all those complications, 1 is left in a class by itself and is neither prime nor composite. Some texts call 1 the generator.

Sieve of Eratosthenes

The Sieve of Eratosthenes is used to develop a list of primes by applying the patterns associated with multiples of counting numbers. A multiple of a number is defined as the number times a counting number. For example, the multiples of 7 are 7, 14, 21, 28, 35, 42, . . . , which is also $1 \times 7, 2 \times 7, 3 \times 7, 4 \times 7, 5 \times 7, 6 \times 7,$ . . . . In this example, 7 is the number under consideration and the counting numbers are 1, 2, 3, 4, 5, 6, ... Some people define multiple to be a whole number times the value in question, making 0 a valid multiple of 7 as well. For this exercise, we will use the counting number definition. Use the following chart to complete the instructions given below it. Although 1 is neither prime nor composite, and therefore will not be part of the exercise, it appears in the chart.

Now think about a rectangle with area 12. You can get 1×12, 2×6, and 3×4 as dimensions—or three different rectangles. The definition of a composite number has to be refined to say two or more rectangles. This discussion is valuable as a means of emphasizing that functional definitions sometimes need to be expanded or altered as horizons are expanded.

What about 1? You can sketch a rectangle that is 1×1, so is it prime? In fact, 1 is neither prime nor composite. The Fundamental Theorem of Arithmetic assures that any number may be expressed as a unique product of prime numbers, excluding order. Thus, $6 = 2 \times 3$ or 3×2 and we are assured that no other product of primes will give an answer of 6. If 1 were prime, then we would have $1 \times 2 \times 3 = 6$, $1 \times 1 \times 2 \times 3 = 6$, and so on. Although it is still the case that the product is 6, the uniqueness part of the definition, which is critical to our number system, would be lost. We need the assurance that a spe-

1	2	3	4	5	6	7	8	9	10
11	12	13	14	15	16	17	18	19	20
21	22	23	24	25	26	27	28	29	30
31	32	33	34	35	36	37	38	39	40
41	42	43	44	45	46	47	48	49	50
51	52	53	54	55	56	57	58	59	60
61	62	63	64	65	66	67	68	69	70
71	72	73	74	75	76	77	78	79	80
81	82	83	84	85	86	87	88	89	90
91	92	93	94	95	96	97	98	99	100

Loop 2. Cross off all multiples of 2 in the chart.

Loop 3. Cross off all multiples of 3 in the chart.

Loop 5. Cross off all multiples of 5 in the chart.

Loop 7. Cross off all multiples of 7 in the chart.

Continue looping each prime and crossing off all multiples in the chart until all primes on the chart are shown.

Your Turn

55. Complete the Sieve of Eratosthenes following the directions given in the text immediately before this exercise. Although this chart stops at 100, it could be continued to any desired value.

56. What is the greatest number of primes in any given row?

57. Would the answer in Exercise 53 change if the chart were extended indefinitely to include more rows or more columns?

58. Next consider the least number of primes in any given row?

59. Would the answer in Exercise 55 change if the chart were extended indefinitely by adding more rows or columns?

60. Create a sieve on a 6-column chart, then answer the questions that follow (the same questions asked for the 10-column sieve). Even though the same questions are asked, the answers will change, thus enhancing understanding.

61. What is the greatest number of primes in any given row of the 6-column sieve?

62. Would the answer in Exercise 58 change if the 6-column sieve were extended indefinitely?

63. Now, what is the least number of primes in any given row of the 6-column sieve?

64. Would the answer in Exercise 60 change if the 6-column chart were extended indefinitely?

The sieves open the door to an interesting question. Assume you have the 10-column sieve. Is it possible to have 10 consecutive composite numbers? The answer is yes, but the table would need to be extended vertically a lot farther. Suppose you consider
$11 \times 10 \times 9 \times 8 \times 7 \times 6 \times 5 \times 4 \times 3 \times 2 \times 1$ (39,916,800). The next counting number after that is 39,916,801 and the counting number after that is 39,916,802. Focusing on 39,916,802, it can be written as 39,916,800 + 2. We know that 2 divides 2 and we know that 2 is one of the factors of 39,916,800. Using the distributive property of multiplication over addition on the set of counting numbers, 39,916,802 $= 2 \times 19,958,400 + 2 \times 1$ or $2(19,958,400 + 1)$, showing that 2 is a factor of 39,916,802. A similar approach can be used for 39,916,803, 39,916,804, . . . , 39,916,811, showing 10 consecutive composite numbers. When dealing with such large numbers, there is a more concise way to write them;
$11 \times 10 \times 9 \times 8 \times 7 \times 6 \times 5 \times 4 \times 3 \times 2 \times 1$, or 39,916,800, is also written 11!. You are seeing correctly. The 11 is followed by an exclamation point—in mathematics, 11! means
$11 \times 10 \times 9 \times 8 \times 7 \times 6 \times 5 \times 4 \times 3 \times 2 \times 1$, and is read 11 factorial.

Divisibility Rules

The discussion about factors and multiples provides the background for a very important concept that is built on another definition. When a mathematician says a number is divisible by another, the assumption is that, when the division is completed, the remainder will be zero.

For example, 36 divided by 9 is 4, and the remainder is zero. This fact might be stated as 36 is divisible by 9 (or 1, 2, 3, 4, 6, 9, 12, 18, and 36, depending on the situation) or 9 divides 36. Notice that divides means there will be no remainder in the answer. As we consider divisibility rules and extensions of the concepts of multiples and factors, this definition is important.

Think about 15. It is divisible by 1, 3, 5, and 15. For now we will focus on the idea that 5 divides 15. Because 5 divides 15, we can be assured that 5 will also divide 30. There are two ways to certify that—one way would be to divide 30 by 5 and determine there is no remainder; the other way would be to express 30 as 2 × 15 and, because we know 5 divides 15, we can see that 5 must also divide 30. This second approach will prove more useful and efficient than the first as we proceed with our discussion. In general, we say that, if a is divisible by b, then we are assured that any multiple of a is also divisible by b. This is an essential concept for the following discussion.

The number 27 can be rewritten as 3 + 9 + 15. The common factor, 3, can be used to rewrite 3 + 9 + 15 as the product of 3 and the sum of the residue of each of the terms, 3(1 + 3 + 5). This shows that the original number is divisible by 3. Examples such as this will aid in understanding and verifying for divisibility rules.

What is the rule for showing a number to be divisible by 2? "The last digit is even." or "The last digit is a 2, 4, 6, 8, or 0." The real question is, "How do you know that to be true?" or "Can you show it?" One of the goals of the Standards is communication, which involves explaining why things work, and producing convincing arguments.

Consider any number xy, where x is any integer and y is any digit. In 7,354, x is 735 and y is 4. The number xy can be written in a quasi-expanded notation as (x)(10) + y. No matter what integer is used for x, (x)(10) must be divisible by 2, because 10 is divisible by 2. Any multiple of 10 will also be divisible by 2. One term of the expanded form is guaranteed divisible by 2. If the other term is also divisible by 2, then a 2 can be factored out of the expanded form and the original number written as 2 times something. Because xy can be written as 2 times something, this verifies that the original number is divisible by 2. But, when can 2 be factored out of both terms? Only when y is even, or 0, 2, 4, 6, or 8, which gives the rule statement.

The divisibility rules for 5 and 10 are similar to that for 2. The digit in the units place must be either 5 or 0 for divisibility by 5. For divisibility by 10, there must be a zero in the units column. You should develop a convincing argument to support these statements.

Understanding divisibility rules for 2, 5, and 10 facilitates the development of the divisibility rule for 4. Because 10 is not divisible by 4, the expanded expression, (x)(10) + y, cannot be used. The number being considered needs to be written as xyz, where x is any integer and y and z are any digits. The number is then written as (x)(100) + yz (note y and z are not multiplied here—they represent the tens and ones places of the number). Because 100 is divisible by 4, attention is turned to the last two places, yz. If this number is divisible by 4, then so is the original number. For example,

$$5,732 = 57(100) + 32$$
$$= 57 (4)(25) + 4 (8)$$
$$= 4[57(25) + 8].$$

If yz is not divisible by 4, neither is the original number, because 4 cannot be factored out of both terms. For example,

5,731 is not a multiple of 4, because 4 cannot be factored out of 31.

For divisibility by 8, the last 3 digits of the number would be set off and added to some multiple of 1000. A rule for 16 can be established, but there is some question about the value of it. In the divisibility rules for 2, 4, 8, and 16, there is a parallel between the exponents of 2 and 10. For divisibility by 2, use 2^1 and 10^1; for divisibility by 4, use 2^2 and 10^2; for divisibility by 8, use 2^3 and 10^3; and for divisibility by 16 use 2^4 and 10^4. Why do you think there is a question about the value of a divisibility rule for 16?

The divisibility rule for 3 uses expanded notation, along with the idea of having a common factor in each term, so the original number can be expressed as a multiple of 3. Suppose you want to know if the 3-digit number xyz, where x, y, and z are digits, is divisible by 3. The rule says to find the sum of the digits. If that sum is divisible by 3, then the original number is also.

Using expanded notation, xyz = (x)(100) + (y)(10) + z. For divisibility by 3, we want to rewrite (x)(100) + (y)(10) + z so that x + y + z is a part of the expression. The challenge is to find a way to rewrite (x)(100) so it is a sum of x and something. If (x)(100) is written as (x)(99 + 1), distributing the x yields (x)(99) + (x)(1) or 99x + x. The x is now an addend. The 99x is a multiple of 3. Using the same technique for (y)(10),

$$
\begin{aligned}
xyz &= (x)(100) + (y)(10) + z \\
&= (x)(99 + 1) + (y)(9 + 1) + z \\
&= (x)(99) + (x)(1) + (y)(9) + (y)(1) + z \\
&= 99x + x + 9y + y + z \\
&= 99x + 9y + x + y + z
\end{aligned}
$$

It is known that 99x and 9y are divisible by 3. If x + y + z is divisible by 3, then 99x + 9y + x + y + z can be written as

3(33x + 3y + w), where 3w = x + y + z, and the original number is a multiple of 3. If the sum of the digits is not a multiple of 3, then the original number cannot be expressed as a multiple of 3.

Divisibility by 9 works like that of 3 except that the sum of the digits must be divisible by 9. Divisibility by 6 uses a combination of the 2 and 3 divisibility rules. The easiest way to use the 6 rule is to see if the number in question is even. If it is not, then the number cannot possibly be divisible by 6. If the number in question is even, then apply the 3 divisibility rule. Consider the prime factorization of 6 for a clue about how this rule works.

Divisibility by 7 provides exploration opportunities for more inquisitive individuals. The rule states, "Double the last digit in the number and subtract that product from the original number after the last original digit has been deleted. If the new number is divisible by 7, the original number is. If the new number is not divisible by 7, the original number is not. The process may be repeated." For example,

2 0 6 5	Double last digit (5)
− 1 0	Subtract 2 × 5 after deleting 5
1 9 6	Repeat the process—double 6
− 1 2	Subtract 2 × 6 after deleting 6
7	Because 7 is divisible by 7, 2065 is.

Your Turn

65. Develop an argument that shows how the divisibility rule for 9 would work with a 4-digit number wxyz.

66. Why does the 6 rule break into an even 3 rule? Explain why a similar rule could or could not be devised for divisibility by 15.

67. Describe a divisibility rule for some number other than those discussed and show why it works.

68. Are divisibility rules limited to integers?

Divisibility by 11 revolves around renaming 10 as $11 - 1$ and using the concept of expanded notation. Consider $(11 - 1)^2$. Expanding yields $11^2 - 2(11)(1) + 1^2$. Because 11 is a factor of two of the terms in the expansion, that part of the sum must be divisible by 11. Expanding $(11 - 1)^3$ gives an expression in which all terms except 1^3 are multiples of 11. The situation is similar for all cases of $(11 - 1)^n$, where n is any counting number—all terms except for 1^n will be multiples of 11. The sign of 1^n will be negative for odd values of n, and positive for even ones.

Using this information to check for divisibility by 11 on the number uvwxyz, where u, v, w, x, y, and z are any digits, uvwxyz would be rewritten as $u(10)^5 + v(10)^4 + w(10)^3 + x(10)^2 + y(10)^1 + z(10)^0$ or as $u(11 - 1)^5 + v(11 - 1)^4 + w(11 - 1)^3 + x(11 - 1)^2 + y(11 - 1)^1 + z(11 - 1)^0$. From the earlier discussion, expansion of this polynomial will yield a set of terms that are multiples of 11 plus some residue. The only terms in question are $- u$, $+ v$, $-w$, $+ x$, $- y$, and $+ z$. Inspection shows the rule to be the rightmost digit minus its left neighbor, plus the next left neighbor, and so on, until all digits are considered. In other words, the sum of every other digit is subtracted from the sum of the rest of the digits (for divisibility, the sign is not important). If that missing addend is a multiple of 11, then the original number is divisible by 11.

Greatest Common Factor and Least Common Multiple

As we embark on this discussion, vocabulary is critical. Looking first at greatest common factor (GCF), examine each of the words:

greatest means biggest, largest

common implies something shared between at least two numbers

factor divides the number being considered

GCF can lead to confusion because we are looking for the greatest common factor of at least two numbers, which ends up being less than at least one of the numbers. Similarly, when considering least common multiple (LCM) we must examine each of the words:

least means littlest, smallest

common implies something shared between at least two numbers

multiple is a counting number times the number being considered

With LCM, we are looking for the smallest value that is a multiple of each number under consideration. It will be bigger than all but perhaps one of them. Intertwined in all of this is the potential confusion about which numbers are factors and which are multiples. Before proceeding with this discussion, we advise you to be certain of your definitions.

The mathematics you learned may have been pretty much self-contained. Each topic was treated at the necessary level and then the curriculum moved on to something else. At times topic were connected, for instance, prime and composite numbers being followed by GCF and LCM. These connections help build a more coherent picture of the world of mathematics.

There is a variety of ways to find LCM and GCF. We start with one you may not have seen. Suppose the exercise is to find the LCM and GCF of 16 and 24. What is a factor of both 16 and 24? You could say 8 or 4, but 2 will do for now. You are left with 8 and 12 from the original numbers and the process is repeated. 2⌐16 24

What is a factor of both 8 and 12?

4|8 12

Two could have been selected again, instead of 4. Eventually, the final pair of numbers will be relatively prime.

Two and 4 are factors of the GCF (8), and the factors of the LCM (48) are 2, 4, 2, and 3. This is much easier to see if the whole presentation is consolidated:

2|16 24
4| 8 12
   2 3

Notice how the 2, 4, 2, and 3 form an "L," indicating the factors of the least common multiple. Notice also that the factors in the vertical part of the "L" are the factors of the GCF of 16 and 24. Notice how this process connects GCF and LCM.

We now turn to methods of finding GCF and LCM that are perhaps familiar to you. As these are discussed, think in terms of how they connect to other mathematical topics. Suppose the task is to find the GCF of 12 and 18. One way to attack the problem would be to list all of the factors of each number:

the factors of 12 are 1, 2, 3, 4, 6, 12
the factors of 18 are 1, 2, 3, 6, 9, 18

Looking for common factors, you have 1, 2, 3, and 6, but the task is to determine the greatest common factor, so the answer is 6.

Listing, although it works, can be cumbersome if the numbers are large. There are other approaches that will shorten and simplify the task. First, we need to introduce a few more terms. Consider the following:

the prime factors of 12 are 2 and 3

the prime factor of 7 is 7

the prime factors of 72 are 2 and 3

the prime factors of 105 are 3, 5, and 7

the prime factor of 16 is 2

the prime factors of 35 are 5 and 7

the prime factorization of 12 is $2 \times 2 \times 3$ or $2^2 \times 3$

the prime factorization of 7 is 7

the prime factorization of 72 is $2 \times 2 \times 2 \times 3 \times 3$ or $2^3 \times 3^2$

the prime factorization of 105 is $3 \times 5 \times 7$

the prime factorization of 16 is $2 \times 2 \times 2 \times 2$ or 2^4

the prime factorization of 35 is 5×7

You should be able to build definitions of factorization and prime factorization from these examples and use exponents in them. When considering the prime factorization of a number, all of the factors are listed, and sometimes exponents can be used to shorten the presentation. When thinking of the prime factors of a number, all prime factors of the number are listed, but each is listed only once.

Although there are different ways of determining the prime factorization of any number, the factor tree is probably the most common. We show some of the ways of determining the prime factorization of 36:

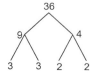 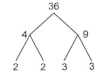 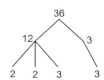 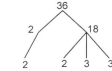

There are other ways this could be done ($36 = 6 \times 6$), but these are enough to meet the needs for this discussion. In each case, we want to list all of the prime factors of 36. How we proceed from the beginning is not important. It is significant, however, that no matter how we initially factor 36, we ultimately end up with the same set of prime factors. Notice that 12 could have been factored as 4×3, but because we know 4 can be factored into 2×2, we expressed the 12 as a product of three primes. You should also notice that although the prime factors can be listed in any order, it is most common and convenient to list them in increasing order. Arranging the prime factors makes it easier to list the prime factorization using exponents ($2^2 \times 3^2$).

The GCF can be found via prime factorization where spacing of the prime factors makes it easier to determine the answer. The prime factors of 18, 24, and 39 are:

$$18 = 2 \times \qquad\quad 3 \times 3$$
$$24 = 2 \times 2 \times 2 \times 3$$
$$39 = \qquad\qquad\quad 3 \times 13$$

Although the spacing may seem strange, it helps us see how to determine the GCF. If a factor is going to be common, it must appear in each of the numbers being considered. Looking at the example, 18 and 24 share 2 as a factor, but 39 does not. Thus, 2 cannot be a common factor of 18, 24, and 39. Only 39 has a factor of 13, which cannot be a common factor of 18, 24, and 39. However, 3 is a factor of all three numbers, 18, 24, and 39, hence, 3 is a common factor for them. This example also can be used to show that once all the prime factors of each of the numbers are arranged and listed with appropriate spacing, one need only look for any col-

umns that have an entry for each number. That column will be a common factor. In this case, the only candidate is 3, which is the GCF of 18, 24, and 39. Consider only 18 and 24:

$$18 = 2 \times \qquad\quad 3 \times 3$$
$$24 = 2 \times 2 \times 2 \times 3$$

Using the column idea, there is a common factor of 2 and another common factor of 3. Because 2 and 3 are common factors for 18 and 24, 6 is the GCF. Another way of explaining this is to say that, if 6 divides 18, its factors divide 18. This could be confirmed by using the listing technique:

the factors of 18 are 1, 2, 3, 6, 9, 18

the factors of 24 are 1, 2, 3, 4, 6, 8, 12, and 24

Checking the list, the common factors are 1, 2, 3, and 6, and the greatest is 6. Notice that 1 is a factor, but not a prime factor.

The exponential expression of the prime factorization provides another way of determining the GCF. Using 18 and 24:

$$18 = 2^1 \times 3^2$$
$$24 = 2^3 \times 3^1$$

The GCF is 6. How can we come up with an explanation from this to match the known answer? Notice that each prime factor is in one of the columns and that the smallest power is 1 in each case. One should conclude that $2^1 \times 3^1$ is yet another way to express the GCF of 12 and 18. Using the other example of 18, 24, and 39:

$$18 = 2^1 \times 3^2$$
$$24 = 2^3 \times 3^1$$
$$39 = \qquad\quad 3^1 \times 13^1$$

The column idea works again and the GCF of 18, 24, and 39 is 3, which agrees with the previous result. Look at one more example:

$$48 = 2^4 \times 3^1$$
$$72 = 2^3 \times 3^2$$

Here again, the column idea is present, but which exponent is selected? Because we are looking for the GCF, what is the largest multiple of 2 found in each number? The answer to that question is 2^3, which indicates that the smallest exponent in each column is the one to be selected when looking for the GCF.

We use a mentality similar to that of GCF to find the LCM of numbers. We can list the multiples:

the multiples of 18 are: 18, 36, 54, 72, 90, 108, 126, 144, . . .

the multiples of 24 are: 24, 48, 72, 96, 120, 144, . . .

Common multiples include 72 and 144, and there is an infinite number of them. The quest is for the LCM, so the choice is 72. The idea of prime factorization could be used as well:

$$18 = 2 \times \qquad 3 \times 3$$
$$24 = 2 \times 2 \times 2 \times 3$$

In this case the LCM is 72, the prime factorization of which is $2 \times 2 \times 2 \times 3 \times 3$. The question becomes one of matching the prime factorization with the column idea. Notice there are 5 columns, three for 2s and two for 3s. Each column value is listed. The LCM of 18 and 24 is $2 \times 2 \times 2 \times 3 \times 3$, or 72. The exponential approach could be used, too:

$$18 = 2^1 \times 3^2$$
$$24 = 2^3 \times 3^1$$

Knowing the answer is 72 comes in handy: $72 = 2 \times 2 \times 2 \times 3 \times 3$, or $2^3 \times 3^2$. Whereas the smallest exponent is used in finding the greatest common factor, the largest is used for the least common multiple. If the task is to find the LCM of 18, 24, and 39:

$$18 = 2^1 \times 3^2$$
$$24 = 2^3 \times 3^1$$
$$39 = \qquad 3^1 \times 13^1$$

The LCM is $2^3 \times 3^2 \times 13^1$, or 936. Pick 3 numbers and find the GCF and LCM of them using each method described here.

Showing how things are intertwined, consider finding all the factors of 72. The divisibility rules help complete the task.

1×72	
2×36	72 is even
3×24	$7 + 2 = 9$, a multiple of 3
4×18	72 is a multiple of 4
6×12	even 3 rule
8×9	number fact
9×8	number fact
12×6	10, 11, and 12 are not factors of 72
18×4	13, 14, . . . , 17 are not factors of 72
24×3	19, 20, . . . , 23 are not factors of 72
36×2	25, 26, . . . , 35 are not factors of 72
72×1	37, 38, . . . , 71 are not factors of 72

Notice the factor list for 72 can be broken into a top half and bottom half, where each pair of factors is reversed in the other half. Produce a similar chart for 96 and you will see the same pattern emerge. Focus on where the reversals start and you should notice that the square root of the number whose factors are being found is between the two central reversed factors (8 × 9 and 9 × 8 in the case of 72). The square root of 72 is approximately 8.49, which is between 8 and 9. When searching for all factors of a number, list the factor pairs, starting with 1 times the number, and proceed to the counting number before the square root of that number. At this point, all the factor pairs are listed.

The counting numbers are traditionally partitioned into primes, composites, and one. Other partitions of the counting numbers provide interesting practice with factors and multiples. Three potentially new terms are perfect numbers, deficient numbers, and abundant numbers. In all three cases, all factors except the number itself, are added. The following are deficient numbers:

> 3   sum of factors excluding 3 is 1
> 5   sum of factors excluding 5 is 1
> 9   sum of factors excluding 9 is
>   1 + 3 = 4 (factors are not repeated)
> 15 sum of factors excluding 15 is
>   1 + 3 + 5, or 9
> 22 sum of factors excluding 22 is
>   1 + 2 + 11, or 14

Studying these examples should lead to the conclusion that the sum of the factors of a deficient number (excluding itself) is less than the number.

The definition of a deficient number should provide a clue to the definition of an abundant number. Some examples of abundant numbers are:

> 12 sum of factors excluding 12 is
>   1 + 2 + 3 + 4 + 6, or 16
> 24 sum of factors excluding 24 is
>   1 + 2 + 3 + 4 + 6 + 8 + 12, or 36

These examples, plus knowledge of deficient numbers, should lead to the conclusion that abundant numbers have a factor sum that is greater than the number itself, even when the number is omitted from consideration.

There is one additional possibility for the sum of the factors of a number (excluding the number itself). A number is said to be perfect when the sum of the factors equals the number. The first perfect number is 6 (1 + 2 + 3 = 6) and the second one is 28 (1 + 2 + 4 + 7 + 14 = 28). The next perfect number is 496. The next few after that are 812, 33550336, 8589869056, 137438691328, and 2305843008139952128. Perfect numbers get large in a hurry, yet they add an interesting twist to how mathematics can be learned and connected to prior work.

Conclusions

There is more to sets and properties than we have given here. This is a beginning for you. Concepts involving the properties of whole numbers, or number theory, provide the foundation for much of the study of higher mathematics. You have seen a few of those ideas discussed and developed. These topics are a part of the basic building blocks for a more extensive study of number theory. As your mathematical growth continues, we encourage you to keep looking for extensions and applications of these ideas while adding to the collection of building blocks. Rest assured, you will see them used throughout this text. Enjoy.

WHOLE NUMBER ADDITION

FOCAL POINTS

- Terminology
- Standard Algorithm
- Partial Sum
- Denominate Numbers

- Horizontal and Vertical Writing
- Expanded Notation
- Left to Right Addition
- Scratch Method
- Any Column First
- Low Stress Addition

Most people believe the standard algorithm they learned in elementary school is the most efficient way to perform addition by hand. Many people think the algorithm they learned is the only way to do addition. The typical addition algorithm, although efficient, is not the most convenient way to approach addition for beginners. The addition algorithm you probably learned for multidigit addition dictates working from right to left, which is not natural for children who are learning to read from left to right. In this section, we will discuss several methods for adding and show you there is no single method that is better than any other.

Some of the methods we will discuss might seem cumbersome to you, but you will find that learning them will increase your understanding of the inner workings of addition. We know you want to become an effective teacher of mathematics. We hope that we can help you deal with the inner workings of arithmetic operations by reminding you of concepts that have become automatic for you over the years since elementary school. Our discussion includes a variety of ways to add whole numbers and is intended to provide insight into the complexities behind the simple idea of "how many altogether."

Whereas full discussions of concrete and semi-concrete approaches will be the focus of your mathematics teaching methods course, they will not be emphasized in this book. You might remember solving simple story problems, perhaps even before you started kindergarten. "If I

have four buttons and you have three buttons, how many buttons would we have if we put them all together?" As a child, you might have counted out four buttons for the first group and three buttons for the second group. After sweeping all of the buttons together as shown in Fig. 2.10, perhaps you counted all the buttons to find that there were seven altogether.

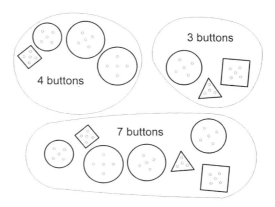

FIG. 2.10.

Number lines are very useful in understanding the inner workings of addition. Because the unit markings on a number line are evenly spaced, the idea of adding "like" terms is introduced before the word "algebra" enters our discussion. The words "start," "first addend," "second addend," and "sum" are helpful, as shown in Fig. 2.11. "Start" will always be at zero. The first vector represents the first addend and placing a second vector in "tip to tail" fashion with the first shows the

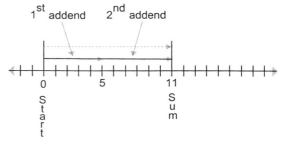

FIG. 2.11.

second addend. "Sum" depicts a point on the number line that represents the answer for the two addends. In summary, to add on a number line, use a vector to represent each addend, always start at the origin, place the tail of the second vector (addend) exactly on the tip of the first vector, and mark the sum clearly.

Your Turn

1. Use the grouping method described in the aforementioned button example to find the total of two sets of elements as a little child might. Use buttons, pennies, chips, or any other manipulative.

   a) A group of three and a group of five
   b) A set of four and a set of eight
   c) An array of two and an array of six

2. Using only addition, write out a simple word problem that would be appropriate for an early childhood addition problem. Use your manipulatives to solve the problem.

3. Use the number line method described previously to show:

   a) $8 + 3 =$ ____
   b) $5 + 4 =$ ____
   c) $7 + 9 =$ ____

Terminology

The language of mathematics is very rich and can seem complicated. You should always use the correct terminology when you discuss mathematical concepts. For this section, two major terms you use without thought are *addend* and *sum*. Numbers that await addition are called addends and the answer for an addition problem is called the sum.

An addition fact involves three numbers, two addends and a sum. Another way of thinking of an addition fact is that three numbers are involved and at least two of them are members of the set of digits, {0, 1, 2, 3, 4, 5, 6, 7, 8, 9}. What is the largest possible addend in an addition fact? What is the largest possible sum for an addition fact? Is it possible to have a nondigit addend in an addition fact? The answer to the first question is 9. The answer to the second question is 18. It is not possible to have a nondigit addend in an addition fact because the sum would also be nondigit, which would violate the definition of having at least two digits in the addition fact.

Please notice that a more in-depth understanding of this definition is possible if we carefully consider the basic concepts that are at the heart of the definition. The ability to sort through definitions in this way is an essential ingredient in the learning of mathematics. As a matter of fact, this addition fact definition can be generalized to cover any operation (+, −, ×, ÷) by saying that a fact involves three numbers, at least two of which must be digits.

The Standard Algorithm

The following discussion of the standard algorithm and the alternate ways of adding that follow are not presented in any particular order. They simply represent different ideas about adding. We encourage you to become adept at using different ways of doing mathematics to increase your mental flexibility.

You may have learned the Standard Algorithm with very little emphasis on understanding—in other words, you were taught only "how to do it." Referring to the following example, you were probably told to first add the numbers in the units column and get 26; write the 2 above the tens column and the 6 beneath the units column. Did you understand that the 2 represents two groups of ten, which is why it is placed at the top of the tens column? Many students are taught to add the digits in the tens, hundreds, thousands, and ten thousands columns as if they were simply adding digits with no explanation or expectation of understanding of place value. As long as they can do the problem and get the right answer, there is little emphasis on knowing why things work as they do, for example:

```
  1 1 2 2
  4 7 3 9 6
  7 0 1 9 4
  5 8 3 0 7
+   2 8 7 9
1 7 8 7 7 6
```

Take a closer look at the problem and determine what happens as you step through the standard algorithm. First, unless the addition facts have been memorized, completion of the problem is difficult. One could count fingers, use tally marks, or some other method, but, if efficient performance of the addition algorithm is expected, the addition facts must be second nature.

Consider the values in the ones column. As you add them, from the top down, the bottom up, or in any other order, you select two addends and get a sum. Once you have that sum, you use it with another addend, creating a new sum. At this point in the process, you may have moved beyond the facts and into the realm of adding a two-digit addend and a one-digit addend. You continue this binary process until all addends have been used. At that point, you have a sum for the units column and use your place value knowledge to write the digits of the sum as you were taught. This process is repeated for the tens column, and then for the other columns, in turn, until the sum is completed.

The columns themselves are quite significant because we often ignore place value as we add. Looking at the units or ones column, you find the sum of 6, 4, 7, and 9 (or 9, 7, 4, and 6 if you add from the bottom up) to be 26. The 6 is written in the ones place of the sum and the 2 is written at the top of the tens column. The 9, 9, 0, and 7 are digits found in the tens column. The task in the problem is to add those digits representing groups of tens, without forgetting the 2 tens generated as an excess of ones. Thus, you add 2, 9, 9, 0, and 7, which yields a sum of 27, representing 27 tens or 270.

Whoa! That looks strange, yet, what we just described is what is going on behind the scenes as you add whole numbers. We will leave this discussion of how you do the problem via the standard algorithm for you to think through on your own. As we look at some other methods of finding the sum, you will gain more insight into what goes on in the background as you add.

Partial Sum

Consider the example we used earlier:

```
  4 7 3 9 6
  7 0 1 9 4
  5 8 3 0 7
+   2 8 7 9
```

The objective is still to find the sum of four multidigit addends, but we are going to change emphasis. Focus on the place value associated with each column and then treat each column as an individual problem. This approach is dependent on ideas generated in the sequence for adding whole numbers, in particular, the concept of adding multiples of tens to multiples of tens, multiples of hundreds to multiples of hundreds, and so on. Even though the format is going to appear strange to you, try to focus on the steps involved and how using partial sums actually simplifies multidigit addition:

```
        4 7 3 9 6
        7 0 1 9 4
        5 8 3 0 7
      +   2 8 7 9
              2 6    Sum of ones
            2 5 0    Sum of tens
          1 4 0 0    Sum of hundreds
        1 7 0 0 0    Sum of thousands
      1 6 0 0 0 0    Sum of ten-thousands
```

The total of the partial sums (26 + 250 + 1400 + 17000 + 160000) can now be found rather easily. The difference between the partial sum method and the standard algorithm is that, because of the emphasis on place value, regroupings are not listed above the respective columns. Aside from rearranging the order of steps somewhat, the problem is essentially done the same as you would do it using the standard algorithm. Although it might look strange in the partial sum format, the problem is easier to do because the regroupings are more logically arranged. Yes, all those zeros might look strange too, but they do clarify what is going on.

Denominate Numbers

Denominate numbers use a numeral and a word that describes the place value of the number. An example of this notation is to write 247 as 2 hundreds 4 tens 7 ones. We can make a quick association from 3 oranges plus 4 oranges to 30 + 40 by saying 3 tens plus 4 tens. You may find this trivially simple, never realizing what a giant leap is involved. You even make the transition from 7 tens back to 70 intuitively. Like partial sums, denominate

numbers are vital to understanding the concepts behind whole number addition.

Using denominate numbers, the addition problem 4567 + 319 + 208 = ? becomes:

```
 4 thousands  5 hundreds 6 tens 7 ones
              3 hundreds 1 ten  9 ones
 +                       2 hundreds 0 tens 8 ones
```

Adding in a column and remembering the 3 oranges plus 4 oranges example, we have 4 thousands 10 hundreds 7 tens 24 ones. You should immediately call on prior knowledge about place value to regroup the 10 hundreds to 1 thousand 0 hundreds and the 24 ones to 2 tens 4 ones. Finally, combine the 1 thousand with the 4 thousands and the 2 tens with the 7 tens. The sum is 5 thousands 0 hundreds 9 tens 4 ones, or 5094. This may seem no less cumbersome than the partial sums method, but it provides a reminder of how important place value is in our arithmetic.

Your Turn

Complete each exercise twice, first using partial sums and then using denominate numbers. Explain how the two algorithms are essentially the same:

4. 4837 + 3519 = ?
5. 647 + 10254 + 9938 = △
6. 24751 + 608 + 93 + 3562 = ♥

Horizontal and Vertical Writing

You should be comfortable with both vertical and horizontal writing while solving exercises. We used a vertical format for showing how to work with partial sums and denominate numbers, and then wrote the exercises in a horizontal format. Which format did you use as you solved the exercises? We could have presented the denominate number example as "4 thousands + 5 hundreds + 6 tens + 7 ones + 3 hundreds + 1 ten + 9 ones + 2 hundreds + 0 tens + 8 ones." This can be conveniently rewritten to group place value names together. Writing "4 thousands + 5 hundreds + 3 hundreds + 2 hundreds + 6 tens + 1 ten + 0 tens + 7 ones + 9 ones + 8 ones" makes the problem very similar to the example in vertical format and touches, once again, on the algebra concept of combining like terms. A person who understands the place value names can add the ones or hundreds first and still correctly complete the exercise.

Your Turn

Use the "other" format for denominate numbers to complete the addition problems. If you used the vertical format before, then try the horizontal format now, or if you used the horizontal format before, then try the vertical format now:

7. 4837 + 3519 = ?
8. 647 + 10254 + 9938 = ☐
9. 24751 + 608 + 93 + 3562 = ☐

Expanded Notation

Expanded notation is a fast way to employ the concept of denominate numbers while using the power of our place value system. Instead of writing a word for the place value, zeros are used to hold the place value. A vertical or horizontal format may be used, and you decide which column to add first. The exercise
2981 + 306 + 247 = ? would be expanded as:

```
   2000 + 900 + 80 + 1
          300 +  0 + 6
+         200 + 40 + 7
```

and addition within columns, gives respective sums of 2000 + 1400 + 120 + 14. The respective column sums could then be expanded giving 2000 + (1000 + 400) + (100 + 20) + (10 + 4). Next, grouping like place values together yields (2000 + 1000) + (400 + 100) + (20 + 10) + 4 or 3000 + 500 + 30 + 4, which is 3534 in standard notation.

Your Turn

Complete the exercises using expanded notation. Do not skip steps. Writing out all the steps will help to solidify the concepts:

10. 4837 + 3519 = ?
11. 647 + 10254 + 9938 = ☐
12. 24751 + 608 + 93 + 3562 = ✎

Left to Right Addition

Adding from left to right makes a lot of sense to some people because they read from left to right. Consider the problem we used earlier to introduce partial sums, but this time work it from left to right.

```
     4 7 3 9 6
     7 0 1 9 4
     5 8 3 0 7
+      2 8 7 9
 1 6 0 0 0 0   Sum of ten thousands
   1 7 0 0 0   Sum of thousands
     1 4 0 0   Sum of hundreds
       2 5 0   Sum of tens
         2 6   Sum of ones
```

The total of the partial sums (160000 + 17000 + 1400 + 250 + 26) can now be found, only this time the exercise was worked from the larger numbers to the smaller numbers, which is often the way real-life problems are approached (depending on the problem situation, we may ignore the smaller partial sums, in effect rounding to a significant value).

You might experience a little difficulty with alignment in this format. Typically, we do not write all those zeros but, if there has been any emphasis on adding multiples of tens, hundreds, and so on, then the idea is fairly simple. One quick solution is to use standard notebook paper rotated 90° from the normal position as a means of keeping values aligned within respective columns.

Your Turn

Complete the exercises using left to right addition. Be sure to use partial sums, denominate numbers, and expanded notation at least once each in this set. Can you determine which exercise is easiest in which method?

13. 4837 + 3519 = ?
14. 647 + 10254 + 9938 = K
15. 24751 + 608 + 93 + 3562 = O

Scratch Method

The scratch method is very similar to the "left to right" method. Rather than listing the partial sums as shown in the "left to right" method, digits are scratched out and replaced by new values as needed. Start working from the left and proceed to the right, one column at a time. In the following example, the sum of the ten thousands column is 160000. The sum of the thousands column is 25000, which is 2 ten thousands plus 5 thousands. The 2 ten thousands are grouped with the 6 ten thousands already present, so scratch out the 6 and replace it with an 8 in the ten thousands column. Continue to the right, scratching out the old value and inserting the new one as needed. The final sum is

read starting from the left and using the new values along with any that are not scratched out.

```
  4 8 9 7 1
  5 6 3 2 0
  1 2 3 4 9
+ 6 9 8 9 9
1 6 5 3 2 9
  8 7 5 3     and the sum is 187539.
```

Your Turn

Complete the exercises using the scratch method.

16. 4837 + 3519 = ?
17. 647 + 10254 + 9938 = Π
18. 24751 + 608 + 93 + 3562 = χ

Any Column First

Anyone with a good understanding of place value might start by adding any column first. The next example is completed in a seemingly random order, but the order could be driven by familiarity with certain facts, groups of digits to be added, or relevance based on a real-life problem. You will notice similarities between this method and partial sums or left to right addition. Without a clear understanding of place value, this method would be very confusing:

```
  4 8 9 7 1
  5 6 3 2 0
  1 2 3 4 9
+ 6 9 8 9 9
      2 3 0 0
1 6 0 0 0 0
          1 9
  2 5 0 0 0
+     2 3 0
1 8 7 5 3 9
```

Your Turn

Examine the exercises and determine if there is a column addition order that is optimal. State the reason for each decision. Then complete the exercise using your column order.

19. 4837 + 3519 = ?
20. 647 + 10254 + 9938 = (
21. 24751 + 608 + 93 + 3562 = #

Low Stress Addition

Suppose the task is to find the sum of 9, 8, and 9, in column addition. Consider what happens in your head as you find this sum. The first part, 9 + 8 is easy because it is a fact, yielding a sum of 17. The next step is to find the sum of 17 and 9, which is not a fact. You have worked this problem, but it probably was formatted as:

```
  1        (regroup 10 ones as one 10)
  1 7
+   9
  2 6.
```

As 17 and 9 are added, what really happens in your head is the 17 is expressed as 10 + 7. The "10" is remembered and the sum of 7 and 9, which is a fact, is determined to be 16. That 16 is actually 10 + 6, so now the aggregate is 10 + (10 + 6) = (10 + 10) + 6 = 20 + 6 = 26. Granted, you do the problem much more reflexively, and much more quickly, than is shown in this example. But, if you think about it, what we described is exactly what you must ask your brain to do for you.

The low stress algorithm eliminates the need to remember all those multiples of ten and keeps the problem as a collection of addition facts. The demonstration below shows the addition of 9 + 8 + 9 + 7 + 9:

```
    9
    8
  1    7   (9 + 8 = 17)
    9
  1    6   (7 + 9 = 16)
    7
  1    3   (6 + 7 = 13)
+   9
  1        (10 from 3 + 9)
       2   (2 from 3 + 9)
+ 4 0      (sum the 10s at the left)
  4 2
```

Does that look strange to you? As with many procedures that are quite simple in use, it takes a bit of explaining. Even if you have to read through the explanation twice, it will be worth your time to learn this simple method. The initial partial sum of 9 + 8 is written below the 8, but spaced out as shown in the example. Actually, you are just writing your scratch work in a different format, as you go. Once the 17 is written, a new problem is done but the emphasis is only on the ones digit from the 17 and the next addend, 9. This maintains the idea of dealing only with addition facts and the sum 16 is listed below the second 9, using the same format as was used for the 17 initially. Once again, the ones digit (6 in this case) from the partial sum, and the next addend (7) are considered, giving a sum of 13, which is written like the 17 and 16 before it were. For the final addition fact, there is a slight difference in the presentation. The ones digit (3) from the last partial sum is added to the next addend (the final 9). The ones digit from the new partial sum is written in the ones column of the answer, where it would normally be found. The tens digit from this new partial sum is written below and to the left of the last addend. Now the tens from each of the partial sums are compiled and, in this example, there are four of them. That total of 4 tens is listed in the sum in its normal location. Typically, the 40 is not shown as a part of the partial sum as we have done, for clarity, in the example. Rather, the problem would be shown as:

```
        9
        8
  1     9     7
  1     7     6
  1     9     3
  + 
  1
 ─────────────
  4     2
```

Although this method might look strange to you, it is extremely appealing to individuals who struggle with column addition. What could appear to be a formidable task is reduced to dealing with a collection of addition facts. The low stress method can be used with more than single digit addends. You only need a little more space between columns and any regrouping from a value is placed at the top of the respective next column. After that, the process is exactly as discussed here.

We are not going to formally assign problems to be done using the low stress method for addition. Rather, we want you to take the responsibility for doing some problems on your own to practice using the method. Without that practice, low stress addition will not become a part of your repertoire.

Conclusions

We hope we have tweaked your interest in the different ways to do addition. We have shown you some of them and encourage you to learn to add using a variety of methods. Of course, there is technology available that provides a fast way of doing all arithmetic. We believe in using technology when appropriate, but we also believe you must have an understanding of how the operations are done. Your responsibilities may include decisions about when technology is appropriate to use and when it is not; these decisions must not be made lightly. As you reflect on this issue, remember that there is more to the world of mathematics than being good at doing arithmetic, but being good at doing arithmetic will help smooth your way into the world of mathematics.

Bibliography

Hutchings, B. (1976). Low-stress algorithms. *Measurement in school mathematics, 1976 yearbook* (D. Nelson, Ed., & R. E. Reys, General Ed.). Reston, VA: NCTM.

WHOLE NUMBER SUBTRACTION

FOCAL POINTS

- Terminology
- Concrete Subtraction
- Denominate Numbers
- Expanded Notation
- Standard Algorithm
- Left to Right Subtraction
- Scratch Method
- Any Column First
- Borrow-Pay Back Method
- Integer Subtraction

Subtraction follows addition in most contexts. Most of the methods used for addition can be altered and used in subtraction. The sequence starts with learning the subtraction facts, which is really just a different way of thinking about the addition facts. Remember that when we say "facts," we imply an operation involving three numbers, two of which are digits. For example, in addition, the two digits are addends and the third number (which may or may not be a digit) is the sum. The subtraction procedures we will discuss here require subtracting a whole number from a whole number, so that a whole number is the result.

Terminology

Subtraction and addition are inverse operations, meaning that subtraction undoes addition and addition undoes subtraction. Connections such as this inverse relation can help you become more comfortable with subtraction. Consider the following arrangement where a subtraction exercise is written vertically and names for the parts are written beside the respective numbers:

Exercise	Historic name	Name connected to addition
8	Minuend	Sum
−3	Subtrahend	Addend
5	Difference	Missing addend

Increasing your mathematics vocabulary is one of the goals of this text, but we feel that vocabulary words should be meaningful. Whereas the words minuend, subtrahend, and difference are descriptive, and historical, they do not strengthen the connection between subtraction and addition. These three words continue to be used. We believe it makes more sense to have a verbal connection between subtraction and addition problems so we will use sum, addend, and missing addend. We will discuss three commonly accepted versions of subtraction: take away, comparison, and add-up.

Focus on the subtraction problem 8 − 3 = ♣. What is the ♣? If you know your subtraction facts, then you can do the problem. If you do not know your subtraction facts, then you could figure it out using a

manipulative with the take away model as shown in Fig. 2.12. In this model, you start out with 8 buttons and literally take three away. Counting how many buttons are left after the removal of the three gives you how many buttons remain.

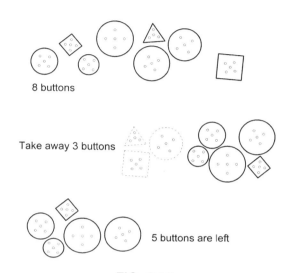

8 buttons

Take away 3 buttons

5 buttons are left

FIG. 2.12.

Subtraction is often used when comparing the cardinality sets. Whereas nothing is literally taken away in such situations, the process involves subtracting the cardinal number of the smaller set from the cardinal number of the larger set. This is often seen in simple word problems like, "Pat has a collection of 8 buttons. Chris has 3 buttons. How many more buttons than Chris does Pat have?" The problem would be done as 8 − 3 = 5, even though nothing has been taken away. This is a different description of the problem in Fig. 2.12.

The missing addend, or add up, approach can be used with buttons too, but it is dependent on knowledge of addition facts, helping to perhaps open your mind to a slightly different way of thinking about subtraction of whole numbers. Suppose the problem is 11 − 6 = ⊗. You know the sum is 11 and that one addend is 6. The task is to determine the missing addend. Asking, "What number, when added to 6 gives 11?" implies that we need to recall an addition fact. You are not starting at 11 and taking away in this scenario. Rather, you are searching your memory banks to determine the specific addition fact that will meet all the requirements of the problem. By doing that, you are identifying the missing addend. Think carefully about how you do some subtraction problems and you might find that this is a technique you subconsciously use. We hope it is one you will now consciously endeavor to employ as you approach subtraction problems in which neither take away nor comparison is involved. A simple word problem of this type might be, "Jesse has saved $14.00 and wants to buy a $21.00 shirt. How much more must Jesse save to be able to buy the shirt?" In this example, the money needed does not exist, so we can't use take away or comparison. We must use our knowledge of addition and determine how much must be added on, we need the missing addend.

Figure 2.13 shows what happens as 8 − 3 = ♣ is done on the number line. You have the starting point of zero and the length of the vector that represents the ad-

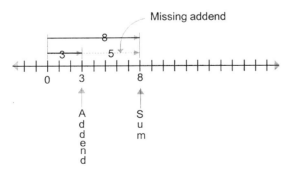

1. Sketch a vector from zero to the sum and label the sum.

2. Sketch a vector from zero to the addend and label it.

3. Sketch a dashed vector from the addend to the sum to show the missing addend.

4. The direction of the motion from the addend to the sum indicates the way the arrowhead should point.

FIG. 2.13.

dend three. The vector from the origin or zero to eight shows the sum. The dashed vector shows the distance between the addend and the sum, or the missing addend. If you think in terms of the missing addend terminology, then you have a known sum of eight and a known addend of three. The thing you do not know is the missing addend. Using the number line model, you can determine the missing addend by counting from the arrowhead of the first vector to the arrowhead of the sum. Right now the arrowheads on the segments might not seem necessary, but this model is very handy when looking at integer operations and we are laying the groundwork for using arrowheads later to indicate positive and negative values.

Your Turn

Do the following problems using the appropriate model:

1. Jo has 14 marbles and loses 8. How many are left?

2. Shawn owns 4 high value stamps, and Sean owns 11 high value stamps. How many more high value stamps does Sean own?

3. Chris has 5 cards left but started with 17. How many are missing?

Concrete Subtraction

Whereas addition is typically presented using a single model, a couple subtraction models are frequently used. We show what is probably the most common one now, but remember, not everyone subtracts this way. This developmental discussion will help you gain a better understanding of what is going on in your head as you subtract. Remember, there are several valid ways of subtracting. Consider the exercise 312 − 147 = ♦. Rarely would it be solved in the horizontal format. Rather you would see it vertically as shown here:

$$\begin{array}{r} 3\ 1\ 2 \\ -\ 1\ 4\ 7 \\ \hline \end{array}$$

Base 10 blocks have three fundamental pieces, as shown in Fig. 2.14: a square with 100 units, usually called a Hundred, or Flat; a bar with 10 units, usually called a *Ten*, or Long; and a single unit, usually called a *One*, or *Unit*.

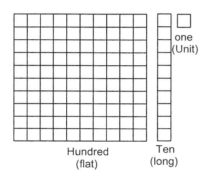

one
(Unit)

Hundred
(flat)

Ten
(long)

FIG. 2.14.

We will show several stages to complete 312 − 147 = ?. The first step is shown in Fig. 2.15. The one Long in the sum (312) needs to be traded for ten Units so there will be enough Units in the sum to allow subtracting 7. Notice how the Long is traded for 10 Units and then a one-to-one correspondence is established between the 7 Units to be taken away and any 7 of the 12 Units in the sum after the trade. Now 5 Units are left. Observe how the regrouping is quite similar to what you would do using a pencil and

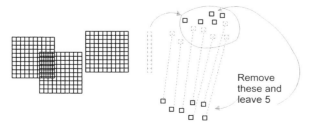

Remove these and leave 5

FIG. 2.15.

paper subtraction procedure where you would cross out the one Ten, write a zero above it, and then write a 12 above the 2.

Next, consider the Tens column. After the regrouping, the sum has no Longs and the addend has a 4 in the Tens column. Figure 2.16 shows how one of the

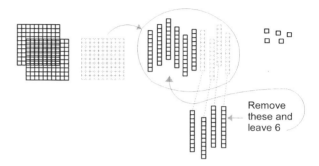

Remove these and leave 6

FIG. 2.16.

Flats in the sum is regrouped to give 10 Longs so the procedure can be completed. Once the regrouping is finished, a one-to-one correspondence is established between any 4 of the Longs in the sum and the 4 Tens in the addend, leaving 6 Longs.

Finally, we will deal with the hundreds. Figure 2.17 shows how that would be accomplished with the Base 10 blocks by establishing a one-to-one correspondence between any one of the Flats in the sum and the Hundred in the addend. Finally, Fig. 2.18 models the missing addend. Granted, you could quickly do this problem abstractly or on a calculator, but

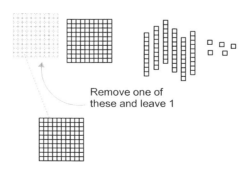

Remove one of these and leave 1

FIG. 2.17.

The missing addend of 147

FIG. 2.18.

it is important that you investigate this procedure using the Base 10 blocks because it shows clearly what is going on in your head as you regroup to subtract. Remembering our discussion about adding any column first, you may wonder why we did not begin by taking away one Flat. By rearranging the discussion and accompanying figures, you'll find that the model is valid whether you begin the exercise with the Longs, Flats, or Units.

Denominate Numbers

With denominate numbers, the problem 312 − 147 would be expressed as (3 Hundreds 1 Ten 2 Units) − (1 Hundred 4 Tens 7 Units). With paper and pencil, the problem could be done with denominate numbers in a manner very similar to that of the Base 10 blocks. Its appearance will also remind you of the standard algorithm for subtraction.

2 Hundreds				
3 ~~Hundreds~~	10 Tens			
	0 Tens	12 Units		
3 Hundreds	~~1 Ten~~	~~2 Units~~	Sum	
−1 Hundred	4 Tens	7 Units	Addend	
1 Hundred	6 Tens	5 Units	Missing addend	

A little investigation should show this procedure to be quite familiar. The one Ten in the sum is traded to make 12 Units, leaving no Tens in the sum. Once that trade is made, the 7 Units are subtracted from the 12 Units. Because we need 4 Tens and there are now no Tens in the sum, one of the Hundreds in the sum is exchanged for

10 Tens, leaving 2 Hundreds in the sum. The 4 Tens in the addend are now subtracted from the 10 Tens in the sum. Finally, the 1 Hundred in the addend is subtracted from the 2 Hundreds in the sum, giving a missing addend of 1 Hundred 6 Tens 5 Units.

Expanded Notation

Expanded notation can also be used to express the sum and addend as (300 + 10 + 2) − (100 + 40 + 7). The scratch notes are similar to the denominate number work:

$$
\begin{array}{r}
200 \quad 100 \quad 12 \\
\cancel{300} + \cancel{10} + \cancel{2} \\
-\ 100 + 40 + 7 \\
\hline
100 + 60 + 5
\end{array}
$$

Notice that the regroupings are shown above the crossed out values, all in one row, getting ever closer to the standard algorithm used by most people.

Standard Algorithm

Finally, we arrive at the standard algorithm, which is probably the most common way of subtracting:

$$
\begin{array}{r}
2 \quad 10 \quad 12 \\
\cancel{3} \quad \cancel{1} \quad \cancel{2} \\
-\ 1 \quad\ 4 \quad\ 7 \\
\hline
1 \quad\ 6 \quad\ 5
\end{array}
$$

You should be able to now connect the standard algorithm back through the sequence of expanded notation, denominate numbers, and the Base 10 blocks themselves.

We spent a lot of time developing that sequence with you. We did it to help you understand what your brain is doing as you subtract. We have assumed that the problem we used for our example is representative of several problem types and that you will transfer the development to all other aspects of whole number subtraction.

Your Turn

4. Shawn scored 512 on a video game and Reggie scored 178 on the same game. How much higher was Shawn's score than Reggie's? Do this problem using each of the stages: concrete, denominate numbers, expanded notation, and standard algorithm. Write a concluding paragraph explaining how the different steps in the various stages are connected across the stages.

Borrow Pay Back Method

This method is another candidate for a standard subtraction algorithm, but it will seem strange to you if you have not done it. You will find it rather easy to do, and quite natural, if you just practice it a little. Consider again 312 − 147 and examine how the borrow pay back method works. Although we will write replacement values in the example, people who use this method rarely write any scratch work:

$$
\begin{array}{ccc}
 & & 12 \\
3 & 1 & \cancel{2} \\
 & 5 & \\
-1 & \cancel{4} & 7 \\
\hline
 & & 5 \\
\end{array}
$$

Here, the 2 Units are "made to be" 12 Units. Essentially, 10 Units have been added to the sum. However, that would change the problem so, to compensate, an additional Ten is added to the 4 Tens that are to be subtracted, implying that 5 Tens must be subtracted. The problem

has not been changed because both the sum and the addend have been increased by 10 giving a net change of zero. The only thing is, we have opted to write that zero a little differently, as shown in the example. Similarly, the 1 Ten in the sum is made to be 11 Tens and the 1 Hundred to be subtracted is changed to 2 Hundreds to be subtracted. Again, we increased both the sum and the addend by the same quantity, so the net resultant change is zero. So, in the Tens column you have 11 − 5, which is 6 Tens—as shown in the sum. Finally, 2 Hundreds are subtracted from 3 Hundreds and the missing addend is 165:

$$
\begin{array}{ccc}
 & 11 & 12 \\
3 & \cancel{1} & \cancel{2} \\
2 & 5 & \\
-\cancel{1} & \cancel{4} & 7 \\
\hline
1 & 6 & 5 \\
\end{array}
$$

As we said, that might look like a strange way to subtract, but it is commonly taught in some areas of the United States and it is the dominant procedure taught in Australia. Check out another example:

$$
\begin{array}{cccc}
 & 13 & 12 & 11 \\
4 & 5 & \cancel{3} & \cancel{2} & \cancel{1} \\
 & 4 & 10 & 8 \\
-1 & \cancel{2} & \cancel{9} & \cancel{7} & 8 \\
\hline
3 & 1 & 3 & 4 & 3 \\
\end{array}
$$

The 1 in the Units place of the sum is made to be an 11 to accommodate subtracting 8. However, that essentially adds 10 Units to the sum and to compensate, another Ten must be subtracted. That is accomplished by changing the 7 Tens to be subtracted to 8 Tens. Once that change is made, the Tens column subtraction is 2 − 8. Again, there is a need to change those 2 Tens to 12 Tens so the subtraction can be completed. That change to 12 Tens mandates that the 9 Hundreds to be subtracted be changed to 10 Hundreds so the problem is not changed. Next, the Hundreds column now asks for 10 to be subtracted from 3, something that is not feasible within the parameters of the take away model of subtraction. So, the 3 Hundreds is made to become 13 Hundreds and the subtraction in the Hundreds column can be completed. Those extra 10 Hundreds in the sum must be compensated for by changing the 3 Thousands that are to be subtracted to 4 Thousands. Now, in the Thousands column, the problem asks for 4 to be subtracted from 5, and because this can be done within the realm of subtraction facts, no compensation or changes are necessary. Similarly, the Ten-thousands column subtraction can be done with no further complications and the missing addend is 31343. As we said earlier, once you try a few, you will get the hang of it; the limitations of a written explanation imply greater complexity than is actually involved in practice.

Left to Right Subtraction

You do not have to start in the right-hand column when subtracting. Starting from the left may seem more natural because almost everything students do except their arithmetic is done working from the left to the right. Doing the problem 312 − 147 in expanded notation (or with the blocks, denominate numbers, etc.) would be started in this manner if you were using the method of starting from the left:

$$
\begin{array}{r}
300 + 10 + 2 \\
- \ 100 + 40 + 7 \\
\hline
200
\end{array}
$$

Now, dealing with the Tens column, there is a need for additional Tens in the sum so one of the 2 Hundreds in the missing ad-

dend must be regrouped into 10 Tens to enable the subtraction. It would look like

$$
\begin{array}{r}
110 \\
300 + \ \cancel{10} + 2 \\
- \ 100 + \ 40 + 7 \\
\hline
\cancel{200} + \ 70 \\
100
\end{array}
$$

and now you would focus on the Units. Again, there are not enough Units in the sum, so one of the 7 Tens in the missing addend has to be regrouped to make enough Units so the subtraction may be completed. The completed exercise would look like:

$$
\begin{array}{r}
110 + 12 \\
300 + \ \cancel{10} + \ \cancel{2} \\
-100 + \ 40 + 7 \\
\hline
\cancel{200} + \ \cancel{70} \\
100 + \ 60 + 5 = 165
\end{array}
$$

Scratch Method

The left to right procedure is quite similar to the scratch method for subtraction and could be considered a developmental step to doing scratch subtraction. The problem would be done as shown, with 165 as the missing addend:

$$
\begin{array}{r}
11 \ 12 \\
3 \ \ \cancel{1} \ \ \cancel{2} \\
-1 \ \ 4 \ \ 7 \\
\hline
\cancel{2} \ \ \cancel{7} \ \ 5 \\
1 \ \ 6
\end{array}
$$

Notice how the 2 from the Hundreds in the missing addend is scratched out. It is replaced with the 1 Hundred below it. Similarly, the 7 from the Tens is scratched out and replaced with 6 Tens below it. This looks very much like left to right subtraction.

Any Column First

This subtraction is quite similar to left to right and yet different because it permits beginning in any column. Regroupings are done as needed. This procedure emphasizes, once again, how important the understandings of place value, regrouping, and subtraction facts are to any subtraction exercise. Starting with the Tens column first would look like:

$$
\begin{array}{r}
{\scriptstyle 2}\ {\scriptstyle 11} \\
\cancel{3}\ \ \cancel{1}\ \ 2 \\
-1\ \ 4\ \ 7 \\
\hline
7
\end{array}
$$

If we move to the Hundreds next, then the situation is simple because no regrouping is necessary. Then, if we do the Units last (although it could have been done second because we are not concerned with the sequence of columns being used), then regrouping is necessary and would look like this:

$$
\begin{array}{r}
{\scriptstyle 2}\ {\scriptstyle 11}\ {\scriptstyle 12} \\
\cancel{3}\ \ \cancel{1}\ \ \cancel{2} \\
-1\ \ 4\ \ 7 \\
\hline
1\ \ \cancel{7}\ \ 5 \\
6
\end{array}
$$

Integer Subtraction

Folklore has it that an elementary-age student developed this method of subtracting. Card games were common in the home and the child often experienced not having enough points on the books to "cover" when someone else "went out." For example, the child might have 3 points on the books when someone else was able to "go out," "catching" the child with 7 points. So, the child was "down" 4, 4 "in the hole," or had a "negative" 4. Similar re-

sults would be generated if the child had 40 points on the books and got caught with 60 when another player "went out." This child was doing subtraction problems in school and the teacher noticed the unusual manner in which the problems were done. The child's work looked like this:

$$
\begin{array}{r}
3\ 1\ 2 \\
-1\ 4\ 7 \\
\hline
5 \\
3\ 0 \\
2\ 0\ 0 \\
\hline
1\ 6\ 5
\end{array}
$$

At first glance, it seems as if the little number is subtracted from the big number, but, somehow, the right answer evolves. The child consistently did problems this way, getting them correct each time. Investigation revealed that the child was in fact "subtracting the little number from the big number" in a column, but was "recording" the values as negative if the addend in a column was greater than the sum value in the column. In this example, the child compiled a positive 200 with a negative 30 and a negative 5, giving a net result of 165 for the missing addend. The name for this method is integer subtraction, because the child was using both positive and negative numbers.

Your Turn

Do the following subtraction problems using each of the following methods: borrow pay back, left to right, scratch, any column first, and integer. Show your regroupings in each style in a manner that would justify a complete explanation:

5. 8314 − 2756
6. 703 − 164
7. How would a problem like 8152 − 1936 impact each of borrow pay

back, left to right, scratch, any column first and integer subtraction?

Conclusions

You have seen a variety of ways to subtract. We encourage you to practice using the different methods. Each one will enhance your understanding of subtraction and build a stronger mathematical background for you.

WHOLE NUMBER MULTIPLICATION

FOCAL POINTS

- Terminology
- Beginnings
- Standard Algorithm
- Partial Product Method
- FOIL
- Lattice Multiplication
- Left to Right Multiplication
- Horizontal and Vertical Writing
- Russian Peasant

Few adults think beyond the standard algorithm and multiplication facts memorized in elementary school. It is not uncommon for people to think that the standard algorithm is the only correct way to multiply, even though they may use their own invented shortcuts in their daily lives. We will discuss several methods for multiplying whole numbers and show you that no one method is better than any other, although one may be more practical than others in any given situation.

Terminology

The language of mathematics uses many everyday terms. Times is no longer linked solely to the idea of events, but is associated with the operation called multiplica-

tion. Product is now more than something to be associated with a brand name or store item. Factor is something beyond an idea or point to be considered. In multiplication, a factor times a factor yields a product. For example, in $3 \times 4 = 12$, both the 3 and 4 are factors and 12 is the product. To express the idea of multiplying the 3 and 4, we say 3 times 4. The product of 3 and 4 could also be written as (3)(4), 3*4, or 3•4. In algebra, the product of 7 and the variable v would normally be written as 7v, but it could also be written as (7)(v), 7(v), or even v7 (v7 is not commonly seen and is usually considered poor notation). In general, numerals are placed before variables, that is, 7v. Rarely will you see 7v written as $7 \times v$ because of the potential confusion between whether the $\times$ is a variable or the times symbol. Once you grasp the concepts behind the language and writing styles, you will better understand the wonderful world of mathematics.

Multiplication depends on an understanding of place value and assumes a command of multiplication facts. The products of all the combinations of digits make up the 100 multiplication facts. Ten of the multiplication facts are doubles (a digit times itself). Remove the doubles from the hundred multiplication facts and 90 are left. However, if the commutative property of multiplication on the set of whole numbers is known, the need to memorize 90 facts is reduced to 45, giving a total of 55 facts that need to be memorized (the 45 plus the 10 doubles).

If you know and understand the role of zero as a factor (zero times any number is zero), then you can eliminate 19 facts. Starting with a new fact table, knowing the role of the multiplicative identity (one times any number is the number itself) decreases the number of multiplication facts to be memorized by another 19. Thus, although there are a total of 100 multiplication facts to be memorized, some basic knowledge can trim that number significantly. Figure 2.19 shows a completed multiplication fact table with a dashed line segment passing along the doubles or major diagonal.

	0	1	2	3	4	5	6	7	8	9
0	0	0	0	0	0	0	0	0	0	0
1	0	1	2	3	4	5	6	7	8	9
2	0	2	4	6	8	10	12	14	16	18
3	0	3	6	9	12	15	18	21	24	27
4	0	4	8	12	16	20	24	28	32	36
5	0	5	10	15	20	25	30	35	40	45
6	0	6	12	18	24	30	36	42	48	54
7	0	7	14	21	28	35	42	49	56	63
8	0	8	16	24	32	40	48	56	64	72
9	0	9	18	27	36	45	54	63	72	81

FIG. 2.19.

Beginnings

The basic concept of multiplication can be modeled in straightforward, everyday contexts. We start with sets of shirts and pants. If you have three shirts and two pairs of pants, how many different outfits can you make (we are not going to be style conscious here, so we do not care about mixing things that might not go well together)? Figure 2.20 shows that you can

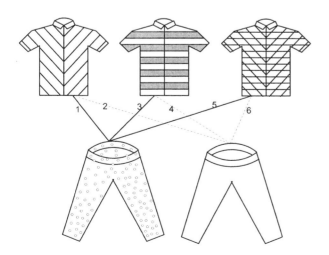

FIG. 2.20.

create six different combinations or outfits. This set representation can be extended to larger numbers and different situations, but the mentality is still the same.

The number line is another way that multiplication can be modeled. If we think in terms of repeated addition, we can describe multiplication as a shortcut way of adding. Perhaps you have heard someone say four threes, when referring to four times three. That verbiage is a clue that four threes are being added together. Figure 2.21 shows how the situation would appear on a number line. We have shown the addends as stops along the way as the product is approached.

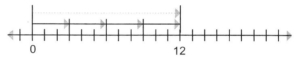

FIG. 2.21.

Standard Algorithm

The standard multiplication algorithm is another process you may have learned without understanding the concept. Consider the following example and then carefully examine our explanation of the process involved in finding the product. You might determine that many of the steps we list are things you do reflexively. Yet, as you investigate what it means to multiply, you need to be aware of each of these steps:

```
  5
    7
    5 8
×   7 9
  5 2 2
4 0 6
4 5 8 2
```

What happened as 58 is multiplied by 79? First you multiply the number in the Units column of the second factor times the number in the Units column of the first factor to get a product of 72. That 72 is really 7 Tens and 2 Units. The 7 Tens are written above the Tens digit of the top factor of the problem and the 2 is written beneath the Units digit of the lower factor. Granted, you know all of that, but did you know or had you ever thought about the terminology and rationalizations? Next you multiply the number in the Units column of the lower factor times the number in the Tens column of the upper factor. This is really 9×50 (although you probably say 9×5) and the product is 450. We know that zero is the additive identity and so, adding it to the 2 you already placed below the Units digit of the lower factor would not change anything. You may not have thought about it in this way before. The product of 450 could be considered as 45 Tens (because $450 = 45 \times 10$), but there is an additional 7 Tens from the earlier multiplication. Add the 7 Tens that were listed above the Tens digit of the top factor to the 45 Tens you just generated and you get 52 Tens. Because that is really 520, write the 52 next to the 2 in the Units column. Then multiply the digit in the Tens place of the lower factor times the digit in the Units column of the top factor and get 560 (it was really 70×8). Perhaps you were taught to write a zero under the 2, being told it was a placeholder. It is a placeholder, but there is a reason for the existence of the zero and you now either know or recall the explanation. Write the 5 above and to the left of the regrouped 7 from before and place the 6 beneath the Tens column of the 522. This happens because the product of 560 is really $500 + 60$ and although you have the ability to write the 60, the 500 will need to be added to more Hundreds about to be generated as the multiplication is continued. Multiply the digit in the

Tens column of the bottom factor times the digit in the Tens column of the top factor and get 3500 (70×50 even though you probably only say 7×5 to yourself), which can be expressed as 35 Hundreds. Add the 5 Hundreds that were regrouped to the 35 Hundreds, getting a total of 40 Hundreds. We know that 40 Hundreds would also be 4000 and adding the 60 to it will not change things, which allows us to write the 40 to the left of the 6. The multiplication problem has been converted to a problem that involves adding 522 and 4060, giving an answer of 4582, which is the product of 58 and 79.

Even today, many students are taught to multiply the digits in the Tens columns as if they were simply multiplying digits without any explanation or expectation of understanding. As long as you can do the problem and get the right answer, little emphasis is placed on knowing why or how things work. How wrong is that? We took the time to carefully explain the steps in a standard multiplication algorithm to help you understand the importance of each of them. It is imperative that you master the behind the scenes workings of arithmetic operations.

Partial Product Method

Partial products are user friendly and provide an intuitive background of what happens during the operation of multiplication. We delayed introducing the partial product method to help you understand the complexities of what you do as you use the standard algorithm for multiplication. The partial product approach to multiplication relies on the two basic concepts: multiplication facts and place value. Although the partial product method of multiplication requires a little more writing, it eliminates regrouping, and could ease confusion. Consider the following example:

```
        5 8
    ×   7 9
        7 2    (9 × 8)
      4 5 0    (9 × 50)
      5 6 0    (70 × 8)
    3 5 0 0    (70 × 50)
    4 5 8 2
```

Each of the four products needed to complete this exercise are present and there is an emphasis on place value; the idea of multiplying a digit by a multiple of ten (9 × 50 and 70 × 8), and the need to find the product of a multiple of ten times another multiple of ten (70 × 50). This is another instance where you could rotate your notebook paper 90° to keep track of your columns.

These partial products could be listed in any order as long as they are all present, but we opted to list them in the same order they would typically appear if the standard multiplication algorithm had been used with the problem. Take a moment to compare this procedure to the standard algorithm, step by step.

Perhaps you are thinking that we should have introduced the idea of partial products before the standard algorithm. We hope you are, because that would indicate you are beginning to pay attention to what goes on behind the scenes. It is important that you understand how multiplication works. If the goal is only to get the product, then we could simply use a calculator, because they do not give wrong products if the correct buttons are pressed. However, calculators cannot think—that continues to be your responsibility.

FOIL

An important bonus of partial products is that they demonstrate the distributive property of multiplication over addition on the set of whole numbers, an important and direct link to algebraic thinking. Emphasize place value by rewriting the exercise we have been doing and apply the distributive property on these factors:

$$
\begin{aligned}
58 \times 79 &= (50 + 8) \times (70 + 9) \\
&= (50 \times 70) + (50 \times 9) \\
&\quad + (8 \times 70) + (8 \times 9) \\
&= 3500 + 450 + 560 + 72 \\
&= 4582
\end{aligned}
$$

You have probably used the FOIL shortcut (Firsts, Outers, Inners, Lasts) in algebra. Partial products require the same procedure as FOIL! If you had learned to multiply whole numbers using partial products, a lot of valuable groundwork for algebra would have been established early.

Your Turn

Use the partial product method of multiplication (in either the vertical or horizontal format) to find the products in the following exercises:

1. 23 × 47 = ☐
2. 519 × 68 = |
3. 803 × 745 = ☐

Lattice Multiplication

So far, we have presented multiplication methods that could be sequenced to assist in learning the standard multiplication algorithm. We think a case can be built for approaching multiplication developmentally by starting with the facts followed by a careful staging of steps, followed by digits times multiples of ten, multiples of ten times multiples of ten, digits times multiples of hundreds, multiples of tens times multiples of hundreds, and so on until the role of place value in products is understood. That staging is necessary if one is to understand why each subsequent row is indented one space to the left as multiplication is performed using the standard algorithm.

Whereas lattice multiplication may or may not be a part of the developmental sequence, you will see that it is closely aligned with partial products and, as such, could be included in the growth progression. Lattice multiplication is an interesting process if you know your multiplication facts and can add. The exercise 436 × 29 is set up for lattice multiplication in Fig. 2.22. The digits of one factor are written above the array of squares,

FIG. 2.22.

starting at the left and going right until you run out of digits. The digits of the other factor are placed to the right of the rows of squares, starting at the top and going down until you run out of digits. Each column and row intersects to form a square, called a *cell*. The diagonals divide each cell into two triangles. Each cell contains a product generated by the digit from its respective row and column. The Tens digit of each product is placed above and to the left of the diagonal and the Units digit of each product is placed below and to the right of the diagonal. Notice that the product 4 × 2 has no Tens. To avoid confusion, a zero is written in the Tens position and the 8 is written in the Units position.

One beauty of lattice multiplication is that only multiplication facts are needed and they can be taken in any order. Once all the cells are filled, ignore the digits out-

side the array (the factors 426 and 39) and add the elements of each diagonal. In the example, starting from the right, the first sum is 4. The sum of the second diagonal is 14 (7 + 5 + 2 or 2 + 5 + 7). Careful examination will show that the actual value is 140, not 14. The 4 from the 14 is written at the base of the diagonal and the 1 is regrouped to the next diagonal. The third diagonal sum is 6 + 2 + 6 + 1, or 15, but the regrouped 1 must be added as well. Write the 6 and regroup the 1. The next sum is 3 + 8 + 0, or 11, plus the regrouped 1, giving 12. The 2 is written at the base of the diagonal and the 1 regrouped to the next diagonal. Finally, the last diagonal is 0 plus the regrouped 1 and the sum is written at the base of the last diagonal as shown in Fig. 2.23.

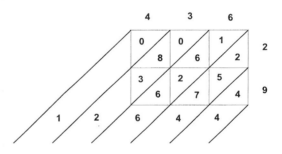

FIG. 2.23.

Look at that same problem done in partial product mode:

```
      436
   ×   29
       54      (9 × 6)
      270      (9 × 30)
     3600      (9 × 400)
      120      (20 × 6)
      600      (20 × 30)
     8000      (20 × 400)
    12644
```

Examine the columns in the partial sum section and you will see the diagonals from Fig. 2.23 except that the zeros are not written. Thus, a connection is made between lattice multiplication and partial products. Because partial products connect directly to the standard algorithm, lattice multiplication is closely related to the standard algorithm. Are you wondering if there is a connection with FOIL, too? We hope you are. If you were wondering about that, then you are beginning to investigate the behind the scenes workings of the arithmetic procedures you perform.

Yes, there is a connection between lattice multiplication and FOIL and it can be demonstrated with this same problem by writing it as (400 + 30 + 6)(20 + 9). Remember that FOIL is really a shortcut for the distributive property of multiplication over addition on the set of whole numbers. Each term from one factor must be multiplied by each term of the other factor. You have (400)(20) + (400)(9) + (30)(20) + (30)(9) + (6)(20) + (6)(9), which is 8000 + 3600 + 600 + 270 + 120 + 54, and there are all the values in the partial product and also in the diagonals of the lattice presentation of the same problem. How about that?!

Left to Right Multiplication

Because of concerns about place value, we have been taught to perform arithmetic operations starting at the right side of the exercise. Partial products make this unnecessary. Think about the example using expanded notation and the distributive property of multiplication over addition on the set of whole numbers and you'll realize that the partial products can be done in any order. Because we read from left to right, working from the left of an exercise has a natural feel or logic to it. The vital roles of place value and multiplication facts continue to be present in this method:

$$
\begin{array}{r}
5\ 8 \\
\times\quad 7\ 9 \\
\hline
3\ 5\ 0\ 0 \quad (50 \times 70) \\
4\ 5\ 0 \quad (50 \times 9) \\
5\ 6\ 0 \quad (8 \times 70) \\
7\ 2 \quad (8 \times 9) \\
\hline
4\ 5\ 8\ 2
\end{array}
$$

You should notice that the only difference between this left to right method and the partial product style is the order in which the partial products are written.

Your Turn

Use lattice, left to right, and the distributive property of multiplication over addition on the set of whole numbers methods to find the products in:

4. $23 \times 47 = \square$
5. $519 \times 68 = \quad .$
6. $803 \times 745 = \sim$

Horizontal and Vertical Writing

You should become proficient with both horizontal and vertical formats while working arithmetic exercises. We used the vertical format for demonstrating the partial product and left to right methods, then wrote the exercises in a horizontal format. As in addition, the argument concerning multiplying from left to right versus multiplying from right to left is one of convention rather than of correctness. We could have presented the last example as $58 \times 79 = (50 \times 70) + (50 \times 9) + (8 \times 70) + (8 \times 9) = 3500 + 450 + 560 + 72 = 4582$. You can multiply partial products exercises in any order, sum them, and still get the correct answer.

Russian Peasant (Simple Halving/Doubling Method)

Consider someone who is struggling to learn how to multiply. Offer the statement, "If you can multiply by 2, divide by 2, and add, you can do any whole number multiplication problem in the world." That challenge seems almost too good to be true and can be used as a diversionary approach for someone looking for an alternate way to multiply. Russian peasant multiplication requires the two factors to be written side by side. One factor is halved (any remainder is dropped), and the other factor is doubled. Each of these results is listed vertically under the respective factors. The halving and doubling continues until the bottom number of the halving column is one. To complete the exercise, even values in the halving column and the corresponding doubled values are crossed out. The numbers that have not been crossed out in the doubling column, including the original factor if appropriate, are added to get the product. Finding the product of 78 and 51 using Russian peasant multiplication would tempt one to start by halving 78. However, the goal is to get to 1 in the halving column, and starting at 51 will require fewer steps:

$$
\begin{array}{rr}
78 & 51 \\
156 & 25 \\
\cancel{312} & \cancel{12} \\
\cancel{624} & \cancel{6} \\
1248 & 3 \\
\underline{2496} & 1 \\
3978 &
\end{array}
$$

The 312 and 624 are not added into the sum because they are associated with even values (12 and 6, respectively) in the halving column. The initial factor of 78 is included in the sum because its associated value (51) is odd.

How in the world does that work, you might ask (we hope this is becoming a part of your routine thought processes now). The answer is rooted in Base 2 notation, which is used to express the halving factor and the problem is represented as $78 \times 110011_2$. That is, $78 \times (32 + 16 + 2 + 1)$. Eight and four are not considered because there is a zero in the 2^3 and 2^2 places, respectively, in the Base 2 notation for 51. Therefore, the rows containing 312 and 624 are eliminated because their respective numbers in the halving column, 12 and 6, are even. The product becomes the sum of 78, 156, 1248, and 2496, which is 3978. The following is a full explanation of the process:

		Halving	Base 2	Multiple of 78
78	51	25 remainder 1	1×2^0	78×1
156	25	12 remainder 1	1×2^1	78×2
$\cancel{312}$	$\cancel{12}$	6 remainder 0	0×2^2	78×0
$\cancel{624}$	$\cancel{6}$	3 remainder 0	0×2^3	78×0
1248	3	1 remainder 1	1×2^4	78×16
$\underline{2496}$	1	0 remainder 1	1×2^5	78×32
3978				

Somewhere in your education you have worked with bases other than 10 and investigated multiplication, although probably not in the Russian peasant format. You are aware of the concepts involved in multiplication and you have seen proofs. Yet, with all that background, each of the ideas about multiplication seems to remain isolated from the others. If you decompartmentalize the things you have learned and think about the processes, then the proof of Russian peasant multiplication is accessible. Much as we would like to, we cannot show you all of these intricacies. You must capitalize on your background and develop the connections between the various mathematical exposures you have had. Only then will your knowledge and understanding of mathematics begin to grow.

Your Turn

Use the Russian peasant method of multiplication to find the products in:

7. 23 × 47 = ☐
8. 519 × 68 = ☐
9. 803 × 745 = ☐

Try This

Here is an interesting mental multiplication trick you can try. Tell me any 2-digit number; I will pick a second number and get the product mentally before you can, using a calculator. Suppose you choose 27. I will choose 23. The product is 621. Try again with a larger number? You choose 74, I choose 76, and the product is 5624.

Magic? No, here's the trick. Whatever number you choose, I choose my number such that the digits in the Tens places match, and the Units digits sum to 10. Multiply the digit in the Tens place times itself + 1. Multiply the Units digits. Now place your answers side by side (Units product on the right) and you are done.

You choose 27, so I choose 23, right? The Tens digits match, and the Units digits sum to ten. The Hundreds digits is the product of (2 + 1) and 2 or 3 × 2 yielding a product of 6. The product of the Units digits is 7 × 3, or 21. Put them together to get 621. The same thing happened for the second example 74 × 76, first think 7 + 1 = 8 and 7 × 8 = 56 hundreds. Then 5600 + 4 × 6 = 5624. Practice and you, too, can Beat the Calculator (a free subscription to Beat the Calculator can be obtained by writing to beatcalc@aol.com and requesting a subscription)!

Conclusions

Combining the multiplication procedures discussed here with the addition procedures discussed earlier provides a robust set of choices for reviewing multiplication. Because people who lack technical skills will be at a disadvantage in our data rich society, you should review the calculators that are available. We believe that calculators should be used judiciously. People who do not understand arithmetic operations are at a disadvantage in our ever-growing technological society, even if they own the best computing equipment available. You will need to decide when to use and when to withhold technology.

Bibliography

Beat the calculator. (2000). Available online at beatcalc@aol.com

WHOLE NUMBER DIVISION

FOCAL POINTS

- Terminology
- Division as a Rectangle
- Repeated Subtraction Division
- Division Algorithm
- Remainders
- Say What?
- Conclusions

You know how to do longhand division by hand, right? Given that, you might wonder why we want to talk with you about it. As with the other whole number operations we have discussed with you, we know you know how to use the algorithms but we want to help you look behind the scenes as you divide and think about what is really going on there. When doing an exercise such as $72\overline{)25704}$, the basic question is, "How many sets of 72 things are contained in 25704 things?"

We want to ask you to do something right now that might help you gain some insight into the difficulties associated with division. Please do the exercise $72 \overline{)25704}$ by hand and focus on the various places where errors can be made. We will tell you the answer is 357 because the answer is not the focus. We would like you to do the exercise while concentrating on looking for places where something could go awry within the various steps needed to achieve the answer.

There should be no question that the division facts must be mastered before attempting an exercise such as $72 \overline{)25704}$.

Otherwise, how could we justify asking you to do it? Skillful use of and understanding of whole number multiplication and subtraction are crucial elements of the standard long division algorithm, along with place value, estimation skills, the ability to round numbers, as well as the use of unusual new formats for the operations being performed.

The first potential error occurs in the ability to estimate the initial partial answer to the problem. You may have been taught to round the 72 to 70 for ease of estimation. If so, rounding is another potential area of difficulty. Most of us would have little problem rounding 72 to the nearest ten and calling it 70, but that process could lead to trouble if we end up estimating too low. Whether or not we round the 72 to 70, our next task is to determine what to take the 70 (or 72) into. We know we cannot divide 2 by 70 in this format. Next consider 25 as a candidate, but that will not work because 25 is less than 70, also. That last statement identifies another potential misunderstanding in the area of place value, a skill that must be present in order to successfully divide. One must know when a number is greater

than or less than another. Moving on, we know that 257 (which actually represents 25700) is greater than 70, so division can now take place. However, we now face a new difficulty. How many 70s are in 25700? Here comes the need for estimation skills. There are approximately three hundred 70s in 25700.

For the rest of the discussion, we will abandon the place value discussion involving how many 70s are in 25700, and use the terminology that is much more common. It should be noted here that, whereas dealing with 70×3 to generate an estimate is much easier than using 72×3, you must realize that there are cases where the rounded 70 would lead to difficulties. For example, if we were trying to determine how many 72s (with 72 rounded to 70) are contained in 213, we would get a false reading. That is, 3×70 is 210, but 3×72 is greater than 213. If you have used the rounding method of division, then you are undoubtedly well aware of this potential difficulty.

Moving along, there are three 70s (or 72s) contained in 257. That implies a new dilemma. Where should the 3 be placed on the vinculum? Of course, it goes above the 7 in the product, but it is rather common to have it incorrectly placed above the 4, as in $72 \overline{)25\overset{3}{7}04}$. Thus, another potential source of error has been located — where to place the first digit of the estimated answer.

Correctly placing the 3 above the 7 in 25704, a new dilemma arises and it involves multiplication. As stated earlier, we assume the multiplication skills are present, but look at the configuration of the multiplication exercise: $72 \overset{\;\;\;3}{\overline{)25704}}$ which is really $72 \overset{\;3}{\big)}$, which is unlike any "regular" multiplication exercise—3 × 72 may be old material, but certainly not in this setup. Such an exercise almost always would have been written as $\frac{72}{\times\ 3}$, almost never as $\frac{3}{\times 72}$, and this format of $72\overline{)}^{\ 3}$ is really unusual. On top of all that, the product is to be placed, thus $72\overline{)25704}^{\ \ 3}$, which is unusual to say the least. Look at how the multiplication problem, 3 × 72 now appears: $72\overline{)25704}^{\ \ 3}$. If an individual does 216 not have command of multiplication skills, this exercise would be next to impossible.

For the sake of discussion, let us suppose that the multiplication can be done and correctly placed. Now a new problem arises. All of the difficulties associated with subtraction requiring regrouping come charging to the forefront. The setting is now $72\overline{)25704}^{\ \ 3}$ and we are lucky 216 because there is no regrouping required performing this subtraction. But the next difficulty appears to be, "How many digits do we bring down after the subtraction is completed?" Do we bring down just the zero or do we bring down 04? There are two schools of thought on that question. Our purpose is not to debate this question, so we will bring down only the zero, making the problem become $72\overline{)25704}^{\ \ 3}$.
$$\frac{216}{410}$$

Now a new monster raises its head. The task is to determine how many 70s (or 72s if we do not round) are contained in 410. No big deal? It is just another divi-

sion exercise? But it is a big deal. Look at the format—$72\overline{)}$ without all of the 410 other writing in there. What if we were just learning to master division and we get this strange setup. If the multiplication expressed as $72\overline{)}^{\ \ 3}$ caused any trouble, then how much worse will the division $72\overline{)}$ be? We will end this discussion 410 now, but you should have the picture. Division is difficult because it involves so many skills from earlier work and a brand new format making previously familiar operations take on a very different look.

Terminology

Earlier we connected addition and subtraction by abandoning traditional terminology and using addend, addend, and sum for addition and sum, addend, and missing addend for subtraction. We will use that same approach here. Many of you have probably learned the division terms to be $divisor\overline{)dividend}^{\ quotient}$. One of the difficulties you might have faced is deciding which number is the divisor and which is the dividend. Connecting the terminology with multiplication makes deciding which number is which much simpler— $factor\overline{)\quad product}^{\ missing\ factor}$. In multiplication, we use factor times factor to get the product. In division, we divide the product by a factor to get the missing factor. The discussion could be summarized by:

Exercise	Historic name	Name connected to multiplication
8	Dividend	Product
4	Divisor	Factor
2	Quotient	Missing factor

Increasing your mathematics vocabulary is one of the goals of this text, but we feel that vocabulary words should be meaningful. Whereas the words divisor, dividend, and quotient are descriptive, they do not strengthen the connection between division and multiplication. Paralleling the discussion about minuend, subtrahend, and difference, we believe it makes more sense to have a verbal connection between division and multiplication problems so we will use product, factor, and missing factor.

Division as a Rectangle

What do you do when you find the area of a rectangle? You multiply the length times the width. Can't all positive number multiplication problems be thought of as finding the areas of rectangles? In a division problem, you would know the area of the rectangle and one dimension; division helps you determine the other dimension of the rectangle. That might seem trivial to you, but you now have the ability to generate a mental image of what division problems look like. Sometimes that helps with understanding what is going on behind the scenes in division. Figure 2.24 shows how knowing the area of the rectangle and one dimension could be used to gain understanding of division. The left rectangle has squares inserted to show how they can help determine the missing factor. The right rectangle, while involving

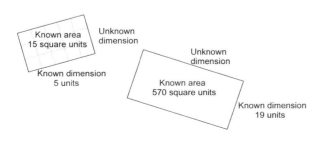

FIG. 2.24.

larger numbers and without the squares, still presents the same idea.

Repeated Subtraction Division

With addition, subtraction, and multiplication, sequences of steps are followed to build what many call standard algorithms. Division is no exception, but often the intermediate step or steps remain hidden. Certainly here the sequence starts with the learning of division facts, which is really just a different way of thinking about the multiplication facts. The investigation of a problem like $2\overline{)24}$ would prove helpful here. This is not a division fact and yet it reveals a lot of insight about division. A simpler problem, also not a division fact, should be considered first—$2\overline{)20}$. Our earlier discussion about the role of zero in multiplication now comes into play, along with the idea of the area of a rectangle. Here, the area is 20 square units and one dimension is 2 units. The missing dimension (missing factor) is determined to be 10 units. That looks a lot like $2\overline{)2}$ and the missing link revolves around the role of zero, much like what was done in multiplication. Skill can be developed with problems like $2\overline{)20}$ or $2\overline{)24}$ using some help from expanded notation and area. We can deal with the area as 24 square units and one dimension of the rectangle as 2 units, and look for the missing dimension. However, we could also consider the problem as $2\overline{)20+4}$, which we could solve as $2\overline{)20+4}^{\,10+2}$. Base 10 blocks help create a mental image of what is happening. Two longs and four units represent the total area. The configuration in Fig. 2.25 also shows that half of the area (we are dividing by 2, remember) would be one Long and 2 Units. Shift the emphasis to place value as shown by the Base 10 blocks and you have 10 + 2 as a dimension of the rectangle. Voila! This is the answer to the division problem, too.

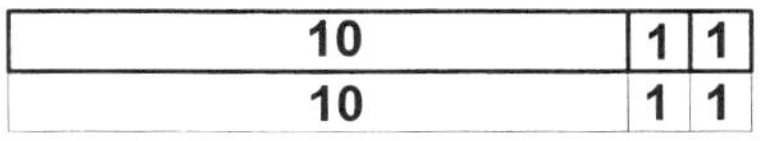

10	1	1
10	1	1

FIG. 2.25.

You might be thinking we went overboard with that last explanation of $2\overline{)24}$, but we felt compelled to draw your attention to the division sequence and its associated missing links. Although $2\overline{)36}$ might appear similar to $2\overline{)24}$, it is quite different. Solving the problem as $2\overline{)30+6}$ with $15+3$ might make sense to you, but it is not sequentially sound to go that route. A more sensible configuration would be $2\overline{)20+16}$ with $10+8$ because of the association with the earlier idea of $2\overline{)20}$ and 16 divided by 2, which is a division fact. We hope that we have drawn your attention to some steps involved in developing the concept of division, some of which you may not have thought about before.

One very significant step in the sequential development of division is the idea of repeated subtraction division. Visualize a pile of 25704 sticks. Are there enough sticks to permit the removal of 72 sticks? You probably laughed at that one, but it is an essential question and the fundamental idea behind the notion of repeated subtraction division. Of course, 72 sticks could be removed from 25704, leaving 25632. Could another bundle of 72 sticks be removed from the stack? Of course!

Could this process be repeated over and over until the initial stack is depleted? Certainly. However, it would take a lot of time and be quite cumbersome. The process can be streamlined somewhat by asking, anywhere along the line, if 10 bundles of 72 sticks could be removed from the stack, or 100 bundles of 72, or 30 bundles of 72, continuing the process by selecting convenient ways of grouping until the stack is gone. This is the idea behind repeated subtraction division—take away conveniently sized groups. As long as you estimate fewer than the maximum number of groups, or exactly right, things are fine. Notice this is significantly different from the typical standard division algorithm, which mandates that all estimates be exactly correct, no more and no fewer. Here are two different looks at $72\overline{)25704}$ done via repeated subtraction division:

```
72)25704                          72)25704
    72       1                        72       1
 25632                             25632
    72       1                       720      10
 25560                             24912
    72       1                       720      10
 25488                             24192
  7200     100                      7200     100
 18288                             16992
 14400     200                     14400     200
  3888                             2592
  1440      20                     2160      30
  2448                             432
  2160      30                     432        6
   288                               0
   288       4
     0
```

You should realize that in each of the two examples, the estimation for the number of bundles of 72 is below the actual amount, until the last step in each problem. Add the values listed to the right of each problem and you get 357, which is the number of bundles of 72 contained in a stack of 25704 sticks. Looking at the two examples should convince you that the convenient and easily spotted multiples could be used any time during the process. The value of being comfortable with multiplying digits by multiples of tens or hundreds should be apparent as well. The "taken out" estimations could be written on top rather than on the side. This is called the *pyramid*, or *stacked*, style, but the process is the same. The advantage to stacking the numbers on top is that as estimation skills get better, the collapsed values look very similar to the standard algorithm:

```
          4
         30                              6
         20                             30
        200                            200
        100                            100
          1                             10
          1                             10
          1                              1
     72)25704                       72)25704
         72                             72
      25632                          25632
         72                            720
      25560                          24912
         72                            720
      25488                          24192
       7200                           7200
      18288                          16992
      14400                          14400
       3888                           2592
       1440                           2160
       2448                            432
       2160                            432
        288                              0
        288
          0
```

Whereas the whole process involved in repeated subtraction division might seem cumbersome, one huge advantage should be jumping out at you. As long as you estimate low or exactly right, the problem can be completed. Contrast that with the standard division algorithm and you should see the advantage of using repeated subtraction division until the exact estimation skills are refined enough to permit moving on to the standard division algorithm.

Your Turn

Do each of the following problems using repeated subtraction division. The ground rule is that you are not permitted to estimate exactly right each time as you do the problems. Write the answers to at least one of the problems in the pyramid format and at least one down the side:

1. $5184 \div 9 =$
2. $37\overline{)2147}$
3. $\dfrac{2495618}{358} =$

Standard Division Algorithm

Did you notice that we wrote the problems in different formats in the exercises? That has not been a discussion point, but we assume you are aware of different ways to write division problems. We mentioned the standard division algorithm earlier. We know that you know how to do long division by hand and are confident in your use of the standard algorithm. Our discussions should have given you some insight into the strengths and weaknesses of the standard algorithm and, more importantly, what is going on behind the scenes as a problem is done. We will do the problem we used as the example for repeated subtraction division via the standard algorithm so you have it as a reference point $72\overline{)25704}$. That should look

```
          357
     72)25704
        216
        410
        360
        504
        504
          0
```

familiar with the possible exception of bringing down only the zero rather than 04 after the first subtraction. Things are fine as long as you estimate exactly correct. Did you check your work on the exercises by working the exercises using the standard algorithm? We know that your time is limited, but suggest that you practice by reworking a couple of them using that tried and true tool.

Technology

Did you do the exercises simply to practice your long division skills? We are betting you did not. Furthermore, we are willing to think that you would have grabbed a calculator to do the exercises if you had been asked simply for the answers. Why would you reach for the calculator? Might you have rationalized that long division is too painful to do, the calculator is faster, and the calculator is a lot more accurate? All of that makes sense to us. Still, a very critical issue has been raised.

When do you use a calculator? We have repeatedly said you need to know the number facts and the basics of the operations. OK, when do you say that a sufficient level of competency has been reached and it is time to use technology? We cannot answer that for you, but we are willing to bet it is somewhere between the division facts and $358\overline{)2495618}$ as far as you are concerned. In fact, the shift point is probably long before here and we sympathize with your decision. Our point here is that technology has a place in all of this. We cannot tell you when to use a calculator. That is your decision. However, when you decide to use or not to use technology, you must be able to defend your position. Saying technology is inappropriate because you had to do a

certain kind of problem by hand is unsuitable. At the same time, deciding to use technology for generating a number fact because it has not been memorized is equally inappropriate. Somewhere between those two is the answer and we are attempting to help you make that into an informed decision, rather than a blanket statement made without forethought.

Remainders

Many division problems do not result in whole numbers. Sometimes a problem with a remainder makes sense and sometimes it does not. For example, if you are dividing a dozen dolls between eight children, a doll and a half does not make much sense; you have four dolls remaining. On the other hand, if you are dividing a dozen cookies between eight children, then each child can get a cookie and a half (if you can get a half a cookie ☺). We will assume that problems posed that have remainders as we discuss decimals would have an application somewhere in the real world.

As you know, the missing factor in division is not always an integer. You have seen the answer for $3\overline{)5}$ expressed as $1\frac{2}{3}$, $1.\overline{6}$, 1.67, and perhaps a host of other ways, including 1 r 2, meaning a missing factor of 1 with a remainder of 2. The idea is that after dividing out as many known factors as possible from the product, there are still some parts left over. Initially, this leftover collection is expressed as a remainder. Later they are expressed as fractions, decimals, or repeating decimals.

Remainders can occur naturally. Suppose 21 people want to take a trip as a group. Assume that all individuals are licensed drivers and any car they elect to use will carry the driver plus three others. Do the division $21 \div 4$ and you get five, but there is one person left. If you are that remaining person and you want to go on the trip, then you do not want to be omitted. Thus, in this case, the remainder is significant and a sixth car is needed. Hopefully, although not germane here, that 21st person will also have some others ride along so there could be three cars carrying three people and three cars carrying four people.

Suppose you have 21 cookies and want to share them with 3 friends so each of you has an equal amount. Doing the problem arithmetically would yield $21 \div 4 = 5$ r 1. As things stand, there is an extra cookie. Certainly it could be divided into four equal parts and shared, which will happen when we get to fractions. The easy solution would be to set that extra cookie aside, or better yet, do the arithmetic ahead of time and simply start with 20 cookies, so that the dilemma is avoided. How you solve the quandary of the extra cookie is not the issue here. The idea of having an extra cookie is our consideration. The solution here is much different than the previous one where a trip was taken. Would you want to be the person who was divided into parts to make the trip? That does not make sense, and yet, dividing the cookie might make sense. Nonetheless, both solutions came out of the same arithmetic exercise.

Certainly remainders could be avoided with careful planning, much like was done in the cookie example. All of the discussion about division of whole numbers prior to this part about remainders actually did that because each missing factor was an integer. Still, the possibility of a remainder does exist and you need to think about how to deal with it. Later you will express them as fractions or decimals.

Some people do not think remainders should be considered. However, as you have seen with the trip and the cookies, there are situations when they are significant. Consider $7\overline{)226}$ (32 r 2) and $9\overline{)290}$ (32 r 2). They imply that $\frac{226}{7} = \frac{290}{9}$ because we get the exact same answer for both exercises. But, $\frac{226}{7}$ is $32\frac{2}{7}$ and $\frac{290}{9}$ is $32\frac{2}{9}$ and you know that $32\frac{2}{7}$ and $32\frac{2}{9}$ are not equal. So what should we do with remainders? You know what they are and how they can show up in real-world situations. You now also see how remainders can connect to nonintegral answers in division.

Say What?

A final concern about division involves the way problems are worded. There are actually two very different questions we might ask: 1) "How many sets of items?" or 2) "How many items per set?" We might think about this while packaging cookies for a bake sale and the stem of the problem could be, "We have 48 cookies for the class sale." If we have a good supply of plastic bags, then we might arbitrarily decide to put three cookies in each bag. This method would be a good example of repeated subtraction division, as we measure out three cookies for each bag. The question would be, "How many plastic bags do we need if we want to have three cookies per bag?" However, if we have only 12 plastic bags, this would not work. In this situation, we know how many sets we need to make, but would need to figure out how to share the cookies among the predetermined number of bags. The question would be, "How many cookies should we put in each of the 12 plastic bags we have?" Although there is no difference in the operation, there is an important difference in the problem solving.

Conclusions

You should have a better understanding of what is going on behind the scenes in division. Of our basic operations, it is easily the most complex because it relies on previous knowledge of both multiplication and subtraction for mastery and requires learning a new format. Still, with careful presentation and thoughtful reflection, division can be understood and managed. Because of the complexities related to division, the question of when to use technology seems worth serious reflection on your part.

EQUIVALENT FRACTIONS AND MULTIPLICATION OF FRACTIONS

FOCAL POINTS

- Concrete Beginnings
- Equivalent Fractions
- Converting an Improper Fraction to a Mixed Number
- Product of a Whole Number and a Fraction
- Product of Whole Number and Mixed Number
- Product of Two Fractions
- Product of a Fraction and a Mixed Number
- Product of Two Mixed Numbers
- Conclusions

Our approach to working with fractions is probably going to be different from what you have seen in the past. We are going to discuss equivalent fractions and then multiplication. Typically, addition of fractions is done after dealing with equivalent fractions. Multiplication of fractions is much easier than addition of fractions. That, coupled with the idea that multiplication is visited as equivalent fraction concepts are developed, prompted us to discuss multiplication of fractions before addition of fractions. Stick with us on this. We are confident you will like what you see.

Concrete Beginnings

People often struggle with the concept of fractions because of fundamental misconceptions. We all have been taught the terms *numerator* and *denominator*, along with their respective definitions. Still, if those definitions are presented only in the abstract, false impressions can be created and the development of mal rules can occur. These are rules people make from their observations that seem to make sense. Because they are generally based on misunderstandings of the ideas presented, they may work only in one situation or perhaps never. Once established, mal rules are often difficult to purge. For example, Fig. 2.26 shows a situation that

FIG. 2.26.

many people accept as a representation of one half. We know that is not a half and yet we participate in situations that often stimulate such impressions. Have you ever been asked if you want the big half or the little half of something? That is a silly question if you think about it. Aren't two halves of something supposed to be equal? Fold a sheet of paper in half. Once you have done that, describe how you know you have created halves.

More than likely, you folded your paper in either hamburger (top) or hot dog (bottom) format as shown in Fig. 2.27. Fur-

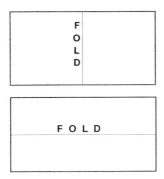

FIG. 2.27.

thermore, you probably rationalized that you knew you had folded the paper in half because the two parts were identical. If we pressed you to discuss the situation more fully, then you would probably say that you knew you had folded the paper in half because the edges of the pieces matched. By this process, you refined your definition to make it clearer. Then, if we showed you Fig. 2.28 you might pause

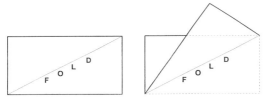

FIG. 2.28.

before agreeing that the paper had been folded in half. A discussion about cutting along the diagonal and rotating one of the triangles would lead to the conclusion that the edges would then match, again confirming that the paper had, in fact, been folded in half. Perhaps reflection would lead to a further revision of the definition, but eventually we get to a working definition of what a half is—a unit is divided into two equal parts and one of those two equal parts is under consideration. The discussion could also include ideas about matching edges yielding areas that are the same.

The representation of a half is $\frac{1}{2}$, where the numerator is 1 and the denominator is 2. The definition clarifies that the denominator represents the number of equal-sized pieces something is divided into and the numerator indicates the number of those equal pieces that is being considered. Notice the operative word is "equal" here. Although we have only developed the idea of $\frac{1}{2}$ concretely, a similar approach could be used to consider additional fractions if you are uncertain of the generalized definition for a fraction.

Equivalent Fractions

The idea of concrete beginnings does not stop with the definition of fractions and a generalized idea of fractions. Exactly what are equivalent fractions? We could tell you, but we are opting to have you see for yourself. Fold a sheet of paper in half either hamburger or hot dog style (but not a diagonal fold for this activity). Open the sheet once you have folded it and shade in one of the two equal-sized pieces. What part of the sheet is shaded? You should say $\frac{1}{2}$ because you shaded one of two equal pieces.

Now close the paper along your fold so the shaded half is inside. Fold the paper in half again, either hamburger or hot dog style. Your model could look like either of the two presentations in Fig. 2.29, although other shading or folding options could occur. There is a significant point brought out by Fig. 2.29. The unit (sheet of paper) has been divided into four equal parts and two of those four are shaded. In other words, $\frac{2}{4}$ of the paper is shaded. But, no additional paper was shaded, so it

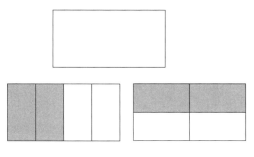

FIG. 2.29.

must be that $\frac{2}{4}$ and $\frac{1}{2}$ are different names for the same quantity. Similarly, if an additional fold is made after refolding the paper twice, as shown in Fig. 2.30, you end

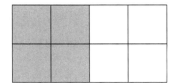

FIG. 2.30.

up with a representation that should convince you that $\frac{4}{8}$, $\frac{2}{4}$, and $\frac{1}{2}$ are different names for the same quantity or, saying it another way, $\frac{4}{8} = \frac{2}{4} = \frac{1}{2}$.

With that background, we can look at something like $\frac{4}{7} = \frac{4 \times 2}{7 \times 2} = \frac{8}{14}$, and recognize the rule you learned some time ago; multiply both the numerator and denominator by the same value to get an equivalent fraction.

Take a huge leap and look at $\frac{24}{36} = \frac{24 \times \frac{3}{4}}{36 \times \frac{3}{4}} = \frac{18}{27}$. Multiply both the numerator and denominator by the same value to get an equivalent fraction is the rule we used. Granted this is unusual, but it is mathematically correct. In the previous example, we found an equivalent fraction to be $\frac{4}{7}$. The result we generated involved larger values for both the numerator and denominator and yet the result, $\frac{8}{14}$, is equivalent to $\frac{4}{7}$. In this example, we have found $\frac{18}{30}$ to be an equivalent expression for $\frac{45}{75}$, but we have expressed the equivalent fraction using smaller values in the numerator and denominator than were used in the original fraction. Whereas $\frac{18}{30}$ is certainly equivalent to $\frac{45}{75}$, it is often preferred that an equivalent fraction to $\frac{45}{75}$ be expressed so that the numerator and denominator use the smallest possible values (also referred to as being relatively prime, which means the largest common factor shared by the numerator and denominator is one). For example, you may have noticed that most standardized tests mandate that all fractions be expressed in simplest terms, even though this might insert the opportunity for additional errors.

For this case, the mandated equivalent fraction would be $\frac{3}{5}$, even though it is only one of an infinite number of fractions that are equivalent to $\frac{45}{75}$. In this example, $\frac{3}{5}$ is the fraction obtained when $\frac{45}{75}$ is simplified to its lowest terms. Sometimes simplified to lowest terms is called the reduced version of $\frac{45}{75}$, but this leads to the notion that $\frac{3}{5}$ is a smaller fraction than $\frac{45}{75}$, which is false. We recommend that you use the phrase simplified to lowest terms rather than reduced to simplest terms or reduced version.

We believe that the phrase "divide out all common factors," is better than either "reduce" or "simplify." Divide out all common factors is more descriptive of what is happening when a fraction such as $\dfrac{45}{75}$ is changed to an equivalent value in which there are no common factors between the numerator and denominator. An understanding of the process of dividing out common factors will be extremely useful in algebra. In this case, you would have $\dfrac{45}{75} = \dfrac{45 \div 15}{75 \div 15} = \dfrac{3}{5}$, a fraction in which the numerator and denominator have no common factors.

To divide out all common factors of $\dfrac{45}{75}$, we could have multiplied both the numerator and denominator by the same convenient value and ended up at the same place: $\dfrac{45}{75} = \dfrac{45 \times \dfrac{1}{15}}{75 \times \dfrac{1}{15}} = \dfrac{\dfrac{45}{15}}{\dfrac{75}{15}} = \dfrac{3}{5}$. Although we have not talked with you about how to multiply whole numbers and fractions, your prior experience should convince you that this is an acceptable, although complex, way to simplify the fraction.

The result of dividing out all common factors of $\dfrac{45}{75}$ is $\dfrac{3}{5}$, which represents the smallest possible values for the numerator and denominator. Another way of saying this is that the numerator and denominator are relatively prime. This statement does not necessarily mean the both values are prime numbers. It simply means that their greatest common factor is one. In $\dfrac{4}{7}$, the numerator and denominator are relatively prime even though 4 is not a prime number.

Your Turn

1. Find an equivalent fraction to each of the following; being sure to show the steps that assure your result is correct:

a) $\dfrac{4}{5}$

b) $\dfrac{6}{18}$

c) $\dfrac{17}{51}$

d) $\dfrac{7}{11}$

e) $\dfrac{24}{96}$

Converting a Mixed Number to an Improper Fraction

If we gave you nine quarters and asked you to count them, you could come up with several different responses, the first of which might be, "One quarter, two quarters, three quarters, four quarters (or one dollar), five quarters, six quarters, seven quarters, eight quarters (or two dollars), nine quarters." Perhaps you would summarize the situation by saying that you counted two dollars and a quarter. Figure 2.31 models this on a number line. You could count on the number line just as you did with the quarters. When you get to $\dfrac{4}{4}$, another name for that point is 1.

Similarly, at $\dfrac{8}{4}$, an equivalent name is 2.

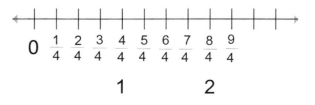

FIG. 2.31.

The point $\frac{9}{4}$ could be called just that, $\frac{9}{4}$, or it could be called 2 and $\frac{1}{4}$, interpreted as two whole things and $\frac{1}{4}$ more. This could be written $2 + \frac{1}{4}$, but it is generally written as $2\frac{1}{4}$, with the plus sign understood, much like when we discussed implicit multiplication (4y rather than 4 × y). We read the understood plus sign as and. This mixed number is two and one fourth. The assumed plus sign is a key element to understanding the process of converting from mixed numbers to improper fractions (a fraction in which the numerator is bigger than or equal to the denominator) or from improper fractions to mixed numbers.

Consider the following conversion:

$$2\frac{5}{8} = 2 + \frac{5}{8}$$
$$= \frac{2}{1} \times \frac{8}{8} + \frac{5}{8}$$
$$= \frac{16}{8} + \frac{5}{8}$$
$$= \frac{16 + 5}{8}$$
$$= \frac{21}{8}.$$

Notice how the first step in the process of converting $2\frac{5}{8}$ to an improper fraction involves inserting that understood plus sign. Next, we give an equivalent fraction for 2, using the appropriate denominator. We remind you that 2 is equivalent to $\frac{2}{1}$, which lets us apply the generalization we developed about multiplying the numera-

tor and denominator of a fraction by the same value to get an equivalent fraction. The rest of the process should seem familiar to you as you recall the basics of fraction addition. The result of this process is $\frac{21}{8}$, an improper fraction.

Converting an Improper Fraction to a Mixed Number

The procedure for converting an improper fraction to a mixed number follows directly from our example of converting a mixed number to an improper fraction, because you work the process in reverse order. Consider the following:

$$\frac{38}{5} = \frac{35 + 3}{5}$$
$$= \frac{35}{5} + \frac{3}{5}$$
$$= 7 + \frac{3}{5}$$
$$= 7\frac{3}{5}$$

The trick is to know how to split $\frac{38}{5}$ initially. Mastery of basic multiplication and division facts is essential here. We need to determine the largest multiple of 5 contained in 38, and we find that $\frac{38}{5} = 7\frac{3}{5}$. Mixed numbers are often useful in helping us understand the quantities involved in problems, whereas improper fractions are generally used when multiplying mixed numbers. Improper fractions are especially useful in algebra.

Your Turn

2. Convert the following mixed numbers to fractions. Please note we have not

discussed any shortcuts you might have learned in the past, so the expectation is that you will not apply them at this point. You need to practice the skills of converting at a basic level so you will gain a full understanding of the shortcuts you might have learned previously.

a) $2\dfrac{5}{8}$

b) $3\dfrac{7}{9}$

c) $13\dfrac{5}{6}$

d) 4

3. Convert the following improper fractions to mixed numbers. Once again, we ask that you practice the skills of converting at a basic level; leave the shortcuts for later.

a) $\dfrac{37}{5}$

b) $\dfrac{49}{9}$

c) $\dfrac{18}{7}$

d) $\dfrac{24}{6}$

Product of a Whole Number and a Fraction

Recall from multiplying two whole numbers that you might have said that 3×4 was three fours. Similarly, we could say that $9 \times \dfrac{1}{4}$ is nine quarters. We write nine quarters as $\dfrac{9}{4}$ and connect $9 \times \dfrac{1}{4}$ with $\dfrac{9}{4}$. Remember that 9 can be written $\dfrac{9}{1}$, so

$9 \times \dfrac{1}{4}$ could be written $\dfrac{9}{1} \times \dfrac{1}{4} = \dfrac{9}{4}$. Connect the ideas here and conclude that, to get the product of $\dfrac{9}{1}$ and $\dfrac{1}{4}$, we could insert an intermediate step to show exactly what is going on. With that step inserted, $\dfrac{9}{1} \times \dfrac{1}{4} = \dfrac{9 \times 1}{1 \times 4}$, which is $\dfrac{9}{4}$. To get the problem done, we place the product of the numerators over the product of the denominators. Another way of generalizing about the product of a whole number times a fraction would be to put the product of the whole number and the fraction's numerator over the denominator. Although this second generalization is an efficient shortcut, the first generalization will work with all fraction products.

Your Turn

4. Find the following products:

a) $9 \times \dfrac{1}{4} = ?$

b) $4 \times \dfrac{1}{9} = ?$

c) $6 \times \dfrac{4}{7} = ?$

d) $97 \times \dfrac{42}{43} = ?$

Product of Whole Number and Mixed Number

You have all the tools for extending the process of multiplying a whole number times a fraction to finding products that involved mixed numbers. Suppose you need to find the product of 4 and $3\dfrac{1}{7}$. You already know how to convert $3\dfrac{1}{7}$ to an improper fraction, getting $\frac{22}{7}$ and the problem becomes $4 \times \frac{22}{7}$. Multiplying the whole number by the fraction's numerator gives $\frac{88}{7}$. If you need to convert the product to a mixed number, then you must decide the largest multiple of 7 that is contained in 88, and $\frac{88}{7} = 12\frac{4}{7}$.

There is another way to find the product of 4 and $3\frac{1}{7}$ that introduces an important concept. Remember that $3\frac{1}{7}$ means $3 + \frac{1}{7}$. So, the problem can be rewritten as $4\left(3 + \frac{1}{7}\right)$. Using the distributive property of multiplication over addition on the set of rational numbers, we get $4(3) + 4\left(\frac{1}{7}\right)$, or $12 + \frac{4}{7}$, which is $12\frac{4}{7}$. The distributive property of multiplication over addition on the set of rational numbers might seem cumbersome to you in this problem, but this is great background work for algebra.

Your Turn

5. Find the following products first by converting the mixed number to an improper fraction and then by using the distributive property of multiplication over addition on the set of rational numbers:

a) $4 \times 3\frac{1}{7} = \square$

b) $6 \times 2\frac{5}{8} = \square$

c) $8 \times 3\frac{7}{11} = \square$

Product of Two Fractions

We have already developed the idea of putting the product of the numerators over the product of denominators when multiplying fractions. That same rule can be used to deal with a variety of problems. The simplest involves two factors, something like $\frac{3}{4} \times \frac{5}{7}$. Multiplying the numerators and denominators would give $\frac{3 \times 5}{4 \times 7}$, or $\frac{15}{28}$. Fraction multiplication exercises are not always that easy to do, but the process is the same each time.

Consider $\frac{3}{7} \times \frac{5}{12}$. The process could be the same as before, giving $\frac{3 \times 5}{7 \times 12}$, or $\frac{15}{84}$. At this point, all of the prior discussion about equivalent fractions comes into play. Whereas getting the product of the numerators and denominators and then dividing out common factors is a valid way to complete fraction multiplication, there is another way. Dividing common factors out first makes the arithmetic simpler, but yields the same final answer.

That is, $\frac{3 \times 5}{7 \times 12}$ could be done $\frac{\overset{1}{\cancel{3}} \times 5}{7 \times \cancel{12}}$, which becomes $\frac{1 \times 5}{7 \times 4}$, or $\frac{5}{28}$. This could have been done as $\frac{\overset{1}{\cancel{3}}}{7} \times \frac{5}{\underset{4}{\cancel{12}}}$, which would become $\frac{1 \times 5}{7 \times 4}$, or $\frac{5}{28}$. To decrease the chances of arithmetic errors, we encourage you to adopt the practice of dividing out common factors at the beginning of the problem.

Multiplication of fractions could involve one or more factors that are improper fractions, but the process is the same. For example, $\frac{3}{7} \times \frac{12}{5}$ becomes $\frac{3 \times 12}{7 \times 5} = \frac{36}{35}$. Depending on the situation, you may need to convert the resultant improper fraction to a mixed number.

A remaining issue with fractions is the situation where more than two factors are involved. Consider $\frac{2}{3} \times \frac{3}{4} \times \frac{4}{5} \times \frac{5}{6}$. There is a hard way and an easy way to do this one. You might show the product as $\frac{2 \times 3 \times 4 \times 5}{3 \times 4 \times 5 \times 6}$, or $\frac{120}{360}$, and then divide out common factors until the answer is $\frac{1}{3}$. Although that method works, it is more efficient to divide out the common factors first; $\frac{\overset{1}{\cancel{2}} \times \overset{1}{\cancel{3}} \times \overset{1}{\cancel{4}} \times \overset{1}{\cancel{5}}}{\underset{1}{\cancel{3}} \times \underset{1}{\cancel{4}} \times \underset{1}{\cancel{5}} \times \underset{3}{\cancel{6}}}$ becomes $\frac{1 \times 1 \times 1 \times 1}{1 \times 1 \times 1 \times 3}$, or $\frac{1}{3}$. In the example, we identified the pairs of common factors that were divided out by using several types of slashes. There are other pairings that could have been used to divide out common factors, but they all would lead to a final answer of $\frac{1}{3}$. If the factors were improper fractions, the process would be the same. The problem $\frac{3}{2} \times \frac{4}{3} \times \frac{5}{4} \times \frac{6}{5}$ is solved $\frac{\overset{1}{\cancel{3}} \times \overset{1}{\cancel{4}} \times \overset{1}{\cancel{5}} \times \overset{3}{\cancel{6}}}{\underset{1}{\cancel{2}} \times \underset{1}{\cancel{3}} \times \underset{1}{\cancel{4}} \times \underset{1}{\cancel{5}}}$, which becomes $\frac{1 \times 1 \times 1 \times 3}{1 \times 1 \times 1 \times 1}$, which is $\frac{3}{1}$, or 3.

Your Turn

6. Find the following products:

a) $\frac{3}{7} \times \frac{5}{12} = \square$

b) $\frac{3}{7} \times \frac{8}{3} \times \frac{14}{64} = \square$

c) Make up an interesting exercise and complete it.

Product of a Fraction and a Mixed Number

The process of multiplying a fraction and a mixed number is not significantly different from finding the product of a whole number times a mixed number. In fact, the problem becomes the product of two fractions if the mixed number is converted to an improper fraction. For example, showing all steps, we might see $\frac{2}{3} \times 4\frac{5}{7} = \frac{2}{3} \times \left(\frac{4}{1} \times \frac{7}{7} + \frac{5}{7} \right) = \frac{2}{3} \times \left(\frac{28}{7} + \frac{5}{7} \right)$ $= \frac{2}{3} \times \frac{33}{7} = \frac{2 \times 33}{3 \times 7} = \frac{2 \times 11}{1 \times 7} = \frac{22}{7}$ or $3\frac{1}{7}$. Although you might want to skip some of these steps, this process will always work. Let's examine the distributive property of multiplication over addition on the set of rational numbers once again. If we introduce the understood plus sign and use juxtaposition, $\frac{2}{3} \times 4\frac{5}{7}$ becomes $\frac{2}{3}\left(4 + \frac{5}{7} \right)$ or $\frac{2}{3}\left(\frac{4}{1} \right) + \frac{2}{3}\left(\frac{5}{7} \right)$, which is $\frac{2}{3}(4) + \frac{2}{3}\left(\frac{5}{7} \right)$, giving $\frac{8}{3} + \frac{10}{21}$. Using equivalent fractions, $\frac{8}{3} + \frac{10}{21}$ becomes $\left(\frac{8}{3} \right)\left(\frac{7}{7} \right) + \frac{10}{21}$ or $\frac{56}{21} + \frac{10}{21}$. Using your skills to add fractions with the same denominators, $\frac{8}{3} + \frac{10}{21} = \frac{8 \times 7}{3 \times 7} + \frac{10}{21} = \frac{56}{21} + \frac{10}{21} = \frac{56 + 10}{21}$ giving a sum of $\frac{66}{21}$. The choice of what to do next often depends on the statement of the problem. As we have said before, there are advantages and disadvantages involved in simplifying this improper fraction, $\dfrac{66}{21} = \dfrac{3 \times 22}{3 \times 7} = \dfrac{22}{7}$, or changing it to the mixed number $3\dfrac{1}{7}$.

Product of Two Mixed Numbers

Our final discussion will involve finding the product of two mixed numbers. In $2\dfrac{3}{4} \times 5\dfrac{6}{7}$, converting to improper fractions makes this a problem similar to those we have considered before. That is, $2\dfrac{3}{4} \times 5\dfrac{6}{7}$ becomes $\dfrac{11}{4} \times \dfrac{41}{7}$ or $\dfrac{451}{28}$, which is $16\dfrac{3}{28}$. The following model shows this problem done in much the same manner as you did whole number multiplication, using the distributive property of multiplication over addition on the set of real numbers:

$$
\begin{array}{r}
2 + \dfrac{3}{4} \\[2mm]
\times\, 5 + \dfrac{6}{7} \\[1mm]
\hline
\dfrac{6}{7} \times \dfrac{3}{4} = \dfrac{9}{14} \\[2mm]
\dfrac{6}{7} \times 2 = \dfrac{12}{7} \\[2mm]
5 \times \dfrac{3}{4} = \dfrac{15}{4} \\[2mm]
5 \times 2 = 10
\end{array}
$$

To complete the exercise, we need only add the partial products,

$$\dfrac{9}{14} + \dfrac{12}{7} + \dfrac{15}{4} + 10.$$

The problem could also be shown another way, if we use the distributive property of multiplication over addition on the set of rational numbers.

$$2\dfrac{3}{4} \times 5\dfrac{6}{7} = \left(2 + \dfrac{3}{4}\right)\left(5 + \dfrac{6}{7}\right)$$

$$= 2\left(5 + \dfrac{6}{7}\right) + \left(\dfrac{3}{4}\right)\left(5 + \dfrac{6}{7}\right)$$

$$= 2(5) + 2\left(\dfrac{6}{7}\right) + \left(\dfrac{3}{4}\right)(5) + \left(\dfrac{3}{4}\right)\left(\dfrac{6}{7}\right)$$

Why, you say, should you have to go through all those steps when we end up with the same partial products? Examining this process will help you understand what you have been doing all these years. An equally significant consideration is that you are establishing a powerful algebraic background.

Your Turn

7. Use both the partial product and distributive methods to complete the following exercises:

a) $2\dfrac{3}{4} \times 5\dfrac{6}{7} = ?$

b) $4\dfrac{5}{9} \times 7\dfrac{11}{13} = ?$

Conclusions

So, there you have it, equivalent fractions and multiplication involving fractions. We hope this experience with fractions has been insightful and helpful in refining your understanding. As you studied the topics in this chapter, fundamental patterns and ideas should have been forming that will provide you a powerful background for your future work.

We suggest that you investigate a variety of calculators, not just brand names, but all levels offered by a manufacturer. You will find that some of them operate with fractions, giving fractions as answers. Some will convert between fractions, decimals, and mixed numbers.

Some use pretty print (vinculum is present), whereas others have special coding to indicate fractions. When and how to introduce these calculators is something you will need to decide.

ADDITION OF FRACTIONS

FOCAL POINTS

- Concrete Beginnings
- Fraction Sums
- Adding Fractions When Denominators Are the Same
- Adding Fractions When the Denominators Are Related
- Adding Fractions When the Denominators Are Relatively Prime
- Adding Fractions When the Denominators Are Not Relatively Prime and One Is Not a Multiple of the Other

We reviewed equivalent fractions and fraction multiplication first because only a few rules are required. Addition of fractions has more rules, but is not difficult to master if you approach the operation carefully and in a logical manner.

Concrete Beginnings

If we gave you three U.S. quarters and asked you what you had, you would probably say, "Three quarters" or "Seventy-five cents." Because a quarter is one fourth of a dollar, the problem could be written $\frac{1}{4} + \frac{1}{4} + \frac{1}{4}$. The answer is known to be $\frac{3}{4}$, so it must be the case that $\frac{1}{4} + \frac{1}{4} + \frac{1}{4} = \frac{3}{4}$. Here we used money to add fractions. Consider the number line in Fig. 2.32, which shows this sum. Each of

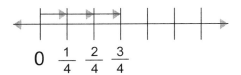

FIG. 2.32.

the three vectors represents $\frac{1}{4}$. Starting at zero, you move $\frac{1}{4}$ of a unit, then you add another $\frac{1}{4}$, followed by a final $\frac{1}{4}$, so that you end up at $\frac{3}{4}$ on the number line. Similar results could be generated with Cuisenaire rods, fraction bars or circles, egg cartons, or other manipulatives that are used with teaching fractions. For a couple of examples, check out:

> http://pegasus.cc.ucf.edu/~mathed/crods.html
>
> http://pegasus.cc.ucf.edu/~mathed/egg.html
>
> http://pegasus.cc.ucf.edu/~mathed/fk.html

We encourage you to investigate using manipulatives to add fractions. They will enhance your understanding and make operating with fractions easier for you.

Adding Fractions When Denominators Are the Same

When adding the three quarters, we know the sum of the addends is $\frac{3}{4}$, however the intermediate step of $\frac{1}{4} + \frac{1}{4} + \frac{1}{4} = \frac{1+1+1}{4}$ was omitted earlier and it holds an essential clue to what is happening in the problem. As you look at the example, you should conclude that, when the denominators of the addends are the same, the numerators of the addends are added and their sum is placed over the common denominator.

This same statement is true if the addends were not unit fractions (fractions with numerators of one). For example, if you had $\frac{2}{7} + \frac{3}{7}$, you would just add the numerators, $\frac{2+3}{7}$ or $\frac{5}{7}$ (note again that the denominator remains constant). On the number line in Fig. 2.33, you see the two

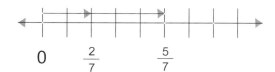

FIG. 2.33.

addends shown with vectors and that the second vector ends at $\frac{5}{7}$. This supports the idea of adding the numerators and putting the sum over the common denominator as a means of expressing the sum. Figure 2.34 shows addends of $\frac{6}{7}$ and

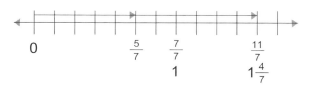

FIG. 2.34.

$\frac{5}{7}$, giving a sum of $\frac{6+5}{7}$, or $\frac{11}{7}$. Notice that equivalent values for $\frac{7}{7}$ and $\frac{11}{7}$ are shown below each.

We suggest that you limit your initial practice of skills to addends that give sums less than one until you are comfortable with this concept, then deal with

sums greater than or equal to one. When a sum is greater than one, it is often necessary to convert an improper fraction to a mixed number. Although that is a skill learned at this stage, it is another step in the problem, and thus, another chance for an error. This step is generally not necessary in algebra classes, but often helps us get a feel for the value of the sum. For example, you may be quite comfortable with a value such as $\frac{3}{2}$, but, depending on the problem situation, $1\frac{1}{2}$ might be easier to understand.

There is another group of addition exercises to be considered when like denominators are involved, and it deals with mixed numbers. If you add a whole number and a mixed number, the task is simple. Consider $5 + 1\frac{4}{7}$. Because $1\frac{4}{7}$ can be written $\left(1 + \frac{4}{7}\right)$, the problem becomes $5 + \left(1 + \frac{4}{7}\right)$. Thanks to the associative property of addition on the set of rational numbers, the problem is $(5 + 1) + \frac{4}{7}$, or $6 + \frac{4}{7}$. We write $6 + \frac{4}{7}$ as $6\frac{4}{7}$, and the exercise is finished.

Suppose the problem involves the sum of a mixed number and a fraction when the denominators are the same: $6\frac{4}{7} + \frac{2}{7}$. The problem can be expressed as $\left(6 + \frac{4}{7}\right) + \frac{2}{7}$ or $6 + \left(\frac{4}{7} + \frac{2}{7}\right)$, which is $6 + \left(\frac{4+2}{7}\right)$ or $6\frac{6}{7}$. If the problem is $\frac{5}{7} + 6\frac{4}{7}$, there is an improper fraction in the sum and the procedure will include the additional step of converting the improper fraction to a mixed number. The problem is written as $\frac{5}{7} + \left(6 + \frac{4}{7}\right)$ and, with applications of the commutative and associated properties of addition on the set of rational numbers, it is changed to $\left(\frac{5}{7} + \frac{4}{7}\right) + 6$. The equivalent value is $6 + \frac{11}{7}$, but we would not write that as $6\frac{11}{7}$, rather we would convert the improper fraction $\frac{11}{7}$ to $1\frac{4}{7}$ changing the exercise to $6 + 1\frac{4}{7}$, and the sum is $7\frac{4}{7}$.

Adding several mixed numbers with like denominators in the fractional parts, like $1\frac{11}{13} + 6\frac{5}{13} + 7\frac{4}{13}$, is an extension of the process. Applying the definition of mixed numbers and the commutative and associative properties of addition on the set of rational numbers, the problem becomes $1 + 6 + 7 + \frac{11}{13} + \frac{5}{13} + \frac{4}{13}$, but this is $14 + \frac{20}{13}$, or $14 + 1\frac{7}{13}$, or $15\frac{7}{13}$. Granted, we skipped some intermediate steps.

You might be wondering why we are taking such small increments as we look at different problem types for adding fractions. We are trying to build a slow, careful sequence that will help you understand and master the whole process of adding fractions.

Your Turn

1. Find each of the following sums, showing the intermediate steps:

a) $\frac{5}{13} + \frac{7}{13} = ?$

b) $2\frac{5}{17} + \frac{8}{17} = ?$

c) $5\frac{11}{13} + 4\frac{5}{13} + 1\frac{7}{13} = ?$

Adding Fractions When the Denominators Are Related

Related denominators occur when one denominator is a multiple of the other. Addition with related denominators involves expressing one fraction in equivalent terms so that both fractions have the same denominator. Because one denominator is a multiple of the other, the common denominator is easy to determine. For example, if you wanted to add $\frac{1}{5}$ and $\frac{1}{10}$, the first step would be to determine that 10 is a multiple of 5 and that the missing factor is 2. At that point, the rule you established earlier for generating equivalent fractions is applied and the equivalent expression of $\frac{2}{10}$ replaces $\frac{1}{5}$, changing the problem to $\frac{2}{10} + \frac{1}{10} = \frac{2+1}{10}$, or $\frac{3}{10}$.

The idea of equivalent fractions is an essential basic theme in proportional reasoning. Part of what we are doing here, and in other related sections of this book, will help you gain a better understanding of proportional reasoning.

Each of the following examples requires determining which denominator to use as the common denominator and setting up the equivalent fraction, then completing the exercise using the procedure for adding fractions with the same denominator. The first example is short, but the second is quite involved, with many steps. We will not provide a detailed discussion. If you do not find the examples easy to follow, then refer back to the section on how to get an expression equivalent to a given fraction, then revisit the discussion about adding fractions or mixed numbers when the denominators are the same:

$$\frac{3}{17} + \frac{9}{68} = \frac{12}{68} + \frac{9}{68}$$

$$= \frac{12 + 9}{68}$$

$$= \frac{21}{68}$$

$$5\frac{3}{11} + 6\frac{7}{44} + \frac{23}{88} = 5\frac{8 \times 3}{8 \times 11} + 6\frac{2 \times 7}{2 \times 44} + \frac{23}{88}$$

$$= 5\frac{24}{88} + 6\frac{14}{88} + \frac{23}{88}$$

$$= 5 + 6 + \frac{24 + 14 + 23}{88}$$

$$= 11 + \frac{61}{88}$$

$$= 11\frac{61}{88}$$

We skipped steps in these examples. If this causes you to struggle with either of the examples, then you should write out each exercise and insert the missing steps needed to enhance your understanding.

Your Turn

2. Do the following problems, showing the intermediate steps you made to get the sum:

a) $\frac{3}{19} + \frac{11}{57} = ?$

b) $5\frac{3}{11} + \frac{23}{88} = ?$

c) $5\frac{3}{13} + \frac{63}{78} + 2\frac{25}{39} = ?$

Adding Fractions When the Denominators Are Relatively Prime

Next, look at fractions with denominators that are relatively prime. An example of an exercise with denominators that are relatively prime is $\frac{2}{3} + \frac{3}{4}$. The greatest common factor of 3 and 4 is 1, so these num-

bers are relatively prime. To complete the exercise, we need a common denominator that is a multiple of 3 and a multiple of 4. Figure 2.35 shows one way that the

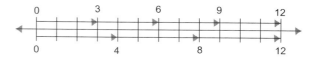

FIG. 2.35.

multiple can be determined using the number line. The vectors above the number line show multiples of 3, whereas the vectors below the number line show multiples of 4. Notice that the left ends of both start at zero, but the tips at 3 and 4 do not match. Because the first 3 vector is short of the end point of the first 4 vector, the second 3 vector is added, giving 6 as the multiple. The second 4 vector is added, giving 8. The process is repeated until the arrowheads of the vectors match exactly. The 3 vectors and 4 vectors match at 12 (and at 24, 36, 48, . . .). We use 12 because it is the least common multiple of 3 and 4. By using 12, we keep the arithmetic simpler, but any multiple of 12 could be used.

Examine Fig. 2.35 and notice that it took four 3 vectors and three 4 vectors to get the arrowheads to match. When we discussed whole number multiplication, we talked about three 4s as another way of expressing 3×4. Aha! We have just developed a rule for finding the least common denominator when the two denominators of the fractions being added are relatively prime. Putting that to work, $\frac{1}{3} + \frac{1}{4}$ is expressed as $\frac{1 \times 4}{3 \times 4} + \frac{1 \times 3}{4 \times 3}$, or $\frac{4}{12} + \frac{3}{12}$. This is now an exercise with like denominators, resulting in a sum of $\frac{7}{12}$.

Another example is $\frac{2}{3} + \frac{5}{7}$.

$$\frac{2}{3} + \frac{5}{7} = \frac{2 \times 7}{3 \times 7} + \frac{5 \times 3}{7 \times 3}$$

$$= \frac{14}{21} + \frac{15}{21}$$

$$= \frac{14 + 15}{21}$$

$$= \frac{29}{21}$$

$$= 1\frac{8}{21}$$

Your Turn

3. Do the following problems, showing the intermediate steps you made to get the sum:

a) $\dfrac{4}{5} + \dfrac{8}{9} = ?$

b) $2\dfrac{4}{5} + 3\dfrac{8}{9} = ?$

c) $2\dfrac{4}{7} + 9 + 3\dfrac{8}{11} + \dfrac{97}{154} + \dfrac{153}{154} = ?$

Adding Fractions When the Denominators Are Not Relatively Prime and One Is Not a Multiple of the Other

Suppose the denominators are 4 and 6, which are not relatively prime because they have a common factor of 2. Certainly the rule about multiplying denominators could be used here, but the product would not be the least common denominator. Depending on the problem, we may elect to go that route, using 24 as the common denominator. The thing is, when the problem is finished, the numerator and denominator of the sum will have a common factor. As we have said before, it is generally accepted that the common

factors are factored out of a fraction. Thus, an additional step would be needed to simplify the denominator.

$$\frac{1}{6} + \frac{3}{4} = \frac{1 \times 4}{6 \times 4} + \frac{3 \times 6}{4 \times 6}$$

$$= \frac{4}{24} + \frac{18}{24}$$

$$= \frac{4 + 18}{24}$$

$$= \frac{22}{24}$$

Most people prefer to work with the least common denominator initially, and we will give you a user-friendly method to find it. In the case of 4 and 6, we list the prime factorization of each, getting 2×2 for 4 and 2×3 for 6. All of the factors are used, but any common factor is used only once. In this case, you have $2 \times 2 \times 3 = 12$, the least common denominator for fractions having 4 and 6 as the denominators. Once equivalent fractions are determined, the exercise is completed exactly as before:

$$\frac{3}{4} + \frac{5}{6} = \frac{3 \times 3}{4 \times 3} + \frac{5 \times 2}{6 \times 2}$$

$$= \frac{9}{12} + \frac{10}{12}$$

$$= \frac{19}{12} \text{ or } 1\frac{7}{12}$$

Your Turn

4. Do the following problems, showing the intermediate steps you made to get the sum:

a) $\dfrac{3}{8} + \dfrac{5}{12} = ?$

b) $5\dfrac{3}{9} + 2\dfrac{11}{12} + 7\dfrac{14}{15} = ?$

Conclusions

Now you have the whole story on adding fractions and mixed numbers. We presented the sequence the way we did to help you build the rules you have probably used for some time. Our goal is to help you realize why you make some of the moves you do as you add fractions. We encourage you to create your own additional problems or seek an alternate source with solutions if you are still a little shaky about adding fractions and mixed numbers in any of the situations presented.

As usual, we advocate the appropriate use of technology. When adding fractions, we ask you to resist the temptation to use technology prior to developing the necessary skills and understandings, because there is so much more than just getting the answer. You need to be more interested in the process at this stage of your development.

SUBTRACTION OF FRACTIONS

FOCAL POINTS

- Same Denominators
- Related Denominators
- Relatively Prime Denominators
- Denominators That Are Not Relatively Prime or Related
- Mixed Numbers

Addition and subtraction are inverse operations of one another, so all the denominator rules for dealing with addition of fractions apply to subtraction involving fractions. You may want to review these rules and the procedures for dealing with different types of denominator combinations. We will restate the appropriate rules and provide some helpful examples with little discussion. We will provide a more elaborate discussion when dealing with mixed number situations.

Subtraction can be modeled on the number line. Figure 2.36 shows how an

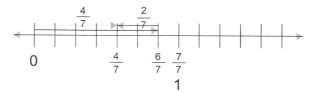

FIG. 2.36.

exercise involving like denominators, such as $\frac{6}{7} - \frac{2}{7}$, would be done using the missing addend approach. The sum is $\frac{6}{7}$ and the known addend is $\frac{2}{7}$. The task is to determine the missing addend, which is $\frac{4}{7}$, as indicated by the dashed vector. Similar results could be generated with Cuisenaire rods, egg cartons, or other manipulatives. We encourage you to use manipulatives to investigate the concepts of fraction subtraction. You will find that the experiences will enhance your understanding and make operating with fractions easier for you.

Same Denominators

The rule for adding fractions when the denominators are the same allows you to add the numerators and put the sum over the common denominator. The rule for subtracting fractions with like denominators is similar, except that you must deal with the numerators in the order in which they are given. Because the commutative property does not hold for subtraction in any set, you must remember that the first numerator is identified with the sum and the second numerator with the given addend. Return to Fig. 2.36 and notice that, in the case of $\frac{6}{7} - \frac{2}{7}$, 6 is the numerator of the sum and 2 is the numerator of the given addend, so you write $\frac{6-2}{7} = \frac{4}{7}$.

Subtraction problems with mixed numbers can involve fractions with denominators that are the same. In $8\frac{9}{11} - 2\frac{6}{11}$, no regrouping is required. Expanding the mixed numbers is one step in completing the exercise. Because $2\frac{6}{11}$ is being subtracted, Fig. 2.37 shows that the distribu-

$$8\frac{9}{11} \atop - 2\frac{6}{11} = \begin{matrix}8+\frac{9}{11}\\-\left(2+\frac{6}{11}\right)\end{matrix} \text{ which is } 8\frac{9}{11} \atop - 2\frac{6}{11} = \begin{matrix}8+\frac{9}{11}\\-2-\frac{6}{11}\end{matrix}$$

FIG. 2.37.

tive property of multiplication over addition in the set of rational numbers causes the given addend to be rewritten. Focusing on each looped section in Fig. 2.38, you see two separate problems. The

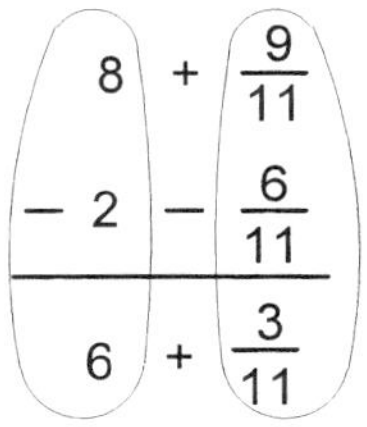

$$\begin{matrix}8 & + & \frac{9}{11}\\ - 2 & - & \frac{6}{11}\\ \hline 6 & + & \frac{3}{11}\end{matrix}$$

FIG. 2.38.

first is whole number subtraction and the second is fraction subtraction where the denominators are the same. In a final step, the missing addend of $6 + \frac{3}{11}$ would be expressed as $6\frac{3}{11}$. This problem could also be done in a horizontal format:

$$8\frac{9}{11} - 2\frac{6}{11} = \left(8 + \frac{9}{11}\right) - \left(2 + \frac{6}{11}\right)$$
$$= 8 + \frac{9}{11} - 2 - \frac{6}{11}$$
$$= (8-2) + \left(\frac{9}{11} - \frac{6}{11}\right)$$
$$= 6 + \frac{3}{11}$$
$$= 6\frac{3}{11}.$$

We realize that this looks like an algebra problem, but feel that showing all the steps this way should clarify the process.

Your Turn

1. Do each of these problems, showing basic intermediate steps:

a) $\frac{7}{9} - \frac{2}{9} = ?$

b) $\frac{4}{5} - \frac{1}{5} = ?$

c) $5\frac{3}{4} - 2 = ?$

d) $8\frac{9}{11} - 2\frac{6}{11} = ?$

e) $5\frac{15}{17} - 1\frac{6}{17} = ?$

2. Discuss what happens if a fraction subtraction problem involves two unit fractions with the same denominator.

Related Denominators

As in addition, subtraction with related denominators involves using equivalent fractions to provide denominators that are the same. Because one denominator is a multiple of the other, determine what factor is needed to provide a multiple of the smaller denominator. For example,

$$\frac{6}{7} - \frac{3}{14} = \frac{12}{14} - \frac{3}{14}$$
$$= \frac{12-3}{14}$$
$$= \frac{9}{14}$$

involves multiplying the

7 by 2 to get a denominator of 14. Because the denominator is multiplied by two, the numerator is also multiplied by 2 to get $\frac{12}{14}$. Take a moment to read through the following subtraction examples:

$$8\frac{6}{11} - 2\frac{9}{44} = 8\frac{24}{44} - 2\frac{9}{44}$$
$$= (8-2) + \left(\frac{24}{44} - \frac{9}{44}\right)$$
$$= 6\frac{15}{44}$$

$$5\frac{6}{17} - 2\frac{9}{34} = 5\frac{12}{34} - 2\frac{9}{34}$$
$$= (5-2) + \frac{12-9}{34}$$
$$= 3\frac{3}{34}$$

Your Turn

3. Do each of these exercises, showing basic intermediate steps:

a) $\dfrac{7}{9} - \dfrac{2}{27} = ?$

b) $\dfrac{4}{5} - \dfrac{7}{10} = ?$

c) $8\dfrac{9}{72} - 2\dfrac{1}{18} = ?$

d) $5\dfrac{15}{17} - 1\dfrac{6}{153} = ?$

4. Discuss what happens if a fraction subtraction problem involves two unit fractions with related denominators.

Relatively Prime Denominators

As in addition, subtraction with relatively prime denominators involves finding equivalent fractions for both the sum and given addend so they have the same denominator. Because the denominators have no common factors, you can make quick work of this by multiplying the numerator and denominator of the first fraction by the denominator of the second fraction, and multiplying the numerator and denominator of the second fraction by the denominator of the first fraction.

For example,

$$\frac{3}{8} - \frac{2}{7} = \frac{3\times7}{8\times7} - \frac{2\times8}{7\times8}$$
$$= \frac{21}{56} - \frac{16}{56} \quad \text{or}$$
$$= \frac{21-16}{56}$$
$$= \frac{5}{56}$$

$$6\frac{7}{9} - 1\frac{3}{8} = 6\frac{7\times8}{9\times8} - 1\frac{3\times9}{8\times9}$$
$$= 6\frac{56}{72} - 1\frac{27}{72}$$
$$= 6 - 1 + \frac{56}{72} - \frac{27}{72}$$
$$= 5\frac{56-27}{72}$$
$$= 5\frac{29}{72}.$$

Once the common denominator is determined, you complete the problem as in previous exercises.

Your Turn

5. The examples we have shown in the text involved two fractions with relatively prime denominators. If the problem involved three (or more) fractions and the only common factor shared by the denominators is one, how would you work the problem?

6. Do each of these problems, showing basic intermediate steps:

a) $\dfrac{5}{8} - \dfrac{3}{7} = ?$

b) $7\dfrac{8}{9} - 3\dfrac{1}{8} = ?$

c) $15\dfrac{11}{13} - 2\dfrac{4}{11} = ?$

d) $\dfrac{3}{4} + \dfrac{2}{3} - \dfrac{7}{11} = ?$

Denominators That Are Not Relatively Prime or Related

Certainly the rule about multiplying denominators could be used when unlike denominators are not relatively prime, but the product would not be the least common denominator. The solution would be a fraction with a numerator and denominator that have a common factor. If you insist that all common factors be divided out, a simplification step would have to be performed. The following examples should help:

$$\dfrac{7}{8} - \dfrac{5}{6} = \dfrac{7 \times 3}{2 \times 2 \times 2 \times 3} - \dfrac{5 \times 2 \times 2}{2 \times 2 \times 2 \times 3}$$

$$= \dfrac{21 - 20}{24}$$

$$= \dfrac{1}{24}$$

or

$$7\dfrac{3}{4} - 2\dfrac{1}{6} = 7\dfrac{3 \times 3}{4 \times 3} - 2\dfrac{1 \times 2}{6 \times 2}$$

$$= 7 - 2 + \dfrac{3 \times 3 - 1 \times 2}{4 \times 3}$$

$$= 5\dfrac{7}{12}$$

Your Turn

7. Do each of these problems, showing basic intermediate steps:

a) $\dfrac{5}{6} - \dfrac{5}{8} = ?$

b) $9\dfrac{1}{4} - 5\dfrac{1}{6} = ?$

c) $7\dfrac{13}{15} - 2\dfrac{7}{18} = ?$

Mixed Numbers

One type of subtraction exercise involving fractions deserves special consideration because of the regrouping that must be done. Consider $4 - \dfrac{5}{7}$. Writing this exercise vertically introduces an alignment that may appear strange $\begin{array}{r} 4 \\ -\ \dfrac{5}{7} \\ \hline \end{array}$. You need to express 4 in a different manner so that the problem will look like one you know how to handle. Although 4 can be written in a multitude of ways, we are going to write it as $3 + 1$ and express the 1 as $\dfrac{7}{7}$.

We want to use $\dfrac{7}{7}$ as an equivalent fraction for 1 because it ensures that the fractions have the same denominator. This changes the problem to a familiar form,

$$\begin{array}{r} 3\dfrac{7}{7} \\ -\ \dfrac{5}{7} \\ \hline \end{array}.$$

The problem could be solved in a horizontal manner, as follows. How to complete an exercise is often a matter of personal preference. We hope that you will practice several different methods, rather than rely on the method you find most comfortable:

$$4 - \dfrac{5}{7} = 3 + 1 - \dfrac{5}{7}$$

$$= 3 + \dfrac{7}{7} - \dfrac{5}{7}$$

$$= 3 + \dfrac{7 - 5}{7}$$

$$= 3\dfrac{2}{7}$$

There is another way to look at this problem. Your experience with missing addends should help you reason that $\frac{5}{7}$ is $\frac{2}{7}$ less than one $\left(\frac{7}{7}\right)$, or that $\frac{2}{7}$ must be added to $\frac{5}{7}$ to generate $\frac{7}{7}$. This line of reasoning is extended when the sum (4 in this case) is made $\frac{7}{7}$ smaller, meaning that the missing addend would include the missing $\frac{2}{7}$ and the remaining 3 from the sum, or $3\frac{2}{7}$. Although it is unlikely that someone would use this process when working with pencil and paper, it is a common technique for mental arithmetic.

A final situation involves an exercise in which both the sum and the given addend are mixed numbers with like denominators. In this special case, the fraction part of the sum is less than the fraction part of the given addend. You will need to do some regrouping before the subtraction can be completed. If the exercise is $6\frac{2}{7} - 1\frac{5}{7}$, the first thing to do is rename the sum so that you can regroup, $5 + 1 + \frac{2}{7}$, which is $5 + \frac{7}{7} + \frac{2}{7}$, or $5\frac{9}{7}$. Now the exercise can be expressed as $5\frac{9}{7} - 1\frac{5}{7}$. Whereas this might look strange, that improper fraction makes the subtraction of the fractional parts possible.

$$5\frac{9}{7} - 1\frac{5}{7} = 5 - 1 + \frac{9}{7} - \frac{5}{7}$$
$$= 4\frac{9-5}{7}$$
$$= 4\frac{4}{7}.$$

Your Turn

8. Do each of these problems, showing basic intermediate steps:

a) $4 - \frac{5}{9} = ?$

b) $6\frac{4}{7} - 1\frac{5}{7} = ?$

c) $6\frac{1}{4} - 2\frac{2}{3} = ?$

Conclusions

Subtraction of fractions and mixed numbers is not difficult once you have mastered the concepts involved with equivalent fractions, addition of fractions, and mixed numbers. We encourage you to think about when and how technology should be used in subtraction of fractions.

DIVISION OF FRACTIONS

FOCAL POINTS

- Concrete Beginnings
- Whole Number Divided by a Fraction
- Fraction Divided by a Fraction
- Mixed number divided by Mixed Number
- Common Denominator Division

Understanding the question is the key to fraction division. If you have 8 divided by 4, the question is, "How many 4s are there in 8?" In mathematics, we often discuss the value of real-world applications. Division involving fractions has real-world applications, but sometimes they are difficult to recognize. Halving a recipe is often mentioned as an example of dividing by a fraction. In reality, when dividing a recipe in half, you are dividing by 2, which although technically is the fraction $\frac{2}{1}$, is not dividing by a fraction as people typically think of a fraction.

Concrete Beginnings

If we have a problem like $3 \div \frac{1}{2}$, a real-life interpretation could be to have a 3-foot long piece of ribbon that is to be divided into 6-inch, or half-foot sections. Figure 2.39 shows the cutting. You see that you

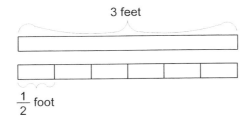

FIG. 2.39.

get 6 pieces of ribbon, each of which is $\frac{1}{2}$ foot long. Translating the situation, we want to know how many $\frac{1}{2}$s there are in 3.

The question now becomes, "How can we get the numbers to match the picture of the cutting?"

Whole Number Divided by a Fraction

Figure 2.39 shows the ribbon has been cut into 6 pieces or $3 \div \frac{1}{2} = 6$. Asking how to get the numbers to match the picture involves another question: "How do we get an answer of 6 when we start with 3?" One answer could be that we find $3 + 3$, which would certainly work. However, we know that multiplication is a short form of addition so we have two threes or 2 times 3. We could also express 2 times

3 as 3 times 2 because of the commutative property of multiplication on the set of rational numbers. Now we have to relate $3 \div \frac{1}{2}$ to 3×2. What has happened? Actually two things have happened. We know that 2 is the multiplicative inverse or reciprocal of $\frac{1}{2}$ and we see that as one thing that is different. The other thing is that the operation has changed from division to multiplication. Because we know that $3 \div \frac{1}{2} = 6$ and $3 \times 2 = 6$, the transitive property of equality tells us that $3 \div \frac{1}{2} = 3 \times 2$. So, as we analyze what has happened in the problem, the conclusion is that if you have a division problem involving a fraction doing the dividing, invert the second number in the problem and then follow the rules for multiplication. Often this rule gets shortened to invert and multiply. We caution you to say the rule properly, invert the second fraction and multiply, which could help avoid misinterpretations. It is important to note here that mathematicians normally do not arrive at a conclusion like invert the second fraction and multiply from so few examples. We assume you are familiar with the idea though, but we did not want to belabor the issue.

Your Turn

1. Do each of these problems, showing basic intermediate steps:

a) $6 \div \frac{1}{2} = ?$

b) $6 \div \frac{1}{3} = ?$

c) $8 \div \frac{1}{2} = ?$

d) $55 \div \dfrac{11}{28} = ?$

e) $144 \div \dfrac{7}{12} = ?$

Fraction Divided by a Fraction

If you have $\dfrac{1}{2}$ divided by $\dfrac{1}{4}$, the question really is, "How many fourths are in a half?" With the Cuisenaire rods, the process becomes one of determining the unit. Figure 2.40 shows that the first rod that is

FIG. 2.40.

"halfable" and "fourthable" at the same time is Purple. Red is a half and White is a fourth. The question was, "How many fourths are in a half?" or, "How many Whites are in a Red?" Two! That is it! There is no discussion of inverting the second fraction. Doing more problems like this shows a pattern, which aid in understanding the rule developed earlier. That is,

$$\frac{1}{2} \div \frac{1}{6} = 3 \Rightarrow \frac{1}{2} \times \frac{6}{1} = \frac{1 \times 6}{2 \times 1}, \text{ which is 3}$$

$$\frac{1}{8} \div \frac{1}{48} = 6 \Rightarrow \frac{1}{8} \times \frac{48}{1} = \frac{1 \times 48}{8 \times 1}, \text{ which is 6}$$

In each of the previous examples, the idea of inverting the second fraction and multiplying gives the correct answer. There is another way to generate that rule.

Multiplying or dividing the numerator and denominator of a fraction by the same value gives an equivalent expression. Consider $\dfrac{1}{2} \div \dfrac{1}{6}$ written in the format of a fraction over a fraction, $\dfrac{\frac{1}{2}}{\frac{1}{6}}$. Multiply both the numerator and denominator of this fraction by 6 or $\dfrac{6}{1}$. Although that might seem like a strange choice, look at what happens: $\dfrac{\frac{1}{2} \times \frac{6}{1}}{\frac{1}{6} \times \frac{6}{1}}$. Focus on the denominator and see that you have the product of a counting number and its multiplicative inverse, which is always 1. So, $\dfrac{\frac{1}{2} \times \frac{6}{1}}{\frac{1}{6} \times \frac{6}{1}}$ becomes $\dfrac{\frac{1}{2} \times \frac{6}{1}}{1}$, or more simply, $\dfrac{1}{2} \times \dfrac{6}{1}$. This is a problem we have done before and the answer is 3. Thus, we have another way of showing that the idea of inverting the second fraction and multiplying for a division problem involving two fractions generates the correct answer. Given the problem $\dfrac{55}{1} \div \dfrac{11}{28}$, it is expressed as $\dfrac{\frac{55}{1}}{\frac{11}{28}}$, which is $\dfrac{\frac{55}{1} \times \frac{28}{11}}{\frac{11}{28} \times \frac{28}{11}}$ and becomes $\dfrac{\frac{55}{1} \times \frac{28}{11}}{1}$, or 5×28, which is 140.

So far, the answers to the problems have always been whole numbers. The answer to a fraction divided by a fraction will not always be a whole number and yet this process will work as a means of solving the problem. For example,

$$\frac{55}{197} \div \frac{11}{28} = \frac{\dfrac{55}{197}}{\dfrac{11}{28}}$$

$$= \frac{\dfrac{55}{197} \times \dfrac{28}{11}}{\dfrac{11}{28} \times \dfrac{28}{11}}$$

$$= \frac{\dfrac{55}{197} \times \dfrac{28}{11}}{1}$$

$$= \frac{5 \times 28}{197}$$

$$= \frac{140}{197}$$

Your Turn

2. We have shown the reasoning behind inverting the second fraction and following the rules for multiplication in division problems involving fractions. Do these exercises using the fraction over a fraction routine.

a) $\dfrac{2}{3} \div \dfrac{3}{4} = ?$

b) $\dfrac{7}{9} \div \dfrac{11}{13} = ?$

c) $\dfrac{8}{11} \div \dfrac{48}{55} = ?$

Mixed Number Divided by Mixed Number

It is important to see patterns in the mathematics you do. Although a problem like $7\dfrac{2}{3} \div 5\dfrac{3}{4}$ might look intimidating, you need only apply one procedure you already know. After converting the mixed numbers to improper fractions, you have a fraction divided by a fraction. So, $7\dfrac{2}{3} \div 5\dfrac{3}{4}$

becomes $\dfrac{23}{3} \div \dfrac{23}{4}$, which could be expressed as $\dfrac{23}{3} \times \dfrac{4}{23}$, or $\dfrac{4}{3}$. You will not always have a common factor like the 23 in this problem, but that should not bother you. Consider $6\dfrac{7}{9} \div 14\dfrac{11}{13}$, which could be expressed as $\dfrac{61}{9} \div \dfrac{193}{13}$. That would be $\dfrac{61}{9} \times \dfrac{13}{193}$, or $\dfrac{973}{1737}$. It so happens that the numerator and denominator of $\dfrac{973}{1737}$ are relatively prime, so there are no common factors to be divided out.

Your Turn

3. Do each of these problems, showing basic intermediate steps:

a) $4\dfrac{7}{8} \div 2\dfrac{5}{6} = ?$

b) $11\dfrac{1}{2} \div 4\dfrac{2}{3} = ?$

c) $4\dfrac{2}{3} \div 11\dfrac{1}{2} = ?$

Common Denominator Division

Before leaving division of fractions, we want to discuss one other way of dealing with the problems. You learned to do division using a format that looks like $6\overline{)42}$. Fractions can also be placed in that format for division. Use old skills—finding a least common multiple (LCM), equivalent fractions, and using the familiar division format to look at the situation. Suppose the problem is $\dfrac{1}{2} \div \dfrac{1}{8}$. We know $\dfrac{1}{2} = \dfrac{4}{8}$. The exercise $\frac{1}{2} \div \frac{1}{8}$, which is $\frac{4}{8} \div \frac{1}{8}$, could be written as $\frac{1}{8}\overline{)\frac{4}{8}}$. The question is still, "How many $\frac{1}{8}$s are in $\frac{4}{8}$?" or, because the denominators are the same, "How many ones are in four?" The completed fraction division would be $\frac{1}{8}\overline{)\begin{array}{c}4\\ \frac{4}{8}\\ \frac{4}{8}\\ \hline 0\end{array}}$.

The equivalent fraction process can be used for any fraction problem. An exercise like $\frac{3}{4} \div \frac{2}{3}$ becomes $\frac{9}{12} \div \frac{8}{12}$, or $\frac{8}{12}\overline{)\frac{9}{12}}$. Do a few like this and you realize you could just do $8\overline{)9}$. Think about finding the least common multiple first and then dividing the numerators as we just described. For some of you, this method seems easier; for others, it may be more complicated. Our point is that there are different ways to view a problem.

An exercise like $\frac{3}{4} \div \frac{2}{3}$ becomes $\frac{9}{12} \div \frac{8}{12}$, but at this point, the development could vary. Rather than expressing it as $\frac{8}{12}\overline{)\frac{9}{12}}$, you could express it as $\frac{9 \div 8}{12 \div 12} = \frac{9 \div 8}{1}$, which becomes $\frac{9}{8}$ or $1\frac{1}{8}$. Notice that this is similar to multiplication of fractions. Expressing the two fractions with the same denominator allows you to divide the numerator of the product by the numerator of the factor. The division in the denominator will always yield one. That might sound strange, but you can see this procedure at work in $\frac{9 \div 8}{12 \div 12} = \frac{9 \div 8}{1}$.

Your Turn

4. Use the least common multiple method to do the following problems:

a) $\frac{2}{3} \div \frac{3}{4} = ?$

b) $\frac{7}{9} \div \frac{11}{13} = ?$

c) $\frac{8}{11} \div \frac{48}{55} = ?$

Conclusions

Here are examples of the types of exercises we have covered in this section:

Whole divided by fraction
$$55 \div \frac{11}{28} = \frac{\cancel{55}}{1} \times \frac{28}{\cancel{11}} = \frac{5 \times 28}{1 \times 1} = 140$$

Fraction divided by fraction
$$\frac{3}{4} \div \frac{5}{7} = \frac{3}{4} \times \frac{7}{5} = \frac{3 \times 7}{4 \times 5} = \frac{21}{20} \text{ or } 1\frac{1}{20}$$

Mixed number divided by mixed number
$$8\frac{3}{5} \div 2\frac{1}{7} = \frac{43}{5} \div \frac{15}{7} = \frac{43}{5} \times \frac{7}{15} = \frac{43 \times 7}{5 \times 15}$$
$$= \frac{301}{75} = 4\frac{1}{75}$$

Least common multiple
$$\frac{5}{19}\overline{)\frac{3}{4}} = \frac{20}{76}\overline{)\frac{57}{76}} \text{ and } \frac{20}{76}\overline{)\begin{array}{c}2\frac{17}{76}\\ \frac{57}{76}\\ \hline \frac{40}{76}\\ \frac{17}{76}\end{array}}$$

Dividing the numerators and denominators when using a common denominator
$$\frac{9 \div 8}{12 \div 12} = \frac{9 \div 8}{1}$$

When all is said and done, these are all very similar. We caution you to do exercises by hand to strengthen your skills and understanding before reaching for your fraction calculator.

ADDITION OF DECIMALS

FOCAL POINTS

- Concrete Beginnings
- Denominate Numbers
- Adding With the Same Number of Places
- Zeros at the End
- Lining Up the Ones
- Expanded Notation

Addition is a familiar topic by the time you get to decimals. The addition facts should be mastered at this juncture and you should have had many experiences adding. You should also understand the basic workings behind addition. If you do not understand what is going on behind the scenes when adding whole numbers, then you may be able to survive adding decimals by sheer force of memory. However, we believe that an understanding of the foundations of addition will serve you better.

Any decimal addition problem could be converted to a fraction addition problem and then the answer converted back to a decimal. However, it is simpler to learn to deal effectively with decimals in their own right.

Concrete Beginnings

A single manipulative can be used for many purposes. You have seen the Base 10 blocks used with whole numbers. Here we will suggest another, equally powerful, application of this manipulative. As you

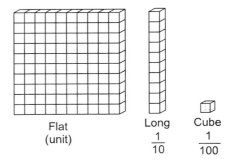

FIG. 2.41.

refer to Fig. 2.41, notice that the Flat now represents 1 whole, the Long represents $\frac{1}{10}$ of a whole, and the tiny Cube represents $\frac{1}{100}$ of a whole. This transition requires that you accept the Flat as the Unit and the Long and tiny Cube as fractional parts of that Unit.

Now consider Fig. 2.42. The Flat is

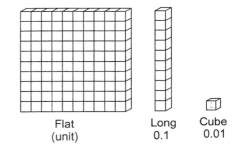

FIG. 2.42.

used as 1 whole, whereas the Long is labeled 0.1 and 0.01 is the label for the tiny Cube. These two figures should establish that 0.1 is the same as $\frac{1}{10}$ and 0.01 is the same as $\frac{1}{100}$ and the foundation for adding decimal numbers through fractions is established. Although the model we have used here can only deal with units, tenths, and hundredths, it provides a good tool for understanding decimal numbers. The set of Base 10 blocks could be extended

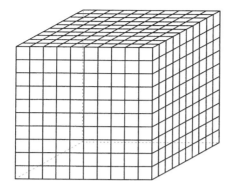

FIG. 2.43.

to make a Big Block as shown in Fig. 2.43, which would be equivalent to 10 of the Flats glued together. If the Big Block is used as a unit, the Flat represents $\frac{1}{10}$, the Long represents $\frac{1}{100}$, and the tiny Cube represents $\frac{1}{1000}$.

As adults, we often read decimal numbers as if they have no connection to fractions. If we see 3.14, we say, three point one four, when the number is actually three and fourteen hundredths. The first reading is quick and easy, but it obscures the fact that 3.14 is another name for a mixed number. Try randomly grouping a handful of Base 10 blocks and reading the result as a mixed number. For example, if you had a group of 3 Flats, 4 Longs, and 7 tiny Cubes when the Flat is the Unit, then you could say, three and four tenths with seven hundredths. You could also say, three and forty-seven hundredths, if you recognize it.

Denominate Numbers

Denominate numbers are handy with decimals, but there is a need for extending the concept of place value. The first place to the right of the decimal point is called tenths. Using denominate numbers to do

whole number addition exercises such as 4567 + 319 + 208, becomes:

4 thousands 5 hundreds 6 tens 7 ones
3 hundreds 1 ten 9 ones
+ _____2 hundreds 0 tens 8 ones.

If that problem is changed to 45.67 + 3.19 + 2.08, it is still done the same way, except the place values for the respective digits have changed and become:

4 tens 5 ones 6 tenths 7 hundredths
3 ones 1 tenth 9 hundredths
+ _____2 ones 0 tenths 8 hundredths.

Once these accommodations for place value are completed, all addition applications from earlier apply. When we use denominate numbers, we don't need decimal points, the numbers are fully described.

Adding With the Same Number of Places

Many decimal addition exercises will look just like whole number addition. Look at the following examples and decide how they are the same as and how they differ from exercises involving only whole numbers:

4.37	10.586	346.9	25.748	5.7
+9.25	+1.378	+427.8	+47.995	+6.2
13.62	11.964	774.7	73.743	11.9

What did you conclude? You probably said something like, "The decimals are lined up in the problem and the decimal goes in that same column in the answer." That is a reasonable and expected conclusion for the examples given. Another way of saying, line up the decimals is line up the ones or units. The advantage is that you learned this while adding whole numbers. Use the same rule here and you eliminate the need to learn a new one.

Zeros at the End

Consider 6.4 + 8.95. This does not look like the examples in the last paragraph because the numbers of digits following the decimal points are not the same. Refer to the Base 10 blocks when the Flat is the unit and consider 6.4. This could be expressed by using 6 Flats and 4 Longs, as shown in Fig. 2.44. But, we know that each Long is equivalent to, or made up of 10 little Cubes. Thus, whereas the 4 Longs represent 0.4, we could trade them for 40 tiny Cubes. This means we could also express 6 Flats and 4 Longs as 6.40, using the tiny Cubes rather than the Longs. We could extend this model by using a Big Block like the one in Fig. 2.43

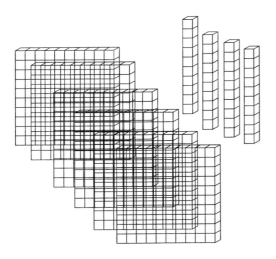

FIG. 2.44.

as the Unit; then a Flat would represent 0.1, a Long 0.01, and the tiny Cube 0.001. This would allow us to use a similar approach to show that 6.4 is equivalent to 6.400. It would then be a logical extension to say that 6.4 is equivalent to 6.4000, 6.40000, and so on. This should lead you to a generalization about zeros after the

last nonzero digit to the right of the decimal point. What would you say? If you said it is acceptable to add as many zeros as you want after the last digit to the right of a decimal point, then you are correct.

The advantage of that last conclusion is that, if an exercise such as 6.4 + 8.95 seems strange or troublesome because the numbers of digits to the right of the decimal points are not the same, a zero can be inserted so that 6.4 + 8.95 is expressed as 6.40 + 8.95. Similarly, the problem could be 6.400 + 8.950, 6.4000 + 8.9500, and so on. Whereas, in general, there is no advantage to putting more zeros to the right, it certainly could happen and the important thing is that the value of the problem would not be changed. Sometimes the zeros after a number indicate precision. For example, in science, there is a reason for putting more zeros to the right. The value 0.010 mm indicates a measurement was accurate to the nearest 0.001 mm instead of 0.01 mm. Additionally, zeros can play a role for significant figures in calculations. For our purposes in this section, zeros to the right of the last nonzero decimal digit only serve as placeholders.

Lining Up the Ones

Perhaps you are more comfortable seeing the problems listed vertically:

$$\begin{array}{llll} 6.4 & 6.40 & 6.400 & 6.4000 \\ +8.95 & +8.95 & +8.950 & +8.9500 \end{array}$$ It is com-

mon to leave out the extra zeros and just do the exercise as $\begin{array}{l} 6.4 \\ +8.95 \end{array}$. Either format is

acceptable. The important thing is to remember that ones are added to ones, tenths are added to tenths, hundredths are added to hundredths, and so on. In this particular exercise, there are 5 hundredths in one addend, and no hundredths in the other addend. We could elect to either represent the no hundredths in that one addend with a zero, or omit the zero and let it be understood that the absence of a digit in the hundredths column means that there are zero hundredths. This same idea is then extendable to any situation, as long as the zeros are placed to the right of the last digit after the decimal point. The rule of lining up the ones is just as applicable as, and more explanatory than, the one you may have memorized about lining up the decimal points. Because you learned to line up the units, or ones, long before you learned to line up the decimal points, you really did not need to memorize that rule.

Look what happens to 4.37 + 9.2 + 10.586 if we forget to line up the ones. The exercise could end up looking like
  4.37
     9.2, in which the decimals are ig-
+10.586
nored and the sum does not make sense. If we merely line up the ones, then the rest of the place values take care of them-
            4.37
selves as is shown here, 9.2 .
           +10.586

The situation can be perplexing if .78 is an addend. All that is necessary is to write .78 as 0.78. When the exercise is 4.37 + 9.2 + 10.586 + 0.78, and we write 0.78 instead of .78, the lining up the ones rule is functional and that zero eliminates a huge
         4.37
         9.2
hurdle: 10.586
         +0.78

Expanded Notation

As we convert from denominate numbers to expanded notation, the focus shifts to a different way of expressing place value. The addends 45.67 + 3.19 + 2.08 are indi-

vidually expanded to become 40 + 5 + 0.6 + 0.07, 3 + 0.1 + 0.09, and 2 + 0.0 + 0.08, respectively. At this point, we are dealing with addition problems we have already handled. Even regrouping is familiar territory. The problem 45.67 + 3.19 + 2.08 is expressed as

    40 + 5 + 0.6 + 0.07
         3 + 0.1 + 0.09
+   2 + 0.0 + 0.08

Your Turn

1. Do the following problems showing any scratch work you generate:

a) 4.36 + 56.789 + 321 = ?
b) 0.3 + 21.4 + 367.963 + 59.6921 = ?
c) 0.1 + 0.01 + 0.001 = ?

Conclusions

We have provided a review that should help you tackle adding decimal numbers in any problem. We have shown you how to start concretely and relate back to whole number addition if necessary. Diligence from you is all that is required now. Don't forget to plan when and how you are going to use technology.

SUBTRACTION OF DECIMALS

FOCAL POINTS

- Concrete Beginnings
- Subtracting With the Same Number of Places
- Zeros at the End

Much of the groundwork for decimal subtraction has already been established. Essentially you are going to encounter only one new idea in this section.

Concrete Beginnings

Base 10 blocks are a nice and effective tool to use to show what is going on with decimal subtraction. If the problem does not involve regrouping, for example, 2.6 – 2.5, Fig. 2.45 shows the subtraction con-

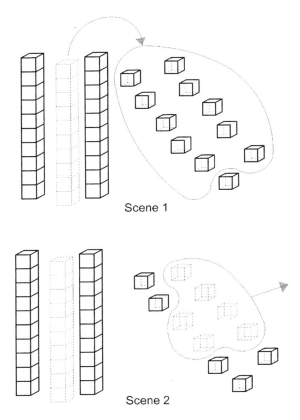

Scene 1

Scene 2

FIG. 2.46.

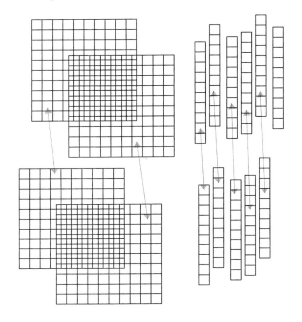

FIG. 2.45.

cretely. In this model, the Flat is the unit and a Long is the tenth. The top row of blocks represents the sum and the bottom row represents the given addend. The double-headed arrows indicate the matching that eliminates the pairings, leaving one Long as the missing addend. Because the Long is designated as a tenth, the missing addend would be 0.1 and 2.6 – 2.5 = 0.1. Vertically, the problem would be shown as: $\begin{array}{r} 2.6 \\ -2.5 \\ \hline 0.1 \end{array}$. Either way is acceptable, however the vertical alignment points out the need to line up the ones.

Figure 2.46 shows how a unit (Long in this case) can be traded for 10 tenths to complete a subtraction exercise such as 3.1 – 0.6. Scene 1 shows one Long in dashed segments to indicate that it is going to be traded for 10 tenths; Scene 2 shows that 6 tenths are removed. The remaining two units and 5 tenths represent the answer. Written horizontally, 3.1 – 0.6 = 2.5, or vertically, $\begin{array}{r} 3.1 \\ -0.6 \\ \hline 2.5 \end{array}$, the missing addend is the same.

Subtracting With the Same Number of Places

Here are a few examples to help you clarify any questions you might have

845.178	23.9814	8712.3
−270.156	−12.3456	−1987.2
545.022	11.6358	6725.1

All of the regrouping procedures are the same as those discussed when we worked with whole number subtraction. Essentially, you can ignore the decimal points and proceed as usual when doing the problem—as long as you line up the ones digits in the sum, addend, and missing addend.

Zeros at the End

Zeros can cause some problems in subtraction, and even more so in decimal subtraction. Actually, the absence of zeros is where the trouble starts. Suppose the problem involves a ragged alignment as in $\frac{34.8}{-2.651}$. The problem is that there is nothing from which to subtract the 0.001 or the 0.05. There is something there to subtract from, but it has not been written. The discussion about putting zeros after the last written decimal digit applies here. An equivalent expression for 34.8 is 34.800, which allows the exercise to be written as $\frac{34.800}{-2.651}$, making the operation more convenient.

There is another ragged alignment problem that can cause you to pause for reflection. Suppose the problem is $\frac{34}{-2.651}$. Because there is an understood decimal point at the right of any whole number, 34 can be written as 34., 34.0, 34.00, 34.000, or with as many zeros as we find convenient. For this problem, 34.000 is helpful in rewriting the exercise so that the sum and given addend have the same number of

decimal places, $\frac{34.000}{-2.651}$, a valid, as well as helpful, alignment for the regrouping that will be required as this exercise is completed.

Your Turn

1. Do each of these exercises using only pencil and paper:

 a) 845 − 270.156 = ?
 b) 23.01 − 2.3456 = ?
 c) 8712 − 19.872 = ?

MULTIPLICATION OF DECIMALS

FOCAL POINTS

- Concrete Beginnings
- Relating to Fractions
- Zeros in Multiplication

We will present a carefully sequenced set of ideas as you broaden your skills with and understanding of multiplication. You should continue to see the cumulative effect of the underpinnings of mathematical knowledge.

Concrete Beginnings

Any multiplication problem is like finding the area of a rectangle. We will expand the set of examples to include positive decimals. When the Long Base 10 block is the unit, the little Cube represents a tenth. Figure 2.47 shows 2 times 0.3 and how 0.6 is the answer. You have two sets that are 0.3 big and end up with one set that is derived from $2 \times 0.3 = 0.6$ as an expression of the situation. Examining the answer, the exercise looks a lot like 2×3,

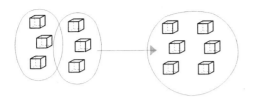

FIG. 2.47.

but a decimal point appears both in one factor and in the product.

Figure 2.48 shows how 4 × 0.3 would

FIG. 2.48.

be done, again with the Long defined as the unit. This time you have four sets that are 0.3 big and when you combine all the elements, you get enough little Cubes to trade 10 of them for a Long and you still have 2 little Cubes left, as shown in Fig. 2.49. The Long is a unit, so we have a unit

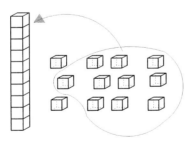

FIG. 2.49.

and two tenths, or 1.2. Thus, 4 × 0.3 = 1.2. Again, the problem looks a lot like 4 × 3, but decimal points are still present.

Using the same mentality, 17 × 0.9 = 15.3 and this is an important problem in the discussion. We are headed toward some conclusions here. First, you should be saying that if there is one decimal point in the problem, then there will be one decimal point in the product. The location of

that decimal point is an issue, however. The 17 × 0.9 = 15.3 problem provides the needed clue. Do the multiplication as if it was 17 × 9 as far as the work is concerned. After you have done the multiplication, count from the right toward the left, one place to locate the decimal point in the product. This will work even with problems like 25 × 0.4, where the product is 10. Doing the problem without worrying about the decimals would give 25 × 4, which is 100. However, considering the decimal points, the answer would be 10.0, which is generally written as 10.

Moving Beyond the Concrete

It is important that you realize we could continue to show various configurations of Base 10 blocks to confirm the results we will discuss. If the problem is 3 × 0.97, the product is 2.91, and the beginnings of a generalization are established. Examine the following examples:

3 × 0.97 = 2.91

3 × 0.978 = 2.934

3 × 0.9568 = 2.8704

3 × 14.35789 = 43.07367

3 × 563.123456 = 1689.370368

You should come up with a generalization that says you count the number of decimal places in the decimal factor, and you will have that many decimal places in the product, COUNTING FROM THE RIGHT in both instances.

The problem 0.4 × 0.3 can be interpreted as taking three tenths of four tenths and is shown in Fig. 2.50. The square is divided into tenths in both directions. Because this figure is two dimensional, a complete column or a complete row of smaller squares would be the

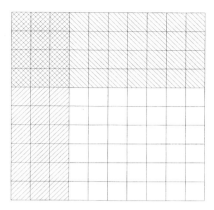

FIG. 2.50.

same as a Long in the Base 10 blocks. Similarly, the big square would be like a Base 10 block Flat and a little square would be like a Base 10 block little Cube. If we considered the big square as the unit, then either a column or a row would represent one tenth and one of the little squares would represent one one hundredth. The top four rows are crosshatched with diagonals going from upper left to lower right. That set of four rows represents 0.4 in the problem. Similarly, the leftmost three columns are crosshatched from upper right to lower left, representing 0.3 in the problem. The small rectangle in the upper left corner of the big square represents three tenths of four tenths. But that rectangle is made up of 12 little squares, each of which represents one one hundredth. So, that three tenths of four tenths of the big square is equivalent to 12 one hundredths. Condensing the notation, $0.4 \times 0.3 = 0.12$, as shown in Fig. 2.50.

Study the following exercises and come up with a generalization about placement of decimals in products, when both factors are decimals:

$0.4 \times 0.3 = 0.12$

$23.4 \times 5.67 = 132.278$

$4.32 \times 1.96 = 8.4672$

$2.3217 \times 3.5 = 8.12595$

$3.428 \times 5.579 = 19.124812$

You should conclude that the total number of decimal places in the factors is the number of decimal places in the product, when counting from the right. That is, because there are four decimal places in the factor, 2.3217, and one more in the factor, 3.5, there must be five decimal places in the product, 8.12595, and they are counted from the right. The multiplication is done as if the decimals were not there and then the count of places locates the decimal point in the product, counting from the right.

One more topic and you should have all you need to do any decimal multiplication problem. Figure 2.51 shows 0.2×0.3 and

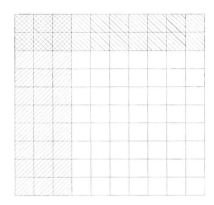

FIG. 2.51.

it helps explain a difficult situation. As in Fig. 2.50, each little square represents one one hundredth. This time the rectangle in the top left of Fig. 2.51 only has six little squares double crosshatched, which represents six one hundredths. So, the completed problem is $0.2 \times 0.3 = 0.06$, and a new situation occurs. Up until now, we have been counting the number of decimal places in the factors and then counting that many places from the right to locate the decimal point in the product. Here, if we do the multiplication without considering the decimals in the factors, the product is six. In order to consider the decimals in the factors and also do our counting from the right in the product, we need to insert a zero to the left of the 6 in the product to get the proper number of places. Thus, 0.06 becomes the expressed factor. Consider the following examples and verify that the generalization works, if zeros are inserted in the product between the first significant digit and where the decimal point needs to be located. As you do this, mental images like Fig. 2.51 could prove helpful:

$$0.2 \times 0.3 = 0.06$$
$$2.1 \times 0.04 = 0.084$$
$$142 \times 0.0001 = 0.0142$$
$$0.04 \times 1.002 = 0.04008$$

Multiplication works the same as before, except for the need to insert zeros in the product to get the right number of decimal places.

Relating to Old Ways

How does decimal multiplication connect with earlier concepts? Recall that multiplication is a short way of adding. The sum $0.4 + 0.4 + 0.4$ is 1.2, as you know. This problem could be interpreted as three sets of 0.4 or three 0.4s, which is really just 3×0.4 and we have expressed the addition problem via multiplication. This scenario could be repeated with any product of a whole number times a decimal.

When the problem involves two decimal factors, repeated addition is abandoned in favor of prior work with fractions. Suppose 0.3×0.4 is the problem. Expressed as fractions, 0.3×0.4 becomes $\frac{3}{10} \times \frac{4}{10}$ or $\frac{12}{100}$, or 0.12 as a decimal. Again, the decimal point location

generalization holds true. In a similar manner, any repeating or terminating decimal multiplication could be converted to fractions and worked out. Of course, somewhere along the line, you might want to shift to a calculator. Our assumption is that before you grab that calculator, however, you do understand how to perform decimal multiplication.

One final thing that might help you involves the distributive property of multiplication over addition on the set of real numbers. A problem like 3×2.4 could be rewritten as $3(2 + 0.4)$, which can be expressed as $(3 \times 2) + (3 \times 0.4)$ and this is familiar material. In this case, the sum of 6 and 1.2 would be 7.2 and, again, it looks like multiplication is done as usual (temporarily ignoring the decimal point in the factor) and then placing the decimal point in the product.

Your Turn

1. Do each of the following problems to practice your multiplication skills when one or both of the factors involve decimals. Although we are proponents of calculator use, you should not use calculators here. You need to practice the skill and be sure you have a handle on decimal multiplication:

$$0.3 \times 4.2 = ?$$
$$14.89 \times 0.005 = ?$$
$$0.002 \times 0.0003 = ?$$
$$12.5 \times 4.2 = ?$$

Conclusions

It is important that you realize multiplication of decimals is done just like with whole numbers. All of the hurdles and challenges encountered there exist here too, with one more: the decimal point placement. We have provided a logical development and connections that should help you make sense of counting from the right in the product until you have the same number of decimal places as were expressed in the factor(s), and put the decimal point there.

DIVISION OF DECIMALS

FOCAL POINTS

- Concrete Beginnings
- Whole Number Divided by a Whole Number
- Decimal Divided by a Whole Number
- Whole Number Divided by a Decimal
- Decimal Divided by a Decimal

You need to be able to do division problems by hand, however, there is debate over how much is enough. It is reasonable to assume that you are comfortable doing something like $3.8 \div 2$ mentally, regardless of the format in which the exercise is presented $\left(2\overline{)3.8} \text{ or } \dfrac{3.8}{2} \right)$. Many authorities in the field of education think that it would be unreasonable to expect you to do $43.81025 \div 796.38624$ either mentally or by hand. We think that, somewhere between those two exercises, a calculator becomes an acceptable tool for finding the missing factor. You, your instructors, and the problem situations in which you are involved will determine when the use of technology becomes appropriate. There is simply no fine line between when pencil and paper work is needed and the use of a calculator is acceptable.

Prior to starting division with decimals, you need to be well founded in the basics of division, place value, equivalent fractions, rounding, approximation, estimation, multiplication, and subtraction. The assumption is that you are functioning well beyond introductory levels with each of these concepts. Building on equivalent fractions, the four categories of decimal division are: $\dfrac{\text{whole}}{\text{whole}}, \dfrac{\text{decimal}}{\text{whole}}, \dfrac{\text{whole}}{\text{decimal}}$, and $\dfrac{\text{decimal}}{\text{decimal}}$. You should realize that each of these four problem types could be expressed as $\dfrac{\text{whole}}{\text{whole}}$ using equivalent fractions. For example, if you are given $\dfrac{7.26}{2.42}$, you might multiply both the numerator and denominator by 100 to get $\dfrac{7.26}{2.42} \times \dfrac{100}{100} = \dfrac{726}{242}$ and eliminate decimal numbers from the exercise. A quick review of place value will remind you that the value you use to create equivalent fractions without decimals will always be an appropriate power of ten. Actually, you may soon realize that the only real necessity is to use an equivalent fraction in which the denominator is a whole number.

Concrete Beginnings

If you and I have 1 Flat and 4 Longs from a set of Base 10 blocks to be divided between us, we will have to trade the Flat for 10 Longs. Once that is accomplished, the task will be to share the pieces equally between us. If we do a one for you and one for me routine until all the Longs are dispersed, then each of us will have 7 Longs. But, what will the Longs be worth? If we are dealing with money, we will trade the dollar (the Flat) for dimes (the Longs) and then each of us will have 7 dimes, or 70 cents. You have seen 70 cents written as $0.70, which is the decimal representation. If the problem statement does not involve money, we would use 0.7 to describe the 7 Longs. Figure 2.52 shows how the situation would be depicted with

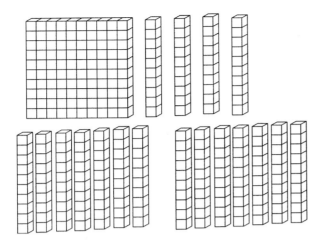

FIG. 2.52.

Base 10 blocks. You start with a Flat and 4 Longs, make the trade and then divide the set of 14 Longs into two sets of 7 each. This is going to be the essence of the discussion that follows. You should create mental images or sketches of the Base 10 blocks as we go through each explanation.

Whole Number Divided by a Whole Number

Initially, the product is a multiple of the factor, so the missing whole number factor represents the exact missing information. When that does not happen, we have a means of expressing the situation. We could say $8\overline{)12}\,^{1\,r\,4}$, which would suffice sometimes. However, in the real world, remainders frequently give way to other ways of telling the story. Certainly $8\overline{)12}$ could be expressed as $\frac{12}{8}$, which could be expressed as $1\frac{4}{8}$ or $1\frac{1}{2}$. As you probably have observed over time, the real world usually deals with decimal

numbers rather than common fractions. So, the task becomes one of expressing $8\overline{)12}$ in terms of decimals. Consider $\frac{12}{8}$, which can be written as $1\frac{1}{2}=1+\frac{1}{2}$. We know that $\frac{1}{2}=0.5$ and, from our addition of decimals discussions, we know $1+0.5=1.5$. Thus, we have generated an equivalent decimal expression for $1\frac{1}{2}$, and we can say that $1.5=1\frac{1}{2}$.

Now the challenge is to make the $8\overline{)12}$ configuration match with $8\overline{)12}\,^{1.5}$, which we know to be the answer. If we are dealing with $8\overline{)120}$, the problem looks like $8\overline{)120}\,^{15}$. The only apparent differences between $8\overline{)120}\,^{15}$ and $8\overline{)12}\,^{1.5}$ is that there is a zero in the units place in $8\overline{)120}\,^{15}$ with no decimal point, whereas $8\overline{)12}\,^{1.5}$ has the decimal point but no zero. But wait a minute! We know there is always a decimal point at the end of any whole number, so 12.0 and 12 must be equivalent. On top of that, we know that we can put as many zeros to the right of the decimal point as we need without changing the value of the number. In other words, 12 = 12.0 is a true statement. Similarly, if we look at the problem with the answer expressed as a remainder, we have $8\overline{)12}\,^{1\,r\,4}$. But that 1 in the missing factor is a whole number, so it has a decimal point to its right. That same decimal point would be to the left of the 5 in 0.5, and voila! The whole thing is coming together. Insert the appropriate missing zero and decimal points and the exercise becomes $8\overline{)12.0}$ with 1.5 above —everything we have been seeing and discussing matches up.

Let's summarize what happened. We started with $8\overline{)12}$, but opted to express it as $8\overline{)12.0}$ instead. We then rationalized that the answer had to be 1.5, so we had $8\overline{)12.0}$ with 1.5 above. The decimal point in the missing factor is directly above the decimal point that was inserted into the product. You may recognize that as a rule you learned long ago, put the decimal point at the end of the product and insert another decimal point directly above it in the missing factor. Look at a few examples in which we have shown all the steps:

```
        49.36              12.25              1.375
  25)1234.00         8)98.00            8)11.000
     100                8                   8
     234                18                  3 0
     225                16                  2 4
       9 0               20                   60
       7 5               1 6                  56
       1 50               40                   40
       1 50               40                   40
          0                0                    0
```

Your Turn

1. Do these problems without a calculator. You should check your work by multiplying the factor times the missing factor:

a) $42\overline{)63}$

b) $12\overline{)18}$

c) $2\overline{)1}$

d) $3\overline{)4}$

Decimal Divided by a Whole Number

Even something like $78\overline{)735.54}$ does not present much of a challenge. Although decimals in fractions are not common, we can express the problem as a fraction, $\frac{735.54}{78}$. Use your knowledge of equivalent fractions to multiply both the numerator and denominator of the fraction by 100, giving $\frac{735.54 \times 100}{78 \times 100}$, or $\frac{73554}{7800}$. We have discussed this type of problem, because it is a whole number divided by a whole number. Your experience multiplying decimals by powers of 10 and knowledge of place value should clarify why we selected 100 as the factor by which to multiply both the numerator and denominator. We see that 100 is the smallest power of 10 that eliminates decimals from the exercise.

You have learned that the decimal point in the product determines where the decimal point is located in the missing factor, so this isn't a new type of problem and there is no need to go through the maneuver of multiplying the numerator and denominator by some power of 10. Instead, with the exercise in the format $78\overline{)735.54}$, apply the technique of aligning the decimal point in the missing factor directly above the decimal point in the product.

Your Turn

2. Complete the following exercises being careful to align the decimal point in the missing factor:

a) $14\overline{)23.456}$

b) $723\overline{)58.92}$

c) $465\overline{)23.1}$

Whole Number Divided by a Decimal

An exercise such as $7.8\overline{)73554}$ may appear to present a little bit more of a challenge. Again, equivalent fractions make even this into a relatively simple task. The problem can be restated as:

$$\frac{73554}{7.8} = \left(\frac{73554}{7.8}\right)\left(\frac{10}{10}\right)$$
$$= \frac{735540}{78}.$$

Once again, an exercise involving a decimal factor is restated as a whole number division exercise. The only hurdle is to determine by what power of 10 to multiply the numerator and denominator of the fraction so that both are whole numbers. Restating the product and given factor as whole numbers does not mean that the missing factor will be a whole number. The decimal point might need to be inserted after the units digit of the product. More than likely, you were taught a rule that said something about moving the decimal point to the right end of the factor and then moving the same number of places to the right in the product. Multiplying the numerator and denominator of the related fraction by the same power of 10 explains why that works and is appropriate.

Your Turn

3. Tell the smallest power of 10 needed to make the factor a whole number:

a) $1.4\overline{)23456}$

b) $7.23\overline{)5892}$

c) $0.465\overline{)231}$

d) $3.54\overline{)679}$

Decimal Divided by a Decimal

The only type of problem remaining involving division and decimals is one such as $7.8\overline{)73.554}$. Once again, the hurdle is to decide by what power of 10 to multiply the numerator and denominator to eliminate the decimal in the factor. Because you already know how to deal with division when the factor is a whole number, it seems logical to use the smallest power of 10 that will do so. In this case, that is 10. So, $7.8\overline{)73.554}$ would become $\left(\frac{73.554}{7.8}\right)\left(\frac{10}{10}\right)$, or $\frac{735.54}{78}$, a problem type you already know how to do. If the original problem had been $0.78\overline{)7355.4}$, then we would have multiplied both the factor and product by 100 and the exercise would be transformed into $\left(\frac{7355.4}{0.78}\right)\left(\frac{100}{100}\right) = \frac{735540}{78}.$

Your Turn

4. Tell the smallest power of 10 needed to make the factor a whole number:

a) $1.4\overline{)234.56}$

b) $7.23\overline{)5892}$

c) $0.465\overline{)2.31}$

d) $3.54\overline{)67.9}$

Conclusions

So there you have it. The hurdles presented by decimal division are taken care of by looking at the problems in a fraction format. Given that understanding, the procedures used for division involving decimals should make sense now. The discussion of decimals and fractions in the last eight sections should have given you both a review and an insight into the workings of the mathematics behind these two fundamental ideas in numeration. We will revisit these ideas one more time in a discussion about ratios and proportional reasoning. Are you grounded well enough to reach for your calculator now?

ADDITION OF INTEGERS

FOCAL POINTS

- Models
- Rules for Adding Integers

Addition of integers provides an interesting extension of the operation of addition. You have already worked with adding wholes, fractions, and decimals. In all of those you used the operation sign, plus (+). Now we extend the operation to include adding signed numbers (positive or negative), and use a plus sign to indicate positive numbers and a minus sign to indicate negative numbers. This extension introduces additional terminology considerations. The "+" can mean add or positive and the "−" can mean subtract or negative. Thus, context becomes important.

With Integers, $4 + 3 = 7$ is rewritten as $^+4 + {}^+3 = {}^+7$, which you should read as, "Positive four plus positive three equals positive seven." This provides reinforcement and practice to help you begin dealing with addition involving negative numbers. Eventually, we will say there is no need to worry about saying, "Positive four plus positive three equals positive seven." It is assumed that numbers written without signs are positive, so we can simply say, "Four plus three is seven."

Models

Initially, the existence of negative numbers has to be established. Traditionally, this is done with discussions about temperature (people in Florida have trouble thinking in terms of temperatures below zero, because water actually freezes at 32°F), below sea level (people in Colorado have trouble identifying with this), debt (too many of us understand this concept), or below ground level. At least one of these real-world examples should give you a feel for the existence of negative numbers. With this notion, we can introduce the other half of the number line by discussing numbers that are mirror images of the whole numbers, with zero serving as the mirror point. This implies that $^-2$ is in the opposite direction of $^+2$ and that these two numbers are equally distant from 0. Figure 2.53 models the

FIG. 2.53.

number line with several integers indicated. It is important that number lines be represented as never ending, with uniform divisions.

One way of showing integer addition involves combining sets of colored chips. Figure 2.54 models integer addition using

Positive 4 plus positive 3 equals positive 7

FIG. 2.54.

black chips for positive numbers. This may remind you adding whole numbers, where we did not care about differences

Negative 4   plus   negative 3   equals   negative 7

FIG. 2.55.

in color. Similarly, Fig. 2.55 models adding a negative four and a negative three with white chips to represent negative values. To add integers that have different signs, consider the real-life concept of money. If you get a dollar from someone, then spend a dollar, your net result is $0.00. This is the dollar version of $^+1 + {}^-1 = 0$. In this model, combining a red chip and a black chip results in no chips, or 0 chips. A one-to-one correspondence between a black chip and a white chip counterbalances them and you can discard them both. Figure 2.56 models the exer-

Positive 4   plus   negative 3   equals   positive 1

FIG. 2.56.

cise $^+4 + {}^-3 = {}^+1$ because three of the black chips in the first set can be put into one-to-one correspondence with three of the white chips in the second set, leaving the single black chip.

The number line is an effective way of developing rules for adding integers. Figure 2.57 shows addition on the number

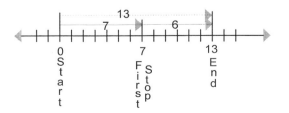

FIG. 2.57.

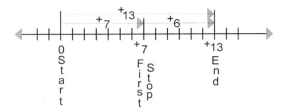

FIG. 2.58.

line using whole numbers. Figure 2.58 shows the same problem using integers. As you compare the two figures, you should notice that the process for doing the problem on the number line with integers is exactly the same as with whole numbers. Figure 2.59 shows $^-7 + {}^-6 = {}^-13$

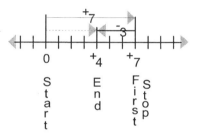

FIG. 2.59.

on the number line. This should make sense in view of your prior experience with adding whole numbers on the number line. In this model, the vectors are pointed in the negative direction, meaning that our ability to model $^-7 + {}^-6 = {}^-13$ is dependent on the inclusion of the negative part of the number line.

Your Turn

1. Do each of the following problems on a number line and record both the problem and the answer in a separate list. State a rule for adding integers when the addends have the same sign:

a) $^+3 + {}^+5 = {}^+8$
b) $^+7 + {}^+6 = {}^+13$
c) $^+4 + {}^+2 = {}^+6$

d) $^-3 + ^-5 = ^-8$
e) $^-7 + ^-6 = ^-13$
f) $^-4 + ^-2 = ^-6$

So far, only number line examples in which the addends have the same sign have been modeled. Next we explore how to model addition on the number line when the signs of the addends are different. Figure 2.60 shows $^+7 + ^-3 = ^+4$ on the

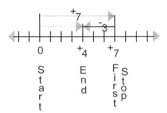

FIG. 2.60.

number line. Notice that the first addend is $^+7$ (7 units long in the positive direction) and the second one is a $^-3$ (3 units long in the negative direction). Tracing along the first addend and then the second addend will lead you to a final position at $^+4$.

The only thing left is to determine how to get from where you start (0) to where you end up ($^+4$). In this case, your net change is four units in the positive direction, yielding a sum of $^+4$. This is shown using a dashed vector.

A companion problem to $^+7 + ^-3 = ^+4$ is $^-7 + ^+3 = ^-4$, which is modeled on the number line in Fig. 2.61. Here, the first ad-

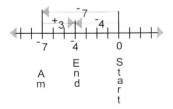

FIG. 2.61.

dend is $^-7$ and the second one is $^+3$, resulting in $^-4$, the sum. You should conclude that if you start at 0 and go four

units to the left, or in the negative direction, you arrive at the sum, $^-4$, shown as a dashed vector.

Your Turn

2. Do some integer addition problems on the number line to ensure you can get the sums. Each of your problems should be similar to those in Figs. 2.60 and 2.61.

Rules for Adding Integers

All arithmetic involves performing binary operations, which means that we operate using two values at a time. Although more than two addends can be considered, integer addition is binary because, no matter how capable you are, you can only deal with two addends at a time. Once the sum of two addends is determined, that sum becomes an addend and the next addend is considered. For example, to complete $^+4 + ^+3 + ^+6$, you begin by adding two of the addends, $^+4 + ^+3 = ^+7$, and then use the result as an addend, $^+7 + ^+6 = ^+13$. You might prefer to do $^+4 + ^+6 = ^+10$ first, but still, only two addends are dealt with at any one time.

The calculator can be an ally in adding when several integers are involved. Do several integer addition problems where the addends have the same sign, while writing the problem and the answer. As you look for patterns, you should generalize the rule for adding integers with the same signs. As you refine the skill of looking for patterns and generalizing, the rule to add the numbers as you normally would and give the answer the common sign, should develop rather quickly.

There are four problem types involved in the addition of integers:

$^+4 + ^+6 = ^+10$

$^-4 + ^-6 = ^-10$

$$^+4 + {}^-6 = {}^-2$$
$$^-4 + {}^+6 = {}^+2$$

Earlier, using the number line, we considered problems where the addends had the same sign. One way to generalize your ideas about adding integers of the same sign is to add the absolute values of the numbers and then to give the answer their common sign. The definition of absolute value involves the idea of "distance from zero," which seems especially relevant as we discuss integers. It means that we can consider two addends having the same sign as two distances that we are going to combine. When you look at the number line, you can tell that ⁻3 is not as far from zero as ⁻5. When you deal with absolute value, you are focusing only on how far the number is from zero, or how long the segment between the number and zero is. You do not care about the direction from zero if the numbers have the same sign. That should add some meaning to the generalization that, when adding numbers that have the same sign, add the absolute value of the numbers and give the common sign to the sum.

After completing work where the signs of the addends are the same, we introduced problems where the addends had opposite signs. We modeled problems where the absolute values of the addends were relatively small so there was little opportunity for distraction. As you do exercises like $^+5 + {}^-3 = {}^+2$, focus on the numbers involved and ask how a two can be the sum of a five and a three. This seems to involve two distances from zero, but in opposite directions. You might conclude that the problem could be restated as $5 - 3 = 2$, or the difference between the distances. Then you might surmise that $5 - 3 = 2$ and $^+5 + {}^-3 = {}^+2$ are two different ways of doing the same problem. Focus on how one can be changed to the

other. You will deduce that the sign of the second number is changed, and the operation is changed from addition to subtraction.

Finally, you must deal with problems such as $^-5 + {}^+3 = {}^-2$. Here, again, you might view this as related to $5 - 3 = 2$, but the operation is addition and the signs are all scrambled around. Returning to our discussion of absolute value, the sum gets the sign of the number with the larger absolute value. Whereas this may not be as immediately apparent as the last example, the same concept is in play—two distances from zero that are in opposite directions. Focus your thoughts on $^+5 + {}^-3 = {}^+2$ and $^-5 + {}^+3 = {}^-2$, and how, in each case, the two different ways of doing the problems can be interchanged. Ultimately, you will conclude that, when adding numbers that have opposite signs, you subtract the smaller absolute value from the larger absolute value and give the sum the sign of the number with the larger absolute value.

Conclusions

Addition of integers is familiar, particularly when the numbers have the same sign. One potential hurdle involves establishing an adequate background about integers and what they are. The number line provides an excellent tool as you work on the concepts of whole numbers and their opposites. The second hurdle centers on the idea that, to add integers with opposite signs, you might intuitively subtract; in one sense, you can use the inverse operation to complete the addition of numbers with opposite signs. Careful development of the addition operation using manipulatives—a calculator, a number line, or all three of these tools—relieves much of the pressure associated with an in-depth understanding of integers. Additional practice is necessary if you are not yet comfortable with these two generalizations that deal with adding integers:

1. When adding integers with like signs, add the absolute values and give the sum the common sign.
2. When adding integers with unlike signs, subtract the smaller absolute value from the larger absolute value, and give the sum the sign of the number with the larger absolute value.

SUBTRACTION OF INTEGERS

FOCAL POINTS

- Models

As was the case with addition of integers, much of the groundwork for subtraction of integers has already been established. We have to make a few adjustments to your knowledge base and you will be adept at subtracting integers. One common interpretation of a rule for subtracting integers says that you change the sign of the second number and then follow the rules for addition. A common rule for adding integers with unlike signs says you subtract. So, to subtract, you think add, which really involves subtracting some of the time. Confused? This section will help you make sense of those statements and develop your own enlightened interpretation.

Models

You can construct a good beginning for the development of subtraction algorithms using white and black chips and the subtraction idea of take away. First, consider the case of a positive number take away a positive number, such as

$^+6 - {}^+2 = {}^+4$, using black chips to represent the positive integers, as shown in Fig. 2.62. A negative number take away a

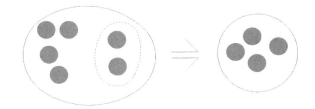

FIG. 2.62.

negative number, such as $^-6 - {}^-2 = {}^-4$, is shown in Fig. 2.63. Take away subtraction

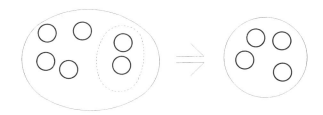

FIG. 2.63.

is straightforward if the sum and addend have the same sign. There are three cases that are not as straightforward and these are the cases that make this model useful.

Suppose the exercise is $^-4 - {}^-6$, as shown in Fig. 2.64. The given set has too few white chips to allow us to take away 6 white chips. The additive identity comes to our rescue! We can increase the num-

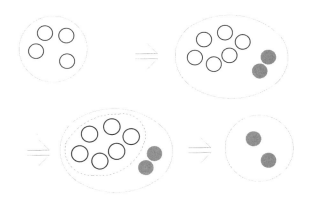

FIG. 2.64.

ber of chips in the set as long as we balance each white chip with a black chip. This is true because $^-1 + {}^+1 = 0$, which can be extended to $^-2 + {}^+2 = 0$ or $^-n + {}^+n = 0$, for any number and its additive opposite. If we increase our set by 2 white chips balanced by 2 black chips, then we have not changed the value of the set, but are able to take away 6 white chips as required by the example.

Take a look at $^-6 - {}^+4 = ?$, which asks us to take 4 black chips away from a set that has only white chips. We can solve this dilemma using the additive identity, inserting 4 black chips balanced with 4 white chips, as shown in Fig. 2.65. Take away

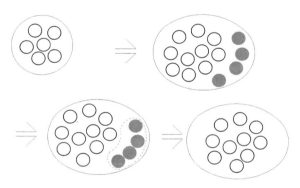

FIG. 2.65.

the 4 black chips to show $^-6 - {}^+4 = {}^-10$. The final case is very similar and uses the additive identity again, as shown in Fig. 2.66. It shows how we can take white chips from a set that contains only black

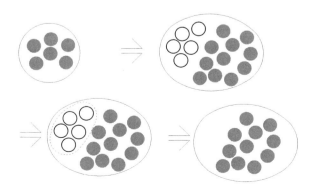

FIG. 2.66.

chips. We express zero by inserting 5 white chips balanced by 5 black chips, and then take away the 5 white chips, which completes the exercise, $^+6 - {}^-5 = {}^+11$.

The number line is a powerful tool for showing how to determine the missing addend in the subtraction of integers. The same format for number line subtraction as was developed in whole number subtraction will be used here. The problem $^+3 - {}^+8 = ?$ is rewritten as $^+8 + ? = {}^+3$. Figure 2.67 shows what this would look like on the number line. The first addend is $^+8$.

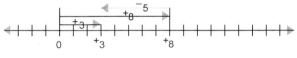

FIG. 2.67.

The sum is $^+3$ and tells you where you want to end. Your number line task is to find the missing addend. In this case, you move five spaces to the left or $^-5$, represented by a dashed vector of length 5 that points in the negative direction.

All number line subtraction exercises could be done in a similar fashion and explained in a similar manner. You have an addend and a sum (solid vectors) and are looking for the missing addend (dashed vector). Your task is to summarize the movement needed to get from the addend to the sum in terms of how many spaces are used and the direction of the motion. Figure 2.68 shows $^+8 - {}^-3 = {}^+11$, whereas Fig. 2.69 shows $^-8 - {}^+3 = {}^-11$.

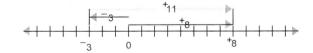

FIG. 2.68.

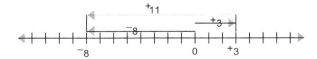

FIG. 2.69.

You need to do several problems of each type on the number line and then generalize a rule from those examples.

Your Turn

1. Do each of the following problems on a number line and record both the problem and the answer. State a rule for subtracting integers.

a) $^+3 - {}^+5 = ?$ b) $^+7 - {}^+6 = ?$
c) $^+4 - {}^+2 = ?$ d) $^-3 - {}^-5 = ?$
e) $^-7 - {}^-6 = ?$ f) $^-4 - {}^-2 = ?$
g) $^-3 - {}^+5 = ?$ h) $^-8 - {}^+2 = ?$
i) $^-10 - {}^+3 = ?$ j) $^+9 - {}^-3 = ?$
k) $^+7 - {}^-5 = ?$ l) $^+6 - {}^-1 = ?$

Conclusions

As we moved through chips and number lines toward abstract concepts, we established the idea that, when subtracting integers, you change the sign of the second number and follow the rules for the addition of integers. Within that setting, four problem types are encountered:

$^+8 - {}^-3 = {}^+11$
$^-8 - {}^+3 = {}^-11$
$^+8 - {}^+3 = {}^+5$
$^-8 - {}^-3 = {}^-5$

You are now an authority on subtracting integers. Your understanding of this concept has been developed through the discussion of take away using black and white chips, followed by work on the number line, and finally arriving at the conclusion that, when subtracting integers, you may change the sign of the addend and then follow the rules for adding integers. Before you continue, take a moment to assure yourself that you understand what is happening in all types of subtraction exercises involving integers.

MULTIPLICATION OF INTEGERS

FOCAL POINTS

- Multiplying Integers

It is helpful, as we try to understand what happens when we operate with numbers, to use our observations to write generalizations—statements that discuss numbers and operations without using specific numbers. The two generalizations you are looking for in this section should develop relatively quickly, given your background with adding integers. Some would argue that we should just tell you the rules, because these generalizations are well established. However, that makes you dependent on an outside source to tell you what to do, limiting the amount of thinking you do on your own. Our goal is to teach you to think through things and developing generalizations from your observations is one element of this type of critical thinking. We don't ask you to reinvent the entire process, but learning to think like an inventor is a valuable skill for a mathematician.

Multiplying Integers

You have already dealt with multiplication as repeated addition, thus a calculator or number line could be used to build the ideas that follow. You have completed exercises such as 4×3. In integer operations, that exercise is $^+4 \times {}^+3$. Figure 2.70 shows $^+4 \times {}^+3$ on the number line, showing 4 vectors each of length $^+3$. The observation that the product of two positive factors is positive should be familiar territory.

A positive factor times a negative factor is shown on the number line in Fig. 2.71 and is very similar to the product of two positive factors. Here, we show a graphic

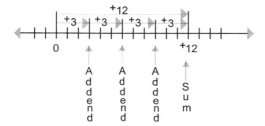

1. Sketch a vector from zero to the sum and label the sum.

2. Sketch a vector for each addend, starting at zero for the first one and then going tip to tail for the rest and label them.

3. Connect zero with the sum using a dashed vector.

4. The arrowhead of the dashed vector points in the direction of travel from zero to the sum.

5. Since this is a repeated addition representation of multiplication, the product is called a sum.

FIG. 2.70.

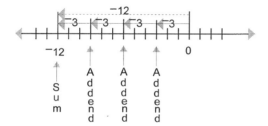

1. Sketch a vector from zero to the sum and label the sum.

2. Sketch a vector for each addend, starting at zero for the first one and then going tip to tail for the rest and label them.

3. Connect zero with the sum using a dashed vector.

4. The arrowhead of the dashed vector points in the direction of travel from zero to the sum.

5. Since this is a repeated addition representation of multiplication, the product is called a sum.

FIG. 2.71.

example of $^+4 \times {}^-3$ and the figure is essentially Fig. 2.70 mirrored at zero; 4 vectors of length 3 in the negative direction. You should generalize that a positive times a negative yields a negative product because of your previous experiences with repeated addition using negative addends.

Multiplication of integers is a binary operation. If more than two factors are involved, then the product of two factors must be found first and then that product becomes one of two factors that generate a new product, until all factors have been

used. For example, when finding the product of $^+2 \times {}^+4 \times {}^+5$, you might find the product $^+2 \times {}^+4$, which is $^+8$. Then you find the product of $^+8$ and $^+5$, which is $^+40$. Given this and your ability to multiply two factors, you will be able to handle more than two factors in a systematic manner. With that assumption in mind, we will consider multiplication of integers using two factors, which requires consideration of four problem types: positive times positive, positive times negative, negative times positive, and negative times negative, taken in that order.

We have already dealt with two of those four possible problem types; a positive factor times a positive factor yields a positive product, and a positive factor times a negative factor yields a negative product. The commutative property of multiplication on whole numbers extends to multiplication of integers. With that in mind, $^-5 \times {}^+6$ can be commuted into $^+6 \times {}^-5$. Therefore, the third problem type can be generalized to a negative times a positive yields a negative product. It should be noted that the factors would have to be commuted before the example could be modeled with a number line. That is, you could not have a negative five vectors that are a positive six long. Once the factors are commuted, the situation would be similar to that shown in Fig. 2.71.

The fourth problem type, which involves two negative factors, presents a little more of a challenge to explain. One way to deal with the situation involves using a calculator and exercise sets, allowing us to generalize from several specific answers known to be correct. Because this type of reasoning leads only to a conjecture, not a proof, it can be useful in situations such as this. Calculators do differ, so care must be taken to insure that the signs of the factors are properly entered and considered as the exercises are done. Working through exercises such as these with your calculator,

$$^-4 \times {}^-3 = {}^+12$$
$$^-5 \times {}^-7 = {}^+35$$
$$^-2 \times {}^-3 = {}^+6$$

will lead you to conclude that, when two factors are negative, the product is positive. Again, although this is not a proof, the conjecture is, in fact, true.

Patterning is another way to develop the idea that a negative factor times a negative factor yields a positive product. Assuming a firm understanding of the other three integer multiplication problem types at this point, we will begin with a product generated using a negative factor with a positive factor. You should read aloud the comment beside each product as it is completed. Each of these comments compares the exercise with the one above it:

$^-6 \times {}^+6 = {}^-36$

$^-6 \times {}^+5 = {}^-30$ Comparing this line with the previous line you say: "1st factor stays the same, ($^-6$); 2nd factor decreases by 1, (from $^+6$ to $^+5$), product increases by 6, (from $^-36$ to $^-30$)"

$^-6 \times {}^+4 = {}^-24$ "1st factor stays the same; 2nd factor decreases by 1, product increases by 6"

$^-6 \times {}^+3 = {}^-18$ "1st factor stays the same; 2nd factor decreases by 1, product increases by 6"

$^-6 \times {}^+2 = {}^-12$ "1st factor stays the same; 2nd factor decreases by 1, product increases by 6"

$^-6 \times {}^+1 = {}^-6$ "1st factor stays the same; 2nd factor decreases by 1, product increases by 6"

$^-6 \times 0 = 0$ "1st factor stays the same; 2nd factor decreases by 1, product increases by 6"

$^-6 \times {}^-1 = {}^+6$ "1st factor stays the same; 2nd factor decreases by 1, product increases by 6"

BINGO! Following the pattern, "1st factor stays the same; 2nd factor decreases by 1, product increases by 6," you just got a positive product out of two negative factors. Using a number pattern such as this, developed from a comfortable concept, can be a powerful way of supporting understandings of abstract concepts until they become a part of our knowledge base.

Your Turn

1. Now that all four types of multiplication problems involving integers have been considered, state two generalizations that deal with multiplying signed numbers.

2. Develop a generalization relating to multiplying more than two integer factors based on the number of negative factors that are involved.

3. State a generalization relating to multiplying two or more integer factors when one of them is zero.

Conclusions

This whole section boils down to two rules to remember when multiplying integers, assuming none of the factors is zero. We have asked you to develop these generalizations and we hope you have, even though we realize you could look them up in the solution section. Remembering those rules is important when doing multiplication exercises involving integers as factors. If you have not digested the process, then the result becomes a mere memorization of disconnected rules provided by someone else. That is not a wise route to the development of your mathematical skills and understandings.

DIVISION OF INTEGERS

FOCAL POINTS

- Division Using Signed Numbers
- Signed Numbers in Inverse Operations

Building on the concepts of whole number division, we now divide using signed numbers. Building on the concepts of integer multiplication, we now discuss how to deal with signed numbers in the inverse operation. Comfort with these two areas ensures quick success with integer division. Remember that multiplication is defined as factor × factor = product and the inverse operation, division, is defined as product ÷ factor = missing factor.

Division Using Signed Numbers

A calculator will be a handy tool for this discussion. For a while, use the division facts for whole numbers to avoid remainders or fractional parts; keep the problems simple as you investigate what happens with signed numbers. Create several exercises in each of the following categories: (a) Positive divided by Positive, (b) Negative divided by Negative, (c) Negative divided by Positive, and (d) Positive divided by Negative. Review your calculator procedures for entering negative numbers. You will see either a +/− or (−) key that is to be used to enter the negative sign for a number. The "minus" key is different from these keys and its use will cause a calculator error or an incorrect response. As you do your exercises, record the problem and answer, being sure to include signs for all of the numbers involved. Look for patterns within the categories and between the categories.

Look at two of the four possible configurations of division problems involving integers. The first one is $^+4\overline{)^+20}$, or $\dfrac{^+20}{^+4} = {}^+5$.

Here in the typical division format, the factor ($^+4$) is outside, the product ($^+20$) is inside, and the missing factor ($^+5$) is on the top of the vinculum. You also see the problem expressed as a fraction with the

product as the numerator and the factor as the denominator, giving the missing factor to the right of the equal sign. The second problem type we consider here is $^-4\overline{)^-20}$, or $\dfrac{^-20}{^-4} = {}^+5$. Both configurations are the same, replacing the factor ($^+4$) and product ($^+20$) with a $^-4$ and $^-20$, respectively. Note that the missing factor ($^+5$) for both problem types remains the same.

One of the remaining two possible problem configurations is $^-4\overline{)^+20}$, or $\dfrac{^+20}{^-4} = {}^-5$. This third problem type follows the same configuration as the other two, this time using $^-4$ as the factor or denominator and $^+20$ as the product or numerator. Here the missing factor is now $^-5$. The fourth problem type, $^+4\overline{)^-20}$, or $\dfrac{^-20}{^+4} = {}^-5$, has $^+4$ as the factor or denominator and $^-20$ as the product or numerator. Again the missing factor is $^-5$.

Signed Numbers in Inverse Operations

Compare these with the exercises you created earlier and do more of each type, writing the problem in fraction form, along with the missing factor. That is, record them all like this: $\dfrac{^-20}{^-4} = {}^+5$ (fraction with $^-20$ over $^-4$ equals $^+5$). How does this remind you of the section dealing with integer multiplication?

Your Turn

1. Considering problems only of the types $\dfrac{^+20}{^+4} = {}^+5$ and $\dfrac{^-20}{^-4} = {}^+5$, for example (positive divided by positive and negative

divided by negative), describe a generalization for working with dividing a product by a factor when their signs are the same.

2. Considering problems only of the types $\frac{^+20}{^-4} = {}^-5$ and $\frac{^-20}{^+4} = {}^-5$, for example (positive divided by negative and negative divided by positive), describe a generalization for working with dividing a product by a factor when their signs are not the same.

Conclusions

This section is relatively short because of previous work in division of whole numbers and multiplication of integers. The connections with these two concepts helped summarize the work with division of integers down to two rules that will cover all situations. Dividing when the product and factor have like signs gives a positive missing factor. Dividing when the product and factor have unlike signs yields a negative missing factor. No new methods for finding missing factors were developed here. We built integer division on the same generalizations about signed numbers that were developed in the section about multiplication of integers. Remember, you should always be looking for connections between and among concepts. This section is an excellent example of reducing the number of concepts that needed to be learned by scaffolding new knowledge onto previously obtained skills.

RATIOS AND PROPORTIONS

FOCAL POINTS

- Rational Numbers
- Ratios
- Percents
- Equivalents
- Proportions
- Cross Products
- Problem solving

Rational Numbers as Ratios

Rational numbers are fractions that can be written as $\frac{a}{b}$, where a and b are integers and b is not zero. The vinculum that we use to define the numerator and denominator of a rational number has multiple meanings. In this section, we use it to help us compare two quantities.

Suppose we want to compare the number of girls to the number of boys in a particular classroom, as in Fig. 2.72. We

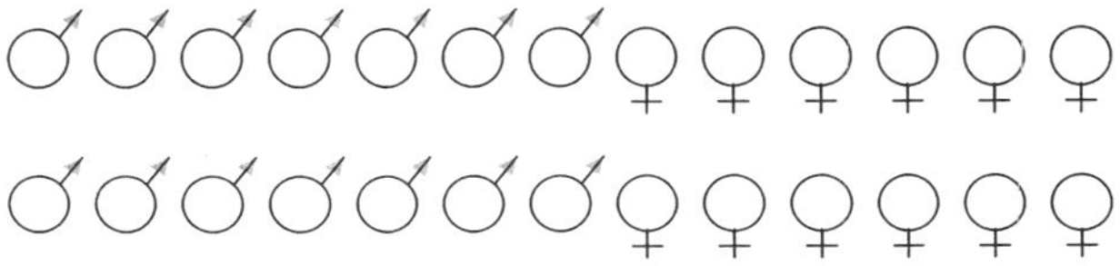

FIG. 2.72.

might satisfy our needs by stating that there are 12 girls and 14 boys. Using a rational number, we could say that the ratio of girls to boys is 12 to 14, which can be written as 12:14, or $\frac{12}{14}$. Although this information might be all that we need, there are several related ratios that might be just as useful, depending on the situation or problem. We might change the order and say that the ratio of boys to girls is 14 to 12, 14:12, or $\frac{14}{12}$; we could say:

there are 6 girls for every 7 boys, 6:7 or $\frac{6}{7}$

there are 7 boys for every 6 girls, 7:6 or $\frac{7}{6}$

there are 12 girls in the class of 26 students, 12:26 or $\frac{12}{26}$

there are 6 girls out of each 13 students, 6:13 or $\dfrac{6}{13}$

there are 14 boys out of a total of 26 students, 14:26 or $\dfrac{14}{26}$

there are 7 boys out of each 13 students, 7:13 or $\dfrac{7}{13}$

In each of these forms, there is an ordered pair of numbers on which we can operate using the properties of fractions. Although we can treat the numbers as if they were fractions, it is not necessarily true that equivalent ratios have the exact same meaning as they do with equivalent fractions. For example, we say that there are 12 girls to 14 boys, but we must say that there are 6 girls for each 7 boys. Notice that $\dfrac{12}{14}$ and $\dfrac{6}{7}$ are equivalent fractions, but do not have the same meaning in the context of our situation because $\dfrac{12}{14}$ not only compares the number of girls to the number of boys, but also tells us exactly how many girls and boys are actually present.

Ratios and proportions react differently than fractions when numbers change, too. If two new girls and one new boy join the class, then the total changes to 29 children, 14 girls and 15 boys. The ratio of new girls to new boys would be $\dfrac{2}{1}$ and the ratio of girls to boys in the class would change from $\dfrac{12}{14}$ to $\dfrac{14}{15}$. We could express that as $\dfrac{12}{14} \oplus \dfrac{2}{1} = \dfrac{14}{15}$. That is OK when dealing with ratios. Think about it and you should be able to come up with a lot of examples like that. Consider the basket-

ball player who made 3 out of 4 foul shots during the first game, 5 out of 9 foul shots during the second game, and 7 out of 7 foul shots during the third game. How would you determine that player's foul shooting percentage? You would form a ratio between the number of foul shots made and the number of foul shots attempted over the three games, or $\dfrac{15}{20}$. But, to get that ratio, you add the numerators of the individual ratios to get the overall foul shots made during all three games and you add the denominators of the individual ratios to get the total number of foul shots attempted during all three games. That is not how you operate with fractions. So, you see, ratios and fractions are treated differently when you operate with them.

Generally, the context will tell you which way to do it. For example, if you operated on these three ratios as fractions, then you would have $\dfrac{3}{4} + \dfrac{5}{9} + \dfrac{7}{7} = \dfrac{581}{252}$, which is about 2.3. Now there is a player you want on your team! Operating this way implies that every foul shot made is worth 2.3 points rather than the normal one point. An answer of 2.3 does not make sense in basketball foul shooting.

Your Turn

1. Write ratios that compare the designs in Fig. 2.73.

FIG. 2.73.

a) Number of ⬭ to number of ♡
b) Number of ☼ to number of ◎
c) Number of ⬭ to total number of items
d) Number of figures that have only straight segments to number of figures that contain curves

Percents

If we take the word "percent" apart, it means per hundred, implying that every number expressed as a percent is actually a ratio with a denominator of 100. If we find that a softball team wins 45% of its games, then that means the team wins 45 out of 100 games, or $\frac{45}{100}$. But does the team have to play 100 games to earn this statistic? Suppose the team only plays 20 games in the entire season; how could we say they win 45% of the time? The key to this issue is in the denominator. If the team wins 9 out of the 20 games, then we can set up a ratio of wins to games, $\frac{9}{20}$. If we multiply this ratio by $\frac{5}{5}$, then we will not change its value because $\frac{5}{5} = 1$, the multiplicative identity. However, we will find that the rewritten fraction, $\left(\frac{9}{20}\right)\left(\frac{5}{5}\right) = \frac{45}{100}$, has a denominator of 100, and that is how the 45% is established.

Suppose we are given the ratio $\frac{6}{15}$ and asked to write it as a percent. We could grab a calculator and divide 6 by 15. This would give us the decimal number 0.4 or, because we want to talk in terms of hundredths, 0.40. We often read a number such as this as "zero point four zero," but if we read it as a decimal fraction we would say "zero and forty-hundredths," which brings to mind the ratio $\frac{40}{100}$ or 40%. However, this procedure does not help us understand what is going on. Put aside the calculator for a moment and see if we can get to $\frac{40}{100}$ by hand. First, simplify the ratio to $\frac{6 \div 3}{15 \div 3} = \frac{2}{5}$. We would like to change that denominator to 100, which can be done by multiplying both the numerator and denominator by 20, $\frac{2}{5} = \left(\frac{2}{5}\right)\left(\frac{20}{20}\right)$, which is $\frac{40}{100}$.

Suppose you are charged a $36.00 restocking fee on a returned item that sold for $250.00. What percentage of your refund does the merchandiser keep? The ratio involved is $\frac{36}{250}$ and it might not be obvious what the numerator would be if the denominator is forced to be 100. However, any power of 10 will allow us to write the number as a percent. Multiplying $\frac{36}{250}$ by $\frac{4}{4}$ gives a product of $\frac{144}{1000}$. Because this denominator has one factor of 10 too many, we divide both the numerator and denominator by 10 to get $\frac{14.4}{100} = 14.4\%$. The merchandiser kept 14.4% of your refund. These examples may contain more steps than you would generally use to solve this type of problem. The extra steps in this last example help us make the point that a ratio does not always have to be a rational number as you typically see them. The ratio $\frac{14.4}{100}$ is a perfectly good and informative number, but it does not fit the classic definition of a rational number, because 14.4 is not an integer. However, multiplying both the numerator and denominator of $\dfrac{14.4}{100}$ by 10 will give $\dfrac{144}{1000}$, which does look like a typical rational number, before common factors are divided out.

Your Turn

2. The following ratios can be changed so that they have denominators that are powers of 10. Use the procedure shown in the examples to write these ratios as percentages.

  a) A bowler got 7 strikes out of the first 20 frames at the bowling tournament. What was the percentage of strikes during the first 20 frames?
  b) Only 18 out of 250 people at the wedding selected chicken. What percent of the people at the wedding selected chicken?
  c) For 135 of the 2500 cars that passed through the tollbooth on Tuesday, an error in the amount of the toll paid was indicated. What percentage of toll errors does this imply?

3. The following ratios cannot be changed so that they have denominators that are powers of 10. Explain why this is true. Use your calculator to write these ratios as percentages. Round to the nearest tenth of a percent.

  a) 19 of 23 students earned passing scores on the first exam. What percentage of the students earned passing scores?
  b) 11 of 18 Matchbox™ cars represent American automobiles. What percentage of Matchbox cars represents foreign automobiles?

Equivalents

One of the big ideas in this section is the notion of equivalence between rational numbers, decimals, and percents. It is important for you to realize that there are equivalencies between each of these topics, not just within each topic. That is, you need to be comfortable with the notion that the common fraction, $\dfrac{1}{4}$, is equivalent to the decimal, 0.25, is equivalent to the ratio, 1:4, is equivalent to 25%.

One way of showing the relations between all of these different representations is by using a chart such as Table 2.1. Examine the relations among the col-

TABLE 2.1

Fraction	Decimal	Percent	Ratio	Graph
$\dfrac{1}{4}$	0.25	25%	$\dfrac{25}{100}$	
$\dfrac{1}{2}$	0.50	50%	$\dfrac{50}{100}$	
$\dfrac{3}{4}$	0.75	75%	$\dfrac{75}{100}$	
1	1.00	100%	$\dfrac{100}{100}$	

umns of equivalents. Observing these connections is a key part of proportional reasoning and you should review the sections about fractions, decimals, and percents if you are not comfortable with this concept.

Proportions

When two ratios are set equal to one another, a proportion is established. Proportions offer us an elegant means of solving many types of problems, but first we must learn to use them with great care. There are 14 shaded squares in Fig. 2.74, which

FIG. 2.74.

has a total of 28 squares. We can set up a ratio to compare the number of shaded squares to the total number of squares, $\frac{14}{28}$. Another ratio describes how much area of the figure is shaded, $\frac{1}{2}$. Whereas the first ratio concerns how many individual squares are shaded, the second ratio concerns the amount of area that is shaded. Because these two fractions are equivalent to one another, we can write

$$\frac{14\text{ shaded squares}}{28\text{ squares}} = \frac{1\text{ shaded area}}{2\text{ areas}}.$$

When dealing with proportions, it is important to remember that ordered pairs are involved. We could write the ratio of total squares to shaded squares, $\frac{28}{14}$, or the ratio of shaded to unshaded squares, $\frac{14}{14}$, but neither of these ratios would be equivalent to $\frac{1}{2}$. A common error people make when working problems that involve proportions is to forget about the importance of the ordered pairs of numbers. We can demonstrate this using an ordinary problem:

If a car can go 300 miles on a single 10-gallon tank of gas, then how far could it go if it had a 20-gallon tank?

To solve this problem, set up a proportion with one value missing—the distance the

car could travel if we doubled the capacity of the gas tank. If we are conscious of the importance of the ordered pairs of numbers, then we would set up the problem as $\dfrac{300\text{ miles}}{10\text{ gallons of gas}} = \dfrac{m\text{ miles}}{20\text{ gallons of gas}}$, where m represents miles traveled, the quantity for which we would like to solve the proportion. In each ratio, the number of miles is on top and the number of gallons is on bottom. We can solve this problem by inspection because doubling the denominator implies that we must double the numerator. The car can go 600 miles on 20 gallons of gas. If we had not paid careful attention to the order in which the numbers should appear, then we might have set up the problem as $\dfrac{300}{10} = \dfrac{20}{m}$. In order to turn 300 into 20, we must divide by 15. If we divide 10 by 15, we find that we cannot go very far if we double the size of the tank. The best way to avoid making this classic error is to write a ratio with words, such as $\dfrac{\text{miles}}{\text{gallons of gas}}$, and then set up all of the numbers in ratios to match.

Your Turn

4. Write two equivalent ratios that represent the quantities in the following statements. Use a letter to represent the missing quantity and set the ratios equal to one another to find that missing quantity.

a) I would like to make 3 identical shirts. My pattern for a single shirt requires 2 yards of fabric. How much fabric should I buy for my 3 shirts?

b) There are 4 tables and 16 chairs in our classroom. If we continue the same arrangement, then how many chairs would we need for 8 tables?

c) A 4-pound turkey requires 1 hour to roast. Assuming all other things are equal, how much time would be required to roast a 16-pound turkey?

Cross Products

In our discussion of ratios and proportions, we have been manipulating fractions. First we wrote fractions to represent the quantities we wished to compare. Then we manipulated fractions so that we could have denominators that were powers of 10 in order to compare using percentages. In the last section, we used equivalent fractions to find missing quantities. As you work with problems that involve ratios and proportions, the numbers may become confusing to manipulate without an additional strategy—that of using cross products. As with all algebraic strategies, this can be used in more than one way. We can use the strategy of cross products to prove or disprove the truth of a proportional statement or we can use the very same strategy to solve a proportion that has one quantity missing.

If a proportion is true, the product of the numerator of the first ratio and denominator of the second ratio will be equal to the product of the denominator of the first ratio and numerator of the second ratio. This is the long way of saying, "Cross multiply." For example, $\frac{105}{180} = \frac{7}{12}$ is a true proportion because $105 \times 12 = 180 \times 7$. However, $\frac{8}{17} \neq \frac{43}{91}$ because $8 \times 91 \neq 17 \times 43$.

If one quantity is missing in a proportion that we consider to be true, we can use cross products to determine the missing quantity. For example, in the proportion $\frac{7}{18} = \frac{a}{63}$, the cross products are

18a and 441. If we set these two products equal to one another and solve for a, we find that a = 24.5.

Your Turn

5. Use cross products to determine if each of the following is a true proportion:

a) $\frac{6}{17}$ = or ≠ $\frac{18}{51}$

b) $\frac{5}{31}$ = or ≠ $\frac{18}{111}$

c) $\frac{8}{19}$ = or ≠ $\frac{144}{342}$

6. Solve the following proportions (if necessary, round to the nearest tenth):

a) $\frac{14}{a} = \frac{5}{3}$

b) $\frac{2}{7} = \frac{b}{147}$

c) $\frac{c}{135} = \frac{14}{27}$

Solving Problems Using Proportions

The father of one of your authors was a magic man. He could stand near a tree, look at his shadow, and tell the height of the tree. When the author was a little child, she only knew that her father could solve the problem without climbing the tree to measure it; she did not know that he was using ratios and proportions! Because the rays of the sun are virtually parallel by the time they create shadows, the shadows of the tree and the man are directly proportional to the heights of the tree and the man, as in Fig. 2.75. If the man's shadow is half as long as the shadow of the tree, then he must be half as tall as the tree. Suppose the man is 6 ft tall and casts a 10.75 ft shadow and the

FIG. 2.75.

tree casts a 21.5 ft shadow. We could use the proportion $\frac{6}{t} = \frac{10.75}{21.5}$ to find that the height of the tree is 12 ft. This is a direct application of the properties of similar right triangles, which are often sketched to solve such problems. If the right triangles are similar, then the same ratio can be used to compare each set of corresponding sides. Assuming that the man and the tree stand perpendicular to their shadows, imagine rays of sunlight to complete the hypotenuse (longest side of a right triangle) of the right triangle as shown in Fig. 2.76. The hypotenuse was not needed for this problem, only the heights and shadows of the man and the tree. In many problems of this type, the hypotenuse will be important.

Ratios and proportions are associated with similar triangles. Comparing the corresponding sides of the similar triangles in Fig. 2.76, we can set up several pro-

portions, such as $\frac{6}{12} = \frac{10.75}{21.5}$, $\frac{6}{12} = \frac{12.3}{24.6}$, $\frac{21.5}{10.75} = \frac{24.6}{12.3}$, and $\frac{10.75}{6} = \frac{21.5}{12}$, which are four of the many possible combinations. We have a great deal of freedom when we set up proportions, as long as we remember that the two ratios represent ordered pairs and must be kept in the same order on both sides of the equal sign.

Your Turn

7. List at least four additional proportions for the triangles in Fig. 2.76.

8. Your recipe for Party Mix calls for 7 cups of wheat cereal, 2 cups of mixed nuts, 2 cups of pretzels, 1.5 sticks of butter, 1 tablespoon of special sauce, and seasoned salt to taste. You find that you have only 1.5 cups of mixed nuts. How much of each of the other ingredients do you use if you want to keep the recipe in proportion?

9. For some incredibly interesting reason, you need to know the height of the telephone pole in front of your home. You know that you are 5.5 feet tall and that you cast a shadow that is 11 feet long. The telephone pole casts a shadow that is 26 feet long. How tall is the telephone pole?

10. Trace the triangles in Fig. 2.76 and label them as follows. Smaller triangle— the shorter leg is 9 cm and the longer leg is 12 cm. Larger triangle—the hypotenuse is 37.5 cm and the shorter leg is 22.5 cm. What is the length of the hypotenuse of the smaller triangle?

11. As a teller in a bank that sells foreign currency, you are responsible for helping customers who are planning for trips abroad. Because the rates change very quickly, you must calculate each transaction separately. A customer asks you how much it would cost to buy 200.00 DM. You check the rate and find

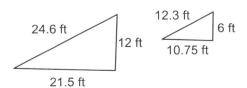

FIG. 2.76.

that $1.00 is worth 1.32 DM. How much will it cost your customer to get the deutsche marks needed for the trip?

Conclusions

You have been introduced some of the myriad uses of ratios and proportions. With this introduction, you may find that you use them intuitively in your daily life—perhaps when shopping, cooking, working on your hobbies, enjoying sports, or working on the monthly budget. As you go through your day, watch for examples of ratios and proportions. You might be surprised to see how many there are.

3
Algebra

Algebra is often thought to be a specific subject area studied in the middle school and beyond. Components of algebra begin to appear early in the curriculum, if only in a problem like 2 + 3 = ?. Algebraically this might be expressed as 2 + 3 = x, but the difference between the two symbols, ? and x, is not major. The study of subtraction problems written in the form ? + 4 = 7 builds a background for an algebra-based solution involving subtracting 4 from both sides of the equation to determine the missing addend. It is possible that algebra and related topics have been part of your world from the beginning of your formal education.

Consider the following problem, which is rich in algebraic opportunities. Pete and Repeat are traveling the 96 miles from Pahokee to Holopow on their bikes. Pete can average 8 miles per hour (mph) and Repeat can average 12 mph. On the following graph, show how far each will have traveled after 1, 2, and 3 hours.

Pahokee ├┼┼┼┼┼┼┼┼┼┼┼┼┼┼┼┼┼┼┼┤ Holopaw

Place the information about the travels of Pete and Repeat into the table.

Hours	1	2	3	4	5	6		
Pete								
Repeat								

If you think of questions like the following, you are beginning to think algebraically:

Describe a pattern for each row of the table.

How far from Pahokee is each rider after 3 hours?

How long will it take each rider to travel 24 miles?

After Repeat gets to Holopaw, how long will it take Pete to get there?

If h is the number of hours traveled, and m is the distance covered in miles, is there a rule that shows the relation between m and h for each rider?

Could I use the rule I just devised to show how far each rider could go in an hour?

How far will each rider travel between the end of hour 4 and the end of hour 5?

If it is 96 miles from Pahokee to Holopaw, how long will it take each rider to complete the trip?

HISTORIC UNDERPINNINGS

Believe it or not, algebra did not simply appear within the last 60 or 100 years or so. The Babylonians were using algebra basics in 2000 BC. It has been discovered that they were solving second- and third-degree equations of the form $x^3 + x^2 = b$ (Eves, 1990) around that time. The Babylonians did not use the letters x or b, nor did they use our current numeral, place value, or exponential systems, which had not been developed yet.

The first records dealing with adding or subtracting the same magnitude on both sides of an equation are found in the Arabic writings of Al-Khowarizmi (Mohammed ben Musa, which means Mahomet, the son of Moses) about 830 AD. Leonardo da Pisa (Fibonacci) introduced some basics of algebra to Italy about 1200 AD, and Robert Recorde introduced it to England in a 1557 AD publication. Even those introductions were not algebra as we know it today, but the ideas, as we know them, were beginning to form. Algebraic methods and notations have been improved and revised through the centuries. Unlike arithmetic, where $3 + 4 = 7$ is constant, algebraic notations like $x + y = z$ take on different meanings in different contexts.

Descartes (about 1637 AD) used symbolic notation to express algebraic calculations. He also used letters at the beginning of the alphabet (a, b, c) to denote known quantities (constants) and letters from the end of the alphabet (x, y, z), particularly x, to indicate unknown quantities (variables). Does this terminology remind you of your high school days?

Organizations such as NCTM suggest that ALL students can learn mathematics. That means all students can learn algebra at the appropriate time in their development. Everyone in our society does not accept this philosophy. Traditionalists say, and many parents agree, "The mathematics I learned and the way I learned it was good enough for me, so it is good enough for my child." Unfortunately, that statement is far from the truth. Limit your skills to computation and you limit your career options. Technology can do the arithmetic after the skills and notions behind the arithmetic are learned. Society needs thinkers, both inside and outside of the box. Today's world is much more mathematical than yesterday's and mathematics is so much more than arithmetic. Productivity in today's world requires greater mathematical abilities and more complex problem-solving skills. Tomorrow's world will be even more mathematical than today's, thus we have a responsibility to help future generations gain insights into the mathematics that will be such a large part of their world. Consider the following example of a primary school algebra problem: $\clubsuit + \diamond = 9$ and $\clubsuit + \diamond + \clubsuit = 11$. The first equation has five solutions in the set of whole numbers, one of which must satisfy the second equation. You might list the addition facts for 9 and try each number pair in the second equation. Another strategy might involve a one-to-one matching of the parts of the equations to see what is duplicated. If one $\clubsuit$ and one $\diamond$ are subtracted from the left side of each equation and 9 is subtracted from each right side, then the correct addition fact can be determined without trying all five pairs of addends. A third strategy might be to replace one $\clubsuit$ and one $\diamond$ in the second equation with 9. Easy you say? Think any second grader could solve this problem? This problem involves solving a linear system of equations, $x + y = 9$ and $2x + y = 11$. The three strategies discussed are guess and check, linear combinations, and substitution.

LAYING THE FOUNDATION FOR ALGEBRA

Although algebra is an abstract way of viewing mathematical concepts, manipulatives can help us understand what is happening. Suppose you have three blocks and another student has seven, as shown in Fig. 3.1. How many blocks do

FIG. 3.1.

you need so that you have as many as the other student? In reality, you are asked to solve a problem of the form $3 + \triangle = 7$, using manipulatives. You are beginning the foundation for algebra as you look for the missing addend. You could line up both sets of blocks as shown in Fig. 3.2. This

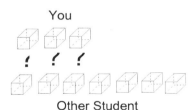

FIG. 3.2.

would allow you to look concretely for a one-to-one correspondence and find the number of blocks needed to have seven. You could add blocks until the number of blocks in each set is the same.

Is there any way to solve $3 + \triangle = 7$ using a calculator? What does this problem mean? Three is the known addend and seven is the known sum. The triangle represents the missing addend, which can be determined by subtracting the known addend from the sum. Subtraction using the missing addend model is the beginnings of algebraic thinking.

Let's kick this idea up a notch and find the missing addend in $3x + \underline{\quad} = 7x$. One way to do this is to use a model similar to the one in Fig. 3.2. The bottom line is that you have three unknowns and you want to know how many more unknowns you will need to have a total of seven unknowns.

The Algebra FX-2.0 calculator, developed by Casio, provides the power of a calculator with an algebraic tutorial. You enter $3 + X = 7$ and, with the push of a button, the calculator supplies an on-screen step-by-step process for solving the problem. With $3 + X = 7$, the first step, subtracting 3 from both sides, will show $3 + X - 3 = 7 - 3$. Next, the calculator will collect like terms on each side of the equation, and $X = 7$.

A computer program called MathXpert (www.mathxpert.com) will solve this problem in a similar symbolic manner. In addition, MathXpert provides a statement and reason for each step taken as a problem is solved. Each of these provides options for step-by-step general hints, specific hints, or automatic complete solutions.

If you want to learn algebra, then technology can be very helpful. Several calculators, such as Casio's fx-9970 or Texas Instruments' TI-89 or TI-92, will solve algebraic problems, but these will not show the intermediate steps involved in the process.

HAVING FUN WITH ALGEBRA

One way to increase enthusiasm for mathematics is to use number tricks. Try this one:

Pick a counting number.
Multiply your number by two.

Add four to your new product.
Subtract 10 from your new sum.
Add six to your new number.
Now subtract your original number.
What did you get?

Figure 3.3 shows a physical model of this number trick.

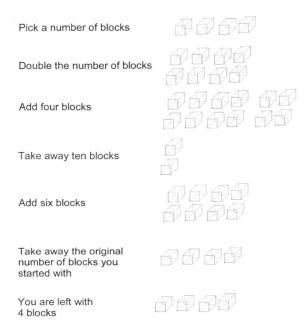

Pick a number of blocks

Double the number of blocks

Add four blocks

Take away ten blocks

Add six blocks

Take away the original number of blocks you started with

You are left with 4 blocks

FIG. 3.3.

Using algebra, we can demonstrate this process using symbolic manipulation and a variable for the original number. This method shows that, no matter what number you pick, you will always end the trick with that number:

Pick a counting number.	n
Multiply the number by 2.	$2 \times n = 2n$
Add 4 to the new product.	$2n + 4 = 2n + 4$
Subtract 10 from the new sum.	$2n + 4 - 10 = 2n - 6$
Add 6 to the new number.	$2n - 6 + 6 = 2n$
Now subtract the original number.	$2n - n = n$
What did you get?	n

There are many number tricks of this sort that can provide entertaining ways of practicing algebraic manipulations. Many have made the rounds on the Internet. One such trick claims that you will end up with your age by following the directions, but that it will only work for the current year. The next time someone sends this type of trick to you, analyze it algebraically and then fix the trick so that it will work for any year. Algebra isn't mathematical magic, it just seems that way until you take a closer look. Number tricks are fun, but you won't be mystified for long if you look at them while wearing your algebra glasses.

Your Turn

1. Do this trick using a specific number and then using x for the number picked.

Pick a number.
Double it.
Add 4.
Divide by 2.
Subtract your original number.

What do you get? If you begin the trick with a different number, will you still get that answer?

2. Do the trick in Exercise 1 using a fraction. Is your answer still the same?

3. Do the trick in Exercise 1 using a negative number. Is your answer still the same?

4. Do this trick using a specific number and then using m for the number picked.

Pick a number.
Double it.
Add 4.
Divide by 2.
Subtract 2.

What do you get? Will this always work? Why or why not?

5. Do this trick using a specific number and then using p for the number picked.

Pick a number.
Triple it.
Add 12.
Divide by 3.
Subtract your original number.

What do you get? Is this problem significantly different from the one given in Exercise 1?

INTEGRATING ALGEBRA

Algebra should be infused throughout the mathematics curriculum. As you have seen, number operations provide foundational underpinnings. In beginning algebra, you learn to simplify expressions such as 4y + 5y by combining like terms. When dealing with 4y + 5y, you get 9y, just as you would get 9 pencils if you were adding 4 pencils and 5 pencils. Think of two groups of identical blocks where one group contains four blocks and the other five blocks. Which problem is algebra? Which problem is arithmetic? Is there really a difference?

As you learn to simplify more complicated expressions, you begin to realize that you cannot combine unlike terms. If you have three apples and four peaches, then can you combine them to give one answer? You could say you have seven pieces of fruit, but the kind of fruit is lost. If you want to know what kind of fruit, then you have to stay with the three apples and four peaches. You could write an expression, 3a + 4p, where a stands for apple and p stands for peach, but you can't simplify the situation beyond that.

Suppose you have three squares and four triangles and a friend has five squares and two triangles. If you combine the sets of figures and arrange the shapes into like groups, how many would be in each group? By writing the expression 3□ + 4△ + 5□ + 2△, you have moved from the concrete situation to a symbolic representation of the problem. Combining like figures will give 8□s and 6△s, which is as far as you can go. That is much like simplifying 3x + 4y + 5x + 2y to 8x + 6y by combining like terms.

In the section dealing with multiplying whole numbers, we discussed partial products and the connection with algebra. Suppose the exercise is:

$$
\begin{array}{r}
1\ 4 \\
\times\ 1\ 2 \\
\hline
8 \quad (2 \times 4) \\
2\ 0 \quad (2 \times 10) \\
4\ 0 \quad (10 \times 4) \\
1\ 0\ 0 \quad (10 \times 10) \\
\hline
1\ 6\ 8
\end{array}
$$

Rather than doing the exercise as shown, we could use expanded notation and write the factors as 10 + 4 and 10 + 2. The problem would still be done the same way but the formatting would be different.

$$
\begin{array}{r}
10 + 4 \\
\times\ 10 + 2 \\
\hline
8 \quad (2 \times 4) \\
2\ 0 \quad (2 \times 10) \\
4\ 0 \quad (10 \times 4) \\
1\ 0\ 0 \quad (10 \times 10) \\
\hline
1\ 6\ 8
\end{array}
$$

As you can see, the rest of the problem is the same but now the factors for each partial product are easier to trace. Figure 3.4 shows this problem done with Base 10 blocks, a reminder of our discussion about multiplication as finding the area of a rectangle.

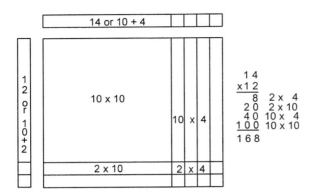

FIG. 3.4.

Now the stage is set for doing an algebra multiplication problem. Rather than 10 + 4 and 10 + 2, suppose you had m + 4 and m + 2 as factors. Using the same format, the problem would be:

$$
\begin{array}{r}
m \ + \ \ 4 \\
\times \quad m \ + \ \ 2 \\
\hline
8 \\
4m \\
2m \\
m^2 \\
\hline
m^2 \ + \ 6m \ + \ 8
\end{array}
\quad
\begin{array}{l}
(4 \times 2) \\
(2)(m) \\
(m)(4) \\
(m)(m)
\end{array}
$$

As you compare the algebra version and the partial product version, things should look similar. Figure 3.5 represents the product of m + 4 and m + 2 and it looks a lot like Fig. 3.4. This problem easily transitions to the FOIL method for multiplying

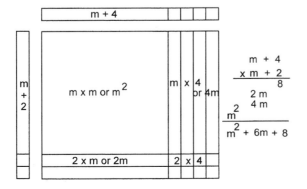

FIG. 3.5.

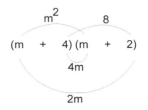

FIG. 3.6.

binomials, as shown in Fig. 3.6. FOIL (Firsts, Outers, Inners, Lasts) is simply a way of remembering to distribute each number in the first binominal to each number in the second binomial. There is nothing special about the order of the letters in FOIL; you could just as efficiently distribute from the right and use LIOF.

PATTERNING

You have dealt with number patterns 2, 4, 6, 8, . . . and 1, 3, 5, 7, . . . saying that they are odd and even numbers. A pattern like 1, 3, 6, 10, . . . is not as easy to classify and yet bowling pins are arranged using the fourth term of this pattern called triangular numbers.

Some patterns are not immediately obvious. Try your hand at this one:

1
11
21
1112
3112
211213
312213
212223

Figure out the pattern before reading on. *We're watching you!* The question is, what is the next term in the pattern. Did you try it? You should, because we are about to tell you the answer and it is better for you to figure out the pattern before we tell you. As you look at it, you need to start at the top and read the first line. What do you see? You saw one one, or 11, which is shown on the second line. Now, read the second line and what do you see? You see two ones, or 21, which is shown on the next line. Read that line and you see one one and one two or 1112. And so it goes. As you read each line, you count the number of ones, then the number of twos, and so on. What you get becomes the next line. Continuing, the line after 1112 should be 3112 to show that the line above contained three ones and one two.

Your Turn

6. What are the next two lines in the pattern 1, 11, 21, 1112, 3112, 211213, 312213, 212223, ? ?

The pattern 1, 11, 21, can be altered. It will start the same, but the fourth term and each one after that will be different from the one used before. It is different because a different pattern is being used:

1
11
21
1211
111221
312213
1311221113

Try to determine the next term in this one before reading on. As we said before, it is better for you to try to figure out the pattern before looking at the answer. In this case, we are reading left to right and reporting what is seen. If the digits are the same, then they are grouped together. Again, read the first line and you see one one. Reading the second line, you see two ones or 21. Reading that third line, you see one two followed by one one, or

1211. Read the fourth line and you see one one, one two, and two ones or 111221.

Your Turn

7. What are the next two terms in the pattern 1, 11, 21, 1211, 111221, 312213, 1311221113, ?, ?

There are a lot of number patterns. We have shown you only a few, but as you begin to sort them out, you are beginning to strengthen your algebra skills.

REPRESENTING SITUATIONS WITH ALGEBRA

Algebraically, we try to express patterns by using a generic expression for any term. Consider the pattern created by the set of even numbers. If n is the ordinal, or positional, number of the term (first, second, third, and so on), 2, 4, 6, 8, . . . can be expressed by 2n. If you need the 87th term in this pattern, then you know it is (2)(87), or 174. Similarly, 2n − 1 can be used to express the pattern of odd counting numbers; if you wanted to know the 87th odd counting number, it would be (2)(87) − 1, or 173. Triangular numbers can be expressed in general by the formula $\frac{n(n+1)}{2}$, which is not as simple to develop.

A pattern you have seen is 1, 4, 9, 16, 25, 36, ... You may recognize this as a beginning of the list of square numbers. Another way of writing them would be 1^2, 2^2, 3^2, 4^2, 5^2, 6^2, ... This format makes it easier to see how the generic term is written. What should it be? If you determined that it should be n^2, then give yourself a pat on the back.

Sometimes we are asked to set up and solve word problems. An important skill is the ability to take the problem apart and use the information given. If the problem is not immediately obvious, then it might be a good idea to look for a pattern. Suppose you are asked to solve the following problem: "In my home town there are two rental companies. I need to rent a jackhammer and would like to spend as little as possible. On Monday, I will need the equipment for 8 hours and on Tuesday I will need it for 3 hours. At Rent It, the cost is a flat fee of $20.00 plus $3.00 per hour. At Get It Here, the cost is $8.00 per hour. What should I do?" A table to compare the cost of the equipment at each rental company would be a good way to look for a pattern.

	Rent It	Get It Here
0 hr	$20.00	$ 0.00
1 hr	$23.00	$ 8.00
2 hrs	$26.00	$16.00
3 hrs	$29.00	$24.00
4 hrs	$32.00	$32.00
5 hrs	$35.00	$40.00
6 hrs	$38.00	$48.00
7 hrs	$41.00	$56.00
8 hrs	$44.00	$64.00
h hrs	20 + 3h	8h

The cost at Rent It is higher at the beginning of the table, but at 4 hours the costs are the same, and Rent It is the better deal after that. The solution to this problem is to rent the equipment at Get It Here for $24.00 on Tuesday and at Rent It for $44.00 on Monday. The more you practice expressing patterns in general terms, the better your algebraic foundations will be.

USING MODELS

Sometimes models make patterns easier to figure out. Look back at 1, 4, 9, 16, 25, 36, ... Switching to exponents was one way of doing it. Figure 3.7 shows how we

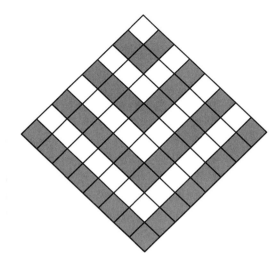

FIG. 3.7.

could have done it with a graphic. At the top is a white unit square representing the first square number. Below that is a shaded V made up of three unit squares which, with the top center white unit square, forms a 2 by 2 square to represent the second square number. The next V is made up by five white unit squares, but if we include all the unit squares above, then the total is nine unit squares. The next V is made up by seven shaded unit squares, but if we include all the unit squares above, then the total is 16 unit squares. Continuing this procedure, you have a 5 by 5 square made up of 25 unit squares, a 6 by 6 square made up of 36 unit squares, a 7 by 7 square made up of 49 unit squares, and an 8 by 8 square made up of 64 unit squares. If we look at the squares in terms of the number of unit squares that make them up, then we would have 1, 4, 9, 16, 25, 36, 49, and 64. But, if we consider the dimensions instead, we have 1^2, 2^2, 3^2, 4^2, 5^2, 6^2, 7^2, 8^2, which connects to our abstract model. The graphic model could be extended to include as many unit squares as we would like, but eventually the advantage of generalizing to the exponential form, and ultimately to n^2, should be apparent.

Wait a minute. Look at Fig. 3.7 again. If you take the number of unit squares making up each V (count the top center white square as the first V), there is another way to express the square numbers. The first square would be one. That square plus the three unit squares in the next V would be $1 + 3 = 4$. Forming a sum for the next V and all those above gives $1 + 3 + 5 = 9$. The whole figure could be described as:

$$
\begin{aligned}
1 &= 1 \\
1 + 3 &= 4 \\
1 + 3 + 5 &= 9 \\
1 + 3 + 5 + 7 &= 16 \\
1 + 3 + 5 + 7 + 9 &= 25 \\
1 + 3 + 5 + 7 + 9 + 11 &= 36 \\
1 + 3 + 5 + 7 + 9 + 11 + 13 &= 49 \\
1 + 3 + 5 + 7 + 9 + 11 + 13 + 15 &= 64
\end{aligned}
$$

Check it out! The model gave a clue to another pattern that can be used to express square numbers—adding consecutive odd counting numbers starting with one. Models can come in handy.

Another type of model that leads to some nice algebraic thinking comes from something that we call *figurate* numbers. Figurate numbers are represented by patterns of dots to model geometric numbers. Figure 3.8 is a model of the square numbers we described earlier.

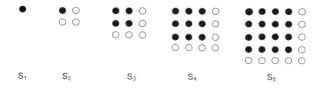

FIG. 3.8.

For the square numbers, the pattern could be identified as $S_n = n^2$, but S_n could also be defined using the pattern $1 + 3 + 5 + \ldots + n$. Sometimes one model is clearer than another—like beauty, clarity is in the eye of the beholder.

Similarly, triangular numbers can be identified using a pattern called $T_n = \dfrac{n(n+1)}{2}$, found by generalizing the model shown in Fig. 3.9. There are other

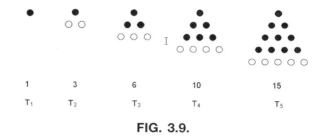

FIG. 3.9.

ways of looking at this pattern. For example, we might say that $T_n = T_{n-1} + n$, that is, any triangular number is just the previous triangular number plus the ordinal number of the triangular number needed: $T_4 = T_{4-1} + 4 = T_3 + 4$. This method requires that you to know $T_3 = 6$. Another nice pattern defined by the triangular numbers is a little more manageable and has a rich mathematical history. We will give the history lesson and then let you make the application to this model.

Carl F. Gauss (1777–1855) was a mathematical prodigy. A story is told that his tutor assigned a considerable amount of work, certainly enough to keep him busy for some time. The assignment was to find the sum of all of the counting numbers through one hundred. Gauss thought about it for a moment, then had the answer to the problem. The instructor was amazed and unprepared for this astonishing outcome. How did Gauss add the numbers so quickly? Certainly in the early 1780s he did not use his electronic calculator! Magic? No, models and patterning!

From his later work, we suspect that Gauss reasoned along these lines. First he listed several counting numbers at the beginning and at the end of the sequence, below that, he listed the same number in reverse order:

$$\begin{array}{c}
1 + 2 + 3 + \ldots + 98 + 99 + 100 \\
\underline{100 + 99 + 98 + \ldots + 3 + 2 + 1} \\
101 + 101 + 101 + \ldots + 101 + 101 + 101
\end{array}$$

This gave him 100 pairs of addends, each with a sum of 101. He quickly found the total to be 10100, but he realized that was twice as much as he needed, because he used each number twice. To rectify the situation, he divided it by two, getting 5050. Is that cool or what?!

Now look at the triangular numbers—does Gauss' trick apply? The first triangular number is one, the second is three, the third is six, and so on. Do you see it? Can you write this algebraically? You saw the answer earlier.

Figurate numbers can be determined for almost any geometric shape. The last of the figurate numbers we are going to model for you are the rectangular numbers. The first rectangular number is 2, the second is 6, the third is 12, the fourth is 20, and so on as seen in Fig. 3.10. The rectangular num-

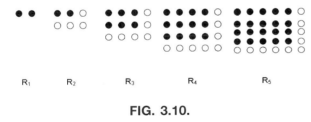

FIG. 3.10.

bers are related to both the triangular numbers and the square numbers. We will leave generalizing this pattern to you.

Your Turn

8. Make a model that shows how Gauss' trick applies to the triangular numbers.

9. Using the model of the rectangular numbers, write a generalizing statement about how to find any rectangular number, R_n.

10. Rewrite the rectangular model to show a relation between the rectangular numbers and the square numbers.

11. Generalize the model you drew about the relation between rectangular and square numbers.

12. How do the rectangular numbers relate to the triangular numbers?

RATE OF CHANGE

Many topics in algebra depend on an understanding of rate of change and how to determine rate of change. A common application of rate of change is the distance formula, $d = rt$ in which the rate, r, can be expressed as $\frac{d}{t}$. Geometrically, when we think about rate of change, we look at rise (change in the y direction) divided by run (change in the x direction). The Greek delta symbol is used to represent change, so algebraically this would be $\frac{\text{rise}}{\text{run}} = \frac{\Delta y}{\Delta x}$. Ordered pairs identifying points on the x–y plane are written in the form (x, y).

Recall the trip Pete and Repeat took as we began this chapter. Pete rode his bike at a rate of 8 mph. At the end of 1 hour, Pete had ridden 8 miles. At the end of 2 hours, Pete had ridden 16 miles, an additional 8 miles, and he rode an additional 8 miles each hour until he got to Hollopaw. If we plot Pete's rate representing distance in miles on the x axis and time in hours on the y axis, it will look like the graph in Fig. 3.11. We start at the first ordered pair (0, 0), representing no miles traveled and no time elapsed. From there, we go up one unit and right eight units until we hit the second point at (8, 1). For each eight miles and 1 hour, we plot a point by rising one and running eight from the previous point. What was the change in y? What was the change in x? Because

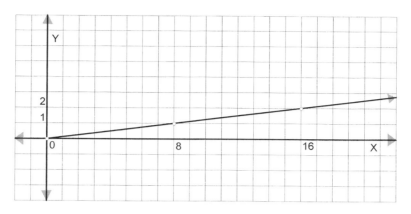

FIG. 3.11.

Pete was riding continuously at a constant rate of $\frac{1}{8}$ hour per mile, we can sketch a line segment that starts at (0, 0), goes through each of the plotted points, and ends at (96, 12).

The rate of change is also called the slope, m and $\frac{rise}{run} = \frac{\Delta y}{\Delta x} = m$. Pete's rate of change, or the slope of the line segment telling us how far Pete had traveled at any given time, is $\frac{\Delta y}{\Delta x} = \frac{1}{8}$. What does this have to do with algebra? The equation for a line can be written in what is known as the slope–intercept form, $y = mx + b$, where m is the slope and b is the point where the graph of the equation intersects the y axis. What if we have two points and we want to figure out the rate of change for a graph? We call the two points (x_1, y_1) and (x_2, y_2). Two distinct points from our discussion about Pete are (8, 1) and (16, 2), where $y_1 = 1$, $x_1 = 8$, $y_2 = 2$, and $x_2 = 16$. We know that the change in the y direction is 1, and by examination we suppose that $y_2 - y_1 = 2 - 1 = 1$. Likewise, we suppose that $x_2 - x_1 = 16 - 8 = 8$. As it turns out our conjecture is correct and

$$m = \frac{\Delta y}{\Delta x} = \frac{y_2 - y_1}{x_2 - x_1} = \frac{2-1}{16=8} = \frac{1}{8}.$$

The equation for the graph of Pete's trip is $y = \frac{1}{8}x + 0$, which tells us that the slope is $\frac{1}{8}$ and the graph intersects the y axis at (0, 0). In Fig. 3.11, we have shown a few points on the graph.

Your Turn

13. Repeat traveled at a rate of 12 mph. Use the information you placed into the table at the beginning of this chapter.

a) Make a continuous graph of Repeat's rate of change using the x axis for time and the y axis for distance traveled.

b) Find m for Repeat by counting $\frac{rise}{run}$ on the line segment.

c) Use the two points from the table for how far Repeat had traveled at 2 hours and at 5 hours and find m algebraically. Does your answer here match your answer for part b?

14. In the word problem about renting a jackhammer, we found a cost pattern for each of the rental companies. For Rent It, the pattern was 20 + 3h ($20.00 plus $3.00 per hour) and for Get It Here, the pattern was 8h ($8.00 per hour).

a) Use the cost pattern for Rent It to write a cost equation for renting the equipment. State the rate of change and the y intercept.

b) Use the cost pattern for Get It Here to write a cost equation for renting the equipment. State the rate of change and the y intercept.

c) At what point would the graphs of these two cost equations intersect?

15. Peggy, a member of this book's dynamic author team, wants to paint her house a particular shade of blue such that the ratio of gallons of blue paint to white paint is 2:3.

a) How many gallons of blue paint and how many gallons of white paint will be needed to mix up 15 gallons?

b) What is the algebraic solution for the slope that represents this color mixture no matter how many gallons of paint are needed?

c) If Peggy would like to make the trim of her house a darker shade of the same color, then how should she change the ratio of the paint mixture?

d) Using the trim mixture you decided on for Peggy, how many gallons of blue paint and how many gallons of white paint would be needed to make 3.5 gallons of paint?

SEQUENCES

There are two interesting types of sequences, which are quite common, that algebra can help explore. One of these sequences is called arithmetic because the difference between any two successive numbers is a constant. The most common pattern is the counting numbers, 1, 2, 3, 4, ... The difference between 1

and 2, 2 and 3, or 3 and 4, and so on is one, a constant or unchanging number. If the difference between each number is called d, then to find the 50th counting number, multiply 50 times d to get 50, the 50th counting number.

Starting at 5, 6, 7, 8, . . . , d would still be 1, but now you use the number you started with to get to the right term in the sequence. If you call the 50th number a_{50}, then the first number would be called a_1. The 50th number in the sequence starting with 5 is four more than the 50th number in the sequence that started with one, so $a_{50} = 54$. Subtract a_1 from 54 to get 49, which is one less than the nth number needed. Let n equal the nth number in the sequence. Then $a_n = a_1 + (n - 1)d$ is the formula for the nth term in an arithmetic sequence.

Another common sequence is the even numbers: 2, 4, 6, 8, ... The difference between any two consecutive numbers is two, so d = 2. Try the formula to see if it works. What is the 137th even number?

$$a_n = a_1 + (n - 1)d$$
$$a_{137} = 2 + (137 - 1)2$$
$$a_{137} = 2 + (136)2$$
$$a_{137} = 2 + 272$$
$$a_{137} = 274$$

Knowing how to find the nth term in an arithmetic sequence, the next step is to be able to find the sum of a certain number of elements in the sequence. What is the sum of the first 10 counting numbers? When n is even the sum can be found by using the following formula: $S_n = \dfrac{n}{2}(a_1 + a_n)$, where a_1 is the first number in the sequence, a_n is the last number in the sequence, and n is the number of terms to be added together in the sequence. Then it follows that:

$$S_n = \frac{n}{2}(a_1 + a_n)$$

$$S_{10} = \frac{10}{2}(1 + 10)$$

$$S_{10} = 5(11)$$

$$S_{10} = 55$$

When n is odd, the formula changes to avoid getting a fractional answer:

$S_n = a_1 + \frac{(n-1)}{2}(a_2 + a_n)$. Try adding the first 11 counting numbers:

$$S_n = a_1 + \frac{(n-1)}{2}(a_2 + a_n)$$

$$S_{11} = 1 + \frac{(11-1)}{2}(2 + 11)$$

$$S_{11} = 1 + \frac{(10)}{2}(13)$$

$$S_{11} = 1 + 5(13)$$

$$S_{11} = 1 + 65$$

$$S_{11} = 66$$

The sum of the first 11 counting numbers is 66.

Your Turn

16. What is the 121st number in the following sequence: 4, 8, 12, . . . ?

17. What is the 326th number in the following sequence: 9, 20, 31, . . . ?

18. What is the sum of the first 84 even numbers: 2, 4, 6, . . . ?

19. What is the sum of the 9th through the 101st numbers in Exercise 16?

A sequence is geometric if each successive term is a constant multiple of the previous term. Another way to think about

this is to say that the ratio of successive terms is a constant; that is, a_2 divided by a_1 is equal to a_3 divided by a_2, and so on. An example of a geometric sequence is: 1, 3, 9, 27, ... To find the nth term in a geometric sequence, multiply the first term by the ratio constant raised to the n − 1 power:

$$a_n = a_1 r^{n-1}$$

Geometric sequences get very large very quickly. For the sake of this discussion, use a small number of terms to avoid calculator overflow. What is the 20th term in the following sequence: 1, 3, 9, . . . ? First decide the ratio of the second to the first term, which is 3:1 or 3. Next plug this information into the formula:

$$a_n = a_1 r^{n-1}$$

$$a_{20} = 1 \cdot 3^{20-1}$$

$$a_{20} = 1 \cdot 3^{19}$$

$$a_{20} = 1 \cdot 1162261467$$

$$a_{20} = 1162261467$$

Wow! The 20th term is already over a billion!

If the ratio constant is less than one, then a geometric sequence gets smaller and smaller like in: 27, 9, 3, ... What is the ratio? What is the 20th term in this sequence? The ratio is $\frac{1}{3}$ and the 20th term is $\frac{1}{43046721} \approx 0.000000023$. Wow, again! The 27 gets really small really fast and is almost what number? The 326th term in this sequence would definitely be almost what number? How is this going to affect the sums calculated next?

One formula summarizes any geometric sequence: $S_n = \dfrac{a_1(1-r^n)}{(1-r)}$. Notice for this formula that there is no need to first determine the nth term. Once the ratio, the first term, and how many terms to sum are known, all the necessary information is present. Find the sum of the first 20 terms in the sequence 1, 3, 9, 27, . . . :

$$S_n = \frac{a_1(1-r^n)}{(1-r)}$$

$$S_{20} = \frac{1(1-3^{20})}{(1-3)}$$

$$S_{20} = \frac{1(1-3486784401)}{(-2)}$$

$$S_{20} = \frac{(-3486784400)}{(-2)}$$

$$S_{20} = 1743392200$$

The sum of the first 20 terms of 27, 9, 3, . . . is:

$$S_n = \frac{a_1(1-r^n)}{(1-r)}$$

$$S_{20} = \frac{27\left(1-\left(\frac{1}{3}\right)^{20}\right)}{\left(1-\frac{1}{3}\right)}$$

$$S_{20} \approx \frac{27(1-0.000000000287)}{\left(\frac{2}{3}\right)}$$

$$S_{20} \approx \frac{27(0.999999999713)}{\left(\frac{2}{3}\right)}$$

$$S_{20} \approx \frac{(29.9999999923)}{\left(\frac{2}{3}\right)}$$

$$S_{20} \approx 40.4999999884 \text{ or } 40.$$

The sum of the first 326 terms of 27, 9, 3, . . . is:

$$S_{326} = \frac{27\left(1-\left(\frac{1}{3}\right)^{326}\right)}{\left(1-\frac{1}{3}\right)}$$

$$S_{326} \approx \frac{27(1-0)}{\left(\frac{2}{3}\right)}$$

$$S_{326} \approx \frac{27(1-0)}{\left(\frac{2}{3}\right)} \text{ or } 40.5$$

Huh, is that what you expected? What does this lead you to believe about this type of geometric sequence? Mathematically, this sum has a limit as n approaches infinity because the contributions made by the ratio raised to the nth power become insignificant to the sum. This is powerful stuff—adding an infinite number of elements from a decreasing geometric sequence and getting a finite answer!

Your Turn

20. What is the 15th number in the following sequence: 5, 10, 20, . . . ?

21. What is the 19th number in the following sequence: 99, 33, 11, . . . ?

22. What is the sum of the first 20 numbers in the sequence: 5, 10, 20, . . . ?

23. What is the sum of the first 500 numbers in the sequence: 99, 33, 11, . . . ?

FORMULAS

Mathematical formulas are algebra based. When you write the general term for a number pattern, you have developed a formula. Some patterns provide information that is so useful that their formulas become standardized. How many formulas have you been asked to memorize in your educational experience? A better question might be to ask you how many formulas you remember.

Think about some formulas you remember. Of all the formulas you have seen, why do you suppose you remembered those specific formulas? Of course, there are many factors that have effects on why we remember particular formulas. The real question is not whether you memorized a formula, it is whether or not you can apply it as you solve a problem. Did you remember some formulas but have no inkling about what they do? Why do you think you remember a formula without remembering its purpose? The following is a list of some common formulas. Did you remember any of these? Did you remember the application of each?

Area

Circle

πr^2 $(\pi \approx 3.14 \text{ or } \dfrac{22}{7},$

r is radius)

Rectangle

$l \times w$ (l is length, w is width)

Square

s^2 (s is side length)

Trapezoid

$\dfrac{b_1 + b_2}{2}h$ (b_1 is one base, b_2 is other base, h is height)

Triangle

$\dfrac{bh}{2}$ (b is base, h is height)

Distance formula

$d = rt$ (d is distance, r is rate, t is time)

Mean

$\dfrac{\text{sum of data points}}{\text{number of data points}}$

Volume

Rectangular Prism (box)

lwh   (l is length, w is width, h is height)

Sphere

$\dfrac{4}{3}\pi r^3$ ($\pi \approx 3.14$, r is radius)

Right circular cylinder

$\pi r^2 h$ ($\pi \approx \dfrac{22}{7}$, r is radius, h is height)

Perimeter of a rectangle

$2(l + w)$ (l is length, w is width)

Pythagorean Theorem

$a^2 + b^2 = c^2$ (a and b are legs, c is hypotenuse of a right triangle)

Formulas come in many different shapes, sizes, and purposes. Think about the pros and cons of memorizing a multitude of formulas. Generally, you are expected to know where to find needed formulas and, above all else, know when and how to effectively utilize the formula.

CONCLUSIONS

Algebra accounts for a large proportion of the Pre-K–16 curriculum. It seems that we are always laying the foundation for algebra concepts, learning algebra concepts, or applying algebra concepts. The representations of problems spiral from concrete to semi-concrete to semi-abstract to abstract—and back again. We need the concrete and semi-concrete models to aid in development and comprehension of the concepts; we move to semi-abstract and abstract models because they are more efficient as problems become more complex. With concrete beginnings and a solid understanding of basic algebraic concepts, the whole subject becomes more familiar, easier to grasp, and ultimately, to understand.

REFERENCES

Eves, H. (1990). *An introduction to the history of mathematics* (6th ed.). Fort Worth, TX: Saunders.

4

Geometry

You might be surprised about how many real-life concepts are included in the study of geometry. Young children experiment with ideas such as over versus under, first versus last, right versus left, and between, without realizing that they are studying important mathematics concepts. Additionally, early attempts at logic, even the common *everyone else gets to do it* arguments that are so popular with children, are geometry topics. A cube is a three-dimensional object with six congruent faces and eight vertices—often called a block. You may also use the term *block* to identify a prism that is not a cube, but, although you may not think of it very often, you can probably identify the differences between a cube and a prism that is not a cube, as shown in Fig. 4.1.

In this chapter, you will review, refine, and perhaps, extend your understanding of geometry. When Euclid completed a series of 13 books called the *Elements* in 300 BC, he provided a logical development of geometry that is unequaled in our history and is the foundation of our modern geometry study. Geometry is a dynamic, growing, and changing body of intuitive knowledge. We will let you explore conjectures and provide opportunities for you to create informal definitions. There will be some reliance on terms and previous knowledge, especially when we get to standard formulas.

UNDEFINED TERMS

Some fundamental concepts in geometry defy definition. If we try to define point, space, line, and plane, then we find ourselves engaging in circular (flawed) logic. The best we can do is accept these fundamental concepts as building blocks and try to explain them.

A fixed location is called a *point*, which is a geometric abstraction that has no dimension, only position. We often use a tiny round dot as a representation of a point. As the series of dots in Fig. 4.2 get smaller and smaller, we observe that the dimensions are diminishing—but any dot that we can see has some dimension,

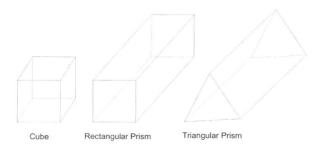

Cube   Rectangular Prism   Triangular Prism

FIG. 4.1.

FIG. 4.2.

even the period at the end of this sentence. The fact that a point has no physical existence does not limit its usefulness, either in geometry or everyday activities. Although a dot covers an infinite number of points, it represents the approximate location of a distinct point so well that we forget the difference and freely identify the dot as a pinpointed location. In mathematics, we label the point represented by a dot with a printed capital letter, for example, the points in Fig. 4.3. The set

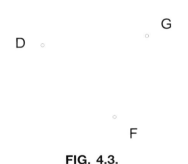

FIG. 4.3.

of all possible fixed locations is called *space*. We have no method of representing space, but we use the concept in mathematics and in real life.

The most direct (straight) path between two points is called a *line segment* and, as shown in Fig. 4.4, the two points, P and

$\overline{PQ}$ means "line segment PQ"

FIG. 4.4.

Q, are called the *endpoints* of the segment. Because the most direct path must be the shortest distance, we say that the segment joining two points must be straight. Unlike a point, a line segment has a dimension because there exists a distance between the points. However, a line segment has only a single dimension, length. Just as we use a dot to represent a point, we trace along the path of a segment to create a physical representation, call it the line segment, and use the endpoints to name it. A tiny line segment drawn above the two capital letters tells us that the figure is a line segment.

A line is a geometric abstraction that infinitely extends a line segment in both directions; it is a straight array of points that has no endpoint. Figure 4.5 shows several models of lines. Sometimes it is convenient to show dots to represent some of the points on the line, but this is not necessary. If a few of the points are shown, then any two can be used to name the line. For example, the line that has points A, B, C, D, and E could be called $\overleftrightarrow{AB}$, $\overleftrightarrow{BA}$, $\overleftrightarrow{CD}$, $\overleftrightarrow{EC}$, $\overleftrightarrow{AE}$, and so on. A lowercase letter could also be used to name the line. It is important to use arrowheads on the model to indicate that the line continues, without end, in opposite directions. The distance you choose to place between the arrowheads is unimportant, because the arrowheads themselves mean that the line has no defined length. When you name a line using two of its points, you must also put arrowheads on the ends of the tiny line segment above the capital letters. Any two points on a line defines a line segment. So, line $\overleftrightarrow{PQ}$ contains $\overline{PQ}$. Similarly, $\overleftrightarrow{AC}$ contains $\overline{AC}$, $\overline{AB}$, and so on.

Sometimes we have a starting point from which we proceed in a single direction. You might think of a beam of light

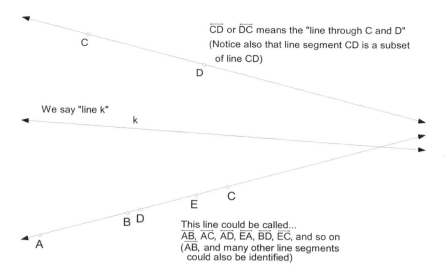

$\overline{CD}$ or $\overline{DC}$ means the "line through C and D"
(Notice also that line segment CD is a subset
of line CD)

We say "line k"

This line could be called...
$\overline{AB}$, $\overline{AC}$, $\overline{AD}$, $\overline{EA}$, $\overline{BD}$, $\overline{EC}$, and so on
(AB, and many other line segments
could also be identified)

FIG. 4.5.

shining out across an ocean from a light-house. Because there is a starting point, it doesn't model a line, and because it continues in a single direction without end, it can't model a line segment. This subset of the points on a line that starts at some point and continues, without end, in a single direction, is a *ray*. To sketch a ray, we first identify the endpoint and then another point in the desired direction, as shown in Fig. 4.6. As you might expect, we use a tiny ray to name the ray and indicate its direction, like $\overrightarrow{KJ}$ or $\overleftarrow{JK}$. The arrow points left over $\overleftarrow{JK}$ and right over $\overrightarrow{KJ}$. Both of these notations identify the same ray and we read the K first, and then the J.

The beginning point of the ray is placed over the letter that is its representative and then another point on the ray is named. In the case of ray $\overrightarrow{AE}$, we could name the same ray with $\overrightarrow{AB}$, $\overrightarrow{AC}$, or $\overrightarrow{AD}$ because each of them starts with A and B, C, D, and E are all points along the path of the ray. Ray AE is different from $\overrightarrow{EA}$ because $\overleftarrow{EA}$ starts at E and passes through A, whereas $\overrightarrow{AE}$ starts at A and passes through E. Did you notice that $\overrightarrow{AE}$ and $\overleftarrow{EA}$ share $\overline{AE}$ and $\overleftrightarrow{AE}$?

The models look similar, but you should not confuse the concepts of rays and vectors. A ray has one endpoint and a direction, but no length. Vector *t*, as shown

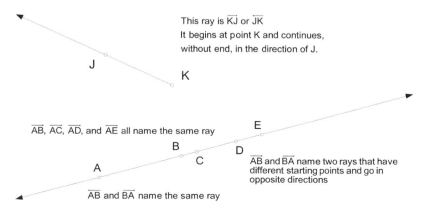

This ray is $\overrightarrow{KJ}$ or $\overleftarrow{JK}$
It begins at point K and continues,
without end, in the direction of J.

$\overline{AB}$, $\overline{AC}$, $\overline{AD}$, and $\overline{AE}$ all name the same ray

$\overline{AB}$ and $\overline{BA}$ name two rays that have
different starting points and go in
opposite directions

$\overline{AB}$ and $\overline{BA}$ name the same ray

FIG. 4.6.

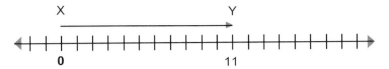

$\overline{XY}$ is a vector that extends from 0 to 11 on a number line

FIG. 4.7.

in Fig. 4.7, has a specific direction and a specific length; in one sense, a vector has two endpoints, the initial endpoint and the terminal endpoint represented by an arrowhead. To help you tell the difference, you must refer to the context of the problem under discussion.

Perhaps the most difficult of the undefined terms in geometry is the idea of a plane. Physical models of geometric planes are everywhere, for example, the surface of a table, wall, or piece of paper. One way to visualize a plane is to use a window glass, because you can see through the surface of the glass, it appears to have no thickness. However, just as a line continues, without end, in opposite directions, a plane continues, without end, in every direction within any two dimensions forms a plane. Just as geometric points, segments, and lines can be represented only by physical models, a geometric plane can be represented only by real-world flat surfaces. You see, a geometric plane is nothing other than a surface; it has absolutely no depth and therefore no visible presence in the physical world. A plane is usually represented by a parallelogram, named with a capital scripted letter, as shown in Fig. 4.8.

Your Turn

1. For each of the following, provide a labeled sketch and explain in your own words:

a) Point Q
b) Line segment ST

c) Line k
d) Plane R
e) Ray UV
f) Vector **u** of length 3 and heading to the right
g) Which of these can be measured?

2. Answer each of the following questions and provide a sketch:

a) How many different lines could you sketch through a single point?
b) How many different lines could you sketch through two points?
c) Is it always possible to sketch one line through three points?

ANGLES

If two rays that go in different directions are joined so they share their endpoint, the result is an angle. The common end-

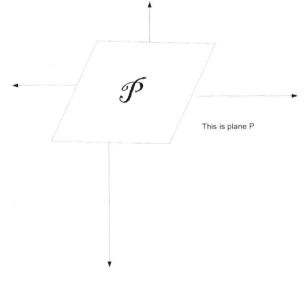

This is plane P

FIG. 4.8.

point of the two rays is called the *vertex* of the angle. The rays are called the *sides*, or *legs*. Sometimes, for the sake of convenience, line segments are used as sides of an angle, but you should understand that any line segment is a part of a ray. The best way to name an angle is to use three points in order—first a point on one leg, then the vertex point, and then a point on the other leg (the vertex letter is always the middle of the three points defining the angle). The symbol for an angle looks like a tiny angle ($\angle$) and sometimes it has a tiny arc drawn across it ($\measuredangle$).

The sides of an angle are rays, so we need not worry about sketching them any specific length. This has implications for our use of the word "congruent" and the symbol that means congruent ($\cong$). Congruent is a very strong word that means figures must be exactly the same shape and exactly the same size. The sides of an angle are rays, so they extend forever no matter how long we make them appear to be. This means that we need only measure the rotations of two angles to decide if they are congruent; in Fig. 4.9,

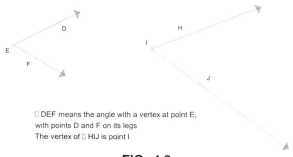

$\square$ DEF means the angle with a vertex at point E, with points D and F on its legs
The vertex of $\square$ HIJ is point I

FIG. 4.9.

$\angle$DEF $\cong$ $\angle$HIJ because they have the same measure, even though we have not sketched the rays to look the same.

Because the legs of an angle are rays, extending forever, an angle divides the plane into three distinct parts, the set of all points that are inside the legs, the set of all points that are on the legs, and the set of all points that are outside the legs. This may not be obvious when you look at an angle, because we draw only a tiny part of each ray. Figure 4.10 shows inte-

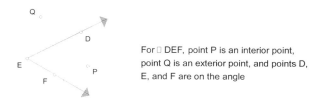

For $\square$ DEF, point P is an interior point, point Q is an exterior point, and points D, E, and F are on the angle

FIG. 4.10.

rior points, like P, are between the rays, exterior points, like Q, are outside the sides, and angle points, like D, E, and F, are on the legs of the angle.

Angles are commonly described by their degree measures. The most common angle found in buildings is the *right angle*, which has a degree measure of exactly 90° and is formed by two lines, rays, or line segments that are perpendicular ($\perp$) to one another. Some other angles are described by their relation to the right angle. Angles with degree measures greater than 0° but less than 90° are called *acute*. Angles with degree measures greater than 90° but less than 180° are called *obtuse*. If two rays are joined at their endpoint and go in exactly opposite directions, then we say that they form a *straight angle*, which measures 180°. See Fig. 4.11 for examples of straight, obtuse, right, and acute angles. Angles can have more than 180°, but the most commonly used ones in daily life are acute, right, obtuse, and straight.

Two of the angles in Fig. 4.11, $\angle$JMI and $\angle$HMI, can be combined to form a right angle. When this happens, we say that the two angles complement one another. Taken one at a time, these angles are acute; however, if you ignore their common leg, then you can see the right angle, $\angle$JMH. Another special relation exists when two angles can be combined to

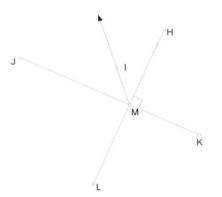

FIG. 4.11.

form a straight angle. In Fig. 4.11, ignore the common leg between ∠KMI and ∠JMI, and you can see the straight angle, ∠KMJ. We say that these two angles supplement one another.

Vertical angles apply some of the things we are have discussed so far. Think of an X and you have two pairs of vertical angles. As you look at that X, the top angle and the bottom angle make one pair of vertical angles. The left and right pair of angles formed by the X make another pair of vertical angles. Gee, that sounds strange: Two horizontal angles are called vertical angles. Do not dismiss that statement too quickly, because the emphasis for vertical angles is how they are formed. Their orientation as far as being vertical or horizontal has nothing to do with how vertical angles are defined. Look at the top and bottom angles in the X. They are both acute and they have the same measure. The same is true for the left and right angles in that X. They are both obtuse and their measures are the same. Could vertical angles be right angles? If you look around as you read this sentence, then you should be able to see examples that would confirm your conjecture.

Your Turn

3. Use a straightedge to sketch an angle. Label a few interior points, exterior points, and points on your angle. Shade the part of the interior that is within the rays you drew. Would this interior shading continue to expand if you continued the rays?

4. Given that $\overline{HL} \perp \overline{JK}$, name every angle in Fig. 4.11; then identify each angle as right, acute, obtuse, or straight. (There are at least 10 angles in the figure.)

5. In Fig. 4.11, explain why there is a tiny box drawn in one of the angles at the intersection labeled with an M.

6. Explain why we need to use three letters to identify any angle in Fig. 4.11.

7. In Fig. 4.11, we say that ∠HMI and ∠HMK are adjacent angles. Write a definition of *adjacent angles*.

8. Write an informal definition for the term *complementary angles*.

9. Write an informal definition for the term *supplementary angles*.

10. Do you think it is possible for two angles to be complementary or supplementary without being adjacent? If your answer is yes, then provide sketches that indicate your thinking.

SIMPLE CLOSED CURVES, REGIONS, AND POLYGONS

A line segment is a straight array of all the points between two given points. You could choose a path that is not straight, but it would not represent the most direct path between the two points. Any path that does not pass through any of its points more than once is called a *simple curve*. As you can see in Fig. 4.12, even segments can be considered simple curves, because part of the path from Point E to Point F is a segment. Curve CD is not simple because it crosses itself at Points H and I.

The simple closed curve is a basic idea for many concepts in geometry. Any

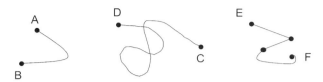

The path from A to B is simple; the path from E to F is simple;
the path from C to D is not simple.

FIG. 4.12.

TABLE 4.1
Polygons

Number of Sides	Name
3	Triangle
4	Quadrilateral
5	Pentagon
6	Hexagon
7	Heptagon
8	Octagon
9	Nonagon
10	Decagon
11	Undecagon
12	Dodecagon
.	.
.	.
.	.
Many	n-gon

curve that returns to its starting point is closed, but a simple closed curve returns to its starting point without crossing any of its points more than once. It does not matter whether we use straight segments or wavy curves; the important idea is that a region on a plane can only be described using a simple closed curve. The points between the legs of an angle are called interior points, but they do not define a finite region because an angle is not a closed figure. Identifying a finite region is important for discussing concepts such as area, which requires two dimensions (usually length and width). A simple closed curve divides the plane into three subsets; the points that are inside the curve, the points that are outside the curve, and the points that are on the curve. In Fig. 4.13, we can identify the exterior

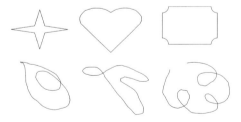

FIG. 4.13.

and interior points for the figures in the top row, but it would be impossible to do the same for figures in the second row.

POLYGONS

Simple closed curves created by connecting straight segments at their end-

points are called *polygons*. Table 4.1 lists the names for several polygons. The prefix *poly-* means "many" and the suffix *-gon* means "side," so we could call these many-sided figures *polygons*, or *n-gons*, no matter how many sides each has. When working with polygons, it is convenient to use more descriptive names to avoid confusion. Whereas some names are familiar, others may not be easy to remember. It is acceptable to use number names for polygons, such as 7-gon and 11-gon. In some cases, you may want to use the general number name, n-gon.

Your Turn

11. Explain why Table 4.1 begins with a three-sided polygon.

12. There are several common polygons, called quadrilaterals, that have four sides. Use the diagram of the quadrilateral family in Fig. 4.14 to answer the following questions:

a) What are the similarities and differences among the special quadrilaterals in Fig. 4.14?

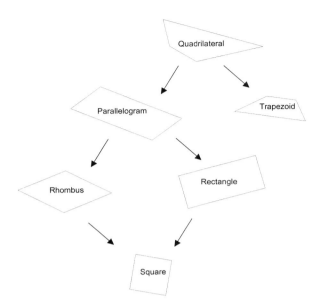

FIG. 4.14.

b) What does it mean if there is not an arrow connecting two quadrilaterals?

c) Is every square a rectangle?

d) Is every rectangle a square?

e) Where does a four-sided figure shaped like a child's kite fit in this diagram?

13. Using a piece of nonelastic string to form a closed loop that is about 2 feet long, make a large model of each polygon in Table 4.1. What do all your models have in common? How do your models differ as you add sides to create new polygons?

Naming Polygons

We use letter names for individual n-gons by listing the vertices. Although it doesn't matter where you start, you must move either clockwise or counterclockwise around the figure to name it. Among the many ways to name the two polygons in Fig. 4.15, you might call the four-sided

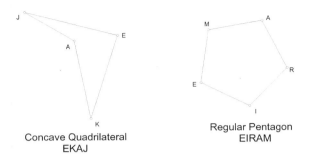

Concave Quadrilateral
EKAJ

Regular Pentagon
EIRAM

FIG. 4.15.

figure EKAJ, JEKA, or AKEJ, and the five-sided figure EIRAM, RIEMA, or AMEIR.

The 4-gon in Fig. 4.15 seems to have been poked in at Point A. You could sketch a line segment connecting Vertex J to Vertex K and it would be completely outside the figure. Although concave polygons such as quadrilateral EKAJ are common, we will confine this informal discussion to convex polygons such as pentagon EIRAM in Fig. 4.15, for which no straight segment joining two vertices extends outside the figure. Most of the common algorithms used with polygons assume that they are convex. A regular polygon, like pentagon EIRAM, has all angles the same measure and all sides the same length.

Your Turn

14. Most of our sketches were created using Geometer's Sketchpad® and we encourage the use of a dynamic software application as you do this exercise. You may complete the sketches using a straightedge and protractor, but it will be a lot more work. Draw and label polygons with the given characteristics. Name the polygons based on the letters at their vertices, and based on their characteristics. Choose from these terms, using each term only once: acute triangle, equilateral triangle, isosceles triangle, obtuse triangle, parallelogram, quadrilateral, rectan-

gle, rhombus, right triangle, scalene triangle, and trapezoid.

a) Three sides with as many right angles as possible.
b) Three sides with as many obtuse angles as possible.
c) Three sides with as many acute angles as possible.
d) Three sides with no sides the same length.
e) Three sides with two sides the same length.
f) Three sides with all three sides the same length.
g) Four sides with no sides the same length.
h) Four sides with two opposite sides parallel and the other two opposite sides not parallel.
i) Four sides with as many right angles as possible.
j) Four sides with all sides the same length and as many obtuse angles as possible.
k) Four sides with opposite sides parallel and as many acute angles as possible.

In addition to sides and vertices, polygons have other important parts. In Fig. 4.16, one diagonal of parallelogram DCBA is shown as a dashed segment. The requirements for a quadrilateral to be a parallelogram are that opposite sides are equal in length, denoted as $m\overline{AB} = m\overline{CD}$ and $m\overline{AD} = m\overline{BC}$, and opposite sides are parallel, denoted by $\overline{AB} \parallel \overline{CD}$ and $\overline{AD} \parallel \overline{BC}$. There are special parallelograms, as shown by the quadrilateral family tree in Fig. 4.14, but DCBA is a general parallelogram. Trace parallelogram DCBA on a piece of paper and cut it out. Cut along the diagonal from A to C and compare the two polygons you have made.

If you repeat this experiment with a few different parallelograms—including rectangles, rhombi, and squares—you can form a conjecture about the relations between parallelograms and triangles. You might trace DCBA again and repeat the experiment using diagonal BD. Although you do not need a formal definition of diagonal of a parallelogram to conduct and understand this experiment, you definitely must know what a diagonal is.

Another important polygonal part is the altitude, or height, of a figure. In a polygon, an altitude can be drawn from any vertex as long as it is perpendicular to the opposite side. In Fig. 4.17, you can see

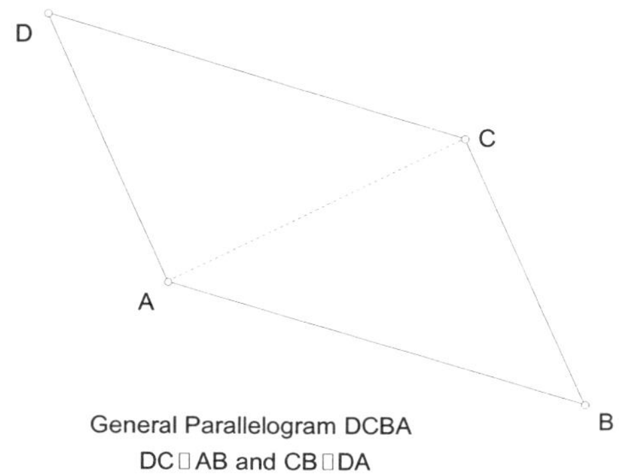

General Parallelogram DCBA
DC □ AB and CB □ DA
DC ≅ AB and CB ≅ DA

FIG. 4.16.

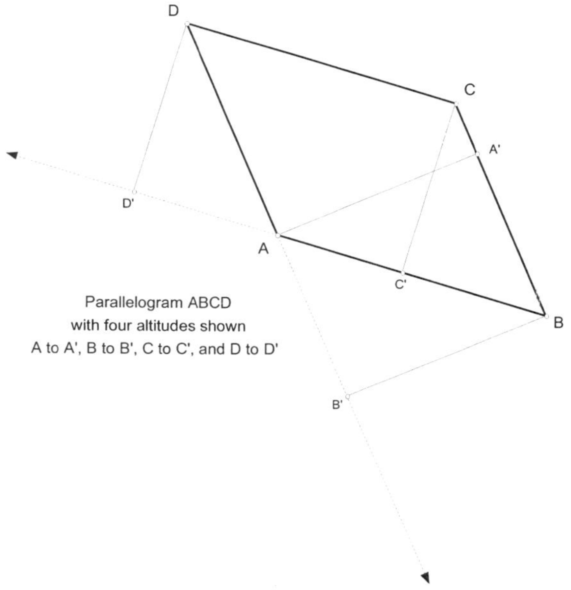

Parallelogram ABCD
with four altitudes shown
A to A', B to B', C to C', and D to D'

FIG. 4.17.

that it is not necessary for an altitude to be inside a figure. Side DA was extended so Altitude BF from Vertex B could be shown and Side BA was extended so Height DH from Vertex D could be shown. Sketches that include several auxiliary segments can be visually confusing. In Fig. 4.17, the parallelogram is shown with thick segments, the altitudes as thin segments, and the side extensions as dashed rays. If you find it more comfortable to view an altitude as a vertical segment, then you may want to rotate the page as you examine the four altitudes of ABCD. Notice that a new point is created where each altitude meets the opposite side (or extended side); for example, the height from Vertex B is perpendicular to $\overrightarrow{DA}$ at F. The sides of ABCD are congruent in pairs, thus you will see that the height of the polygon depends on your orientation as you view the sketch.

Your Turn

15. Write an informal definition for each term.

a) Side of a polygon—How many sides does a 12-gon have?

b) Vertices of a polygon—How many vertices does a 7-gon have?

c) Diagonal of a polygon—How many diagonals does a 5-gon have?

d) Altitude of a polygon—How many altitudes does a 3-gon have?

CIRCLES

Some people consider a circle to be a special polygon—with an infinite number of infinitely short sides. Others prefer to put the circle in a special category all its own. Because a circle is a simple closed curve, it divides the plane into three sets of points (inside the circle, outside the circle, and on the circle). When you used a piece of string to model the polygons in Table 4.1, did your model start to look a bit like a circle as you added more and more sides without changing the length of the string? It is easy to see the connection with polygons. However, as you look at circles, such as the one shown in Fig. 4.18, you do not see infinitely short sides, only smooth and perfectly rounded curves, making it easy to argue that circles should have their own category.

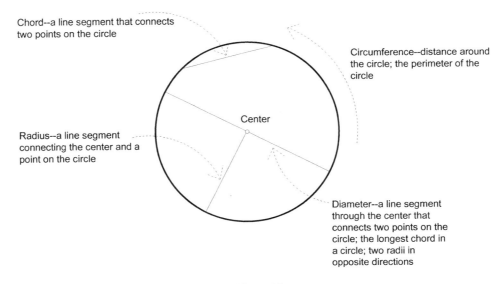

Chord--a line segment that connects two points on the circle

Circumference--distance around the circle; the perimeter of the circle

Center

Radius--a line segment connecting the center and a point on the circle

Diameter--a line segment through the center that connects two points on the circle; the longest chord in a circle; two radii in opposite directions

FIG. 4.18.

Sometimes people refer to circular pieces of material as circles—perhaps a coin, poker chip, or other disk. In fact, these items are right circular cylinders; they may be very short cylinders, but they are not figures in a plane and they have more dimensions than do circles. A circle is a point and every member of the set of points is the exact same distance from the center in the plane. The circular array of points is the circumference of the circle. The circle is the ring. The set of points inside the ring is not the circle; it is the interior of the circle. Similarly, the points outside the ring are not the circle; they make up the exterior of the circle. A circle has no substance, so the best way to model a circle is with a wire ring. Of course, the wire of the ring has thickness, but it represents a much better model of a circle than a solid plastic disk.

There are several important terms associated with circles, some of which are shown in Fig. 4.18. The diameter is a segment that joins two points on the circle and passes through the center. A radius is half a diameter and goes from the center to any point on the circumference. A chord is a line segment that joins any two points on a circle. The diameter is the longest chord of a circle. A few additional terms are shown in Fig. 4.19. A sector of a

circle is a pie-wedge region bounded by two radii and an arc. A segment is a region bounded by a chord and an arc.

Your Turn

16. Use the information in Fig. 4.18 and Fig. 4.19 to write your own informal definitions for the following terms:

a) Center
b) Chord
c) Circle
d) Circumference
e) Diameter
f) Radius
g) Sector
h) Segment

CONSTRUCTIONS

Classic constructions, completed with nothing more than a compass and straightedge (not a ruler), are elegant and beautiful in form. However, the basic concepts of construction can be introduced using paper folding. For this, you need a straightedge, a pencil, and some paper. Waxed paper, tracing paper, or meat patty paper are best, because these are thin and show the creases of the construction well. We have selected a few standard geometric constructions for you to try using paper folding. Many more can be accomplished using this method, although the more complex constructions are actually easier to complete using a compass and straightedge. An introduction to construction using paper folding will strengthen your understanding and improve your level of confidence. Geometer's Sketchpad® or another dynamic software application could be used to generate additional conjectures once you have mastered the basics.

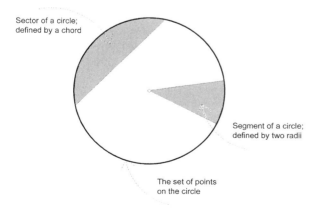

Sector of a circle; defined by a chord

Segment of a circle; defined by two radii

The set of points on the circle

FIG. 4.19.

Your Turn

17. Use a straightedge and a sharp pencil to score a line segment on your paper, labeling the endpoints A and B. Fold the paper so that A and B coincide and crease it. What geometric figure have you made? Place a few points at random positions on the crease and label them C, D, E, and F (be sure that one of the points is at the intersection of the crease with $\overline{AB}$). From each of these points, one by one, compare the distance to A with the distance to B. What might you conjecture based on this construction?

18. Start on a new piece of paper with $\overline{AB}$. Place a point C on the segment, not very near the center. Fold the paper through point C so that the parts of $\overline{AB}$ on either side of C coincide and crease it. How does this figure compare with the one in Exercise 16? How does it differ?

19. Start on a new piece of paper with $\overline{AB}$. Place a C somewhere off $\overline{AB}$ and fold the paper through C so parts of $\overline{AB}$ lie on top of each other and crease it. How does this figure compare with the ones in Exercises 16 and 17? How does it differ?

20. Start on a new piece of paper with $\overline{AB}$. Place points C and D on the segment. Using first C and then D, follow the instructions in Exercise 19. How does each of these two creases meet $\overline{AB}$? What conjecture can you make about these two creases?

21. On a new piece of paper, score an angle on your paper; label the vertex B and the rays *t* and *s*. Fold the paper through B so Rays *t* and *s* coincide and crease it. What construction have you completed? If you used an acute angle, try this again with an obtuse angle—if you used an obtuse angle, try it again with an acute angle. Finally, try it again with a right angle.

22. Using only a compass and straightedge, construct a triangle and the altitude to one side of the triangle. Does this apply any of the paper folding work you just did? (You might want to use Geometer's Sketchpad® or some other dynamic software for this one.)

THIRD DIMENSION

All the figures we have discussed so far are planar. They range from a point, which has no dimension, to a segment, which has one dimension, to a rectangle, which has two dimensions. The third dimension is a vital part of geometry, opening the door to real-world concepts like capacity. An initial step into the third dimension is learning to represent things that have length, width, and depth in a two-dimensional medium—your paper. Following a few procedures won't make you an artist, but it will help you create useful sketches. If you already have methods for sketching that are more comfortable, then feel free to use them or try the procedures presented here.

To sketch a sphere, start with a circle and imagine how the sphere would sink into and protrude from the paper. Sketch a solid curve to represent the bulge and a similar dashed curve to represent the unseen part of the sphere. The sphere in Fig. 4.20 seems to bulge down toward the viewer.

To sketch a right circular cylinder as shown in Fig. 4.21, start with an oval or

FIG. 4.20.

FIG. 4.21.

football shape and a copy of that shape for the top and bottom. Sketch line segments forming the left edge and right edge. When the upper and lower ovals are vertically aligned, the figure is a right circular cylinder. Dash the arc representing the unseen part. If the ovals are not vertically aligned, then the cylinder is not a right circular cylinder. If the segments representing the vertical edges aren't straight, then the figure seems to wiggle. Right circular cylinders are common in geometry classes, but all sorts of cylinders exist in the world.

To sketch a cone, start with an oval or football shape and a point directly over the center of the shape. Sketch segments connecting the apex (top) with the left-most and right-most points of the football and dash the unseen curve, as shown in Fig. 4.22. If the apex is not directly over

FIG. 4.22.

the center or if the figure on the bottom does not represent a circle, then it will not represent a right circular cone.

To sketch a rectangular prism, start with a rectangle. Make a copy of the rec-

tangle a little to the right and a little above the original. Sketch line segments to connect the corners of the two rectangles, top left to top left, top right to top right, bottom left to bottom left, and bottom right to bottom right. Make the edges that would not be seen into dashed segments, as shown in Fig. 4.23.

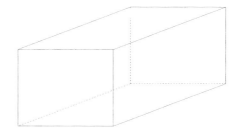

FIG. 4.23.

Perhaps the most challenging three-dimensional figure to sketch is the pyramid. Consider a right hexagonal-based pyramid. Start with a hexagon that appears regular, but is in perspective, and a point directly over its center. Sketch a line segment to connect each vertex of the hexagon with the apex. Dash segments that represent unseen edges, as shown in Fig. 4.24.

FIG. 4.24.

Once you gain confidence with sketches such as these, you will be able to produce other figures. Sketching these shapes will help you understand the connections between polygons and three-dimensional figures. With practice, you will develop additional techniques for creating even better and more useful sketches.

Your Turn

23. All of the figures in this discussion were sketched as if we were viewing them from above and in the front. Sketch each figure as if you were looking at it from below and in the front.

COORDINATE GEOMETRY

In algebra, coordinate geometry is called *graphing*. It is unfortunate that topics in mathematics sometimes are taught in isolation, divorced from natural connections. Perhaps coordinate geometry is one area of subject matter integration you have recognized. You knew about the coordinate plane before your geometry course—you just called it the x–y system, rectangular plane, or Cartesian plane. We place two number lines perpendicular to one another at their zero points and call the intersection the origin of the axis system, as shown in Fig. 4.25. This system divides the plane into four quadrants. Both the x and y coordinates of a point are positive in the first quadrant, the x coordinate is negative whereas the y coordinate is positive in the second quadrant, both coordinates are negative in the third quadrant, and the x coordinate is positive whereas the y coordinate is negative in the fourth quadrant. Because the coordinates are always listed as an ordered pair, with the x coordinate first, every address on the coordinate plane can be clearly provided. The name of the x coordinate is abscissa and the name of the y coordinate is ordinate; although these names aren't used very often, they provide another way to think of the ordered pair in alphabetical order. Other concepts, such as slope and intercepts, are clarified with the visually orientated geometric approach. In algebra we learn about slope by first counting the rise

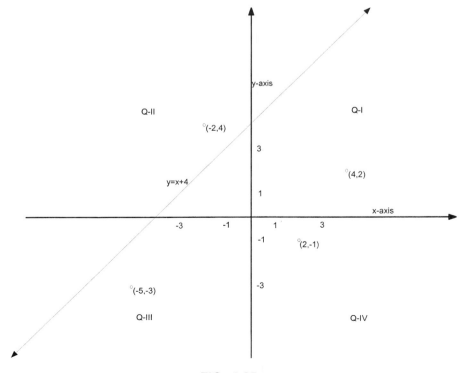

FIG. 4.25.

and the run and then learning the slope formula. We learn about intercepts by looking for the place where a line crosses the y axis or the x axis.

Coordinate geometry can be useful in other areas of study, such as statistics. Did you ever think about a histogram as a geometric figure? You need a coordinate plane with a vertical axis and a horizontal axis to construct a histogram, bar chart, or even a pictogram. You also need a coordinate plane if you want a scatter plot.

TRANSFORMATIONS AND SYMMETRY

We will consider rigid transformations, called *isometries*, because they preserve size and shape. We will not discuss transmography, although these amazing transformations are the basis for many of the special effects for movies, television, and video games. Special effect experts change the figure point by point to transform an image from one appearance to another. Parts of the image are changed by sliding, rotating, flipping, stretching, or shrinking. Because there is no set factor for all the transformations, it is often impossible to recognize any part of the original image after it has been transformed.

Translations, rotations, reflections, and glide reflections are transformations that preserve shape and size and can create images that have symmetry. As a beginning, compare your left hand with your right hand. Did you find that they are very similar, but have opposite orientation? This is an example of symmetry created by reflection. For a completely different type of symmetry, consider a wallpaper pattern that repeats. If you cut out a piece of the wallpaper and slide it up or down, you will find it matches a new section exactly. This is an example of symmetry cre-

ated by translation or sliding. A third type of symmetry can be seen on fancy car wheels. As a wheel turns, the same image is seen over and over. This is an example of symmetry created by rotation or turning. We will not expect you to create patterns or tessellations such as M. C. Escher did, but we do recommend that you read about this artist/mathematician and review some of his famous images, many of which were created using transformations. Information can be found at http://www.mcescher.com.

Translations preserve not only size and shape, but also orientation. When we translate (or slide) a triangle with vertices at (3, 4), (4, 1), and (1, 2) four steps to the left and two steps down, we have a triangle that appears identical, except that it has vertices at (⁻1, 2), (0, ⁻1), and (⁻3, 0), as shown in Fig. 4.26. The two triangles, the

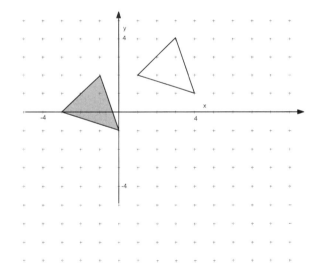

FIG. 4.26.

original and the copy, or image under the transformation, demonstrate translational symmetry. To make the translation clearer, the image is shaded.

Rotations preserve size and shape, but the orientation changes as we turn the figure about a given point called the *center*

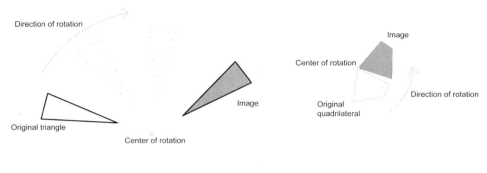

FIG. 4.27.

of rotation. The triangle in Fig. 4.27 has been rotated 130° clockwise. The two dashed figures indicate the rotation. The image, or copy, has been shaded. The center of rotation may be near or far from the figure; it may even be on or inside the figure as it is in the quadrilateral in Fig. 4.27, which shows a rotation of 80° counterclockwise about a vertex of the figure (the image has been shaded).

An axis of symmetry, reflection line, or mirror is required to reflect a figure. As with the point of rotation, this axis may be far from the figure, near the figure, on the figure, or even inside the figure. In Fig. 4.28, the mirror is indicated by a thick line

shaded image is different from that of the original figure, size and shape have been preserved. Additionally, the original hexagon and its image are equally distant from the line of reflection.

The last transformation, and perhaps the most fun one, is the glide reflection. In Fig. 4.29, a pattern of footprints was cre-

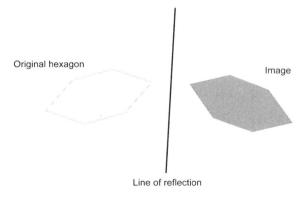

FIG. 4.28.

segment, over which the figure on the left has been flipped to create a congruent, but reversed image on the right. You can see that, whereas the orientation of the

FIG. 4.29.

ated from a single original sketch. For each image, the original is either translated or both translated and reflected. Can you figure out which is the original sketch? Do you think each of the images is congruent to the original? Can you find the mirror line?

Your Turn

24. Consider the following capital letters of our alphabet:

A B C D E F G H I J K L M N O P Q R S T U V W X Y Z

a) Determine which have reflectional symmetry about a vertical mirror within the letter.
b) Determine which have reflectional symmetry about a horizontal mirror within the letter.
c) Determine which have rotational symmetry within the letter.
d) Do any of the letters have more than one type of symmetry within the letter?
e) Do any letters have all three types of symmetry within the letter?
f) Do any have no symmetry within the letter?

CONCLUSIONS

We have highlighted some important topics in geometry. It will be up to you to determine which topics in geometry are like comfortable old clothes and which topics are more like scratchy new wool sweaters. You need to work on the scratchy topics until you soften them up.

5
Measurement

What is the first thing that comes to your mind when you hear the word "measurement"? Do you think about how many gallons of gasoline you had to buy yesterday, how many miles you must travel to get to class, how many minutes you will be in class, how many dollars will be in your next paycheck, how many ounces of potato chips are in a bag, how warm it will be today, or even how many square yards of carpet you had to buy to cover your bedroom floor? Perhaps you considered one or more of these without thinking of the word "measurement."

Measures are important in our world and we are so comfortable with the concepts that we often accept and understand the information without much thought. Have you ever considered how much the gasoline in your tank weighs, how many times your left front tire revolves as you drive to class, how many seconds you spend in class, what your net salary per hour is, or how temperature is related to humidity? These are all *valid measures*, you just don't think of them as relevant to your daily life.

The measurement concepts that are so familiar to us have developed over many years. Primitive people used rudimentary methods to measure distances for their foraging or hunting boundaries, but there were no standard units. Figure 5.1 repre-

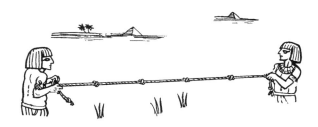

FIG. 5.1.

sents ancient Egyptians, who lived along the Nile River and used standard linear measures and elaborate survey methods to mark and remark their crop boundaries as the river flooded and receded, taking and restoring cropland. The Babylonians looked to the stars to measure the length of a year; their calculations were surprisingly accurate and their methods of astronomical observations are the basis for calculations today.

TERMINOLOGY

Many early measurement techniques were based on human anatomy, as shown in Fig. 5.2, making standardization problem-

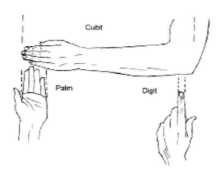

FIG. 5.2.

atic. For example, the cubit (length from elbow to longest finger tip) was a linear measure common to several cultures, but each defined it differently. The Egyptian Royal Cubit, used to build the pyramids, was 20.63 inches, whereas the Greek Olympic Cubit was 18.93 inches.

An argument for the inherent fairness of a standard system of measures can be made using a tale of two tailors. Tailors once measured cloth using the distance from the tip of one outstretched arm to the center of the chest as a unit. Who would want to pay more for a suit just because a tailor, like the one in Fig. 5.3, had

FIG. 5.3.

short arms? In 1130 AD, with the regulation of trade in mind, King Henry I of England decreed the distance from the point of his nose to the end of his thumb to be the lawful yard. Later, King Henry VII commissioned a bronze bar, 3 feet long, and ruled that to be the standard yard.

As we shift our attention from the everyday world to the mathematics content in Pre-K–16 classrooms, we must acknowledge that the terminology associated with even basic measurement concepts is often approached differently in the classroom. Dichotomous terminology, such as biggest and smallest, can be doubly confusing, for certainly the biggest kitten is not as large as the smallest elephant. Comparison can be either quantitative or qualitative and a brief review of such concepts and the related terminology is necessary at this time.

Your Turn

1. Make a list of all the measurement words you can think of in 30 seconds. Share your list with classmates.

2. Make a list of all the dichotomous measurement words you can think of in 30 seconds. Compare your list with those of your classmates.

3. Find a subtle example of confusing dichotomous terminology using the terms larger and smaller.

4. When can the smallest be larger than the biggest? When can the biggest be smaller than the smallest?

ATTRIBUTES

Consider the different attributes possessed by a measurable object. When we find the dimensions of an object, we choose a unit of measure, but we also make a qualitative decision about the attribute we want to consider. A pound of feathers weighs the same as a pound of chocolate, but they do not have the same volume. A backyard might be completely enclosed using 250 feet of fencing, but the cost will differ according to the height and style of fencing that is selected. The choices we make, including those related to measurement, are based on experiences and prior knowledge.

Your Turn

5. When you say that a beach ball is bigger than a bowling ball, what attributes are you ignoring?

6. What attributes, other than the number of square yards required, influence the cost of carpeting?

7. Attribute Blocks™ help children learn the terminology and concepts of differences. The 60-piece set includes squares, rectangles, circles, triangles, and hexagons, in two sizes, three colors, and two thicknesses. List at least 10 different ways by which Attribute Blocks™ could be sorted.

SYSTEMS

Some metric units, such as kilowatt of electricity, appear regularly in the United States. The system used in general communication has many names: inch/foot/pound, U.S. Standard, U.S. Common, and English Customary. Ironically, we encounter both systems and get around using either name by saying things like a carton of milk, which can be taken to be a liter or a quart. On top of that, measures in both units are listed on many containers. For example, a bottle of water shows 16.9 FL OZ, 1.06 PT, and 500 mL. Although both the metric and inch/foot/pound were adopted as official measurement systems in the United States long ago, many American adults prefer to use the inch/

foot/pound system. President Ford signed a voluntary Metric Conversion Act in 1975. Soon after that, metric speed limit signs appeared on our interstate highways, but they have long since disappeared. Yet, the dual system lives on. Mechanics must still maintain two complete sets of tools in order to repair cars. Many cars have speedometers that list both systems. Digital gauge systems in many cars allow selection of systems. Measuring cups are dual-scaled, with ounces and milliliters.

Few examples of the problems we experience with this dual system are as costly as the crash of the Mars Climate Orbiter in 1999. Findings by NASA's internal review indicated that the spacecraft was not placed in the proper orbit because one team of scientists was using the inch/foot/pound system and the other team was using the metric system. This failure of communication between the spacecraft team in Colorado and the mission navigation team in California resulted in faulty data for critical maneuvers, destroying an opportunity for scientific gain and costing American taxpayers millions of dollars. Such problems are likely to continue until we all learn to be cognizant of the units being used, no matter the system. This is significant because the United States is the only industrialized nation, and one of a few nations in the world, that is not using the metric system of measure.

The inch/foot/pound system of measurement was the result of attempts to standardize measures. In the 14th century, King Edward decreed that three kernels of barleycorn, taken from the center of the ear, would be an inch or one twelfth of a foot. If we accept the Greek legend that Hercules' foot was the original basis for this measure, it must have measured 36 kernels of barleycorn. Learning to use the inch/foot/pound system is no easy task! We use words such as ounce or quart for both liquid and dry measures, and there are confusing relations between and within the units used for length, weight, and capacity as shown in Table 5.1.

TABLE 5.1
Commonly Used Inch/Foot/Pound Abbreviations

Quality	Measure	Symbol	Comparisons
length	inch	in	12 in = 1 ft
	foot	ft	3 ft = 1 yd
	yard	yd	1760 yd = 1 mi
	mile	mi	5280 ft = 1 mi
capacity	teaspoon	t	3 t = 1 T
	tablespoon	T	16 T = 1 c
	cup	c	2 c = 1 pt
	pint	pt	2 pt = 1 qt
	quart	qt	4 qt = 1 gal
	gallon	gal	
weight	ounce	oz	16 oz = 1 lb
	pound	lb	2000 lb = 1 T
	ton	T	

The metric system grew out of a need for more coherent measurement and the International Bureau of Weights and Measures was established in 1875. During the French Revolution, French scientists led the way and the system we call SI (le système international d'unités) is the result of many decades of effort to establish a system that uses Base 10. All metric measures within a unit concept are related using powers of 10, so this is the system preferred by scientists around the world. Once you master the units for lin-

ear measures, mass, and capacity the prefixes will begin to make sense. We use Greek prefixes, such as tera (10^{12}), giga (10^9), mega (10^6), kilo (10^3), hecto (10^2), and deca (10^1) for measures that are greater than the unit and Latin prefixes, such as deci (10^{-1}), centi (10^{-2}), milli (10^{-3}), micro (10^{-6}), nano (10^{-9}), and pico (10^{-12}), for measures that are smaller than the unit. Of course, there are many orders of magnitude greater and smaller than these, but we commonly use only the few shown in Table 5.2.

The scientists developing the metric system had the advantage of starting from scratch. In 1791, the French Academy of Sciences defined the meter as one ten millionth of the length of the meridian through Paris from the north pole to the equator. Whereas the original prototype missed this target by 0.2 of a millimeter (flattening of the earth due to its rotation caused a miscalculation), this length was accepted as the standard. The definition of a meter has changed several times and in 1983 the definition was standardized to be the distance traveled by light through a vacuum during $\dfrac{1}{299{,}792{,}458}$ second. Note that only the definition of a meter changed, not the length. This interconnecting system has helpful relations among the measures for length, mass, and capacity. At sea level, one milliliter of pure water at 4° Celsius weighs one gram and has a volume of one cubic centime-

TABLE 5.2
Commonly Used Metric System Prefixes

Prefix	Value	Numerical	Linear	Capacity	Weight
kilo	thousands	10^3 = 1000	km	kL	kg
hecto	hundreds	10^2 = 100	hm	hL	hg
deka	tens	10^1 = 10	dam	daL	dag
unit	one	10^0 = 1	m	L	g
deci	tenths	10^{-1} = 0.1	dm	dL	dg
centi	hundredths	10^{-2} = 0.01	cm	cL	cg
milli	thousandths	10^{-3} = 0.00	mm	mL	mg

ter. Because our ability to precisely measure mass has improved over the decades, we know that this relation is not perfect, but rather an incredibly close approximation.

UNITS, TOOLS (INSTRUMENTS), AND PRECISION

Linear Measure

Almost anything can be used as a linear measuring unit. You could measure the length of this book in paperclips or erasers. A standardization problem would result if you used large paperclips or new erasers and your classmate used small paperclips or partly used erasers. Measuring with nonstandard units is an interesting activity and makes the point that standardization is important. It also reminds us that it is critical to always provide both parts of the measure—how many and what unit.

Once you have moved beyond nonstandard measuring devices and picked up a ruler, precision becomes an issue. Whereas it may seem natural to begin measuring at zero, it isn't necessary. You can place the length you want to measure anywhere along the rules. The smaller reading subtracted from the larger reading will be the length. Of course, if you place one end of the length to be measured at the origin, the smaller reading will be zero (this process is called *predetermining the measure*). Be careful, however, because on some rulers, the origin is at the edge, whereas on others it is indented slightly. The first issue of precision is to know your tool. After that, the degree of precision required will be determined or assigned by the task at hand. For some tasks, you may need to be accurate to within one half or one fourth of an inch,

but such estimates might be considered sloppy for others. Many rulers also provide graduated marks for eighths and sixteenths of an inch, with halves indicated by the longest mark and sixteenths indicated by the shortest. Some tools are calibrated to even smaller parts of an inch. We have used inch/foot/pound in this discussion, but similar comments could be made about metric and we encourage you to learn both systems.

Your Turn

8. Measure the height of your coffee cup using anything except a ruler. Would you want to use a new pencil as your unit?

9. Measure the length of a room in paces. (The Romans figured 1000 paces were a mile and defined a pace as two steps or about 5 feet.) Would it have made sense to use a new pencil as the unit?

10. Trace your hand and wrist. How many measurements can you discuss in reference to your tracing? Measure the trace in inches, then in centimeters. Which unit was easier to use? What is the finest degree of precision you can reach with your ruler?

11. Measure the line segments in Fig. 5.4 to the finest degree of precision avail-

FIG. 5.4.

able to you in the inch/foot/pound system and the metric system. Measure the distances AB, AC, AD, AE, BC, BD, BE, CD, CE, and DE.

12. What is the total length of a corner shelf that is 5 yd 1 ft 9 in along one wall and 4 yd 2 ft 7 in along the other wall? Be careful as you regroup the measures in your solution.

FIG. 5.5.

13. What is the total length of a corner shelf that is 5 m 10 cm 5 mm along one wall and 4 m 44 cm 5 mm along the other wall?

14. Use a piece of string to measure the distance an ant would walk around the outer edge of the leaf in Fig. 5.5. Compare your string measure to a ruler to find the distance.

Area

A concrete way to review the concept of surface area is to make square tiles for measuring area. You should make square tiles using different colors of paper for square inch tiles and square centimeter tiles. A square inch is much larger than a square centimeter, so you need fewer square inch tiles to cover a surface. Making both types of tiles will highlight the idea that you have to decide what unit you are going to use as you measure, reinforcing the idea that the units are just as important as the numbers in measurements. You may not be able to accurately tile irregular shapes, so you will need to establish a few estimating procedures.

A similar way to measure area involves printing square grids on transparency sheets. When you place the grid on a surface of an object, an outline can be traced and the squares—and parts of squares—inside the outline can be counted to estimate the area of the object. The leaf in Fig. 5.6 has an approximate area of 10 square cm or 1.25 square in.

The right angles so evident in square tiles or grids remind us that the heights and bases used in algorithms must be perpendicular to one another. You may

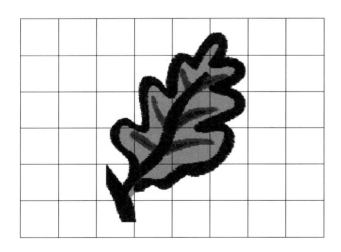

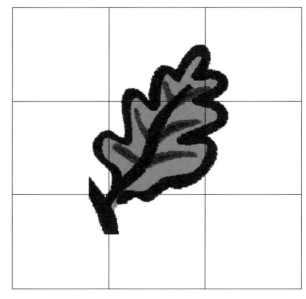

FIG. 5.6.

find that the familiar area algorithms are more obvious after you have explored the concept of area in this way.

Your Turn

15. Make a set of unit square tiles for measuring area using any unit you like. Find an everyday item with a flat surface and estimate the area of the flat surface by tiling. You may need to use partial tiles. How do you know this is a good estimate?

16. Create a one foot square showing 144 square inches. Create a 1 yard square using 9 square foot tiles.

17. Find the perimeter of each region in Fig. 5.7 using your string and a centimeter ruler; then find the area of each by counting and estimating the number of squares covered by each.

18. At some point, the string and grid paper are replaced by measures that lead to formulas for perimeter and area. From your previous experience with algorithms, identify these common formulas and tell the meaning of each letter and symbol.

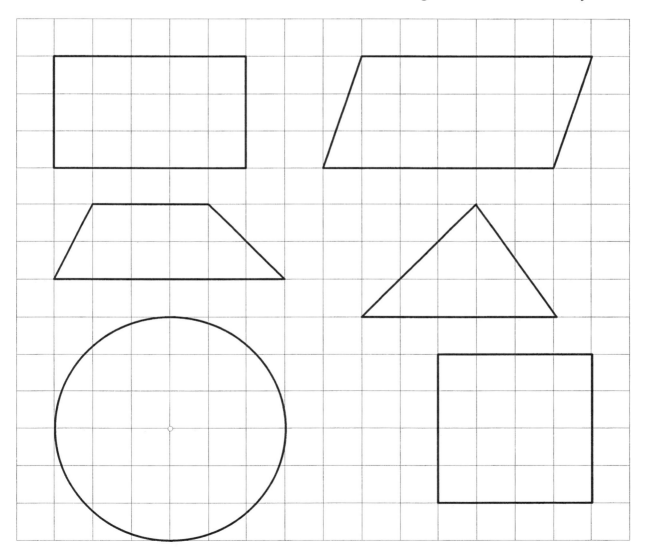

FIG. 5.7.

a) $A = l \cdot w$

b) $P = 2l + 2w$

c) $A = s^2$

d) $P = 4s$

e) $A = \frac{1}{2}b \cdot h$

f) $A = \frac{1}{2}h(b_1 + b_2)$

g) $P = ns$

h) $A = \frac{1}{2}ans$

i) $A = \pi r^2$

j) $C = 2\pi r$

19. Use the appropriate algorithms in Exercise 18 to check your measures and estimates in Exercise 17.

20. Which algorithms in Exercise 18 were not helpful in completing Exercise 17?

21. Why is there no algorithm in Exercise 18 for finding the perimeter of the trapezoid or the triangle? Do you think perimeter algorithms are needed?

As you were completing Exercises 17 and 18, did you notice that, in Fig. 5.7, the triangular region has exactly one half as much area as the rectangular region? A closer look at the area algorithms for these two figures confirms this relation, because the terms *length* and *base* or *width* and *height* are used interchangeably. You might have noticed that there is not a separate algorithm for the area enclosed by a parallelogram. What happens if you use the slant height (not the height because it is the slanted side) of the parallelogram to find the area? You could rearrange the squares enclosed by the parallelogram to form a rectangle (which, is a parallelogram with right angles). For the parallelogram in Fig. 5.8, think of making a cut through Vertex A that is perpendicular to Side DC. The resultant right triangle is moved to the other end, creating a rectangle. You don't have to chop up a region defined by a parallelogram to find its area. However, it is handy to use the terms base and height instead of length and width. Whereas either of the two algorithms $A = l \cdot w$ and $A = b \cdot h$ can be used,

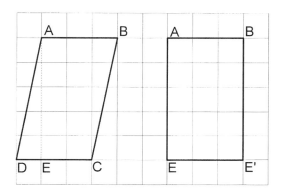

FIG. 5.8.

the second reminds us not to use the slant height when dealing with area.

The algorithm for finding the area of a triangular region works even if the base and height (or altitude) of the triangle are determined by a parallelogram that is not a rectangle, such as the triangular region shown in Fig. 5.9. For triangular region

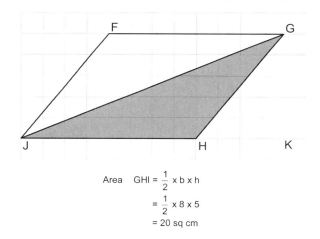

Area $GHI = \frac{1}{2} \times b \times h$

$= \frac{1}{2} \times 8 \times 5$

$= 20$ sq cm

FIG. 5.9.

GHJ, the base is determined by $\overline{JH}$ and the altitude is determined by the dotted perpendicular from G to K. Even though this altitude is completely outside of the region defined by triangle GHJ, it is the height of the triangle.

Consider the triangular region in Fig. 5.10, in which the altitude from Vertex N to Side MP is provided. The decision to use $\overline{NT}$ as the height and $\overline{MP}$ as the base

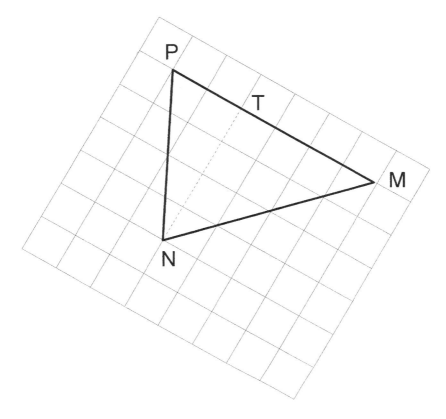

FIG. 5.10.

is arbitrary. Any one of the three sides could be used as the base, but you would need to use the altitude to that side as the height. The region in Fig. 5.10 is on a grid so that you can count the squares to estimate the area, then use a centimeter ruler to measure the two perpendicular segments (base and height), and use the formula to confirm your estimate.

We included a circular region in Fig. 5.7, even though the formulas for circumference and area are difficult to discover based on measuring with string or counting squares. Additionally, the two circle algorithms look very much the same, each has two constants, π and 2, and the variable r. The only difference in appearance is that the 2 is a factor in the circumference formula and an exponent of the variable in the area formula. Just remember that area is measured in squares and

that r^2 will help you remember which formula is for area.

Did you use 3.14 or $\frac{22}{7}$ for π in Exercise 17? Either approximation is adequate for most Pre-K–16 applications. New computers are often used to determine π to more and more decimal places. As we write this, 51.5 billion decimal places for π have been determined, by the time you read this it will be many more. Still, the decimal number for π does not terminate or repeat. This continues to confirm that π is an irrational number. If you used a calculator as you completed the exercises, then perhaps you used the π button. Did you notice how many decimal places of π were involved? Some calculators provide only a few, and others provide 8 or 12 decimal places in this approximation.

A short experiment will help you understand π. Cut a piece of string to measure the diameter of the circle in Fig. 5.11. How

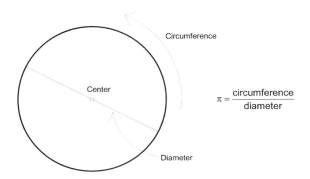

FIG. 5.11.

many times must you use this measure to trace the circumference of the circle? It isn't easy to be accurate with a piece of string, but this experiment will strengthen the idea that π is the ratio of the circumference of a circle to the diameter of the circle. Why not take the string around and across the top of a can?

The area of any polygonal region can be determined. We have standard formulas for parallelograms, trapezoids, and triangles, and any polygonal region can be sectioned into parts for which we can use these standard formulas. The pentagon in Fig. 5.12 has been sectioned into triangles

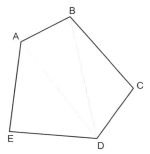

FIG. 5.12.

gles ABD, BCD, and DEA. If the polygon is not regular, we would want to use a sectioning procedure to determine the area of the region. Of course, we aren't limited to using only triangles, but they

provided a convenient sectioning of pentagon ABCDE.

The area formula from Exercise 18, $A = \frac{1}{2}ans$, is an extension of the idea of dividing polygons to find their area. If a polygon is regular, such as the hexagon in Fig. 5.13, then it can be sectioned into congruent triangles that have a common vertex at the center of the polygon. The base of each triangle is a side of the polygon and, because the polygon is regular, the bases have the same measure. The common vertex is at the center of the polygon, thus the altitudes of the triangles have the same measure. We call this common measure the *apothem* of the polygon and it is shown as a dashed segment in Fig. 5.13. Two of the three vari-

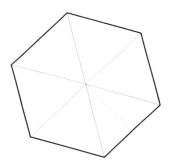

FIG. 5.13.

ables in the formula have been explained, a stands for the length of the apothem (altitude of the triangles) and s stands for the length of a side (base of the triangle). The third variable, n, tells the number of triangles that are needed, in this case 6.

Your Turn

22. Use the formula, $A = \frac{1}{2}ans$, to find the area of a region defined by a regular octagon with sides of length 4 cm and an apothem of length 4.828 cm.

Volume

Just as area is directly measured using a two-dimensional model, volume can be measured using a three-dimensional model. For example, how many rolls of quarters will it take to exactly fill your sock drawer? You might decide that you need to break your unit roll into 40 subunits or disks in order to completely fill the space and obtain a reasonably close approximation of the volume. Perhaps you would like a more convenient unit, such as a cube. How many sugar cubes will it take to fill your coffee mug? If your mug is a cylinder rather than a right, rectangular-based prism, then you will find that you must develop (or recall) some estimation strategies. As you stuff the cubes in the cup, some of them will be out of sight.

In our discussion about area, we talked about covering a region with unit squares. For volume, we could use a unit cube whose face is the same size as the unit square that was used to discuss area. Suppose a rectangle is 8 units long and 3 units wide. From the area work, the rectangle would be covered by exactly 32 unit squares. We could place a unit cube on each of those squares, as shown in Fig. 5.14, and now a wondrous thing has hap-

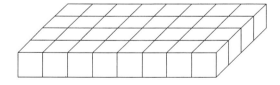

FIG. 5.14.

pened. That rectangle we used to discuss area is still visible (the tops of the cubes), but there is now a depth factor as well. Counting the cubes, rather than the top face of each cube, tells us that the figure has a volume of 32 unit cubes. We have a length of 8 units, a width of 4 units, and a

height of 1 unit, giving a total of 32 unit cubes. If a second layer of cubes is placed on top of the first, then the length is still 8 units, the width is still 4 units, but the height is now 2 units, and now we have used 64 unit cubes. A pattern is emerging:

$$32 = 8 \times 4 \times 1$$
$$64 = 8 \times 4 \times 2$$

The model could be made taller by following this pattern of adding a layer of 32 unit cubes for each unit increase in height. The prism in Fig. 5.15 has a

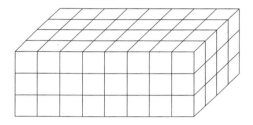

FIG. 5.15.

height of 3 units and a volume of 96 unit cubes. The top faces of the models in Fig. 5.14 and Fig. 5.15 have areas of 32 square units, but the volume in Fig. 5.15 is three times the volume in Fig. 5.14. The pattern defined by this layering means that the volume is found by multiplying the area of the top face by the number of layers. A familiar formula may come to mind: $V = l \times w \times h$, where the length times the width is the area of the top face. The terms *length*, *width*, and *height* can be replaced with other terms, such as *base*, *height*, and *depth*, but the idea of three dimensions is the critical issue. As a matter of fact, we can glue the cubes together and stand the prism on a different face, as shown in Fig. 5.16. Now the area of the top face is $3 \times 4 = 12$ unit squares and the prism is 8 layers tall, but the volume is still 96 unit cubes. Moving the prism around does not change the

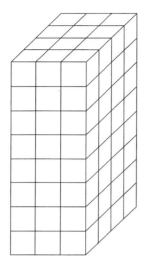

FIG. 5.16.

measures, so it doesn't matter what we call the three measures.

Figure 5.17 is reminiscent of the figures we used while discussing the formula for

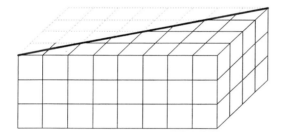

FIG. 5.17.

the area of a triangle. In this case, the area of the top face of the prism is 32 unit squares and the area of the triangle formed by slicing straight down through two opposite corners is 16 unit squares. You might suspect that there is a similar connection between the volumes of the rectangular prism and the triangular prism—that the volume is halved when that cut is made. If we use the idea of multiplying the area of the top face by the number of layers, the suspicion is confirmed. Because the area of the top face is halved, the volume is halved. Does this mean that we need to write a new formula

each time we use a prism with a different top face? Well, each formula will require only the area of the top face and the height. Consider the skew trapezoidal prism in Fig. 5.18 and think about how we

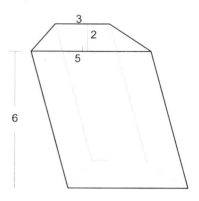

FIG. 5.18.

can find the volume. The top face is a trapezoid, so we need that area formula and the height:

Area of top face:
$$A = \frac{h(b_1 - b_2)}{2}$$
$$A = \frac{2(3 + 5)}{2}$$
$$A = 8 \text{ unit squares}$$

Volume of prism:

V = Bh   (B = area of top face or
                 A above)

V = (8)(6)

V = 48 unit cubes

Your Turn

23. Build a cube using 27 unit cubes. Use any unit cube, even a sugar cube.

a) What are the linear measurements associated with this cube?
b) What are the area measurements associated with this cube?

24. Use 24 cubes to answer the following:

a) How many different rectangular prisms can you form using the 24 unit cubes?
b) Do all of the prisms have the same volume?
c) Use your prisms to justify the volume formula, $V = lwh$, for rectangular prisms.
d) Add the areas of the six faces to determine the total surface area for each of your prisms. Do they all have the same surface area?

25. Consider a solid cube that is 6 unit cubes in height, width, and depth. If you paint the six faces of this large cube, each unit cube may have no, one, two, or three painted faces, depending on its location in the cube.

a) How many of the unit cubes will have paint on at least one face?
b) How many of the unit cubes will have only one face painted?
c) How many of the unit cubes will have two faces painted?
d) How many of the unit cubes will have three faces painted?
e) How many of the unit cubes will have 4, 5, or 6 faces painted?
f) How many of the unit cubes will have no faces painted?

Rectangular prisms are handy for exploring the concept of volume because, if you stay with unit measures for the length, width, and height, as we have done, you can build convenient models. In the real world, volume won't always be that convenient. However, if you remember that the height must be perpendicular to the base, the formulas should not be too confusing. In the following exercise

set, we have provided several formulas with sketches. As you work through the exercises, see if you find connections among the formulas. We have limited our discussion to some degree, because the exercises involve figures with regular bases and perpendicular sides. We know there are volumes where the bases will not be regular polygons and the sides will not be perpendicular to the base, as the sketches in Fig. 5.19 show. However, we

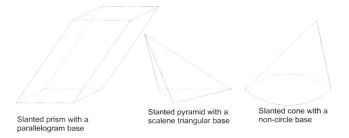

Slanted prism with a parallelogram base

Slanted pyramid with a scalene triangular base

Slanted cone with a non-circle base

FIG. 5.19.

feel that the exercises we have provided are sufficient and that you will be able to locate formulas for nonregular volumes when the need arises.

Your Turn

26. The formula for the volume of a right circular cylinder is $V = \pi r^2 h$, or the area of the circular top face times the height. Use the information in Fig. 5.20 to find the volume of the cylinder.

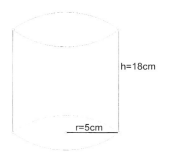

h=18cm

r=5cm

FIG. 5.20.

27. The formula for the volume of a right circular cone is $V = \dfrac{1}{3}\pi r^2 h$. Use the information in Fig. 5.21 to find the volume of the cone.

FIG. 5.21.

28. How do the volume formulas in Exercises 26 and 27 compare?

29. To find the volume of a regular right polygonal prism, find the area of the top face and multiply by the height. For this exercise, use the formula $V = \dfrac{1}{2}asnh$ to find the volume of the right hexagonal prism in Fig. 5.22.

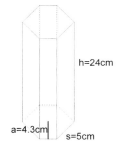

FIG. 5.22.

30. The volume of a pyramid also depends on the number of edges on the base. Use $V = \dfrac{1}{3}s^2 h$ and the information in Fig. 5.23 to find the volume of the right square pyramid.

Capacity

Volume, or capacity, is not always measured in cubic units. When was the last time

FIG. 5.23.

you stopped by a service station to buy a cubic yard of gasoline? The word "gallon" was derived from an Anglo French word, *galon*, and was standardized by the English in 1215 AD for measuring grain and wine. A gallon represents 213 cubic inches of liquid. When you must consider capacity using the inch/foot/pound system, denominate numbers are useful in dealing with inch/foot/pound units. Consider this example of an addition problem that involves regrouping cups to pints, pints to quarts, and quarts to gallons:

9 gallons	3 quarts	1 pint	1 cup
+ 5 gallons	2 quarts	1 pint	1 cup
14 gallons	~~5 quarts~~	~~2 pints~~	~~2 cups~~
	~~1 gallon~~ 1 quart	~~1 quart~~	~~1 pint~~
15 gallons	2 quarts	1 pint	

Several regroupings are required to complete this exercise. In the first line below the vinculum, you see the sum, 14 gallons, 5 quarts, 2 pints, and 2 cups. In the second line, the 5 quarts have been regrouped to 1 gallon 1 quart, the 2 pints have been regrouped to 1 quart, and the 2 cups have been regrouped to 1 pint. In the third line, the 1 gallon from the quarts column has been added to the 14 gallons, the 1 quart from the pints column has been added to the 1 quart, and the 1 pint from the cups column has been moved to the pint column. The result of all this regrouping is an answer of 15 gallons, 2 quarts, and 1 pint.

The capacity unit for the metric system is Liter. Perhaps the most well-known metric measure in the United States is 2 Liters, which is a little more than half a gallon. Many household measuring cups have inch/foot/pound on one side and metric measures on the other. On the handy 4-cup measure, you will find that the 1 L or 1000 mL mark is a bit higher than the 4-cup mark, 750 mL is a bit more than 3 cups, 500 mL is a bit more than 2 cups, and 250 mL is a bit more than 1 cup. As any cook will tell you, the differences in these measures have little effect on a finished meal. You just need to practice using the other side of the measuring cup to become comfortable with either capacity measure. Any measure is only as accurate as the measurer.

Weight

Do you know why we speak of weight when using the inch/foot/pound and mass when we use the metric system? In physics, mass is a measure of the inertia of a body and weight is mass multiplied by gravity. This implies that a body has no weight without gravity, whereas the mass of a body remains constant—with or without gravity. Because we do most of our weighing here on earth, we often use the terms *mass* and *weight* interchangeably. The best experience we can provide in this area is to suggest that you weigh lots of things using a simple balance. If you have access to a precision instrument and a mass set, then it is fun to measure exactly how many grams that special gold chain or bracelet actually masses. Again, denominate numbers can be used to simplify arithmetic operations that involve regrouping weight units in the inch/foot/pound system. For example, find the difference between the weight of a one ton, six hundred pound, fourteen ounce car and a two ton, one hundred pound, nine ounce car:

```
 1 ton   2099 pounds
           99 pounds  25 ounces
 2 tons   100 pounds   9 ounces
-1 ton    600 pounds  14 ounces
         1499 pounds  11 ounces
```

To complete the subtraction, 100 pounds needs to be regrouped to 99 pounds and 16 ounces so we can subtract 14 ounces from the 9 ounces plus the 16 ounces. In a similar manner, 2 tons needs to be regrouped to 1 ton and 2000 pounds so we can subtract 600 pounds from the 99 pounds plus the 2000 pounds.

Your Turn

31. Name everyday items that you could use to approximate each of the following: 1 g, 1 kg, 1 oz, 1 lb, 1 ton
32. What is the sum of 8 tons 1700 pounds 13 oz and 5 tons 980 lb 6 oz?

The metric unit for mass is the gram. A bar mass set may contain bars for 1 g, 2 g, 5 g, 10 g, 50 g, 100 g, 500 g, and 1 kg. A gram is also defined in terms of one cubic centimeter of pure water at sea level in ideal conditions at 4° Celsius, so you can imagine that it represents a very small mass. When buying groceries, such as coffee, it is handy to know 500 g is approximately 1 pound. The 500 g of coffee would be about 2 cups.

Time

Do you have an intuitive understanding of time? How long is a minute when someone says, "Wait a minute." What does a salesperson mean when asking, "May I have a minute of your time?" Using a watch or clock that shows the passage of seconds, close your eyes and see if you can tell when exactly one minute has passed—no fair counting or peeking! Try this little experiment with your friends of different ages.

Some people seem to struggle with learning to tell time using an analog clock. You may argue that it isn't important to tell time with an analog clock: After all, who has bothered to learn to use a sundial recently? The skills used in learning to tell time with an analog clock will be useful. A clock face with 60 divisions helps with the concept of elapsed time. Consider a delicate surgical situation, where even seconds count. You might need to determine how much time elapses between 11:42:51 AM and 2:07:08 PM. A convenient way to complete this as a subtraction problem is to use the military 24-hour clock, which keeps counting up from 1200 hours, or noon, to 2400 hours, or midnight. In our example, 11:00 in the morning is just 1100 hours, but 2:00 in the afternoon is 1400 hours:

```
   13            66
                  6          68
  ̶1̶4̶ hours       ̶7̶ minutes    ̶8̶ seconds
 −11 hours      42 minutes   51 seconds
   2 hours      24 minutes   17 seconds
```

Using denominate numbers reminds us that regrouping 1 hour results in 60 minutes and regrouping 1 minute results in 60 seconds. In this example, 1 minute was regrouped to allow the subtraction of 51 seconds, then 1 hour was regrouped to allow the subtraction of 42 minutes.

For everyday problems involving elapsed time, we usually count or estimate. To determine the elapsed time from 11:45 AM to 2:15 PM, you could count the 15 minutes until noon, then the 2 hours and 15 minutes after noon, and determine that 2 hours and 30 minutes elapsed.

Your Turn

33. Explain why you would know that a clock with one hand pointed directly at the 9 and the other hand pointed directly at the 3 was broken.

34. What other measure uses Base 60? Is there a connection between these two measures?

35. Use denominate numbers to determine how much time elapses between 9:24:13 AM and 1:15:08 PM? (Don't forget that, on the 24-hour clock, you can use 13:00 for 2:00 PM.)

Money

How did you learn about money? Do you even remember? Most people seem to have picked up the concepts of our monetary system before entering school. Some confusion is possible when children or adults first encounter our system of coins. Shel Silverstein's poem, shown in Fig. 5.24, provides a humorous reminder of this confusion.

A few children may prefer a shiny nickel over a dull old quarter, but we hope that most will prefer the new golden dollar to any other coin. Even with our variety of size and value in coins, it can be seen that our monetary system is an application of Base 10: penny (10^0), dime (10^1), dollar (10^2) ten dollar (10^3), hundred dollar (10^4).

Your Turn

36. List as many different ways as you can think of to use U.S. coins to make a dollar.

37. How much change should you receive if you have a $10 bill and the amount you must pay is $4.15? How many different ways might you receive the change?

Smart
Shel Silverstein

My dad gave me one dollar bill
'cause I'm his smartest son,
    and I swapped it for two shiny quarters
'cause two is more than one!

And then I took the quarters
and traded them to Lou
    for three dimes-I guess he don't know
that three is more than two!

Just then, along came old blind Bates
and just 'cause he can't see
he gave me four nickels for my three dimes,
and four is more than three!

And I took the nickels to Hiram Coombs
down at the seed-feed store,
and the fool gave me five pennies for them
and five is more than four!

And then I went and showed my dad,
and he got red in the cheeks
and closed his eyes and shook his head-
too proud of me to speak!

FIG. 5.24. From "Where the Sidewalk Ends" (p. 35) by S. Silverstein, 1974, San Francisco: Evil Eye Music, Inc.

(Please remember that 585 pennies might not be reasonable, but is possible.)

Temperature

We know when it is too warm or too chilly. There are two commonly used scales to help us describe temperature. The Fahrenheit scale is probably the one with which you are most familiar, but the other is the Celsius scale. Another scale, often used by scientists, is called Kelvin. Anders Celsius, the Swedish astronomer, suggested using a Base 10 scale comparing two common fixed points, the melting point of thawing snow and the boiling point of water. He wanted to use 100° for the freezing point and 0° for the boiling point. His scale, turned upside down, is what we use today, and the scale is named after him.

Figure 5.25 shows the two scales side by side, with the boiling and freezing points lined up. There are formulas for converting between Fahrenheit and Celsius, but many thermometers have both scales. Although using the conversion formulas is good practice for algebra, you may want to just read the scale you need and skip the conversion.

Your Turn

38. Using Fig. 5.25, find the boiling point and the freezing point of water at sea level in degrees Fahrenheit and degrees Celsius.
39. Using Fig. 5.25, determine the comfort range for humans in degrees Fahrenheit and degrees Celsius.

Angle Measure

About 2000 years ago, the astronomer Claudius Ptolemy divided a full rotation into 360 equal parts, which we now call degrees. The protractors you have used represent only half a rotation and therefore

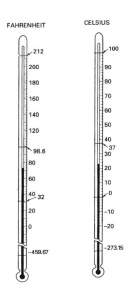

FIG. 5.25.

indicate 180°, which is sufficient for beginning geometry. Later in the study of mathematics, there are discussions of angles with degree measures greater than 180° and two other units of measure for rotation are introduced, radians and gradients. As with any measurement concepts, the units are part of our answer. When we say that an angle measures 45°, we are using denominate numbers in a practical way.

To use a protractor, such as the one represented in Fig. 5.26, place the origin

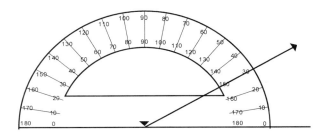

FIG. 5.26.

of the protractor (the point of the wedge in the very center on the straight edge) on the vertex of the angle, lining up one leg of the angle with the straight edge of the protractor. The other leg of the angle indicates the number of degrees of rotation

the angle represents. The angle superimposed on the protractor in Fig. 5.26 measures 30°. Most protractors have 10° between each number so that we can measure angles to within 1°.

Can you name the angle that occurs most often in our daily lives? Can you express the same concept two more ways? We are intrigued when we see a corner that is not a right angle. Carpenters use an instrument called a square to verify right angles and we can express the same concept by using the terms perpendicular and 90°. The definitions of acute and obtuse depend on our knowledge of right angles. A common error is to read the wrong scale when using a protractor. To overcome this tendency, always decide whether an angle appears to be acute, right, obtuse, or straight before you measure. The angle in Fig. 5.26 appears to be an acute angle, but the ray goes through two rules, 150° as well as 30°, and we must make a decision about which scale to use. In this case, a measure of 150° does not make sense for our acute angle. Notice that the correct scale is the one that counts up as we follow the rotation from the first leg, at 0°, toward the second leg, at 30°.

Your Turn

40. How many degrees are in one full rotation?

41. Do the lengths of the legs of an angle have any meaning in degree measure?

42. Is there a special name for an angle of 180°?

43. Identify each named angle in Fig. 5.27 as less than, exactly, or greater than 90°, then measure the angles using a protractor.

Angles are created if two lines, rays, or segments intersect. An application of an-

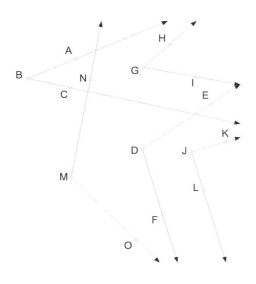

FIG. 5.27.

gle measure occurs when parallel lines are cut by a transversal (a line in the same plane as the parallel lines that intersects each of the lines). Figure 5.28 shows that

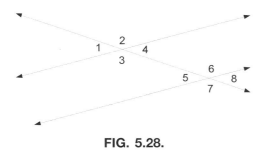

FIG. 5.28.

eight angles are formed when a transversal cuts through two parallel lines. You can determine the measure of each of those eight angles after making only one measurement. Suppose you measure Angle 1 and find that it is 35°, then Angles 4, 5, and 8 also measure 35°. Angles 1 and 4 are formed by the same pair of lines, share a vertex, and are directly opposite one another across that vertex—they are called *vertical angles* and they have the same measure. Angles 1 and 5 have the same orientation, each is above one of the parallel lines and has the transversal as the second leg—they are called *corre-*

sponding angles and they have the same measure. That accounts for four of the eight angles. For the other four, notice that Angles 1 and 2 are supplementary, if Angle 1 measures 35°, then Angle 2 must measure 145° (recall that the measures of supplementary angles add up to 180°). If Angle 2 measures 145°, so do Angles 3, 6, and 7. There you are! Eight angle measures determined by measuring only one.

Another application of angle measure occurs when we examine the interior angles of polygons. There are several ways to demonstrate that the three interior angle measures in any triangle total 180°. You might use your protractor to measure and total the interior angles of many, many triangles. You might cut out many, many triangles and tear off the vertices of each, lining them up to form a straight angle as shown in Fig. 5.29. A quick and

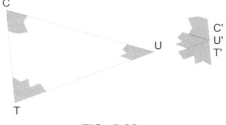

FIG. 5.29.

convincing demonstration is to use dynamic geometry software such as Geometer's Sketchpad®.

The sum of the measures of the interior angles of any polygon can be determined by sectioning the polygon into triangles, as was done in Fig. 5.12. The measures of the interior angles of each triangle total 180°, thus you only need to know how many triangles are involved. For the pentagon in Fig. 5.12, the sum of the measures of the interior angles is $3 \times 180 = 540°$, whereas for the parallelogram in Fig. 5.9, the sum of the measure of the interior angles is $2 \times 180 = 360°$.

Your Turn

44. Given that Angle 1 measures 48°, Angle 10 measures 90°, Angle 20 measures 115°, and Line m is parallel to Line n, use your knowledge of perpendicular lines, parallel lines, supplementary angles, complementary angles, and triangles to determine the measure of each angle in Fig. 5.30.

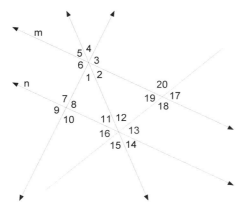

FIG. 5.30.

Pythagoras is credited with discovering a special relation among the sides of right triangles. The Pythagorean Theorem is an application of the concept of perpendicular lines or segments. The Pythagorean Theorem says that the sum of the squares of the measures of the two legs of a triangle is equal to the square of the measure of the hypotenuse if and only if the triangle is a right triangle. This means that we can apply the Pythagorean Theorem to any right triangle. It also means any triangle with measures that satisfy the Pythagorean Theorem is a right triangle. Fig. 5.31 shows one way of understanding the theorem. It also shows the geometric model of a number to the second power, because the squares on the three sides represent $a^2 + b^2 = c^2$. In a right triangle, the hypotenuse is the longest side and the square drawn using the hypotenuse as a side has the greatest area. Its area is equal

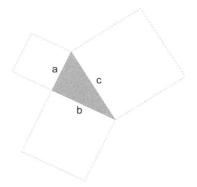

FIG. 5.31.

to the sum of the areas of the squares drawn using the two sides that are legs of the right angle. The implication of the theorem is that the length of the third side of a right triangle is determined as soon as the lengths of any two sides are known.

Pythagorean Triples represent a class of right triangles that have whole number measures for all three sides. A common Pythagorean Triple is 3-4-5, because $3^2 + 4^2 = 5^2$. In other words, this set of measures satisfies the Pythagorean Theorem, determining a right triangle. As shown in Fig. 5.32, any multiple of 3-4-5 determines another right triangle.

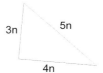

FIG. 5.32.

Your Turn

45. Find and confirm five more Pythagorean Triples.

For generations, students in algebra classes have been required to memorize the distance formula: $d\sqrt{(x_2 - x_1)^2 + (y_2 - y_1)^2}$. But did you think you would find it in the measurement chapter? Unless a teacher has helped you connect this formula to the Pythagorean Theorem, you probably are wondering if we are getting forgetful. Examine the individual parts of the formula and you will see the connection!

First, consider a triangle with legs that are 6 units and 3 units. Substituting these values into the Pythagorean Theorem will determine the length of the hypotenuse.

$$a^2 + b^2 = c^2$$
$$6^2 + 3^2 = c^2$$
$$36 + 9 = c^2$$
$$45 = c^2$$
$$\sqrt{45} = c^2$$
$$c \approx 6.7 \text{ units}$$

Now, place that same problem on a coordinate plane, as shown in Fig. 5.33,

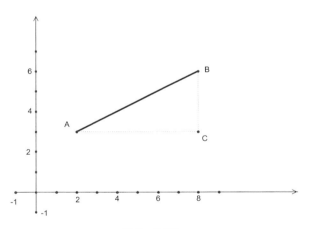

FIG. 5.33.

and the question might become, "What is the distance between (2, 3) and (8, 6)?" To use the distance formula, you still must begin by substituting values into the formula:

$$d = \sqrt{(x_2 - x_1)^2 + (y_2 - y_1)^2}$$
$$d = \sqrt{(8 - 2)^2 + (6 - 3)^2}$$
$$d = \sqrt{6^2 + 3^2}$$

$$d = \sqrt{36 + 9}$$
$$d = \sqrt{45}$$
$$d = 6.7 \text{ units}$$

Compare the last 4 lines using the Pythagorean Theorem with the last 4 lines using the distance formula. They look a little different, but the arithmetic is the same. The horizontal displacement, $(x_2 - x_1)$, is one leg of a right triangle and the vertical displacement, $(y_2 - y_1)$, is the other leg. The distance between the two given points is the hypotenuse of the right triangle. Use a couple of Pythagorean Triples from Exercise 45 to check your understanding of this connection.

Dimensional Analysis

Sometimes it isn't possible to measure using the units desired for reporting. In an experiment using a matchbox car and a ramp, it would not be reasonable to measure speed in miles per hour (mph) because neither the distance traveled nor the time period involved would be great enough. However, you can determine the average speed of the little car in mph by measuring the distance in feet and the time in seconds. Suppose you start the stopwatch when the car is released at the top of the ramp and find that it covers 14 feet of ramp in 0.2 seconds. Using dimensional analysis, you can figure out the average rate of change for your matchbox car in mph. The beauty of dimensional analysis is that it sounds so serious and you already have the skill you need to use it—it is a straightforward application of fraction multiplication and ratios. You will also need to know, or look up, unit comparisons in order to complete the procedure. You can find the length comparison needed for this example in Table 5.1 and you will need to remember that $\dfrac{60\,\text{sec}}{1\,\text{min}}$ and $\dfrac{60\,\text{min}}{1\,hr}$. We will show the matchbox car problem in two formats that are in common usage:

$$\frac{14\,\text{ft}}{0.2\,\text{sec}} \times \frac{1\,\text{mi}}{5280\,\text{ft}} \times \frac{60\,\text{sec}}{1\,\text{min}} \times \frac{60\,\text{min}}{1\,\text{hr}} = \frac{50400\,\text{mi}}{1056\,\text{hr}} = \frac{47.7\,\text{mi}}{1\,\text{hr}}$$

$$\frac{14\,\text{ft}}{0.2\,\text{sec}} \left|\; \frac{1\,\text{mi}}{5280\,\text{ft}} \;\right|\; \frac{60\,\text{sec}}{1\,\text{min}} \;\left|\; \frac{60\,\text{min}}{1\,\text{hr}} \right. = \frac{50400\,\text{mi}}{1056\,\text{hr}} = \frac{47.7\,\text{mi}}{1\,\text{hr}}$$

Your Turn

46. How do the two formats demonstrated compare? How do they differ?

47. How did the units go from feet per second in the first column to miles per hour in the last column?

48. If it is reported that a matchbox car had an average speed of 30 mph, how many feet did it travel in 1 second?

Conclusions

As you read this chapter, you may have felt that you were reading about history, science, arithmetic, geometry, algebra, or even trigonometry. The concepts of measurement are absolutely vital to our study in many areas of mathematics and science. Close your book for a moment and try to list all of the areas of life outside the classroom that are somehow impacted by the concepts of measurement. What are some of the roles that measurement plays in, for example: construction, medicine, commerce, manufacturing, accounting, computers, transportation, landscaping, real estate, art, music, cooking, parenting, entertainment, and taxes—or any other activities you listed? We hope that you will always think about measurement in terms of uses and never think of it as a stand-alone concept or skill.

6
Data Analysis and Probability

DATA COLLECTION AND REPRESENTATIONS

FOCAL POINTS

- Data and Where to Get It
- Representations of Data
- Venn Diagrams
- Percentages
- Circle Graph
- Line Plot
- Bar Graph
- Line Graph
- Histogram
- Frequency Polygon
- Box and Whisker Plot
- Scatter Plot
- Stem and Leaf Plot

As citizens of the 21st century, we live in a data rich world. It would be hard to find someone who has not heard of or, more likely, participated in at least some sort of opinion poll. Do you like this candidate or that one? Do you like this cola or that one? Do you like this restaurant or that one? On and on, we are inundated with questions, percentages, circle graphs, bar graphs, and a myriad of other data bits when we watch the news on television, listen to the radio, or even talk with friends. You do a course evaluation survey at the end of each class; you are asked for input about the course's usefulness, knowledge gained, and your instructor's presentation clarity, availability, and concern for you. The data center

people analyze the responses and provide a summary to your instructor, who then uses the information to improve the course for future students.

Data and Where to Get It

In order to perform any type of statistical analysis, you need data. Data collection provides the information to be analyzed so questions can be answered about some situation. Statisticians follow strict rules for the proper collection of data so final analyses and generalizations are valid. If data is collected or used improperly, then conclusions are not valid. For our purposes, we will discuss the attributes of random samples and convenience samples. Data are not only collected and used by statisticians for formal studies. For example, do you check the inventory of canned goods in your cupboards to make a shopping list before you leave for the grocery store? If so, you collect and analyze data! Is your inventory a random sample or a convenience sample? What is the proper use of your data?

If you wanted to know how many 45-year-old people in the United States responded to the 2000 U.S. Census, you would go to the Census and count how many people were 45 years old on that date. If we wanted to know how many people in the United States have green telephones in their kitchens, we would need to figure out another way to get the information. Random sample data collection is a powerful tool because it allows a representative sample of a population to be used to infer or generalize about the entire population.

Perhaps you are thinking to yourself, "So what?" or "Why is that important?" Two quick reasons are time and money. Only governments can afford to do a census of the entire population, especially one as large as that of the United States. A small random sample is both affordable and takes far less time than asking millions of people the same question. Furthermore, if the sample is taken properly, the results can be generalized or used to make predictions about the entire population. At times, you might be asked to consider your classmates as a population. You will see that collecting data from the entire class provides more robust information than just collecting a sample from this population. Collecting the sample will be faster and easier for you and will give you a feel for differentiating the ideas of sample versus Census.

Random samples require careful planning and design. The classroom data we suggest you use for this fundamental excursion into statistical analysis is not a random sample; any grouping of your classmates will represent a convenience sample. Convenience sampling can be used to explore fundamental ideas, but should not be used for generalization purposes. Data gathered from your classmates will be convenient and handy for our use, but we caution you to NOT generalize the data you collect from your classmates to other sections of students taking this course, other courses, or to your school as a whole. Because random sampling techniques are beyond our reach, there will be times when we will say, "Suppose these data WERE randomly collected, what inferences could you make about the popu-

lation?" It is important that you know the difference between randomly collected data and convenience samples.

The most data rich source in any classroom is the students! Heights, weights, birth months, birth dates, favorite colors, preferred games, or desirable foods all provide rich, meaningful, data. We recommend that you be particularly sensitive about the types of data you collect; some types of information may be too personal for comfort. Think about your current classmates, what kind of data will you be able to gather just by observation? What kind of data will not be available without communicating with individual classmates?

Your Turn

Collect the following convenience data, by observation only, from your classmates in this course, your classroom or building for this course, and from the environment in which you currently live:

1. Gather three types of data about your classmates, for example: How many of your classmates are wearing glasses? How many of your classmates are wearing shoes?
2. Gather three types of data about the room or building in which you are taking this class, for example: How many desks/tables are in the room? How many ceiling tiles are there?
3. Gather three types of data about the environment in which you currently live (dorm, house, apartment, etc.), for example: How many books? How many chairs?

Representations of Data

Statistical data can be represented in a variety of ways. Data appears in several formats. You can show a plethora of information in Venn diagrams. Look in your newspaper. You will see budget items relating to headline stories, car prices, store advertisements listing sales, discounts, bargains, and so on. But, it does not stop there. Go to the financial section and you will see charts, tables, line graphs, circle graphs, and bar charts. Check out the sports section. Box scores, batting averages, foul shooting percentages, good fishing locations, and more are there. Data! It is almost anywhere you look. You just need to learn to spot it.

Venn Diagrams

Raw data, or data that have been collected, but not analyzed, are seldom useful. Venn diagrams provide a handy method of organizing information so that analysis is possible. This brings up the idea of sets. Recall the information you studied earlier about the different types of properties that sets have and how they can be depicted in Venn diagrams. We will use some of those same ideas to enrich your understanding of statistics. Perhaps, when responding to the question for data about your classmates, you noted that 15 people wore glasses and 15 did not, 20 were female and 10 were male, and 30 people wore shoes. You could represent your data using a Venn diagram like the one in Fig. 6.1.

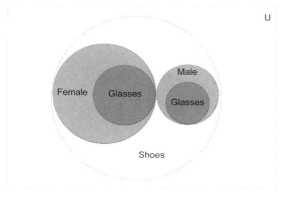

FIG. 6.1.

Percentages

Another way to represent data is to use proportional reasoning, such as percentages and circle graphs. In order to find the percent of information in each category of collected data, divide the number of observations of interest (people who wear glasses, gender, or footwear for this example) by the total number of subjects for this example. To convert the decimal number to a percentage, multiply by 100. We obtained the percentage in the top row of Table 6.1 by writing a ratio with 15 as the nu-

TABLE 6.1

Category	Observations	Percentage
Glasses: Yes	15	50%
Gender: Female	20	66.67%
Shoes: Yes	30	100%

merator (the number of people who wear glasses) and 30 as the denominator (the total number of people in the class). An equivalent form is $\frac{50}{100}$, which means 50 per 100, or 50%. For the second row, we used the data to write $\frac{20}{30} = \frac{66.\overline{6}}{100}$, or approximately 66.67%. For the third row, we did not find an equivalent fraction, because 100% of the people were observed wearing shoes. Organizing data in a table will be a helpful first step as we explore other ways of representing data.

Circle Graph

Figure 6.2 shows another way to represent our classmate data. Half of the circle graph is shaded to show that 50% of the classmates wear glasses. You can think about why we shaded half of the circle in at least two ways. We wrote a ratio,

50%
Wear Glasses

66.67%
Women

100%
Wear Shoes

FIG. 6.2.

$\dfrac{15 \text{ glasses wearers}}{30 \text{ classmates}}$, and used the equivalent ratio, $\dfrac{50 \text{ glasses wearers}}{100 \text{ classmates}}$, which is 50 per 100, or 50%. If you think of the ratio as a fraction and remove the common factors, we have $\dfrac{1}{2}$, exactly the part of the circle we shaded. Another way to think about 50% is to use its decimal equivalent, $\dfrac{15}{30} = 0.50$, and again exactly half the circle is shaded.

Line Plot

A line plot is often used to efficiently represent data. We will use a set of data to answer the question, "How many keys do you have with you today?" The following data set, ranging from 1 key to 8 keys, was obtained from a convenience sample of 30 people:

1	3	5	7	1
2	2	2	3	3
3	5	5	6	3
5	2	2	4	4
8	3	2	2	7
2	2	3	3	4

To represent this data using a line plot, a horizontal line is marked in even steps from 0 to 10, as shown in Fig. 6.3. Then each data point (the number of keys reported) is plotted using an "x" or other mark (e.g., balloons, stars, diamonds) to represent each time a number of keys oc-

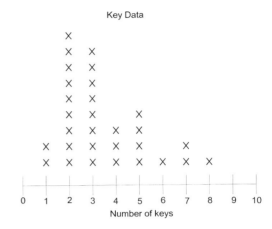

FIG. 6.3.

curs. The resultant plot allows us to see summary information about the data easily. What number of keys occurs most often? What number occurs least often? Did anyone in our sample have no keys?

Bar Graph

What if we extended our key survey to several groups of people? A line plot would not be very convenient if the sample included a hundred or more people. A bar graph is similar to a line plot and is much more practical for large data sets (more than 40 data points). Instead of counting the number of data points in each column as in the line plot, you read the total for each column using the scale provided in the bar graph. In Fig. 6.4, nine

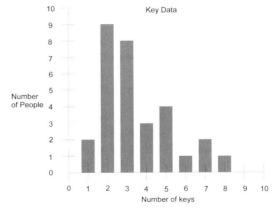

FIG. 6.4.

people carry two keys, whereas only one person carries six keys.

Occasionally, bar graphs are constructed with horizontal bars instead of vertical ones. Rotate your book so that Fig. 6.4 is turned 90° counterclockwise to see how a horizontal bar graph might look. The figure's text would need to be reoriented if we decided to actually make Fig. 6.4 into a horizontal bar graph. Additionally, we could elect to have the bars extend to the right instead of the left.

Your Turn

Use a tally technique to collect the following data about you, your classmates, and your professor: wear eyeglasses, gender, wear shoes, have cats or dogs, number of keys. Condense your data into a table similar to Table 6.1:

4. Using proportional reasoning, what percentage of the people in your class: wear glasses; are male; wear shoes; have cats; have dogs; have 3 keys?

5. Construct circle graphs to represent the data you collected about eyeglasses, shoes, and pets.

6. Construct a line graph to represent the number of keys each person in the class reported.

7. Construct a bar graph to represent the number of keys each person in the class reported.

Line Graph

A line graph is constructed using the same axis system as a bar graph, a horizontal and a vertical axis. Look at the bar graph used for the key data collected in Fig. 6.4. We will construct a new graph by placing a point at the top middle of each bar. After marking these points, connect them with dashed line segments in order from left to right as seen in Fig. 6.5.

When our data represents discrete rather than continuous information, we connect the data points with dashed line segments. Discrete data includes only information that is counted with whole numbers. Think of a digital clock. It flips minute to minute (assuming the absence of a second display), not showing any point along the continuum between minutes. An analog clock models continuous data, be-

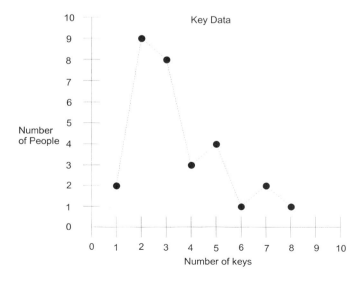

FIG. 6.5.

cause the minute hand sweeps from minute to minute, passing through every point on the continuum. We use solid line segments when the graph contains continuous information. A line graph provides a good feel for when data has a sharp turn upward or downward. For this reason, it is frequently used to show economic outcomes and forecasts for stocks and bonds, where anticipating dramatic ups and downs is important. Because you are probably not in this course to become a stock analyst, you will most likely use this information in your future career to graph student test results and behavior data.

Histogram

One popular way to represent statistical data is by using a histogram, which is similar to a bar graph. For the histogram, one axis shows range, class, or category and the other axis gives the frequency of each category. If you are thinking, "I could have made a histogram out of the classmate data by labeling all of the categories," then you are absolutely right! The data are graphed vertically and horizontally in histograms in Fig. 6.6.

Frequency Polygon

Just as the bar graph lead into a line graph, a histogram leads into a frequency

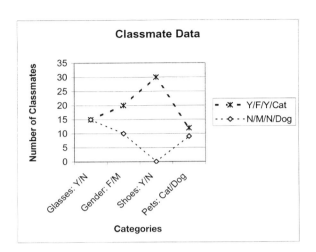

FIG. 6.7.

polygon. Figure 6.7 is a frequency polygon of the classmate data, which comes from the frequency table found in Table 6.2. Whereas this graph looks a bit like a

TABLE 6.2

Category	Y/F/Y/Cat	N/M/N/Dog
Glasses: Y/N	15	15
Gender: F/M	20	10
Shoes: Y/N	30	0
Pets: Cat/Dog	12	9

quadrilateral, an actual polygon, not many frequency polygons actually look like closed figures.

Consider how you go about creating a frequency polygon for the data about how many keys people report. You will need a

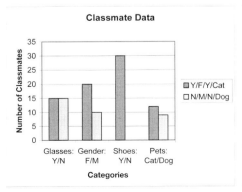

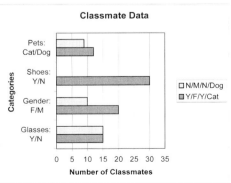

FIG. 6.6.

histogram as your basis. One way to simplify the task is to group the individual frequencies into equal ranges like 1–3, 4–6, 7–9. Notice that these ranges are distinct and do not overlap one another. It is important that no piece of data fit into more than one range of the histogram. Table 6.3 shows the frequency distribution for the key data tabulated according to the new ranges.

TABLE 6.3
Key Data

Class	Frequency
1–3	19
4–6	8
7–9	3

Figure 6.8 is a frequency polygon of the data in Table 6.3. It is a good representa-

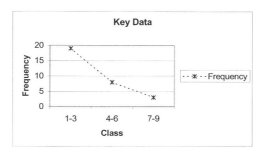

FIG. 6.8.

tion of how many keys a classmate is likely to have. You might have elected to use different ranges, such as 1–2, 3–4, 5–6, and 7–8 to create an equally effective frequency polygon. The frequency distribution for this set of ranges is shown in Table 6.4.

TABLE 6.4
Key Data

Class	Frequency
1–2	11
3–4	11
5–6	5
7–8	3

Your Turn

Use the tables of classmate data you created earlier:

8. Construct a line graph from the data you collected about how many keys your classmates had with them.

9. Construct a horizontal histogram for the data you collected about eyeglasses, gender, shoes, and pets.

10. Construct a frequency polygon for the data you collected about eyeglasses, gender, shoes, and pets.

11. Construct a table for your key data with equal classes and tabulate the frequency of each. From the table construct a frequency polygon for the key data. Compare and contrast the information in the frequency polygon and the line graph you made earlier. Which graph do you believe summarizes the data best, and why did you make that selection?

Box and Whisker Plot

A box and whisker plot is based on the range and quartiles of the data. The range of the data is plotted as the whisker, a line segment that begins at the lowest value and ends at the highest value in the data. A rectangular box is constructed on top of the whisker and spans the middle 50% of the data. The left side of the box is positioned at the value of the first quartile and the right side of the box is located at the third quartile. The second quartile, the median, or middle value is marked with a dot on the whisker and a line segment across the box. Figure 6.9 is the box and

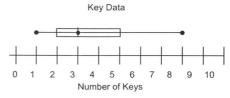

FIG. 6.9.

whisker plot of the key data. The data ranges from 1 key to 8 keys, with a median value of 3 keys. The middle 50% of the data is from 2 keys to 5 keys. We will discuss, in detail, how to obtain each of these points and give you a turn at constructing a box and whisker plot in the next section.

Scatter Plot

Suppose we want to investigate a relation between one type of data and another. For your classmates, is there a relation between the year their cars were manufactured and how many keys they report? Additional information is required, so you must re-poll the class and organize the data as shown in Table 6.5. You can't simply ask for the last two digits of their model year, because you can't match the model year with the key data for any individual.

Now that we have the data in an appropriate table, we can plot it using Car Year on a horizontal axis and Number of Keys on a vertical axis as shown in Fig. 6.10. Is

TABLE 6.5
Car Year Versus Keys Data

Classmate	Car Year	Keys
1	82	1
2	82	1
3	83	2
4	83	2
5	85	2
6	85	2
7	86	2
8	87	2
9	87	2
10	89	2
11	89	2
12	81	3
13	90	3
14	91	3
15	95	3
16	96	3
17	97	3
18	98	3
19	97	3
20	98	4
21	97	4
22	96	4
23	95	5
24	96	5
25	97	5
26	95	5
27	99	6
28	99	7
29	98	7
30	99	8

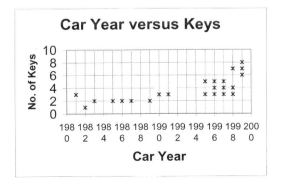

FIG. 6.10.

there a relation between someone's car model year and the number of keys they carry? If you said to yourself, "According to the scatter plot, it seems the newer the car a person has the more keys they will carry," give yourself a pat on the back! Way to go!

You might suspect that the data was purposely contrived to support that conclusion. A trend where both values increase is a positive relation. How would the scatter plot look if students carried fewer keys as they obtained newer cars? A trend where one value increases while the other decreases is a negative relation. How would the scatter plot look if there were no relation between the age of a student's car and the number of keys carried? Work with a partner or group to figure out how these two plots might look. Chances are you will be asked to create such a plot when it is your turn.

Stem and Leaf Plot

Stem and leaf plots are similar to line plots, because you can reclaim all of the original data points after organizing them. A stem and leaf plot is also handy as a first step in creating a box and whisker plot. A stem and leaf plot organizes data in two parts: a *stem*, which is one or more digits, and a *leaf*, which is always composed of single digits. It is necessary to include a key with this plot so that it can be interpreted properly.

One thousand rainbow-colored centimeter cubes were brought into the classroom. Each class member took one handful of centimeter cubes and counted them. The number of cubes they collected is shown in Table 6.6. The "Key 1|5 = 15" is used to interpret the plot. The stem represents digits in the tens place and the leaf represents digits in the units place. Because all of the centimeter cube data can be represented with two digits, this is sufficient. If the stem and leaf plot were about the altitudes of the Rocky Mountains, it would look the same. But the key would look like this: Key 1|5 =

15000, where the stem part represents digits in the ten thousands place and the leaf part symbolizes digits in the one thousands place.

A stem and leaf plot always starts with a decision about how many digits the stem will require. An examination of the rainbow centimeter cube data from Table 6.6 gives us the information. Which digits are needed in the stem? Why don't we need digits other than 2, 3, and 4 for the stem? For the leaf part of the plot, we list the units digit in the row with its respective tens digit, without comas between data points, as shown in Fig. 6.11. Why is there no need for punctuation to separate the data points?

The data in a stem and leaf plot are generally organized so that the leaf entries go from smallest to largest. The plot in Fig. 6.11 is called an unordered stem and leaf

TABLE 6.6
Cm Cube Data

Number of Cubes	Number of Cubes
40	25
20	41
31	20
23	32
25	25
40	39
24	26
37	30
27	28
40	32
27	22
21	22
31	38
28	42
35	29

Cm Cube Data

Stem	Leaf
4	0 2 1 0 0
3	0 1 2 2 1 5 8 7 9
2	2 5 7 0 3 2 5 0 8 4 1 5 7 6 8 9

Key 1|5 = 15

FIG. 6.11.

plot, an intermediate step often necessary for large data sets. After getting all the leaf digits into their correct row, order them to get the final stem and leaf plot as shown in Fig. 6.12. Although each class member's

Cm Cube Data

Stem	Leaf
4	0 0 0 1 2
3	0 1 1 2 2 5 7 8 9
2	0 0 1 2 2 3 4 5 5 5 6 7 7 8 8 9

Key 1|5 = 15

FIG. 6.12.

handful of centimeter cubes is shown in the stem and leaf plot, it isn't possible to reconstruct Table 6.6 because we didn't keep track of what count went where. In this hypothetical situation it is unimportant, but if your professor lost the grade book and were trying to recreate it from a stem and leaf plot, even though your grade is listed, your professor would have no idea what grade belongs to you!

Your Turn

Re-poll your classmates and keep track of the model year of each person's car along with how many keys they each have. Place the data into an appropriate table and do the exercises that follow:

12. Construct a scatter plot for your data using car year versus keys.

13. What, if any, relation do you see between the model years of your classmates' cars and the number of keys they had?

14. How would a scatter plot look if there were a positive relation between the model years of your classmates' cars and the number of keys they had?

15. How would a scatter plot look if there were a negative relation between the model years of your classmates' cars and the number of keys they had?

Conclusions

There are an unlimited number of data types that can be collected from your data rich classmates and classrooms. Nonetheless, you should not limit yourself to these convenience samples. If you have Internet access, then you can locate and analyze random samples from the National Education Longitudinal Study (NELS) database, Nielson television program ratings, or other Web sites. Although information found on the Internet should not be trusted

without regard to the source, even analyzing invalid information can be informative.

Although we had you plot or graph everything by hand in this section, technology may assist you. Most of the graphs and all of the tables in this section were made using Microsoft Excel®. When and where will you use technology in making graphs and tables. It is important to remember that even if you use technology for assignments, you may be asked to take tests without it.

Data can be represented in a wide variety of ways. Some data is better organized in a line plot or stem and leaf plot, whereas other material is better summarized using bar graphs, histograms, and so on. Sometimes the choice of representation is not clear and you will have to make judgments based on your experience and understanding. Welcome to the wonderful and robust world of statistics!

DATA ANALYSIS AND STATISTICS

FOCAL POINTS

- Measures of Central Tendency and Scatter

    Mean
    Median
    Mode
    Range
    Variance
    Standard deviation
    Quartiles
    Statistics
    Assumptions
    Generalizations

Collecting data and summarizing data with a variety of representation tools was fun, but the fun doesn't stop there! Now you need to analyze the data to make sense of it and draw some conclusions.

As you explore the measures of central tendency and scatter, it is important that conclusions are supported by the data. We will discuss statistics, random samples, assumptions, and generalizability.

Measures of Central Tendency and Scatter

Measures of central tendency help us determine where the central part of the data is located. Statisticians recognize that under different circumstances, different measures of the central part of the data are more helpful or more meaningful than others. Sometimes the mean is the best measure of central tendency; other times it is the median or the mode. As you go through this section, think about the different measures and decide when each would be more beneficial than the other in a given situation.

The type of data we have can also influence which measure of central tendency is the most appropriate measure to be used. Data comes in a variety of forms. Some data is nominal or categorical, such as the color of each student's car in your class or the different types of candy collected in a bag of Halloween treats. Other types of data are seen as being ordinal in nature. Ordinal data is data that can be placed into a logical order like low, medium, and high or infant, toddler, child, teenager, adult. The last type of data we routinely gather is interval ratio data. Interval ratio data is data that comes in the form of numbers, such as those associated with measurements of time, distance, area, or volume and test scores. With nominal data, we are limited to only finding the mode of the data, with ordinal data we can determine the mode and the median. Interval ratio data is the only type of data we are able to determine all three (mean, median, and mode) measures of central tendency.

Scatter is a term used to describe how the data points are spread out within the data set. One measure of scatter is the range; others are variance and standard deviation. Quartiles also give you a feel for how spread out the data is in a set. Just as with measures of central tendency, the data type determines whether or not measures of scatter are appropriate. Nominal data usually do not have measures of scatter, unless they are also ordinal. Ordinal data can have a range determined and quartiles, but not variance or standard deviations. Only interval ratio data meets the requirements for having all of the scatter values calculated. Understanding these concepts along with the measures of central tendency will help you better understand, analyze, and interpret statistical information.

Mean. Mathematics and statistics often define words differently from how they are used in everyday language. Before you can talk the talk of statistics, you must examine some everyday words that are defined differently in mathematics and statistics. The first is *mean*, which has nothing to do with kicking someone in the leg or providing meaning for an unclear communication. This is an instance where mathematics is like a foreign language and a new definition for an everyday word must be added to your vocabulary.

The mean is probably the most commonly used measure of central tendency. Many people are aware of the term and think of it as the arithmetic average of a group or set of numbers. For example, your grade may be the mean of your test scores; if there are five tests during a course, add your five scores and divide by five. A mean (μ) can be taken of an entire population, but is far too costly and time consuming in most instances, or a mean ($\bar{x}$) can be calculated from a sample. You will stick to finding $\bar{x}$ (read "x bar").

Students like to compare grades with the class average to get some sense of how they are doing in a course. Although it might be interesting to look at your classmates' grades while we explore this topic, confidentiality issues outweigh whatever benefit might be derived from such an exercise. Instead, we will take another look at the data gathered earlier when we asked how many keys people reported:

1	3	5	7	1
2	2	2	3	3
3	5	5	6	3
5	2	2	4	4
8	3	2	2	7
2	2	3	3	4

The key data here represents a sample of the number of keys students at the school possess. How do we calculate the mean number of keys? To calculate $\bar{x}$ for this sample, we find the sum of all of the data points and divide by the number of data points we added, $\bar{x} = \dfrac{x_1 + x_2 + x_3 + \ldots + x_n}{n}$. In the numerator, x_1 represents the first data point to be added, x_2 the second, and so on until the last term, x_n. The sum is divided by the number of terms, n. This can be stated more concisely using a summation symbol: $\bar{x} = \dfrac{\sum\limits_{i=1}^{n} x_i}{n}$, where the Σ means to add all the data points and x_i represents each value, starting with x_1 for the first and going on to x_n for the last.

If we read the data points from left to right across each row, then $x_1 = 1$; $x_2 = 3$; $x_3 = 5$; $\ldots$; $x_n = 4$; and $n = 30$. Using $\bar{x} = \dfrac{\sum\limits_{i=1}^{n} x_i}{n}$ we have:

$\bar{x} = \dfrac{104}{30}$, which is $3.4\overline{6}$ or ≈ 3.47

The mean number of keys is approximately 3.47. But we ask, does this answer make sense? We used the formula correctly, but can you have 3.47 keys? In the real world, you have three keys, or you have four keys. Do you think anyone carries 0.47 of a key?

Sometimes it makes sense to give decimal answers for weights or temperatures, but it does not when we are talking about keys, people, or any other discrete object. What does two thirds of a person look like? When we are calculating the mean for items that must be thought of in terms of whole numbers, it is appropriate and necessary to always round to the next whole number. This type of estimating is different from the regular rule for rounding, which you probably learned as round down if the decimal is less than 0.5 and round up if the decimal is 0.5 or more. The mean rounding rule says always round to the next whole number for discrete data, so that 3.1 rounds to 4 the same as 3.9 rounds to 4. That being said, what is the mean number of keys someone had in their pocket?

Median. The next measure of central tendency, median, also has a different meaning when we use it mathematically. Median does not describe the grassy part dividing a highway that you are routinely cautioned to keep off. Median, as a measure of central tendency, refers to the middle value after the data points have been put in order from highest to lowest or lowest to highest. Sometimes we call the median the *positional average*, because it is the data value located at the mean distance from one end of the data to the

$$\bar{x} = \dfrac{1+3+5+7+1+2+2+2+3+3+3+5+5+6+3+5+2+2+4+4+8+3+2+2+7+2+2+3+3+4}{30}$$

other. When you have an odd number of terms, the median is the data point in the exact center of the ordered data. If there is an even number of data points, then the median is found by taking the average of the two middle terms in the ordered data.

One clever way of making sure that you get the correct median, after putting the numbers in order, is to slash out data points on each end, in pairs, working toward the center. If you are careful when ordering the data and slashing out terms, then this method gets you what you are looking for every time. Consider the following data about keys reported by people in two different sample groups: Group A: 1, 2, 3, 1, 2, 1, 2, 3, 5, 7, 8, 5, 8, 7, 4, 4, 5, 8, 9 and Group B: 1, 2, 3, 1, 2, 1, 2, 3, 5, 7, 8, 5, 8, 7, 4, 4, 5, 8, 9, 9. Using this method you can find the median for Group A:

Group A: 1, 2, 3, 1, 2, 1, 2, 3, 5, 7, 8, 5, 8, 7, 4, 4, 5, 8, 9

1 1 1 2 2 2 3 3 4 4 4 5 5 5 7 7 8 8 8 9	First put the terms in order
X 1 1 2 2 2 3 3 4 4 4 5 5 5 7 7 8 8 8 X	Cross out both end terms
X X 1 2 2 2 3 3 4 4 4 5 5 5 7 7 8 8 X X	Cross out the next inner terms
X X X 2 2 2 3 3 4 4 4 5 5 5 7 7 8 X X X	Cross out the next
X X X X 2 2 3 3 4 4 4 5 5 5 7 7 X X X X	And so on . . .
X X X X X 2 3 3 4 4 4 5 5 5 7 X X X X X	
X X X X X X 3 3 4 4 4 5 5 5 X X X X X X	
X X X X X X X 3 4 4 4 5 5 X X X X X X X	
X X X X X X X X 4 4 4 5 X X X X X X X X	
X X X X X X X X X 4 4 X X X X X X X X X	Only the median, 4, is left

The median for Group A is 4 keys. Typically, when using this procedure, only one the last row would be visible. This model was created to show the work that was done, starting from the top and working down.

When finding the median for Group B, there are two terms in the middle of the ordered data. The mean of these two terms is the median for Group B. The last step would look like this:

X X X X X X X X X 4 5 X X X X X X X X X

$$\frac{4+5}{2} = \frac{9}{2} = 4.5$$

The median for Group B is 4.5. Notice that 4.5 is not a value listed in the original data and that you will need to apply the rounding scheme to conclude that the median for Group B is 5 keys. The median will not always be equivalent to a data point, it just happened to be true this time.

The median is not affected by extreme values the way the mean is and often provides a more useful measure of the central tendency of the data. The mean for the data in Group A is 4.47 or 5 keys and the mean for Group B is 4.70 or 5 keys. If you replace the last 9 in each group with 1000, the medians will remain the same, but the means will shift dramatically to 56.63 or 57 keys and 54.25 or 55 keys, respectively. Similarly, one really expensive home in a neighborhood can skew or shift the mean value, whereas the median value for a home in a neighborhood remains constant. This is something you should think about when you are shopping for a house. Ask for the median price of homes in a neighborhood, not just the mean or average price.

Mode. Mode is not a mode of transportation—or "a la mode," the ice cream for your desert—when we are speaking mathematically. Mode is another measure of central tendency. Mode refers to data that appear most often in the set. A data set has exactly one mean and one median. But, there may be zero, one, two (bimodal), or more modes in any given set of data.

There are several ways to find the mode. Which column has the most data points in Fig. 6.3? Which bar in Fig. 6.4 represents the most data points? Which peak in Fig. 6.5 represents the most data points? Two keys? Then two keys is the mode for that key data. Which leaf entry occurs most often in Fig. 6.12? The centimeter cube data has two modes, 25 cubes and 40 cubes; it is a bimodal data set.

Consider the data we used to find the medians for Groups A and B. There are four modes present in each data set. The one, two, five, and eight occur three times each, making them the modes for the data sets. Modes come in handy when you need information that might be obscured by the mean or median. Suppose you surveyed the students at your school to find the location of the best tasting pizza. Which measure of central tendency should you use to decide which pizza is the best? Do you want to eat at the mean, the median, or the mode restaurant in town? You can meet me at the mode because that is where the most people go and that indicates it is the best!

Range. The range is the most common measure of dispersion, rather than central tendency. The range measures how the data is spread and is calculated by subtracting the smallest data point from the largest data point. Unfortunately, like the mean, it is adversely affected, or skewed, by extreme values. Going back to the Group A data, the largest value is 9 and the smallest is 1, and the range is $9 - 1 = 8$. In our discussion about median, we introduced the idea of changing the last 9 in the data set to 1000. If we do that, the range is $1000 - 1$, or 999, which shows how one extreme value can significantly affect this measure of dispersion.

Your Turn

1. Find the mean, median, mode, and range of the key data you collected from your classmates.
2. Find the mean, median, mode, and range of the rainbow centimeter cube data.

Variance. Variance is a much better measure of spread or dispersion for a set of data, because variance is not affected as strongly as the range by extreme values. We will be asking you to find the sample variance (s^2) rather than the population variance (σ^2). We talked earlier about how only governments and large corporations have the money necessary to collect data on entire populations. Although you will not be asked to compute or work with the population variance (σ^2), we want to remind you that it is different from the sample variance (s^2). You will not generally find the variance mentioned in statistical reports, but it is an important intermediate step in finding the standard deviation.

To find the variance for a given set of data, first determine the mean of the data. Look at the key data reported by students in Group C: 1, 2, 3, 1, 2, 1, 2, 3, 5, 7, where $\bar{x} = 2.7$ or 3 keys. For the purposes of calculating the variance, we need to use the mean as calculated, even though no one had 0.7 of a key. The variance is based on the actual arithmetic mean, not the practical mean, so we must use $\bar{x} = 2.7$ to calculate variance.

One of the best ways to manage the calculations needed to find variance is to organize the data in a spreadsheet, either by hand, using a calculator, or computer application. Subtract the mean from each data point as shown in Table 6.7. Notice that the sum of all the $x_i - \bar{x}$ values is zero, because $\bar{x}$ represents the arithmetic average. This implies a need to do something else to the information in the $x_i - \bar{x}$ column in order to obtain meaningful information. This is accomplished by squaring each value in the $x_i - \bar{x}$ column before finding the sum.

For small data sets like Group C, the calculations are not too troublesome to do by hand; calculate each of the $(x_i - \bar{x})^2$ values for Table 6.7 and compare your results with Table 6.8. Next sum all of the $(x_i - \bar{x})^2$ values. The final step, which is also shown in Table 6.8, is to divide the

TABLE 6.7
Computing Variance

Keys	$x_i - \bar{x}$
1	−1.7
2	−0.7
3	0.3
1	−1.7
2	−0.7
1	−1.7
2	−0.7
3	0.3
5	2.3
7	4.3
Sum = 27	0
Mean = 2.7	

TABLE 6.8
Computing Variance

Keys	$x_i - \bar{x}$	$(x_i - \bar{x})^2$
1	−1.7	2.89
2	−0.7	0.49
3	0.3	0.09
1	−1.7	2.89
2	−0.7	0.49
1	−1.7	2.89
2	−0.7	0.49
3	0.3	0.09
5	2.3	5.29
7	4.3	18.49
Sum = 27	0	34.1
Mean = 2.7	Variance =	3.41

sum in the $(x_i - \bar{x})^2$ column by the number of data points, 10 for this data set, yielding a variance of 3.41, or $s^2 = 3.41$. A commonly used formula for this calcula-

tion is: $s^2 = \dfrac{\sum\limits_{i=1}^{n}(x_i - \bar{x})^2}{n}$, which is exactly

what is shown in Table 6.8. Now that we know the variance of the data for Group C, you might be asking, "Isn't there an easier way of getting this answer?" There is another way, but it is up to you to decide which you think is easier.

The second way of calculating the variance is one you might have discovered for yourself after doing many of these cal-

culations by hand. First find the mean of the data as before. Then square each of the data points, and add those squares, as shown in Table 6.9. Next, multiply the square of the mean by the number of data points which, for this example, would be $10(2.7)^2$. Subtract this product (72.9) from the sum of the squares (107) and divide the difference by the number of data points (10). What did you get? This for-

mula is: $s^2 = \dfrac{\sum\limits_{i=1}^{n} x_i^2 - n\bar{x}^2}{n}$.

TABLE 6.9
Alternate Method for Computing Variance

Keys	x_i^2
1	1
2	4
3	9
1	1
2	4
1	1
2	4
3	9
5	25
7	49
Sum = 27	107
Mean = 2.7	
$\bar{x}^2$ 7.29	
$n\bar{x}^2$ 72.9	
variance 3.41	

Standard Deviation. Standard deviation is directly related to variance. The standard deviation for the population (σ) is calculated in the same way as for a sample (s). Comparing the symbols for variance of a sample (s^2) and standard deviation of a sample (s) should make you sigh with relief. Finding the standard deviation from the variance is not much work. We calculated the variance for Group C to be 3.41. The standard deviation for Group C is the square root of 3.41 or s = 1.85. The formula we use for standard deviation is $s = \sqrt{s^2}$. Combining this with the variance formula you prefer results in $s = \sqrt{\dfrac{\sum\limits_{i=1}^{n} (x_i - \bar{x})^2}{n}}$ or

$$s = \sqrt{\dfrac{\sum\limits_{i=1}^{n} x_i^2 - n\bar{x}^2}{n}}.$$

The standard deviation is an important measure of dispersion. As a matter of fact, we say that the mean and the standard deviation, together, are necessary and sufficient statistics to describe or summarize an entire data set. This is true because, in Fig. 6.13 you can see that 68% of the data in a set are within plus or minus one standard deviation (±1s) from the mean; approximately 95% of the data are within plus or minus two standard deviations (±2s) from the mean; and nearly 100% of all data in a set are contained within plus or minus 3 standard deviations (±3s) of the mean. Figure 6.13 is

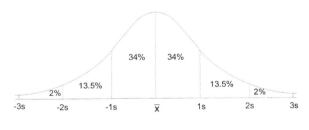

FIG. 6.13.

known as a normal curve. When a random set of data is normally distributed, you can make assumptions and predictions.

A data point falling outside two standard deviations ($\bar{x} \pm 2s$) is considered to be an outlier or an unexpected input. When we were discussing the median values and ranges for Groups A and B, we purposely introduced an outlier, 1000 keys, to show what affect an outlier can have on the mean and the range while not affecting the median or mode. Sometimes it is easy to recognize an outlier. In our example, 1000 keys is a pretty extreme data

point. However, if the data point is only one or two values outside the expected range, it may be difficult to spot. Look at the key data for Group C. How many of the data points are within one, two, or three standard deviations of the mean? Are there any outliers? Are any of the data points farther than 1.85, 3.70, or 5.55 from the mean of 2.7 keys?

Your Turn

Use the first 10 key data points reported by your classmates to answer the following:

3. Find the variance of the sample using both formulas. Calculate each by hand and then verify your results using a software application.
4. Find the standard deviation for this sample of your data.
5. Look back at your full data set for the key data. Are there any outliers based on the standard deviation of the sample?
6. Does this sample accurately represent the whole class? Why or why not?

Quartiles. Quartiles? What are quartiles and why do I have to know about them? You need to be comfortable with quartiles so you will be able to adequately and comfortably discuss standardized test scores. Quartiles are directly related to percentiles. So naturally the next question is, "What's a percentile? Is it like a percent?"

Percentiles should only be used when there is a very large data set, like scores from a whole state or at least scores from several school districts. You may have taken a standardized test on which you scored in the 85th percentile. Did you think that meant you made an 85% on the exam? Nope, you might have gotten 90% or 60% of the problems correct, but you did better than 85% of the other people who took the exam. Another way to think about it is that only 15% of the people taking the exam got more right answers than you did.

The 50th percentile is approximately equal to the median score. A box and whisker plot, such as the one in Fig. 6.14, is often used when discussing the results of standardized tests. Remember, for the box and whisker plot we needed five things: the lowest score, the highest score, the second quartile (the median score), the first quartile (the median of the scores below the median), and the third quartile (the median of the scores above the median). If the median or second quartile is equivalent to the 50th percentile, then you might guess that the first quartile is the 25th percentile and the third quartile is the 75th percentile. This connection between percentiles and quartiles points out the usefulness of quartiles as well as box and whisker plots.

Data points falling outside of two standard deviations are considered outliers. But what if you only have a box and whisker plot? Aha! We can determine outliers by using the interquartile range (IQR). The IQR is found by subtracting the first quartile (Q_1) from the third quartile (Q_3) or $Q_3 - Q_1 = IQR$. The expected range is calculated by subtracting 1.5 times IQR from the first quartile, and adding 1.5 times IQR to the third quartile [$Q_1 - 1.5IQR$, $Q_3 + 1.5IQR$]. Any data point outside these values is considered an outlier. Figure 6.14 is the box and whisker plot developed for the key data.

Without peeking back, use Fig. 6.14 to determine what value represented the first quartile. What value represented the second quartile or median? What value represented the third quartile? You should have said 2 keys, 3 keys, and 5 keys, respectively. Using this information, $Q_1 = 2$ and $Q_3 = 5$, the IQR is $5 - 2$ or 3. Because the product of the IQR and 1.5 is 4.5, $Q_1 - 1.5 (IQR) = -2.5$, and $Q_3 + 1.5 (IQR) = 9.5$ for the expected range. What were the fewest and most keys present according to the Fig. 6.14? The outliers would be outside the interval [-2.5, 9.5]. Did anyone have fewer or more keys than expected? The left side of the interval is a negative number; what meaning does this have for the data set? What is the fewest number of keys that would be considered an outlier?

Your Turn

Use your key data for the following problems:

7. Find the first, second, and third quartiles.
8. Find the IQR.
9. Create a box and whisker plot.
10. Determine the expected range using the IQR and identify any outliers.

Statistics

Statistics are based on samples from populations and if the samples are collected properly, they allow us to make generalizations about the entire population fairly accurately. Using samples is both a cost effective and efficient way of finding information about an entire population. When you make generalizations about the population, however, certain assumptions go along with this process.

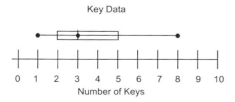

Key Data

Number of Keys

FIG. 6.14.

It is important for you to be aware of these assumptions and when it is and is not appropriate for generalizations to be made about a population.

Assumptions. Assumptions play an important role in the statistics you create, no matter what procedure you use. Nothing invalidates research and wastes more hard work faster than breaking a statistical assumption. If these assumptions are so critical, then why did we wait until now to talk about them? We needed to develop your statistical vocabulary to provide common ground on which to build. Assumptions must be verified or qualified for a given data set. The data representations you have been learning can be examined to determine whether assumptions are holding or failing.

Whereas it is beyond the scope of this course to talk about all the assumptions made in statistical analysis, some of them are critical to daily survival in a data rich society. When you find the mean, variance, and standard deviation for a given set of data you make some assumptions. First you assume that the data is interval ratio data or that the spaces between the numbers are fixed and the numbers have meaning. This meaning is not arbitrarily assigned, such as blue equals one, red equals two, but meaning that develops from the data collected, such as test scores or numbers of keys.

Second, you assume the data was derived from a random sample. Data collected in your classroom represents a convenience sample. To get a truly random sample of students is a rather complicated process. It is okay to use the data and make calculations based on nonrandom samples in order to learn the processes. It is not okay to break the assumption outright or ignore it for convenience sake when doing research.

The last assumption you make when calculating a mean, variance, and standard deviation is that the data is evenly or normally distributed and there are no extreme values or outliers falsely skewing or shifting the mean. Although we found no evidence of outliers in the key data, the box and whisker plot showed that the key data are skewed, indicating that the data are not normally distributed. Remember when we replaced the last 9 in the Groups A and B data with 1000? Certainly, that outlier had a profound impact on the mean value. Sometimes we are allowed to assume a data set is normally distributed if the data set is large enough. In general, a data set must have a minimum of 30 random data entries in order to be assumed normally distributed.

There are other assumptions in statistics, some of which seem quite obvious. For example we assume that every circle graph represents 100%. Not 99% or 101%, but exactly 100%. When you use a pie chart or circle graph in which the sector values total more or less than 100%, you violate the assumption for a circle graph.

Generalizations. Your classmate data was a convenience sample, as opposed to a random sample. The data is useful for learning procedures, but this violation of the second required assumption implies that we should not attempt to generalize the information to any population. All of the assumptions must be met in order to have any generalizability for a given set of data. Whereas most people in the sample we provided had two keys, we cannot say that most people, in general, carry two keys.

As you read and study research, it is important for you to be a critical thinker. Tainted generalizations, due to statistical assumption violations, will make the researcher look pretty silly. It may not be obvious during casual reading, but important assumptions are often ignored or deliberately broken in published articles, invalidating the conclusions drawn by the researchers or authors. We want you to recognize this fact, so that you can make decisions based only on reliable and sound data analysis.

Conclusions

You should understand that a statistic is a random sample of data that can be generalized to a population by looking at measures of central tendency and dispersion, as long as assumptions have not been violated. Some measures of central tendency and dispersion, like the mean and range, are adversely affected by extreme values. Values like median, mode, variance, and standard deviation are not as affected by outliers. Percentiles, quartiles, and medians are related to one another and are helpful in describing and interpreting data. Sometimes data is normally distributed and sometimes it is skewed. Recognizing these foundational concepts as you read data analyses will help you be a discriminating consumer of research.

COUNTING AND PROBABILITY

FOCAL POINTS

- Factorial
- Permutations
- Combinations
- Independent
- Dependent
- Conditional Probability
- Lottery
- Odds

Many people think that the words "probability" and "statistics" are synonymous. They are related, but they are also very different. Statistics are numerical data that has been tabulated and organized to provide reports or information. When we talk about probability, we discuss the outcomes of experiments and how those outcomes might be used to make predictions. This often involves counting how many different ways there are of combining events. Some fundamental ideas about independence or dependence of data will be presented. After we have explored this vocabulary and worked some problems, we will explore lotteries. You can decide for yourself if playing is a good idea.

Factorial

Factorials provide a convenient and short way to write products of several related factors. The mathematical notation used to indicate this operation is an exclamation point placed to the right and adjacent to a number, 5! is shorthand for writing $5 \cdot 4 \cdot 3 \cdot 2 \cdot 1 = 120$. We say that $n! = n(n-1)(n-2)(n-3) \ldots 3 \cdot 2 \cdot 1$. The easiest way to remember this is to think of a countdown and then multiply all the numbers together.

Many of the problems we do involve dividing a factorial by another factorial or two factorials. These can be done by hand or with a calculator; this is an instance where you are smarter than the calculator because you have the ability to do higher order thinking. The calculator does the exercise by finding 10!, then 7!, and then $3628800 \div 5040$. As you do some of these by hand, you will gain an understanding of what is happening. We begin this exploration by looking at $\dfrac{10!}{7!}$.

$$\frac{10!}{7!} = \frac{10 \cdot 9 \cdot 8 \cdot 7 \cdot 6 \cdot 5 \cdot 4 \cdot 3 \cdot 2 \cdot 1}{7 \cdot 6 \cdot 5 \cdot 4 \cdot 3 \cdot 2 \cdot 1}$$

1st Expand each factorial

$$\frac{10!}{7!} = \frac{10 \cdot 9 \cdot 8 \cdot \cancel{7} \cdot \cancel{6} \cdot \cancel{5} \cdot \cancel{4} \cdot \cancel{3} \cdot \cancel{2} \cdot \cancel{1}}{\cancel{7} \cdot \cancel{6} \cdot \cancel{5} \cdot \cancel{4} \cdot \cancel{3} \cdot \cancel{2} \cdot \cancel{1}}$$

$$\frac{10 \cdot 9 \cdot 8}{1} =$$

2nd Divide out common factors

$$10 \cdot 9 \cdot 8 = 720$$

3rd Find the product

$$\frac{10!}{7!} = 720$$

The computation of 10! ÷ 7! shows how you are smarter than a calculator. You can divide out common factors—the calculator cannot. This becomes significant when you encounter something like 500! ÷ 499! The calculator gives up, even some big fancy ones overload and quit. But, with the previous process, you can get the answer, 500, because all factors are common except the 500.

Next look at an exercise that has two factorials in the denominator: $\frac{10!}{4! \cdot 6!}$

$$\frac{10!}{4! \cdot 6!} = \frac{10 \cdot 9 \cdot 8 \cdot 7 \cdot 6 \cdot 5 \cdot 4 \cdot 3 \cdot 2 \cdot 1}{4 \cdot 3 \cdot 2 \cdot 1 \cdot 6 \cdot 5 \cdot 4 \cdot 3 \cdot 2 \cdot 1}$$

1st Expand each factorial

$$\frac{10 \cdot 9 \cdot 8 \cdot 7}{4 \cdot 3 \cdot 2 \cdot 1} =$$

2nd Divide out common factors

$$\frac{10 \cdot 3 \cdot 7}{1} =$$

$$10 \cdot 3 \cdot 7 = 210$$

3rd Find the product

$$\frac{10!}{4! \cdot 6!} = 210$$

There is one more example that will help you gain a good understanding of how this operation works. After the common fac-

tors in $\frac{13!}{9! \cdot 7!}$ are divided, the result will be a fraction instead of a whole number.

$$\frac{13!}{9! \cdot 7!} = \frac{13 \cdot 12 \cdot 11 \cdot 10 \cdot 9 \cdot 8 \cdot 7 \cdot 6 \cdot 5 \cdot 4 \cdot 3 \cdot 2 \cdot 1}{9 \cdot 8 \cdot 7 \cdot 6 \cdot 5 \cdot 4 \cdot 3 \cdot 2 \cdot 1 \cdot 7 \cdot 6 \cdot 5 \cdot 4 \cdot 3 \cdot 2 \cdot 1}$$

$$= \frac{13 \cdot 11}{7 \cdot 2 \cdot 3 \cdot 1}$$

$$= \frac{143}{42}$$

$$\frac{13!}{9! \cdot 7!} = \frac{143}{42}$$

A few more things about factorials before we move on. First, 0! = 1 by definition. Second, 1! = 1 because in 1!, 1 is the only factor. Third, for your work in this book, ⁻5! is written as ⁻1(5!) = ⁻1(5 · 4 · 3 · 2 · 1), then ⁻1(120) = ⁻120. As mentioned earlier, factorials get really big really fast and calculators are handy when dealing with them. Some calculators have a factorial key; for others, you have to enter the individual factors. Some calculators can handle 50! or even 150!, but it may take a while to come up with the number because it is so huge. Some calculators will express such huge results in scientific notation and may use front-end estimation. For example, 200! = 7.88658E374 or 7.89 × 10^{374} to two significant digits. Again, the exciting part is that you are smarter than your calculator!

What?! Yes! That is because you can do many problems that your calculator cannot! How can this be so? Revisit 500! divided by 499! or $\frac{500!}{499!}$. Examine what we are saying:

$$\frac{500!}{499!} = \frac{500 \cdot 499!}{499!}$$

$$= \frac{500}{1}$$

$$= 500$$

$$= \frac{500!}{499!} = 500$$

You don't have to write out all of the factors if you see a relation between the factors in the numerator and denominator. You can complete many outrageous problems by hand, or with the aid of your calculator after making a few adjustments. For $\frac{500!}{495!}$, think of 500! as $500 \cdot 499 \cdot 498 \cdot 497 \cdot 496 \cdot 495!$, because you can divide out the common factor of 495!. Then use your calculator to find $500 \cdot 499 \cdot 498 \cdot 497 \cdot 496 = 30629362512000$. All right!

Your Turn

Simplify each of the following by hand. Check your answers using a calculator or some other form of technology. It will be helpful to you if you become comfortable doing these types of problems using both methods.

1. $3!$
2. $8!$
3. $0!$
4. $\frac{12!}{6!}$
5. $\frac{7!}{5!}$
6. $\frac{11!}{4!}$
7. $\frac{9!}{3! \cdot 6!}$
8. $\frac{13!}{7! \cdot 5!}$
9. $\frac{15!}{9! \cdot 11!}$

Permutations

How many different ways can you order three colored blocks that are red (R), purple (P), and blue (B)? There are only three objects, so you can make a list to figure out all the different ways to order R, P, and B. Try it. You should get: RPB, RBP, PRB, PBR, BRP, and BPR. There are exactly six ways to arrange the three blocks. Add a green (G) block to the R, P, and B ones. Now how many arrangements? Wow! There are many more than six different ways to order four blocks. Isn't there an easier way to determine how many arrangements there are? Yes!

Finding the total number of different ways to order a given set of objects is called a *permutation*. The notation for this operation can be written in two different ways, $P(n, n)$ or $_nP_n$. Here comes the cool arithmetic to all of this. $P(n, n) = n!$, where n is the number of objects in the set to be arranged. So, instead of using trial and error, and a lot of time, to figure out how many different ways to order R, P, B, and G, just do the arithmetic: $P(4, 4) = 4! = 24$. There are 24 different ways to order R, P, B, and G blocks.

Of course, sometimes we only want to see how many different ways there are to rearrange part of a set at a time. How many different ways could 5 students be chosen from a class of 30 students? Our notation changes to $P(n, r)$, or $_nP_r$, where n is the total number of objects in the set and r is the number of things to be arranged. (Note that n is always at least as large as r.) You could say that you are looking for how many different ways to arrange n things taken r at a time. This formula involves a fraction: $P(n, r) = \frac{n!}{(n - r)!}$.

Speaking like a statistician, read, "The permutation of n choose r, is n factorial divided by n minus r the quantity factorial."

Suppose you want to know how many distinct ways you can order subgroups of 5 out of a total group of 30. You would be looking for $P(30, 5)$:

$$P(30, 5) = \frac{30!}{(30 - 5)!}$$
$$= \frac{30!}{25!}$$
$$= \frac{30 \cdot 29 \cdot 28 \cdot 27 \cdot 26 \cdot 25!}{25!}$$
$$= \frac{30 \cdot 29 \cdot 28 \cdot 27 \cdot 26}{1}$$
$$= 17100720$$
$$P(30, 5) = 17100720$$

Did you notice that this is the procedure you learned for division problems with factorials?

Combinations

When you looked for all the different ways to order the R, P, and B blocks, the order you placed them in was important. That is RPB was different from BPR. When you look at forming combinations, order is not important, because rearranging the pieces doesn't increase your count. The letters A through G are used to name musical notes, the seven major tones. For this exercise, define a chord as having three notes and CEG sounds exactly the same as GEC. How many different chords or combinations of three different notes can be formed (not taking into account that some will sound awful) using the seven major tones? We could try to find them all by trial and error as we initially did for finding permutations, but you should guess that there is a formula to help us with the arithmetic.

Combinations are expressed as $C(n, r)$ $= \dfrac{n!}{r!(n-r)!}$. Combinations are related to permutations. Multiplying this formula by r! returns you to the formula for permutations. This also indicates that there will be fewer combinations than permutations if we are using the same numbers. When working with combinations, n must be larger than r. To see why, try working through the formula when n = r. Did you get 1? Well, there is only one way to combine the entire set, all other arrangements are duplicates.

Back to our musical note problem, how many combinations of three notes out of seven notes are there?

$$C(7, 3) = \frac{7!}{3!(7-3)!}$$

$$= \frac{7!}{3! \cdot 4!}$$

$$C(7 \cdot 3) = 35$$

There are 35 different combinations of chords that can be made using the major tones A through G.

Your Turn

For each of the following problems:

a) Determine whether the problem requires a permutation or a combination for its solution.
b) Give your reasoning for choosing that function.
c) Find the solution to the problem.

10. Suppose the rainbow colors could come in any order. How many different patterns of colors of the rainbow (ROYGBIV) could there be?

11. A certain guitar has 12 strings. In how many different orders can a guitarist pluck any 5 strings on this guitar?

12. How many different pairs of colors can be made using colors of the rainbow (ROYGBIV)? (We understand that you would not wear or be seen in some of these combinations, but we do want you to consider and count them all.)

Independent

We are ready to discuss probability. We are a society of risk takers and the ideas of chance and the percent chance of being a winner or a loser permeates our culture. We say things like "fat chance," "sure thing," or "take a chance" on a regular basis. The weatherperson reports there is a slight chance of rain or a strong possibility of thunderstorms in the area. But how much do we really know about probability and what it really means?

All probabilities lie between zero and one inclusive. If something has no chance of occurring, or is impossible, then we say it has a probability of zero. If something will always happen, or if it must occur, then it has a probability of one. All of the other probabilities can be expressed as common or decimal fractions between zero and one. Another way to think about this is that all of the probabilities are between 0% and 100%, inclusive.

Okay, now we know a little bit about probabilities, but how do we figure out the probability that something will occur? We are going to take a look at experiments and their outcomes, and then figure out the probability of a particular outcome. We will assume that the possible outcomes are uniformly likely to occur. This may seem to be a fairly sophisticated statement and not all experiments have this quality, but for now it is enough to get your feet wet.

One popular experiment with equally likely outcomes is a fair coin toss, where the outcomes are either a head (H) or a tail (T). Each coin toss is independent (it does not rely on the result of any other coin toss). The set containing all of the possible outcomes is called the *sample space*. The sample space for a fair coin toss is {H, T}. The cardinality of this sample space is two. Because both outcomes are equally likely to occur, the probability of getting a head is one out of two, one half, 0.50, or 50%, and the probability of getting a tail is one out of two, one half, 0.50, or 50%. Notice that the sum of the outcomes is one, or 100%, as it always will be.

Another popular experiment is rolling a fair die. Each roll is independent of another roll and each face is equally likely to be on top. The sample space of the outcomes for rolling a fair die is {1, 2, 3, 4, 5, 6} and the probability of rolling a 1 is one out of six, one sixth, approximately 0.167, or approximately 16.7%. The probability of rolling either a 2, 3, 4, 5, or 6 is also one out of six. Notice that the fractions give exact answers, whereas the decimal equivalents and percents require rounding. If you like using decimal equivalents or percents, then you will have to use great care to be sure that the total of all the probabilities is 100%.

Another common experiment involves drawing a card from a fair standard deck of playing cards. A standard deck has four suits, hearts (H), diamonds (D), clubs (C), and spades (S), and 13 cards in each suit, ace (A), 2, 3, 4, 5, 6, 7, 8, 9, 10, jack (J), queen (Q), and king (K). Thus, the sample space could be written {AH, 2H, 3H, . . . , 10H, JH, QH, KH, AD, 2D, 3D, . . . , 10D, JD, QD, KD, AC, 2C, 3C, . . . , 10C, JC, QC, KC, AS, 2S, 3S, . . . , 10S, JS, QS, KS}. The sample space has 52 cards, with each card having $\frac{1}{52}$ chance of being selected. But what are the chances of drawing an ace (A) if you don't care about the suit?

In order to figure out this problem, we look back to the original sample space to find the sample space for a success. The sample space for a success is {AH, AD, AC, AS} and the cardinality of the success is four. To find the probability of a success, you divide the cardinality of a success (n) by the cardinality of the entire sample space (s) or $\frac{n}{s}$. The probability of drawing an ace, from a fair standard deck of playing cards is $P(A) = \frac{4}{52} = \frac{1}{13} \approx 0.077$.

In general, the probability of a success in any experiment is found by dividing the cardinality of the success of the event by the cardinality of the entire sample space or $P(n) = \dfrac{n}{s}$, where n represents a success, or the cardinality of a success sample space, and s represents the cardinality of the entire sample space. We can use that information to go back and explore some more complicated ideas about rolling a fair die. How do we determine the probability of rolling a single fair die where an event is a roll of less than 3?

$P(n < 3)$

$(n < 3) = \{1, 2\}$

$s = \{1, 2, 3, 4, 5, 6\}$

$P(n < 3) = \dfrac{2}{6}$

$P(n < 3) = \dfrac{1}{3}$

What happens if the success sample sets overlap? Finding the probability of drawing a king (K) or a heart (H) will require us to use some of the ideas about intersections of sets and unions of sets:

$P(K \cup H) = P(K \cup H) - P(K \cap H)$

$(K \cup H) - (K \cap H) =$

$\{KH,KD,KC,KS\} \cup \{AH,2H,3H, \ldots,$
$10H,JH,QH,KH\} - \{KH\} =$

$\{KH, KD,KC,KS,AH,2H,3H, \ldots,$
$10H,JH,QH\}$

$s = \{all\ 52\ cards\}$

$P(K\ or\ H) = \dfrac{16}{52} = \dfrac{4}{13} \approx 0.308$

What do you think would happen if our experiments had multiple parts? Instead of tossing a coin once, suppose we toss two coins once. What are all the possible

outcomes for the sample space? List them and see if you get four possible outcomes: {HH, HT, TH, TT}. Four is the cardinality for the sample space. If you tossed three fair coins, what is the sample space? Watch for a pattern so you can determine the cardinality of a sample set for tossing any given number of coins. The sample space for tossing three fair coins is {HHH, HHT, HTH, THH, HTT, THT, TTH, TTT}. What is the pattern? Can you fill in the question marks in Table 6.10? Generalize the pattern and deter-

TABLE 6.10

Number of Coins Tossed	Cardinality of the Sample Space	Pattern
1	2	2
2	4	2 × 2
3	8	?
. . .	. . .	. . .
n	?	?

mine the cardinality for the sample space for tossing six fair coins.

A tree diagram could be used to determine the cardinality of a sample space. A word of caution on tree diagrams—if your notation is sloppy or if you write very large, then you are likely to make errors using this method. Although a tree diagram becomes cumbersome if you flip more than three coins, many people favor this method for its ease of use. As long as you are careful, it will serve you well. Figure 6.15 shows how the tree diagram works. To determine the probability of a given outcome, multiply the probability of each toss along a direct path to the desired outcome. For example, to find the probability of HT, consider the tree diagram for tossing two coins; the path to the first H has a probability of 0.5 and the path to the T that follows (down and to the right of the H) has a probability of 0.5. Multiply 0.5 × 0.5 = 0.25, and there you have it, the probability

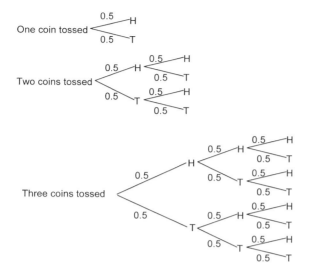

FIG. 6.15.

of tossing HT in a two-coin toss experiment is 0.25, or one fourth.

We now have a convenient rule. When the probabilities of individual outcomes are independent (one does not rely on another), multiply the respective probabilities together to get the final probability of a success. That may not sound like a very big deal, but mathematically and for ease of obtaining probabilities it is huge! Consider the following scenario and you will see. There are 10 marbles in a bag. Five of the marbles are red (R), 3 are Violet (V), and 2 are blue (B). The probability of drawing a R out of the bag is $P(R) = \frac{5}{10} = \frac{1}{2}$, or 0.5; the probability of drawing a V out of the bag is $P(V) = \frac{3}{10}$, or 0.3; and $P(B) = \frac{2}{10} = \frac{1}{5}$, or 0.2 is the probability of drawing a B. What is the probability of drawing RRVVB, in any order, as long as each time a marble is drawn it is placed back into the bag before the next marble is drawn? Because no draw depends on the results of another draw, the events are independent. P(RRVVB) = 0.5 × 0.5 × 0.3 × 0.3 × 0.2, or 0.0045. The probability of

drawing 2 red, 2 violet, and 1 blue, in any order, is 45 out of 10000. Doesn't seem very likely, does it?

A hidden idea we just explored with independence is randomness. When we flip a coin, roll a die, pick a card (with replacement), or draw a marble (with replacement), we do so at random. Randomness is a statistical assumption. As we are finding probabilities, it is assumed that the outcomes occur randomly. If a coin is tossed 10 times, resulting in four H and six T, does that mean the coin wasn't a fair coin? No, it means that, in order to approach the theoretical probability, P(H) = 0.5 and P(T) = 0.5, a large number of coin tosses, like 1000, or more, are needed. Even with 1000 tosses, there is no guarantee that you will get 500 H and 500 T. Theory and practice are not necessarily the same.

Your Turn

13. What is the cardinality of the sample space for each of the following?

a) an experiment tossing 5 coins
b) an experiment rolling 3 dice

14. What is the probability of obtaining the following outcomes from the experiments in Exercise 13?

a) HHTHT
b) 352

15. There are R = 3 marbles, O = 4 marbles, Y = 4 marbles, G = 2 marbles, B = 1, I = 3 marbles, and V = 3 marbles in a bag. What is the probability of drawing BORG from the given bag of rainbow marbles when there is replacement?

Dependent

We will explore one aspect of dependence using nonreplacement. Our focus will be on experiments such as drawing cards from a standard deck or drawing marbles from a bag without replacing the item before drawing again. When drawing without replacement, the total number of cards or marbles in the bag decreases with each draw. How does this affect the probabilities?

We start by exploring 10 marbles in a bag. Five of the marbles are red (R), 3 are violet (V), and 2 are blue (B). The probability of drawing a R out of the bag the first time is $P(R) = \frac{5}{10} = \frac{1}{2}$, or 0.5, the probability of drawing a V out of the bag the first time is $P(V) = \frac{3}{10}$, or 0.3, and the probability of drawing a B out of the bag the first time is $P(B) = \frac{2}{10} = \frac{1}{5}$, or 0.2. What is the probability of drawing RRVVB, in any order, when a marble is drawn it is not placed back into the bag? We are still going to multiply the probabilities of each individual outcome together, but this time we have to adjust the probability of each successive draw to reflect its dependence on the previous draw.

$P(R_1) = \frac{5}{10} = \frac{1}{2}$, just as before, but $P(R_2)$ $= \frac{4}{9}$ because now a red marble has been removed, changing the number of total marbles and the number of red marbles left in the bag. The probability of drawing a V is affected, so $P(V_1) = \frac{3}{8}$, which affects the next draw, so $P(V_2) = \frac{2}{7}$. Our last draw is a B, but now there are only 6 marbles left in the bag and 2 are blue, so $P(B) = \frac{2}{6} = \frac{1}{3}$. Now we have all the information we need and we multiply each probability together, $P(RRVVB) =$ $\frac{1}{2} \times \frac{4}{9} \times \frac{3}{8} \times \frac{2}{7} \times \frac{1}{3} = \frac{1}{126} \approx 0.0079$. With re-

placement, P(RRVVB) = 0.0045. With which method are you more likely to achieve a desired outcome? This is just something for you to ponder.

For a dependency example involving drawing three cards without replacement, $P_1(A \cup H) = \frac{16}{52} = \frac{4}{13} \approx 0.308$ for the first card drawn. For the second draw, $P_2(A \cup H) = \frac{16}{51}$ if no H or A was drawn and $P_2(A \cup H) = \frac{15}{51} = \frac{5}{17}$ if a H or A was pulled on the first draw. For the third draw, the pattern continues $P_3(A \cup H) = \frac{16}{50} = \frac{8}{25}$ if neither the first nor the second draw was a H or A, $P_3(A \cup H) = \frac{15}{15} = \frac{3}{10}$ if only one of the other draws was a H or A, and finally $P_3(A \cup H) = \frac{14}{50} = \frac{7}{25}$ if both the first and second draws were H or A. For the sake of simplicity, stick to the idea that each draw was H or A. Then $P(A \cup H)$ $= \frac{4}{13} \times \frac{5}{17} \times \frac{7}{25} = \frac{28}{1105} \approx 0.0253$. Card experiments get complicated when there is no replacement, but you now have the background to handle different cases.

What would the P(AH, AC, or 3H) be if cards were not replaced, assuming each draw was a success? $P_1(AH, AC, 3H) = \frac{3}{52}$, $P_2(AH, AC, 3H) = \frac{2}{51}$, and $P_3(AH, AC, 3H) = \frac{1}{50}$. Now P(AH, AC, 3H) = $\frac{3}{52} \times \frac{2}{51} \times \frac{1}{50} = \frac{6}{132600} = \frac{1}{22100} \approx 0.0000452$. Although the probability of drawing three cards, any ace or heart, without replacement is approximately 0.0253, the probability of drawing the AH, AC, or 3H in any order is much smaller. Things are not as likely to happen as you might think.

Your Turn

16. What is the probability of drawing BORG from the given bag of rainbow marbles when there is no replacement? There are R = 3 marbles, O = 4 marbles, Y = 4 marbles, G = 2 marbles, B = 1, I = 3 marbles, and V = 3 marbles in the bag.

17. What is the probability of drawing an AD through 10D, any J, or a 3S from a fair standard deck of 52 playing cards when there is no replacement and five cards are drawn? Consider that each draw was a success.

Conditional Probability

Sometimes we are given information or know things that influence how we calculate the outcome of an experiment. Having advanced information limits or refines the sample space. Suppose that there is a 20% probability of rain today. Given that it is already cloudy and thundering increases the probability that it is going to rain, compared with not having this information. Knowing some conditions prior to calculating the probability of an occurrence increases the probability of a success. When you are asked the probability of some event, given some information, it is written P(A|B), which is read "the probability of A given B."

We start with the sample space for a three-coin toss experiment: {HHH, HHT, HTH, THH, TTH, THT, HTT, TTT}. What is the probability of obtaining two heads and one tail, in any order? There are three such possibilities: HHT, HTH, THH, thus P(two heads and one tail) = 0.375. What is the probability of two heads and one tail, given the first toss was H? There are only two elements of the sample space that fit the criteria: HHT and HTH. Knowing that

the first toss was H eliminates any element for which H was not listed first. Then our new sample space is {HHH, HHT, HTH, HTT}. Thus, P(two heads and one tail|H first toss) = 0.5 for this conditional statement.

Your Turn

18. What is the probability of drawing a 10H card, given that a red card was drawn?

19. What is the probability of rolling a 2 on either of two dice, given that the sum of the dice is 7?

20. What is the probability of drawing a red K card, given that a black card was drawn?

Lottery

Suppose there is a lottery for which you pick 6 out of 55 numbers. This lottery involves 55 individually numbered, identically weighted, ping-pong balls in sealed bin. They mix the balls using compressed air and then capture 6 balls, one at a time. You win the lottery if you have picked, in any order, all 6 captured numbers. The lottery sponsor is only going to charge you a dollar for a chance to win. Such a deal!

Or is it?

$$P(\text{winner}) = \frac{1}{55} \times \frac{1}{54} \times \frac{1}{53} \times \frac{1}{52} \times \frac{1}{51} \times \frac{1}{50}$$

$$= \frac{1}{20872566000} \approx 0.000000000048.$$

Up until now we have only looked at the probability of a success, but this is as good a time as any to take a look at the likelihood of a failure. In this case,

$$P(\text{losing}) = \frac{54}{55} \times \frac{53}{54} \times \frac{52}{53} \times \frac{51}{52} \times \frac{50}{51} \times \frac{49}{50} = \frac{49}{55} \approx 0.891.$$

Hey, wait a minute, that is the probability of not getting a single one of the numbers. We shouldn't go wait in line just yet.

We need to explore this lottery probability a bit further. This particular lottery will also pay small amounts of money for three, four, or five numbers correctly picked. The probability of getting three numbers is

$$P(3 \text{ numbers}) = \frac{54}{55} \times \frac{53}{54} \times \frac{52}{53} \times \frac{1}{52} \times \frac{1}{51} \times \frac{1}{50}$$

$$= \frac{1}{140250} \approx 0.00000713.$$

The probability of getting four numbers is

$$P(4 \text{ numbers}) = \frac{54}{55} \times \frac{53}{54} \times \frac{1}{53} \times \frac{1}{52} \times \frac{1}{51} \times \frac{1}{50}$$

$$= \frac{1}{7293000} \approx 0.000000137.$$

The probability of getting five numbers is

$$P(5 \text{ numbers}) = \frac{54}{55} \times \frac{1}{54} \times \frac{1}{53} \times \frac{1}{52} \times \frac{1}{51} \times \frac{1}{50}$$

$$= \frac{1}{386529000} \approx 0.00000000259.$$

The probability of not winning any of smaller prizes is calculated by subtracting the probability of winning from one. So the probability of not getting any money at all for any lottery ticket is the complement of getting three numbers or

$$P(3 \text{ numbers})' = 1 - \frac{1}{140250} = \frac{140249}{140250}$$

$$\approx 0.99999287.$$

We will let you figure out the likelihood of losing for the other amounts. We will also let you decide if you want to wait in line for a lottery ticket.

Odds

What are the odds that we would wait until the end to discuss odds? Asking about the odds of something occurring is fairly common in our culture. The thing to remember is that, although probability and odds are related, they are not equivalent. This is be-cause the odds in favor of something occurring is $\frac{m}{m'}$, where m equals the cardinality of a success and m′ is the complement of m or the cardinality of a failure. In other words, m + m′ = n, where n is the cardinality of the sample space. The probability of a favorable odds ratio is found by $\frac{m}{m+m'} = \frac{m}{n}$. The odds against something occurring are $\frac{m}{m'}$ and the probability of the odds against something happening is $\frac{m'}{m+m'} = \frac{m'}{n}$. One important difference between odds and probability is that the odds ratio can be larger than one, whereas the probability ratio is always between zero and one, inclusive.

What are the odds in favor of rolling a five using a fair die? We know the probability is $\frac{1}{6}$. We know that a fair die has only one face with five dots, so m = 1. The complement of m is m′, which can be found by subtracting m from the cardinality of the sample space. Here n = 6, so m′ = n − m or m′ = 6 − 1 = 5. Thus, the odds in favor of rolling a five using a fair die are 1:5. The odds against rolling a five are 5:1. You notice we use different notation here. We include this to help you become comfortable with seeing different notation. The probability of the odds for rolling a five is $\frac{m}{m+m'} = \frac{1}{1+5}$, or 1:6, and the probability of the odds against rolling a five is $\frac{m'}{m+m'} = \frac{5}{1+5}$, or 5:6. Notice again that the odds against rolling a five are greater than one, and the probability of the odds against rolling a five remain less than one.

Your Turn

For each of the following find:

A. The odds in favor of the event

B. The odds against the event

C. The probability of the odds in favor of the event

D. The probability of the odds against the event

21. Drawing a black card from a fair standard deck of 52 playing cards?

22. Flipping two coins and obtaining HT?

23. Drawing BORG from the given bag of marbles when there is replacement? There are R = 3 marbles, O = 4 marbles, Y = 4 marbles, G = 2 marbles, B = 1, I = 3 marbles, and V = 3 marbles in the bag.

Conclusions

You have just been through several mathematical ideas as they relate to counting and probability. We have endeavored to open your eyes and increase your mathematical prowess in these two areas. You know the difference between a permutation and a combination and when to use them. You have explored independent and dependent probability. You have even looked at how the lottery works and the difference between an odds ratio and a probability ratio. It has been said that the lottery is a tax on the mathematically illiterate. Is the lottery worth it?

7
Problem Solving

Ever have any problems? How did you solve them? As you ponder that for a moment, think about the steps you took to resolve whatever situation you were in. Problem solving in mathematics uses techniques similar to those you apply to real-life problems. Problem solving is one of the core ideas in mathematics and the main thing that mathematicians do. Because we all experience problems of one nature or another, learning how to be a good problem solver is important for everyone.

Problem solving is central to all disciplines, and one reason for including mathematics in every Pre-K–20+ curriculum. According to NCTM, "in everyday life and in the workplace, being a good problem solver can lead to great advantages" (2000, p. 52). Do all situations in mathematics require problem solving? No. Most of the exercises you completed in this book represented guided practice as you walked through the process of figuring out how to use unfamiliar algorithms or reflected on the processes behind familiar ones. We did that to raise your comfort level in doing mathematics. In this chapter, however, to guide you too much would be a disservice to you and the topic. We will guide you through definitions and some general guidelines, but you will have to use your own thinking to solve the problems.

WHAT MAKES A PROBLEM A PROBLEM?

Not every situation we encounter requires problem solving. If we asked, "How much is four plus three?", you would say seven. In fact, you might roll your eyes if we implied that this was something for which you needed problem-solving techniques. However, one person's firmly understood fact might be another person's problem. Even the most difficult problem becomes just another exercise once you unlock the solution. Exercise and problem are often interchanged, but we distinguish between them by saying that an exercise is practicing an algorithm or technique, whereas a problem has no immediate or obvious solution. So what makes an exercise into a problem? How do you know when something will require problem solving? What makes a good problem solver?

In order for a situation to be a problem for you, first it has to be something you cannot answer by blindly applying a regular algorithm to get a viable answer. Four plus three could require problem solving for a child learning addition, but for you it is not problem solving. This criteria is important and means that, if you already have done a particular type of problem, even if you had to do problem solving to get the answer, it is no longer a problem for you. It might still be a problem for others who have not seen it or resolved it.

The second requirement is that a problem needs to engage you or get your attention. If you are not engaged, or do not accept the challenge the problem presents, then you will not attempt it. Anyone can be turned off if the problems presented are too difficult or if the learner does not have the necessary background to attempt a solution. Problems must be challenging, appropriate, and engaging for the learner.

The third requirement for problem solving is tenacity—you must work on the problem long enough to come up with a solution. Making one or two attempts at a new problem is rarely sufficient for finding a viable solution. It is important to make conjectures (guesses that can be tested) about a problem as you work through it. Conjectures, even when they are wrong, often lead to a solution as they may eliminate false paths or provide insights to other possibilities. Sometimes we call this attribute stick-to-itiveness.

POLYA'S STEPS

George Polya (1898–1972) is credited with outlining steps for solving a problem. Polya stated there are four phases required for a person to solve a problem, as shown in Fig. 7.1. The first step is to understand the problem. That is, the learner must read and correctly interpret the problem. You are probably saying to yourself, "Well, of course you have to understand the question before you can begin to solve the problem. How could you even start if you didn't understand?"

Polya's second step is to make a plan, which will help you solve the problem. We

Polya's 4 Steps for Problem Solving

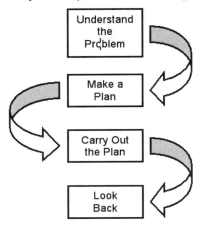

FIG. 7.1.

will discuss strategies that can be used in problem solving later. Any plan you develop will be based on your prior knowledge and experiences and may combine your ideas in new or different ways. Nonetheless, you may be saying, "Of course the next step is to make a plan. What else would you do next?"

Polya's third step is to carry out the plan. Your plan may require revision or perhaps you will scrap it and develop a new plan after attempting to carry out your original one. You may even go back to make sure you understood the problem correctly, make an entirely new plan, and then try carrying it out. You are probably saying to yourself, "Duh? How else would you ever get a solution?"

We distinguish between the words answer and solution. The answer to four plus three is seven. When you solve a problem, you come up with a solution. There may be more than one solution for a problem. A solution also implies that there is some sort of rationale or reasoning behind your method.

Polya's fourth step is to look back and make sure that your understanding, plan, and execution of the plan resulted in a solution that makes sense and resolves the original situation. This is the time to look for errors. You should also examine your solution for faults in your plan or difficulties in the execution of your plan. Are you saying, "I know I should always check my answers, but sometimes I forget or get in a rush?"

Polya's four steps for problem solving make good sense. Understand the problem, make a plan to solve the problem, carry out the plan, and look back and check your answer. It seems like just plain common sense. Then why do we struggle with problem solving? Take a look at Fig. 7.2, which indicates the interconnected-

Polya's 4 Steps for Problem Solving Interconnectedness

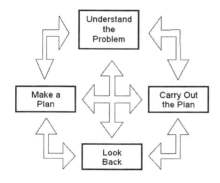

FIG. 7.2.

ness of the four problem-solving steps and you will begin to see that, although the steps themselves seem simplistic, their interconnectedness and interdependence veil a complexity the steps themselves do not necessarily evoke.

STRATEGIES

Now that we have discussed what makes a problem a problem and the steps you take to find a solution to a problem, you are ready to explore different strategies for solving problems. Will we give every possible strategy? No. The strategies we are about to discuss, just like Polya's

problem-solving steps, will seem natural and, for the most part, straightforward. These, coupled with your continued growth in problem solving, should provide the tools you will need to become an effective problem solver.

Probably one of the most popular strategies used by students is guess, test, and revise. After reading, your plan for solving the problem is to guess, test the solution, and then revise your guess according to the results of testing. For example, try solving Riddle Me This #1: "I am a number between one and twenty. I can be written as a base raised to a power to obtain myself. Exchange the base and the power and you still get me. The base is not equal to the power. What number am I?"

You can start by guessing any number, say four, our first conjecture. We test four and find that four is two to the second power. The power and the base are equal. Looking back, four is not the solution. You could guess nine as your next conjecture. Nine is three to the second power, but two to the third power is eight, not nine, so looking back, nine doesn't work either. If you guess six, well there is no easy way to figure out what power you would raise a number to for six, so that one gets eliminated in the testing phase. Continue to guess, test, and revise until you solve the riddle.

How'd you do? You probably started thinking about using another strategy to help keep track, like making a list. Did you make a list of the numbers between 1 and 20? Another handy strategy for this problem is eliminating impossible answers. Did you cross out one and the prime numbers? That would leave 4, 6, 8, 9, 10, 12, 14, 15, 16, 18, and 20. What could you do next?

Giving you the answer will not assist you in building problem-solving skills, but without the answer, how can you check your work? We think the simplest way around this is to put the solutions for each of the text discussions in a section called "Riddle Me This." That way you can have someone else check the solution to see if you are right. Of course, after following Polya's four steps, you already know your solution is right!

We are trying to help you think about your thinking, a process called *metacognition*. Thinking about your thinking and being able to communicate about your thinking is one of the NCTM process standards. Many standardized tests now require explanations. It would be wise for you to articulate your thinking process to your partners in class. Verbalizing your thinking helps clarify it. When working in a group, it helps in two ways: first, by letting you know others were thinking similar things and, second, knowing what others are thinking reduces overlap in the group effort.

Making a chart or a table can be helpful in solving some problem types. Riddle Me This #2: "Suppose you are in charge of a 128-team single elimination softball tournament for which all tie games will go into extra innings until a winner is determined. If no team forfeits a game, how many games will have to be played before the winner is declared?" What categories will you need for your chart or table? Would software be helpful?

You may have played in tournaments and recall the diagrams used to pair teams. If that is part of your previous knowledge base, then you might try solving the 128-team tournament problem by drawing a picture or diagram. In many ways, your past experiences and comfort level with a particular type of strategy determines whether or not you use it. We encourage you to draw pictures as a strategy, because they often provide insight that makes a difficult appearing problem easier.

One of the key strategies used for any problem is looking for a pattern. Most mathematics is based on one type of pattern or another. Before you see the pattern, solving the problem seems improbable, if not impossible. Once you see the pattern, the problem may become trivial. Looking for a pattern is a subgoal of almost every problem-solving strategy. You might think of the tournaments in which you have played and use them as examples for the 128-team problem, even if they involved far fewer than 128 teams. Using a simpler version of a problem can provide the needed insight for solving a complicated or complex problem.

Some problems lend themselves to solutions involving algebraic models. Restating the problem to use an algebraic strategy more effectively sometimes helps. Take a look at Riddle Me This #3: "If the length of the Loch Ness monster is 20 meters long plus half of its own length, how long is Nessie?" Your understanding of the English language is important in solving problems such as this. Certainly this problem begs for an algebraic model, but would restating the problem help you avoid an error during the process of translating the English into the algebraic model? Whereas phrases add descriptive information and clarity to English sentences, they are sometimes movable or removable in mathematical situations.

Some people shy away from doing story problems because they struggle with forming algebraic models. Problems in the real world are not stated in mathematical terms. Understanding the English structure of problems goes a long way toward helping you become more proficient at solving problems, because it helps you translate situations into algebraic terms.

Have you ever wondered what purpose the answers in the back of your book might have—other than to see if you are right? One reason we provide a solution manual (not just answers, but how we got them) is to give you the opportunity to work backward. Sometimes, if you know the answer, then you can work your way back to the question.

Riddle Me This #4: "You have been contracted to use gold to guild the page numbers in a reproduction of an ancient manuscript, starting with page 1. Because of the expense and time required for this process, you will be paid by the number of digits you guild. If you guild a total of 642 digits, how many pages did you number in the manuscript?" Try your hand at using the working backward strategy to come up with a solution for this problem.

Did you figure it out? Perhaps the very first strategy for solving any problem is to use reasoning to determine how to proceed. Few problem-solving strategies work well in isolation. One of the important aspects of the reasoning strategy is the estimation of a solution and checking the reasonableness of a solution. An estimate of 500 pages for Riddle Me This #4 should seem unreasonable to you. Why? Did you use Polya's step number four, looking back, before you looked up the answer? If so, you put the reasoning strategy to good use. Every time you check back you are using this strategy!

Riddle Me This #5: "In the early days of movie making, a villain might do things that cannot be done in real life. In today's movie making, directors often use consultants to avoid this type of blunder. A director has asked you to determine if it is reasonable for the villain to grab a $1,000,000 ransom, in one-dollar bills, and run. You know a dollar bill weighs about one gram. Is the scene reasonable?"

COLLECTION OF PROBLEMS

The difficulty level of any particular problem is dependent on the background knowledge of the problem solver. Difficult for one person may be easy for another, not because one is smarter but because they have had experiences with a type of problem or have the background and tools to solve the problem. Another influencing factor, and a big key to solving almost any problem, is how much tenacity a problem solver possesses. One or two attempts at a problem are often insufficient. Take a look at all of the problems here. Anyone can do "easy" problems. These may not be so easy. Take this opportunity to challenge yourself to do these problems, even the ones you perceive as "difficult." Please note they may not be arranged in ascending degree of difficulty for you:

1. Take an ordinary sheet of paper and fold it in half. Fold it in half a second time. Fold it in half a third time. If you could continue folding it in half 50 times, how high will the stack of paper be?

2. A farmer had 26 cows. All but 9 died. How many lived?

3. A uniform log can be cut into three pieces in 12 seconds. Assuming the same rate of cutting, how long will it take for a similar log to be cut into four pieces?

4. How many different ways can you add four odd counting numbers to get a sum of 10?

5. What is the sum of the first 100 consecutive counting numbers?

6. How many cubic inches of dirt are there in a hole that is 1 foot deep, 2 feet wide, and 6 feet long?

7. How many squares are there in a 5 by 5 square grid?

8. A little green frog is sitting at the bottom of the stairs. She wants to get to the 10th step, so she leaps up 2 steps and then slides back 1. How many leaps will she have to take if she follows this pattern until she reaches the 10th step?

9. If there are 7 months that have 31 days in them and 11 months that have 30 days in them, how many months have 28 days in them?

10. There are exactly 11 people in a room and each person shakes hands with every other person in the room. When A shakes with B, B is also shaking with A; that counts as ONE handshake. How many handshakes will there be when everyone is finished?

11. TTTTTTT9 What number does this represent?

12. There are 9 stalls in a barn. Each stall fits only 1 horse. If there are 10 horses and only 9 stalls, then how can all the horses fit into the 9 stalls without placing more than one horse in each stall?

13. You are given 5 beans and 4 bowls. Place an odd number of beans in each bowl. Use all beans.

14. You are to take a pill every half hour. You have 18 pills to take. How long will you be taking pills?

15. If you got a 40% discount on a $150.00 pair of sport shoes and 20% off a $200 set of roller blades, what was the percent discount on the total purchase (assuming no taxes are involved)?

16. Where should the Z be placed and why?

17. Estimate how old will you be in years if you live 1,000,000 hours?

18. A child has $3.15 in U.S. coins, but only has dimes and quarters. There are more quarters than dimes. How many of each coin does the child have?

19. There are three children in a family. The oldest is 15. The average of their ages is 11. The median age is 10. How old is the youngest child?

20. A famous mathematician was born on March 14, which could be written 3.14. This date is the start of a representation for pi. It is interesting that this mathematician was born on "pi day." Give his name.

CONCLUSIONS

Polya provided the general four-step process for solving problems. We added a group of common strategies and insights into what makes a situation a problem versus an exercise. We also gave you opportunities to practice Polya's four-step process and use a variety of strategies to solve problems as they were presented to you. As you solve a greater variety of problems and use different strategies, your problem-solving abilities will grow. It is up to you to become a good problem solver, but like any other worthwhile endeavor becoming a good problem solver requires interest and practice on your part.

BIBLIOGRAPHY

NCTM. (2000). *Principles and standards for school mathematics*. Reston, VA: Author.

Polya, G. (1957). How to solve it (2nd ed.). Garden City, NY: Doubleday Anchor.

8
Reasoning and Proof

In a regular conversation, how many times have you heard, "That seems logical,"—once, twice, a lot of times? Try to recall why the statement was made. Most likely it was made because the conversation followed some sort of procedure or outlined a step-by-step process that seemed to make sense. In mathematics, we use truth tables to determine if statements are true or false. In some ways, your intuition about logic will serve you well as you explore the ideas behind reasoning and proof. However, you may find that, when dealing with compound statements, the rules of formal logic differ from everyday conversation.

AND

"And" statements in logic are called conjunctions and they are linked to the idea of intersection. The symbol logicians use for "and" statements is ∧, which makes sense, as it closely resembles ∩, the in-tersection symbol for sets. Whereas any variables can be used to make logical statements, you will find that logicians are fond of the letters p and q when they talk about ideas in general. Using the letters p and q to represent sentences or parts of sentences shortens our work. For example, use "Today is Friday" for p and "It is sunny" for q. Our first logical expression p ∧ q is read "p and q". But what does p ∧ q mean? Inserting the sentences into the situation helps sort out the meaning, based on what is said in English.

We can figure out whether p ∧ q is a true statement or a false statement by assigning truth values for p and q. A truth table is the tool of choice for this procedure. To construct a truth table, you assign one of two values to p and to q—true (T) or false (F). It is possible to say whether the statements, "Today is Friday," and "It is sunny," are true or false. Because either statement might be true or false while the other is true or false, there are several possible combinations. Table 8.1 organizes every combination of true and false for p and q. The third column helps us interpret the meaning of the compound statement p ∧ q. We can generalize from this table that a conjunction is true only

TABLE 8.1

p	q	p ∧ q
T	T	T
T	F	F
F	T	F
F	F	F

when both p and q are true. In other words, everything must be true or the statement using "and" is false. If you are reading this on a sunny Friday, the conjunction is true. Otherwise, one or both of the statements is false and the conjunction is false.

You have already explored the commutative property of addition on different sets of numbers. Do you think p ∧ q = q ∧ p? Why do you think so? Does it seem logical to you? What would the truth table look like? Does your hypothesis match Table 8.2?

TABLE 8.2

q	p	q ∧ p
T	T	T
F	T	F
T	F	F
F	F	F

Will the idea of the associative property of addition on different sets of numbers, also hold true as conjunctions are considered? We will use r as the third letter for this property. In other words, is p ∧ (q ∧ r) equivalent to (p ∧ q) ∧ r? A truth table for three variables is shown in Table 8.3.

TABLE 8.3

p	q	r
T	T	T
T	T	F
T	F	T
T	F	F
F	T	T
F	T	F
F	F	T
F	F	F

Your Turn

1. Using p, q, r, and the truth table in Table 8.3, determine if the associative property is true for conjunctions. In other words, does the following statement hold: p ∧ (q ∧ r) = (p ∧ q) ∧ r. (Hint: You will need columns for both q ∧ r and p ∧ q.)

2. Using what you have learned about probability, what is the probability of getting:
   a) a true "and" statement (p ∧ q) with two variables?
   b) a true "and" statement with three variables?
   c) a false "and" statement with two variables?
   d) a false "and" statement with three variables?

OR

Just as conjunctions, which use "and" as the connecting word, are related to intersections of sets, statements using "or" as the linking word are related to unions of sets. Logicians call "or" compound statements disjunctions and use the symbol ∨ which is similar to the symbol for union (∪) used when operating on sets. Take a look at Table 8.4. How is the result of p ∨

TABLE 8.4

p	q	p ∨ q
T	T	T
T	F	T
F	T	T
F	F	F

q, read p or q, different from p ∧ q (p and q)? You might find it helpful to compare and contrast Table 8.4 with Table 8.1 as you think this through. We can generalize from Table 8.4 that a statement using "or" as the linking word is true as long as at least one of the variables is true. In other words, the only time a disjunction is false is when all of the variables are false, just as the only time the union of two sets is empty is when both sets are empty. Does

Table 8.4 make sense based on the English using "It is Friday" for p and "It is sunny" for q?

IF, THEN

Compound statements connected using "if" and "then" are called conditional statements and are written p → q, read, "If p, then q." English sentences aid understanding these, also. This time we will use "You live in North America" for p and "You live in the United States" for q. Four different possibilities exist:

> If you live in North America (true), then you live in the United States (true).
>
> If you live in North America (true), then you live in the United States (false).
>
> If you live in North America (false), then you live in the United States (true).
>
> If you live in North America (false), then you live in the United States (false).

The conditional statement for all four of these is: If you live in North America, then you live in the United States. The "if" portion of the statement is called the antecedent, or hypothesis, of the condition and the "then" part is called the consequent, or conclusion, of the condition. The first of the four possibilities, "If you live in North America (true), then you live in the United States (true)," would make sense, because both the antecedent and the consequent of the condition are true, the conditional statement is true.

Looking at the second of the four possibilities, "If you live in North America (true), then you live in the United States (false)," implies that you live in North America, but do not live in the United States. In other words, if you live in Canada, the original compound statement is false. This may seem counterintuitive at first glance. Remember that we are dealing with a very specific case here. We have to stick strictly with what is written in the original compound statement and must not reword, make leaps of faith, or assume Canada into the statement. In this case, the statement is that you live in North America and also in the United States. The conditional statement is false because the antecedent is true and the consequent is false.

The third statement is "If you live in North America (false), then you live in the United States (true)." You might think that this has to be false because, if you do not live in North America, then how could you live in the United States? Well, maybe you live in Hawaii! Logically, when we look at a conditional statement, if the antecedent is false, and the consequent is true, then the statement is true.

Finally, the fourth statement, "If you live in North America (false), then you live in the United States (false)", is a true statement because if you do not live in North America, most likely you do not live in the United States. You could live in Hawaii, but, when the antecedent is false and the consequent is false, the conditional statement is logically true. Thus, if the antecedent is false, then the conditional statement will be true regardless of whether or not the consequent is true or false. All four of these situations are summarized in a truth table in Table 8.5. Did you notice that the only time a conditional statement is false is when the antecedent is true and the consequent is false?

TABLE 8.5

p	q	$p \to q$
T	T	T
T	F	F
F	T	T
F	F	T

NEGATIONS

Logicians have devised a concise way for reversing the meaning of a statement. Negation is used to convey the message that the opposite of what was said is what was meant. That is, if you say, "It is sunny," then the negation is, "It is not sunny." Similarly, if you say, "It is not sunny," the negation is, "It is sunny." We say that negation changes the truth value of a variable or statement. Although the symbols ~p, p′, –p, and $\tilde{p}$ can be used to show negation, the most common one is ~p. Table 8.6 shows the truth table for the negation of a variable.

TABLE 8.6

p	~p
T	F
F	T

You can think of the negation as acting like the minus sign in front of a number. You know that –(–p) = p is true, so it follows then that ~(~p) = p. How about ~(~(~(~(~p))))? Because there are an odd number of ~ signs (5 in all), then ~(~(~(~(~p)))) = ~p.

TAUTOLOGIES

Take a look at Table 8.7. Each entry in the last column is True. This special case is called a tautology, which has to be true all the time. In Table 8.7, the column with (p ∧ q) → (p ∨ q) has all true values. Com-

TABLE 8.7

p	q	p ∧ q	p ∨ q	(p ∧ q) → (p ∨ q)
T	T	T	T	T
T	F	F	T	T
F	T	F	T	T
F	F	F	F	T

paring the first and second columns with the last column, the statement (p ∧ q) → (p ∨ q) is true no matter what truth values are assigned to statements p and q. Tautologies represent basic laws of logic.

The commutative and associative rules for conjunctions you explored earlier are always true, and form two tautologies, (p ∧ q) ↔ (q ∧ p) and p ∧ (q ∧ r) ↔ (p ∧ q) ∧ r, respectively. The symbol ↔ is read, "If and only if," and is similar to the equal symbol used with ~(~p) = p. Another tautology is implied in the discussion about negation, ~(~p) ↔ p. Were you able to understand the uses of the two symbols (implies [→] and logically equivalent [↔]) that we have been using?

LOGICAL EQUIVALENCE

Compare Table 8.8 with Table 8.9. Notice that the truth values for the p ∨ q column

TABLE 8.8

p	q	p ∨ q
T	T	T
T	F	T
F	T	T
F	F	F

TABLE 8.9

p	q	~p	~p → q
T	T	F	T
T	F	F	T
F	T	T	T
F	F	T	F

and the ~p → q columns are the same. When this happens, the two compound statements are said to be logically equivalent, symbolized by ↔. Putting two logically equivalent statements in a truth table will always generate a tautology, such as the one in Table 8.10. This allows the replacement of a statement with a logically

TABLE 8.10

p	q	p ∨ q	~p → q	(p ∨ q) ↔ (~p → q)
T	T	T	T	T
T	F	T	T	T
F	T	T	T	T
F	F	F	F	T

equivalent statement without affecting the truth value of the original compound statement. As you move through higher stages of proof, this capability will become a very handy tool.

Your Turn

3. Experiment with the different types of logical expressions that have been discussed. Find at least two different tautologies that have not already been discussed. Make a truth table for each to prove it is a tautology.

INFORMAL PROOFS

Proof can be a strange word, at times. It carries various assumptions and meanings with it, and sometimes it is difficult to discern the exact meaning. There is a need for proof in the study of mathematics. Otherwise, we arrive at incorrect conclusions. Mathematical proofs come in a variety of formats, the most fundamental of which is an informal proof. With an informal proof, we might see compelling evidence that something is so but, at this level, it is possible that an exception exists somewhere.

Consider the medians of a triangle as shown in Fig. 8.1. A median is a segment

that connects a vertex with the midpoint of the side opposite the vertex. It looks as if the three medians in each of the triangles are concurrent (meet at a common point). If you use a dynamic geometry program and move the vertices of a triangle around, then the medians will appear to be concurrent. As compelling as this might be, it is not a proof. We can only prove by example if we do every possible example and, even with a dynamic geometry program, you can't examine all possible triangles. Zoom in really close to a suspected point of concurrency—could there be a tiny triangle formed where the point of concurrency appears to be? In this particular example, we know that will not happen, because a formal proof has been done to show that the medians of any triangle are concurrent. Although the formal proof is beyond the scope of this discussion, you need to realize the significance of that last statement.

Whereas you are unable to prove that any particular statement is true by using any number of examples (unless you do every possible one), you are able to disprove any statement with one single counterexample. This is not only true for an informal proof, but for any formal proof as well. Proof and disproof by counterexample are powerful devices in a mathematician's tool belt. You can show that the set of digits is not closed for multiplication using a counterexample such as 3 × 4 = 12. A mathematician might write this proof: Suppose the operation of multiplication is closed on the set of digits. Arbitrarily choose 3 and 4 to multiply together, yielding 3 × 4 = 12. Because 12 is not a digit, we have a contradiction. Thus, the operation of multiplication is not closed on the set of digits. (QED, *quid errata demonstratum*—the proof is finished, which was to be shown, quite easily done, quit exit desist.)

FIG. 8.1.

Your Turn

Informally prove or disprove the following statements:

4. The operation of addition is closed on the set of whole numbers.
5. The operation of addition is closed on the set of digits.

BEYOND THE INFORMAL PROOFS

Formal proofs can explain many things. Do what is asked in each of the following steps:

Pick a number.
Triple it.
Add 12 to the product.
Divide the sum by 3.
Subtract your original number.
What is the result?

If you followed the instructions, and did all arithmetic correctly, then you should have ended up with 4. Many people, young and old, are fascinated by number tricks. Often, after expressing amazement, they will ask if it always comes out that way. That is a paraphrasing of a request for a formal proof. In this particular case, algebra is helpful to see how and why the trick works:

Pick a number.	Let x be the number
Triple it.	3x
Add 12 to the product.	3x + 12
Divide the sum by 3.	$\frac{3x + 12}{3} = \frac{3(x + 4)}{3} = x + 4$
Subtract your original number.	x + 4 − x = 4
What is the result?	4

This trick will work no matter what number you pick for x. Can you explain why?

The next time you hear a number trick, you should ask yourself why the number trick works. We have used number tricks as examples several times. It would be good practice for you to see if you can figure out how they all work. The more skill you develop in determining how things work, the more successful you will be in your pursuit of mastering the wonderful world of mathematics. As you investigate how things are put together, you are beginning to formalize proofs.

Without proof, sometimes you arrive at false conclusions. For example, look carefully at each of the following problems, trying to find some things that are true for each example:

$$\frac{1}{2} + \frac{1}{3} = \frac{5}{6}$$

$$\frac{1}{3} + \frac{1}{4} = \frac{7}{12}$$

$$\frac{1}{5} + \frac{1}{3} = \frac{8}{15}$$

In each case, the denominator of the sum is the product of the denominators of the addends. Also, in each case, the numerator of the sum is the sum of the denominators of the addends. Will this always work? You might wonder why no one has explained fraction addition this way before because this looks a lot easier than the set of rules you learned. We kind of set you up for that one—in these special problems, only unit fractions are being added. If the problem had been $\frac{2}{5} + \frac{1}{3}$, then the answer would have been $\frac{11}{15}$, and in this more general case, the procedure does not work. We set you up to think something would be true and then showed you it was not to amplify the need for proof. Remember, it takes only one example where something is false to prove that it is untrue.

Here is another example in which we move beyond an informal proof. Given the set of numbers in Fig. 8.2, select any one

13	22	(40)	17
20	29	47	(24)
(6)	15	33	10
21	(30)	48	25

FIG. 8.2.

of them and eliminate all the other numbers in the row and column occupied by that number. There will still be some numbers left, so select one of those and eliminate all the numbers in the row and column in which that number appears. You will still have four numbers that have not been crossed out. Select one of them and cross out all the numbers in its row and column. Now you have one number left. Select it, too. The sum of the four numbers you selected is 100. Are you wondering how that worked? We will show you (prove to you) why the answer for this problem will always be 100.

Look at Fig. 8.3. You see that 33 has been selected as the first number and all

	4	13	31	8
9	13	22	40	17
16	20	29	47	24
2	6	15	(33)	10
17	21	30	48	25

FIG. 8.3.

the other values in its row and column of the original table have been crossed out. But Fig. 8.3 has some additional numbers that were not shown in Fig. 8.2. That is because this is an addition table. The numbers in the row and column that were

hidden in Fig. 8.2 are the addends, but the shown numbers are the sums of the addends in any given row and column. When the row and column for 33 are eliminated, so are the addends (the shaded 31 and 2 in this case). Those addends will not be used again in this application. Selecting another number and eliminating its row and column will eliminate two more of the initial addends. When all four numbers are selected, all eight of the original addends will have been accounted for. We knew the answer had to be 100 (barring arithmetic errors). It does not matter which numbers you pick, because $17 + 2 + 16 + 9 + 4 + 13 + 31 + 8 = 100$.

Your Turn

6. Make up a 5 by 5 addition table like the one show in Fig. 8.2 (be sure the addends are hidden) and give it to someone who is not in this class to do, following the directions given for Fig. 8.2. Record their reaction to the trick.

Two-Column Proof

After discussing informal proofs, we moved to a new level where we started showing why things work. The next step in that progression is the formal, two-column proof. In this approach, a statement is given, accompanied by a reason, for each step that is taken in a logical argument, taking you from a beginning point to a conclusion. All forms of proofs, including two-column proofs, have strict rules that must be followed. Statements that are given to you as a part of the problem are accepted as true. Next, you have a set of rules (axioms, theorems, and postulates) that you are permitted to use. These will be statements that you have proven earlier or know to be true. This framework is used to build an argument to support your proof.

For example, suppose that you wanted to prove that, for all real numbers, a, b, and c, if a = b, then it must be the case that $\frac{a}{c} = \frac{b}{c}$ as long as c ≠ 0. Before beginning a formal proof, you need to determine what is given. In this case, you have that a, b, and c are real numbers, a = b, and c ≠ 0. Those facts, along with prior work, are all you have to use as you start your formal, two-column proof:

Statement	Reason
a = b	Given
c ≠ 0	Given
$\frac{a}{c} = \frac{a}{c}$	Reflexive property of equality
$\frac{a}{c} = \frac{b}{c}$	Substitution of b for a

You might say it all makes sense and you knew that. Well and good! However, as we build a formal system, we need to go beyond what makes sense and is intuitive to establish a carefully developed set of ideas and rules that build an unshakeable foundation. It should be noted that some proofs would have combined the two givens into one step. That decision is left to personal preference.

You might wonder why we opted to give an algebra proof as our first example of a formal proof. We did this because most people have not seen two-column proofs unless they took high school geometry. The exposure to two-column proofs in high school geometry courses can be both intimidating and formidable. If, on the other hand, students are exposed to proofs, both informal and formal, before getting to high school geometry, then two-column proofs can be much more palatable.

Reconsider the trick where you picked a number, tripled it, added 12, divided the sum by 3, and subtracted your original

number. We replicate the explanation of that trick below, but replace the x with a triangle, which might make the whole approach appropriate for elementary school students. The point is, proofs should be started much earlier in the curriculum than students currently experience. Early experience with proofs, at appropriate levels, would be a huge asset for students taking subsequent classes that emphasize proof.

Pick a number.	Let Δ be the number
Triple it.	3Δ
Add 12 to the product.	3Δ + 12
Divide the sum by 3.	$\frac{3\Delta + 12}{3} = \frac{\cancel{3}(\Delta + 4)}{\cancel{3}} = \Delta + 4$
Subtract your original number.	Δ + 4 − Δ = 4
What is your number?	4

A proof of this sort, shown after students have been intrigued by the trick, could spark the beginning of something wonderful.

Pick any two odd counting numbers and multiply them. Repeat the process with different pairs of numbers until you arrive at a conclusion about the respective products. The conclusion you just generated is something that appears to be true, based on your observations of several similar problems. Suppose, however, that you wanted to prove your conjecture.

Statement	Reason
a, b ∈ {1, 3, 5, 7, . . .}	Given
a = 2x + 1, x ∈ {0, 1, 2, 3, . . .}	Dfn. of odd number
b = 2y + 1, y ∈ {0, 1, 2, 3, . . .}	Dfn. of odd number
ab = (2x + 1)(2y + 1)	Substitution
(2x + 1)(2y + 1) = 4xy + 2x + 2y + 1	Algebra
4xy + 2x + 2y + 1 = 2(2xy + x + y) + 1	Factoring
2(2xy + x + y) + 1 is odd	Dfn. of odd number
4xy + 2x + 2y + 1 is odd	Substitution
(2x + 1)(2y + 1) is odd	Substitution
ab is odd	Substitution
☺	QED

It is important that you start proving things you know to be true so you can build the skills that will help you prove things you do not know to be true. It is like you are training for some athletic event — you need to get the right muscles tuned up before you take on the challenge of the event.

Paragraph Proof

The two-column proof is not the only way to prove things. They are handy when things are long and complex. Sometimes a paragraph can be written as a means of presenting the logic involved. Suppose you are given Fig. 8.4, in which ACB is

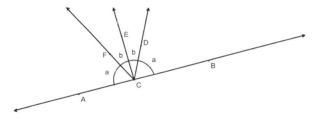

FIG. 8.4.

a straight line and there are the 4 angles shown as a, b, b, and a. A paragraph proof that m∠ACE = 90° could be developed.

Given that ACB is a straight line, $m\angle a + m\angle b + m\angle b + m\angle a = 180°$. So, $2m\angle a + 2m\angle b = 180°$ or $2(m\angle a + m\angle b) = 180°$ and $m\angle a + m\angle b = 90°$. But $m\angle a + m\angle b = m\angle ACE$. So, $m\angle ACE = 90°$. QED ☺

Like we said, paragraph proofs are acceptable and a matter of preference. One argument against them is that the reasons for the steps are not presented. They can be inserted with each part, but then the proof is really a two-column proof, just not written in columns.

Indirect Proof

You may have been using a form of indirect proof for some time without realizing it. Consider the multiple choice question, "When was the classmate you just met born?" The four options for your answer are: (a) 1492, (b) 1776, (c) 1983, (d) 2054. You can arrive at the conclusion indirectly. It is highly unlikely that individuals in your class are over 100 years old, and that rules out answers a and b. Similarly, it is highly unlikely that one of your classmates would have been born in 2054, because that would imply the individual is a time traveler. Thus, answer d is not an option. This process of elimination leaves c as the only logical answer and you would say your new classmate was born in 1984. In an indirect proof, all the possibilities under consideration are examined. Rule out each item that contradicts some fact or rule. If all options except one can be eliminated, then it must be accepted that the one remaining option must be true, and the proof is complete.

CONCLUSIONS

The basic ideas of proof have been established. You need to start asking why things work out as they do in the world of mathematics. Then, after you ask, you need to begin a course of investigation that will logically answer your question. You will find that, with repeated effort, the activity will become easier and easier for you. Like any routine, you learn to excel through practice. Get ready. Get set. Go!

9
Communication

"I know what I want to say but can't find the words." Have you ever said that to anyone? How frustrating it is to be unable to put knowledge into a concise set of words. We do not use only words to communicate. We use gestures, body language, objects we hold and point to, things we refer to, and a host of other means, all designed to get our message across.

OK! If you checked the Table of Contents, you found that this chapter is the shortest in the whole book. Please do not assume this chapter is less important because it is shorter than the others. Mathematics as communication has been discussed implicitly on almost every page so far! We include this chapter because we want you to think explicitly about mathematics as communication.

Most of us have learned mathematics by observing teacher demonstrations. Perhaps that is why things like Cuisenaire rods, Base 10 blocks, dynamic software, and models seem foreign to you. There are places where teacher telling is an appropriate method of instruction. But, it is not the only way.

How do teachers communicate? The following vignette will help make a point. A teacher is explaining something to a class. After the presentation is completed, the teacher asks for questions. The dialogue between the teacher and a student is:

S: "I don't get it."

T: (The teacher is quite patient with all such questions. The explanation is repeated, almost verbatim from the first one.)

S: "I still don't get it."

T: (The explanation is repeated again, still calmly and patiently, again, almost verbatim.)

S: "I still don't get it."

T: (Exasperation is beginning to show but patience persists and again, the material is covered, almost verbatim.)

S: "I still don't get it."

T: (Finally, pushed beyond the limit) "Haven't you been listening?"

The teacher is failing miserably when it comes to communication. Perhaps a verbatim explanation is in order the first time the student asks for clarification. However, after that, it should be clear that a communication gap is present. One solution is to explain the material a different way. That mandates that you understand mathematics. Do you see now why we have been presenting so many different ways of approaching topics? Maybe this student needs to see the concept at a concrete, semi-concrete, or semi-abstract stage. Something different needs to be done. It is the teacher's responsibility to portray knowledge in a manner that is understandable. Teacher telling is not necessarily equivalent to student learning.

We were mighty hard on the teacher as we went through the discussion. The student bears some responsibility to communicate, too. "I don't get it," is not very helpful or specific. We can develop better communication by trying to elicit more specific comments. Ask things like, "Where did you begin to get confused?" or "Tell me what you do understand." These questions begin to force thinking about what is going on and to express ideas more specifically.

You probably have never considered mathematics as communication. Learning to do mathematics, without understanding how and why it works, is merely learning to complete a mechanical task; any computer can do the mathematical manipulations quickly and accurately, but only a human can understand and explain the how and why. Mathematics is an essential way of expressing ideas and we all, at one time or another, communicate quantitative and qualitative ideas, arguments, concepts, or requirements. Even as you discuss the fact that you must take some college courses dealing with mathematics in order to earn your elementary school teaching degree, you are using mathematics to communicate. Students tell us many things as we try to lead them to view mathematics as a way of communicating. "No one ever asked me to explain how I got the answer," "I never got to discuss my answer with someone else before," or "I know what I want to say but can't find the words" are comments heard repeatedly. Mathematical communications are embedded in each of the following:

Negotiate with a bank teller about how you want your change

Explain how to navigate through a building to a given location

Brag about how quickly you traveled

Boast about what great gas mileage your car gets

Sketch a map

How can we promote mathematical communication? Begin by asking for explanations of the mathematics being done. Promoting communication must be an ongoing process. It cannot be a one-time shot. Continually build verbal and written explanations of concepts. Learn how to ask questions.

Earlier we mentioned Gauss' procedure for finding the sum of the first 100 consecutive counting numbers. We provided a discussion of how Gauss communicated with himself to solve the problem. He knew what questions to ask and how to answer them. That is communication!

Discovery has a place in learning how to communicate mathematically. That is one reason why we have talked so much about investigation of patterns. Many things can be extracted from a set of numbers when a pattern is spotted, sometimes even going to the point of generating a formula that works for all similar situations. That is really one of the things mathematics is all about—reducing a set of experiences to a formula or rule that makes the solving of similar problems simple. Then, when it is generalized, it is easily communicated.

An unwanted tradition is inherent in the world of mathematics. Ask someone what they think of when you say mathematics and most people will say numbers, arithmetic, or formulas. Think back over the mathematical instruction you had in the Pre-K–16 environment. Most of it probably focused on numbers. How many times did you write an explanation of how to do a problem? Had you heard of a paragraph proof before the section on Proof and Reasoning?

We could go on, but you get the point. Communication is everywhere: in mathematics, in your daily conversation, in the real world, and in the list of responsibilities that you inherit as a future teacher.

Your Turn

1. Write a paragraph explaining how you would add 842 + 136. Put the paragraph aside and don't look at it for 24 hours. Is your paragraph organized and coherent? Does it concisely explain what you did and why you did it?

2. Exchange paragraphs with a classmate. Do you understand that person's explanation? Ask questions that might help the person clarify their explanation.

3. Compare the two paragraphs, identifying the strong points of each. Reason together logically about disputed points.

4. Using the strong points of each, collaborate to write a paragraph that is better than either of you wrote alone. Ask someone who is not in your class to use the paragraph to complete the addition problem.

10
Connections

People often see mathematics as being a collection of independent skills or activities. Individuals who visualize mathematics as a bunch of unrelated facts, skills, and procedures to be memorized cannot attain mathematical maturity. Mathematics is not a collection of separated topics; it should be viewed as a comprehensive and coherent science without which human progress would be severely limited.

INDEPENDENT OR INTERCONNECTED TOPICS

Why do people have trouble thinking of mathematics as interconnected and interdependent concepts? One culprit is the curriculum that is taught in the United States. It is common for mathematics to be taught as a collection of topics that have no apparent connection. Do you remember how you learned your multiplication facts? Was there any discussion about how 3×5 is a shortcut method of adding $5 + 5 + 5$? Even if the repeated addition definition for multiplication is mentioned early in the curriculum, the connection is made simply to help children with the transition from addition to easy multiplication facts, it soon fades away. Although there are other ways to define multiplication, the repeated addition method strengthens the connection to prior work. One of the most effective ways to learn any subject is to take a new topic and relate it to previously mastered work. The reference makes the new work seem familiar and, therefore, not so frightening. As the connections between addition and multiplication are strengthened, the learner may discover the advantage of using multiplication as a shortcut, abandoning the old method in favor of the new approach. This may not happen immediately. A learner may not see much advantage to abandoning $5 + 5 + 5$ in favor of 3×5, but might not be overly thrilled to do 9×47 in repeated addition form ($47 + 47 + 47 + 47 + 47 + 47 + 47 + 47 + 47$). If using repeated addition to complete 9×47 is preferred, then that is OK. It might be considered a less preferred method, but it is a valid strategy. Perhaps we can convince the learner to change routines by giving problems with larger factors. Ultimately, everyone will be ready for an easier way to do the problem. At that point, we are happy to provide the world's slickest, quickest way to do the problem—multiplication. Mission accomplished and connection made.

Stick with multiplication a little longer. The problem 3×5 could be solved using an array as shown in Fig. 10.1. Counting the unit squares is a reasonable way to determine how many are needed. A discussion could focus on 3 rows with 5 squares in each row, 3 sets of 5, or three fives—each of which provides a total of

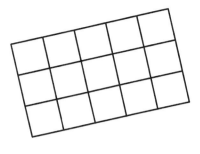

FIG. 10.1.

15 unit squares. The example could also be viewed as 5 columns with 3 squares in each column, 5 sets of 3, or five threes. Such a discussion provides a verbal transition that solidifies the connection between addition and multiplication. Have you noticed the connections that have been made throughout this text? We have been building them with you throughout our discussions. We purposely waited until now to call this to your attention. We wanted to show you how easily connections can be inserted into the curriculum.

HOW ARE THINGS CONNECTED?

We used Fig. 10.1 as a means of generating a multiplication fact, but it also models the area of a rectangle that has a base of 5 units and a height of 3 units (or is that a length of 3 and a width of 5?) and an area of 15 square units. How is it that the picture is the same and yet we are moving from the concept of multiplication to the area of a rectangle? Surprise! Connections! Hold on, we are not done. The product of almost any 2-factor multiplication exercise can be expressed as the area of a rectangle (would ⁻3 × ⁻4 give the area of a rectangle?). Suppose the dimensions are 3.5 units and 6 units. Figure 10.2 models this situation. Sure, there are partial squares, but two of the 6 partial squares can be put together to make another square because each partial square is a

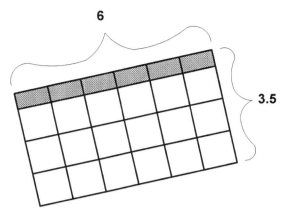

FIG. 10.2.

half of an original square. Do that three times, add the 18 squares that are clearly whole, and you end up with a total of 21 squares. What is the product of 6 and 3.5? It better be 21. By the way, the results are the same if you use $3\frac{1}{2}$, or $\frac{7}{2}$, as the factor to be multiplied by 6. The numbers can be made to look more complex but the story is the same—you end up with the area of a rectangle when you do a two-factor multiplication problem. Now you have another connection—from repeated addition through multiplication to areas of rectangles. During your work in this text, you connected between decimals, improper fractions, and mixed numbers in multiplication. These simple, as well as much more complex, connections abound in mathematics. You only have to learn to recognize them. Few mathematical concepts can be understood in total isolation.

Another connection grows from the array definition used for multiplication and area of a rectangle. We have said that the dimensions in Fig. 10.2 were 3.5 units by 6 units. We counted the unit squares, but we did not extend the discussion of dimensions to the product of 21 unit squares. An important part of learning about area involves understanding what is happening with the units. This can be established by remembering what happened when you learned addition facts by combining 3 blocks and 2 more blocks to get 5 blocks. That verbiage is fairly natural and many students will say it reflexively as they do the problem or answer the question. Extend that to the idea of finding the sum of 3 inches and 2 inches. For some reason, there is a temptation to omit the inches and just give 5 as the sum. Recording the answer as 5 inches is significant and must not be overlooked. The connection can be strengthened when working with something like Fig. 10.3. A key element of the discussion is the length of the resultant vector, which is the sum of the two shorter ones. When the answer is given as 5, an immediate question should be, "5 what?" so that the units are emphasized.

This discussion can be extended to area problems (grid paper is handy here). The readiness skill for dealing with units grows from experiences such as our discussion about Fig. 10.3. In the two-

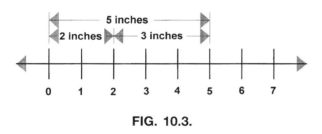

FIG. 10.3.

dimensional concept of area, the unit is a square, so area is expressed in terms of how many little squares it takes to cover the shape. The central issue involves not only how many little squares are needed, but also the length of a side of a little square. If the length of the side is an inch, then the area discussion can be built around square inches. You have connected the little square to square inches, the unit for area discussions. If the length of the side of a unit square is changed to a foot, the discussion must be built around square feet. It takes 144 inch

squares to cover a foot square, thus important information is contained in the unit provided. Depending on the problem, the length of the side of a unit square might be a meter, centimeter, yard, mile, or paperclip. Sometimes we use the word unit as a placeholder. Initially we write the area for the rectangle in Fig. 10.2 as 21 square inches or 21 square units. Eventually, the notation is shortened to 21 units^2 or even 21 u^2. This shorter notation should be allowed only after the idea of including units in every answer is firmly entrenched and the concept of exponents has been developed. Did you notice a connection to the concept of denominate numbers during this discussion?

How can unit squares be used to express the area of a figure other than a rectangle? Connecting the area of a triangle to the area of a rectangle helps. Start with a sheet of rectangular paper and fold the paper along the diagonal, as shown in Fig. 10.4. Cutting along the fold and rotating

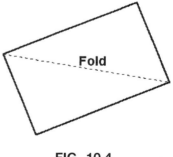

FIG. 10.4.

one piece shows that the two triangles have the same area. One of the triangles has an area that is half of the area of the original rectangle and the formula $\frac{base \times height}{2}$, or $\frac{bh}{2}$, is established. Understanding this connection does not come as quickly as the time you took to read those last two sentences. Some students will struggle to see how the little squares can fit in a triangle. A different de-

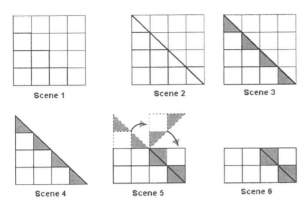

FIG. 10.5.

velopment of this, as shown in Fig. 10.5, might help. Scene 1 shows a rectangle, which happens to be a square with an area that equals 16 u². Scene 2 shows a diagonal along which we might fold the rectangle in half. Scene 3 shows the little triangles, which are half unit squares, shaded. Half of the rectangle is removed in Scene 4 to make it easier to see the triangle. Mentally visualize the little triangles being paired together to make squares. The area of the triangle can be counted—and is 8 square units, exactly half the area of the rectangle. Scenes 5 and 6 might help some people with the visualization, but might confuse others because the triangle has been rearranged into a rectangle. Scene 6 shows that none of the pieces are changed in size. Again, the area is exactly half of the original rectangle.

If repeating decimals are explored, then a rule is provided, and the discussion is terminated long before the connections between topics are understood. Often a shortcut is provided for converting repeating decimals, such as $0.\overline{6}$ or $0.\overline{123}$, to common fractions. The rule states that you count the number of digits involved in the repeat and write a fraction with that number of 9s in the denominator and the repeated value as the numerator. So $0.\overline{6} = \dfrac{6}{9}$, $0.\overline{57} = \dfrac{57}{99}$, or $0.\overline{123} = \dfrac{123}{999}$. In this

set of three examples, each of the fractions has common factors. Both the numerator and denominator divided by 3 for starters (use the divisibility rule for 3 as a quick check of that statement).

Regretfully, using the rule stops short of showing connections. Why does the rule work? How did they come up with using so many 9s as a denominator? Algebra answers those questions. For example, take a look at $0.\overline{57}$.

Let $x = 0.\overline{57}$, which we will call equation 1.

If we multiply both sides of Equation 1 by 10, we get $10x = 5.\overline{75}$, Equation 2.

If we multiply both sides of Equation 1 by 100, we get $100x = 57.\overline{57}$, Equation 3.

Although we could multiply by any value, Equations 2 and 3 provide the direction we need. Using some algebraic skills, consider the following:

$$
\begin{array}{ll}
100x = 57.\overline{57} & (3) \\
-\quad x = 0.\overline{57} & (1) \\
\hline
99x = 57 & \text{Subtract (1) from (3)} \\
x = \dfrac{57}{99}. & \text{Solve for } x
\end{array}
$$

This process explains the derivation of the 9s rule. If Equation 2 had been used rather than Equation 3, we would have had

$10x = 5.\overline{75}$ (2)

$- x = 0.\overline{57}$ (1), which presents a problem. When Equation 3 is used, the values to the right of the decimal place in both equations line up under each other. That is, there is a 5 subtracted from a 5 or a 7 subtracted from a 7, regardless of the place value and that assurance exists no matter how far the repeat is extended. The subtraction is easy because despite the place where the subtraction is started, the missing addend is zero. On the other hand, if Equation 2 is used, the decimal places do not line up properly for the subtraction.

That gives a part of the whole picture but there are other problem types that need to be discussed. Suppose the task is to convert $4.\overline{86}$ to a fraction. With expanded notation, $4.\overline{86}$ becomes $4 + 0.\overline{86}$ and when the rule is applied, $4.\overline{86} = 4\frac{86}{99}$. This does not address the all-important question of how that works. The other way to do this problem is use the process of multiplying $x = 4.\overline{86}$ by some power of 10. The question of which power to use is answered by the need to align the 8s and 6s to the right of the decimal point so the subtraction will yield zeros only to the right of the decimal point:

$$
\begin{array}{r}
100x = 486.\overline{86} \\
- \quad x = \quad 4.\overline{86} \\
\hline
99x = 482 \\
x = \dfrac{482}{99} \text{ or } 4\dfrac{86}{99}
\end{array}
$$

The important distinction between the two methods is that the rule did not show why the answer came out as it did.

Although these examples do not exhaust the discussion on converting a repeating decimal to a fraction, it has shown how one topic within mathematics can be used to develop understanding in another. We encourage you to explore this topic in greater depth. As we learn mathematics today, these explanations are critical to overall understanding of what is happening. And, at the same time, connections are amplified.

CONCLUSIONS

In the multiplication of whole numbers section of this text, we discussed partial products, a connection to algebra. We discussed patterns in several places and ended with extensions, rules, or formulas. More connections. They are everywhere and all you have to do is notice them. You might find that you will actually get excited about some of the connections you see and the mathematics you are learning and discovering in the world around you. Aaaahhhhhh, connections, they really are everywhere!

11

Representation

- Different Ways of Saying the Same Thing

I am one of the authors of this book. My name is Douglas Kent Brumbaugh. I have been addressed as Doug most of my life. In my younger days, if I was not behaving as I should have been, I heard Douglas. If I was more out of line, I heard Douglas Kent. If I was pushing the envelope to the limit, I heard Douglas Kent Brumbaugh. My dad and my grandfather wanted to name me Mike, but they lost that discussion. Undaunted, they called me Mike. My friends awarded several different nicknames to me; many of my high school students called me Coach and some of my college students address me as Doc B. Over the years, I have answered to all of them. I am still me, no matter what I am called.

DIFFERENT WAYS OF SAYING THE SAME THING

The notion of representation is something like all my names discussed earlier. "The term representation refers both to process and product—in other words, to the act of capturing a mathematical concept or relationship in some form and to the form itself. . . . Moreover, the term applies to processes and products that are observable externally as well as to those that occur 'internally,' in the minds of people

doing mathematics" (NCTM, 2000, p. 67). Figure 11.1 shows how a child showed

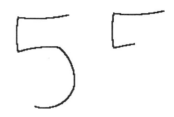

FIG. 11.1. Principles and standards for mathematics (p. 67), by National Council of Teachers of Mathematics, 2000, Reston, VA: Author.

her age to be 5 and one half. It appears as if the girl has begun to establish a feel for the idea of a half by how she writes the second part of her age. Her style seems strange and yet, apparently, she knows that she is 5 and some more, and that the more is a half. She seems to be attempting to convey that message by writing half of the numeral 5. It makes sense, doesn't it? And yet we adults would write 5.5 or $5\frac{1}{2}$ and might not have understood her representation without an explanation.

Representation consistently moves from concrete to abstract as new concepts are encountered and understood. The ultimate goal is to have you function abstractly with your mathematical understandings because that is the most convenient and accepted way to communicate about such things. On the other hand, the main idea is to communicate the idea under consideration. As your understanding of a mathematical concept increases, you progress to a more sophisticated or acceptable representation of the idea.

Young children represent numbers of objects using sets of items. They move on to using pictures of the sets, tally marks to represent the pictured objects, and finally to a numeral, which is a shortcut way of showing the tally marks—which represent the pictured objects, which represent the objects themselves. The last sentence describes parallel developments that might take years to accomplish, depending on the complexity of the concept being considered. Think back through the things covered in this text. You should be able to conjure up ideas that show the development of the different representations.

Technology comes into play as a means of representing ideas too. Consider fractions. Throughout this text, we have been careful to represent fractions with horizontal vinculums. But many calculators express three fourths as ¾. Some calculators will show three fourths as 3⌋4 and a few show the pretty print form of $\frac{3}{4}$. Many will shift the representation to 0.75 with the touch of a button. You become comfortable with one way, but easily gravitate to another because you understand that all those forms are different ways of saying the same thing. Those are only some of the ways to represent $\frac{3}{4}$.

Throughout this text, we have depicted or modeled different mathematical situations. Those have all been representations. We gave you examples of representations and did not tell you we were doing it. Now, as you look back over the semester, you should be able to see a variety of representations of different concepts. What is the best way to resolve questions about representation? Ask, "What did you mean when you wrote. . . ?" Sometimes the representation used is actually the goal of an activity, but many times we just need to understand the representation without judging it or requiring that it fit neatly within our preconceived notion of how it should look.

CONCLUSIONS

Howard Eves, a friend and world-class geometer and mathematical historian, has said, "If you have algebra without geometry you have answers to questions nobody would ask, and if you have geometry without algebra you have questions you cannot answer." You might be asking why we would mention algebra and geometry here, as you reach the end of this text about elementary school mathematics. This, however, is not the end of your learning about mathematics or how to communicate about it. With that in mind we leave you with our hope for you . . .

Let your adventure begin.

MaryE, Peggy, & Doug/Mike

BIBLIOGRAPHY

Eves, H. (January 26, 2002).

National Council of Teachers of Mathematics. (2000). *Principles and standards for school mathematics*. Reston, VA: Author.

Index

Solutions Manual

2: NUMBER AND OPERATIONS

Sets

1. Based on the examples in Figs. 2.1 and 2.2, write a definition of what looping the elements of a set means.

Answers may vary. You are going to put a fence around all of the elements of the set. When you are finished, it is clear what does and does not belong in the set.

2. Define a *finite set*.

Answers may vary. When you count the number of elements in the set, you stop counting at some point. If you can stop counting, no matter how large the number is, the set is finite.

3. Define an *infinite set*.

Answers may vary. When you count the number of elements in the set, you can never stop counting because there are always more elements to be counted, no matter how large the number becomes.

4. Define a *subset*.

Answers may vary. In each case, the first set is completely contained in the second set, making it a subset of the original set. Notice that a subset may be all or part of the original set.

5. Define a *proper subset*.

Answers may vary. A proper subset is part, but not all, of a set.

6. Define an *improper subset*.

Answers may vary. The only improper subset is the set itself. The definition of a proper subset gives a clue as to why the set itself is improper. Part, but not all, indicates that either some or no elements of the set must be in the subset.

7. Define *cardinality*.

Answers may vary. The cardinality, or cardinal number of a set, tells the number of elements in the set.

8. What is the cardinality of the empty set?

Zero. There are no elements in it.

9. What is the cardinality of $\{\phi\}$?

One. There is one element in the set. It just so happens that the element is ϕ, which is used to represent the empty set. However, in this setting, that ϕ becomes an element of a set and takes on a different meaning. You could think of it as one of the Greek letters just like you would say that {A} has a cardinality of one.

10. What is the cardinality of {BMW}?

One. There are no commas between the letters so the three are considered one element, how does this compare to {P, e, g, g, y}? ☺

11. Generalize the pattern established by the total number of subsets, as the number of elements in the set is increased one element at a time.

$\{2, 4, 8, 16, \ldots\}$ can be written many ways, but one convenient one for this exercise is $\{2^1, 2^2, 2^3, 2^4 \ldots 2^n\}$, where "n" represents the cardinality of the set. The generalization would that when the number of elements in a set is known, the number of subsets can be determined. Once the number of subsets is known, you also know the number of improper subsets and the number of proper subsets (always one less than the number of subsets because there is always one improper subset for any set with cardinality of at least one).

12. A set with 11 elements will have _____ subsets, _____ of which are improper, and _____ of which are proper.

A set with 11 elements will have 2048 subsets, 1 of which is improper, and 2047 of which are proper.

13. Is there a case where the number of proper and improper subsets will be equal? Is there more than one case? Why or why not?

Yes. The set {A} has one proper subset, {}, and one improper subset, {A}. Because no set has more than one improper subset, there can be no other case where the number of proper and improper subsets will be equal. In our Base 10 numbering system, only 1 + 1 = 2.

14. Define *equal sets* and *equivalent sets*.

Equal sets have the same cardinality and the exact same elements, although they may not necessarily appear in the same order. Equivalent sets have the same cardinality, but the elements are not all the same.

15. Which tells you more about two sets, equal or equivalent? Why?

Equal is the stronger statement because it tells you that both the cardinality and elements are the same. Equivalent only assures that the cardinalities are the same.

16. Define *overlapping sets*.

Overlapping sets have some elements in common. Generally, those with one set contained within another (like {1, 2, 3, 4} and {2, 3}) are excluded from this definition.

17. Define *disjoint sets*.

Disjoint sets have no common elements.

18. Define *partitioned sets*.

Sets may be partitioned according to some definition. For example, the counting numbers can be partitioned into odd numbers and even numbers. When a set is partitioned, each element is in one and only one of the subsets.

19. Define *complements of sets*.

The complement of a subset is everything that is in the original set except for the elements of the subset itself. The complement of a subset and the subset are disjoint and together include every element of the set.

20. Define ∪ (the *union of sets*).

When the union of two sets is formed, all of the elements in any set are listed in the union set. If an element is in more than one of the sets being joined by the union, then it is shown only once in the resultant union set.

21. Define ∩ (the *intersection of sets*).

The intersection of sets is all elements common to all of the sets being considered. If the sets being considered are disjoint, then the union will be the empty set.

22. Define X (*set multiplication* or *set product*).

The set product of two sets is a set of ordered pairs with the first element in the ordered pair coming from the first set in the product and the second element of the ordered pair coming from the second pair. That is why {1, 2} × {A, B} = {(1, A), (1, B), (2, A), (2, B)} and {A, B} × {1, 2} = {(A, 1), (B, 1), (B, 2), (A, 2)} look different. Their respective elements are ordered pairs, so (A, 1) is different from (1, A) because the order is different.

23. Define *relative complement* (set subtraction).

The relative complement of one set is found by subtracting the intersection of that set from a second set. The relative complement of A to B or the complement of A relative to B is written B − A = B − (B ∩ A).

24. State a generalization about the cardinalities of sets and their union.

If the sets in the union are disjoint, the sum of the cardinalities of the sets will equal the cardinality of the union. For example, {1, 2, 3} ∪ {A, %} would be 3 + 2 in terms of cardinalities of the sets. The union would be {1, 2, 3, A, %}, which has a cardinal number of five. We know that 3 + 2 = 5. If the sets in the union are overlapping, then addition cannot be shown. {1, 2, A} ∪ {A, %} = {1, 2, A, %}, but the cardinalities are 3, 2, and 4, respectively. We know that 3 + 2 ≠ 4.

25. State a generalization about the cardinalities of sets and their set product.

The cardinality of a set product will be the product of the sets involved. For example, in {A, 1, &} X {♣, ∇} = {(A, ∇), (1, ∇), (&,∇), (A, ♣), (1, ♣), (&, ♣)}, the cardinality of {A, 1, &} is 3, the cardinality of {♣, ∇} is 2, and the cardinality of {(A, ∇), (1, ∇), (&, ∇), (A, ♣), (1, ♣), (&, ♣)} is 6 [remember, (A, ∇) is one element of the set] and 3 × 2 = 6.

26. Describe what the universal set might be for each of these examples given previously of unions and then construct a Venn diagram that accurately depicts each statement:

a) {1, 2, 3, 4} ∪ {5, 6, 7} = {1, 2, 3, 4, 5, 6, 7}

Universal set = digits

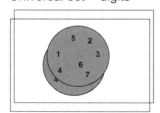

b) {1, 2, 3} ∪ {4} ∪ {7, 8, 15} = {1, 2, 3, 4, 7, 8, 15}

Universal set = counting numbers less than 20

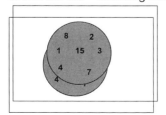

c) {1, 2, 3, 4} ∪ {5, 6, 4} = {1, 2, 3, 4, 5, 6}

Universal set = digits

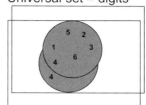

27. Describe what the universal set might be for each of these examples given previously of intersections and then construct a Venn diagram that accurately depicts each statement:

a) {1, 2, 3, 4} ∩ {5, 6, 4} = {4}

Universal set = digits

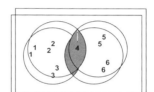

b) {1, 2, 3, 4, 5} ∩ {3, 4, 5} = {3, 4, 5}

Universal set = digits

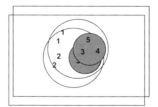

c) {1, 2, 3, 4} ∩ {5, 6, 7} = { }

Universal set = digits

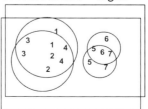

Let A = {1, 2, 3, 4}, B = {1, 2, 3, 4, 5}, C = {5, 6, 4}, and D = {3, 4, 5}.

d) A – C = {1, 2, 3}

Universal set = digits

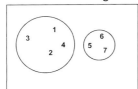

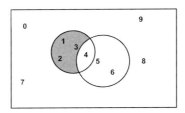

e) C – A = {5, 6}

Universal set = digits

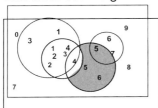

f) B – D = {1, 2}

Universal set = digits

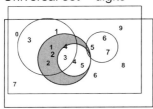

g) D – B = { }

Universal set = digits

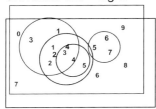

28. Describe what the universal set might be for each of these examples given previ-

ously of set multiplication and then construct a Venn diagram that accurately depicts each statement:

a) {1, 2} × {A, B} = {(1, A), (1, B), (2, A), (2, B)}

Universal set = digits and Latin alphabet

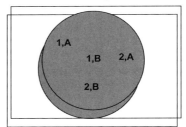

b) {A, B} × {1, 2} = {(A, 1), (B, 1), (B, 2), (A, 2)}

Universal set = digits and Latin alphabet

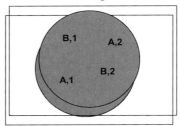

c) {A, 1, &} × {♣, ∇} = {(A, ∇), (1, ∇), (&, ∇), (A, ♣), (1, ♣), (&, ♣)}

Universal set = digits, Latin alphabet, playing card suits, &, and ∇

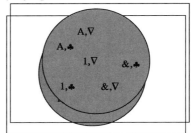

29. Let the universal set for each of these examples be the set of digits and then construct a Venn diagram that accurately depicts each statement:

Let A = {1, 2, 3, 4}, B = {1, 2, 3}, C = {5, 6, 7}, D = {3, 4, 5}, E = {4}, and F = {7, 8, 9}.

a) A′ ∪ C = {0, 5, 6, 7, 8, 9}

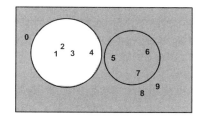

b) A′ ∩ D = {5}

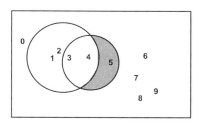

c) C − F′ = {7}

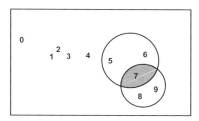

d) (A − D) ∪ B′ = {0, 1, 2, 4, 5, 6, 7, 8, 9}

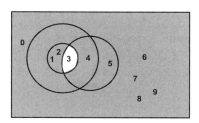

30. We know 2 + 2 = 2 × 2 as discussed with the commutative property of addition on the set of counting numbers. Are there any other examples that will react similarly?

Yes. 0 + 0 = 0 × 0.

31. Is there a situation where commutativity of subtraction on some set would exist?

Yes. As long as the elements are the same. 7 − 7 = 7 − 7 = 0.

32. Is there a situation where commutativity of division on some set would exist?

Yes. As long as the elements are the same. 9 ÷ 9 = 1 = 9 ÷ 9.

33. Generalize the idea of commutativity of operations for some set in words.

Answers may vary. Pick two elements and operate on them. Reverse the order of the elements under the same operation and the answer will be the same.

34. We know 2 + 2 = 2 × 2 as discussed with the commutative property of addition on the set of counting numbers. Are there any examples that will work like that for associativity?

Yes. Use zeros throughout.

35. Is there a situation where associativity of subtraction on some set would exist?

Yes. Use zeros throughout.

36. Is there a situation where associativity of division on some set would exist?

Yes. Use all ones.
For each of 34 through 38, select True or False and explain the reason for your choice.

37. Generalize the idea of associativity of operations for some set in words.

Answers may vary. You can switch which elements you operate with first, but you will still get the same result.

38. The even counting numbers are closed for addition.

True. Answers may vary on the why by giving a lot of examples. It is assumed that these students have completed at least high school algebra, if not college algebra, and thus they could do something like 2y and 2z are guaranteed even for any y and z as elements of the counting numbers. Their sum, 2y + 2z could be expressed 2(y + z), which is also guaranteed to be even.

39. The odd counting numbers are closed for addition.

False. Answers may vary. 2y = 1 is guaranteed odd as is 2z + 1. Adding gives 2y + 2z + 2 = 2(y + z + 1), which must be even.

40. The even counting numbers are closed for multiplication.

True. Given 2y and 2z as even, (2y)(2z) = 4yz = 2(2yz), guaranteed even.

41. The odd counting numbers are closed for multiplication.

True. Given 2y + 1 and 2z + 1 as guaranteed odds, then (2y + 1)(2z + 1) becomes 4yz + 2y + 2z + 1. Three of the terms are even but that 1 at the end forces the sum to be odd.

42. Give a set that is closed for addition and describe why it is so.

Answers will vary.

43. Give a set that is closed for multiplication and describe why it is so.

Answers will vary.

44. Would the commutative property for addition have a negative impact on the situation if we insisted that it hold true while we discussed closure?

No. Actually, many mathematicians prefer to define closure to include commutativity for the operation because of advanced situations where the property may not hold.

45. Generalize the idea of closure of operations for some set in words. Don't forget about division and subtraction.

Answers may vary. Take any two elements of a set, operate on them and the result must be an element of the given set.

46. Generalize the idea of the identity element for an operation for some set in words.

Pick an element out of a set, operate on it with the identity element and the result will be an element in the set.

47. Generalize the idea of the inverse element for an operation for some set in words.

Pick an element out of the set, operate on it with its operative inverse and the result will be the identity element for that operation in that set.

48. In general, is there a left distributive property of multiplication over subtraction in the real numbers?

Yes. It reacts just like addition.

49. In general, is there a right distributive property of multiplication over addition or subtraction on the set of reals?

Yes. It reacts just like addition.

50. In general, is there a left distributive property of division over addition in the reals?

No.

51. In general, is there a right distributive property of division over addition in the set of real numbers?

No. It will work for something like (8 + 4) ÷ 2, which is 12 ÷ 2 or 6. Applying the distributive property of multiplication over addition from the right, (8 + 4) ÷ 2 becomes (8 ÷ 2) + (4 ÷ 2) = 4 + 2 = 6.

52. Generalize the idea of the distributive property for multiplication over addition for some set in words.

Answers will vary. Take the element outside the parentheses and operate with it on each element inside the parentheses, adding the resulting products.

53. Using the following examples, write a definition of multiple and a definition of factor:

Multiples of 12 are 12, 24, 36, 48, . . .

Multiples of 5 are 5, 10, 15, 20, 25, . . .

Multiples of 7 are 7, 14, 21, 28, 35, . . .

Multiples of 2 are 2, 4, 8, 16, 32, 64, 128, . . .

Factors of 12 are 1, 2, 3, 4, 6, 12

Factors of 7 are 1, 7

Factors of 100 are 1, 2, 4, 5, 10, 20, 25, 50, 100

Factors of 36 are 1, 2, 3, 4, 6, 9, 12, 18, 36

Answers will vary. A multiple of a number is that number times any counting number. Some say a multiple is that number times any whole number, making zero be a multiple of every number, sometimes referred to as the "trivial case." Still others say that a multiple of a number is that number times any integer.

A factor of a number is any counting number that divides the given number. Here, "divides" means that when the division is done, the remainder is zero.

54. What conclusions can you draw from your table?

Answers will vary. Some numbers have only one way of making a rectangle and others have more than one way. Eventually, the one way numbers will be called primes and the more than one way numbers will be called composites.

55. Complete the Sieve of Eratosthenes following the directions given in the text immediately before this exercise. Although this chart stops at 100, it could be continued to any desired value.

Yes.

56. What is the greatest number of primes in any given row?

There can never be more than three after the first row. Consider columns for this discussion. The columns headed by an even number will always contain only even numbers. Thus, those five columns after the first row cannot contain a prime, eliminating five

columns from discussion. Similarly, the columns headed by 5 and 10 will always contain only multiples of five, eliminating those columns. This leaves three columns that could contain a prime number.

57. Would the answer in Exercise 53 change if the chart were extended indefinitely to include more rows or more columns?

Yes. If you go far enough, like to 105!, it is possible to have over 100 consecutive composite numbers, giving at least eight rows of consecutive composite numbers in a 10-column sieve. Ranted, they are going to be mighty big numbers.

58. Next consider the least number of primes in any given row?

That number could be zero, if you consider something like 12!

59. Would the answer in Exercise 55 change if the chart were extended indefinitely by adding more rows or columns?

Answers will vary, but it is yes in both cases. As columns are added, even headings will be eliminated from consideration as holders of prime numbers, as explained in Exercise 56, as would be the case for multiples of five. Still, there would be more columns that could contain a prime.

60. Create a sieve on a 6-column chart, then answer the questions that follow (the same questions asked for the 10-column sieve). Even though the same questions are asked, the answers will change, thus enhancing understanding.

1	2	3	4	5	6
7	8	9	10	11	12
13	14	15	16	17	18
19	20	21	. . .		

61. What is the greatest number of primes in any given row of the 6-column sieve?

After the first row, two. The second, fourth, and sixth columns will always hold values that are multiples of 2. The third column will always hold values that are multiples of 3. That leaves, at most, two columns that could contain a prime.

62. Would the answer in Exercise 58 change if the 6-column sieve were extended indefinitely?

Yes. See Exercise 57.

63. Now, what is the least number of primes in any given row of the 6-column sieve?

Zero. See Exercise 57.

64. Would the answer in Exercise 60 change if the 6-column chart were extended indefinitely?

Yes.

65. Develop an argument that shows how the divisibility rule for 9 would work with a 4-digit number wxyz.

Consider a 4-digit number, wxyz, where w, x, y, and z are any digit:

$$wxyz = 1000w + 100x + 10y + z$$
$$= (999 + 1)w + (99 + 1)x + (9 + 1)y + z$$
$$= 999w + w + 99x + x + 9y + y + z$$
$$= 999w + 99x + 9y + w + x + y + z$$
$$= 9(111x + 11x + y) + w + x + y + z$$

This shows that the divisibility depends on the sum of the original digits. Only if the sum + w + x + y + z is divisible by 9, will the original number be divisible by 9.

66. Why does the 6 rule break into an even 3 rule? Explain why a similar rule could or could not be devised for divisibility by 15.

The prime factors of 6 are 2 and 3. Thus, if both are met, the number must also be divisible by 6. A similar argument would be made for 15.

67. Describe a divisibility rule for some number other than those discussed and show why it works.

Answers will vary.

68. Are divisibility rules limited to integers?

In the sense of our discussion, yes. However, they are often employed in fractions, for example, to determine if there is a common factor that exists between the numerator and denominator.

Whole Number Addition

1. Use the grouping method described in the previous button example to find the total of two sets of elements as a little child might. Use buttons, pennies, chips, or any other manipulative.

a) A group of three and a group of five (XXX ∪ XXXXX → XXXXXXXX)
b) A set of 4 and a set of 8 (XXXX ∪ XXXXXXXX → XXXXXXXXXXXX)
c) An array of two and an array of six

```
X      X  X  X       X  X  X  X
   ∪              →
X      X  X  X       X  X  X  X
2  +        6     =        8
```

Answers may vary, but one possible representation is given with each part.

2. Using only addition, write out a simple word problem that would be appropriate for an early childhood addition problem. Use your manipulatives to solve the problem.

Answers may vary. The manipulative response should be similar to those demonstrated.

3. Use the number line method described previously to show:

a) 8 + 3
b) 5 + 4
c) 7 + 9

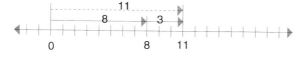

4. 4837 + 3519 = ?

```
  4 thousands +  8 hundreds + 3 tens +  7 units
+ 3 thousands +  5 hundreds + 1 ten  +  9 units
  7 thousands + 13 hundreds + 4 tens + 16 units
     which becomes
  8 thousands +  3 hundreds + 5 tens +  6 units
```

5. 647 + 10254 + 9938 = △

```
                         6 hundreds + 4 tens + 7 units
   1 ten thousand + 0 thousands + 2 hundreds + 5 tens + 4 units
 +                    9 thousands + 9 hundreds + 3 tens + 8 units
 1 ten thousand + 9 thousands + 17 hundreds + 12 tens + 19 units
     or
   2 ten thousands + 0 thousands + 8 hundreds + 3 tens + 9 units
     or 20839
```

6. 24751 + 608 + 93 + 3562 = ♥

```
   2 ten thousands + 4 thousands + 7 hundreds + 5 tens + 1 unit
                              6 hundreds + 0 tens + 8 units
                                            9 tens + 3 units
 +                3 thousands + 5 hundreds + 6 tens + 2 units
 2 ten thousands + 7 thousands + 18 hundreds + 20~tens + 14 units
     or
   2 ten thousands + 9 thousands + 0 hundreds + 1 ten + 4 units
     or 29014
```

7. 4837 + 3519 = ?

4 thousands + 8 hundreds + 3 tens + 7 units + 3 thousands
  − 5 hundreds + 1 ten + 9 units =

4 thousands + 3 thousands + 8 hundreds + 5 hundreds + 3
  tens + 1 ten + 7 units + 9 units =

7 thousands + 13 hundreds + 4 tens + 16 units =
8 thousands + 3 hundreds + 5 tens + 6 units

8. 647 + 10254 + 9938 = ☐

6 hundreds + 4 tens + 7 units + 1 ten thousand +
  0 thousands + 2 hundreds + 5 tens + 4 units +

9 thousands + 9 hundreds + 3 tens + 8 units =

1 ten thousand + 0 thousands + 9 thousands + 6 hundreds
  + 2 hundreds + 9 hundreds + 4 tens + 5 tens + 3 tens + 7
  units + 4 units + 8 units =

1 ten thousand + 9 thousands + 17 hundreds + 12 tens + 19
  units =

2 ten thousands + 0 thousands + 8 hundreds + 3 tens + 9
  units

9. 24751 + 608 + 93 + 3562 = ☐

2 ten thousands + 4 thousands + 7 hundreds + 5 tens +
  1 unit + 6 hundreds + 0 tens + 8 units + 9 tens + 3 units +
  3 thousands + 5 hundreds + 6 tens + 2 units =

2 ten thousands + 4 thousands + 3 thousands + 7 hundreds
  + 6 hundreds + 5 hundreds + 5 tens + 0 tens + 9 tens + 6
  tens + 1 unit + 8 units + 3 units + 2 units =

2 ten thousands + 7 thousands + 18 hundreds + 20 tens +
  14 units =

2 ten thousands + 9 thousands + 0 hundreds + 1 ten + 4
  units

10. 4837 + 3519 = ?

4000 + 800 + 30 + 7 + 3000 + 500 + 10 + 9 =
4000 + 3000 + 800 + 500 + 30 + 10 + 7 + 9 =
7000 + 1300 + 40 + 16 =
8000 + 300 + 50 + 6

11. 647 + 10254 + 9938 = ☐

600 + 40 + 7 + 10000 + 0 + 200 + 50 + 4 + 9000 + 900 + 30
  + 8 =

10000 + 0 + 9000 + 600 + 200 + 900 + 40 + 50 + 30 + 7 + 4
  + 8 =

10000 + 9000 + 1700 + 120 + 19 =
10000 + 9000 + 1000 + 700 + 100 + 20 + 10 + 9 =
10000 + 10000 + 0 + 800 + 30 + 9 =
20000 + 0 + 800 + 30 + 9

12. 24751 + 608 + 93 + 3562 = ⅋

20000 + 4000 + 700 + 50 + 1 + 600 + 0 + 8 + 90 + 3 + 3000
  + 500 + 60 + 2 =

20000 + 4000 + 3000 + 700 + 600 + 500 + 50 + 0 + 90 + 60
  + 1 + 8 + 3 + 2 =

20000 + 7000 + 1800 + 200 + 14 =
20000 + 7000 + 1000 + 800 + 200 + 10 + 4 =
20000 + 8000 + 1000 + 0 + 10 + 4 =
20000 + 9000 + 0 + 10 + 4

13. 4837 + 3519 = ?

```
    4837
  + 3519
    7000
    1300
      40
      16
    8356
```

14. 647 + 10254 + 9938 = K

```
    647
  10254
+  9938
  10000
   9000
   1700
    120
     19
  20839
```

15. 24751 + 608 + 93 + 3562 = O

```
  24751
    608
     93
+  3562
  20000
   7000
   1800
    200
+    14
  29014
```

16. 4837 + 3519 = ?

```
    4837
+   3519
    7̶346
     8  5
```

17. 647 + 10254 + 9938 = Π

```
    647
  10254
+  9938
  1̶9̶7̶2̶9
   2083
```

18. 24751 + 608 + 93 + 3562 = χ

```
  24751
    608
     93
+  3562
  2̶7̶804
    901
```

19. 4837 + 3519 = ?

Answers will vary.

20. 647 + 10254 + 9938 = (

Answers will vary.

21. 24751 + 608 + 93 + 3562 = #

Answers will vary.

Whole Number Subtraction

Do Problems 1, 2, and 3 using both the take away model and number line.

1.   Jo has 14 marbles and loses 8. How many are left?

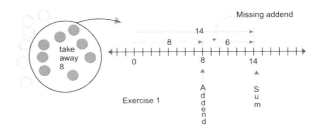

Exercise 1

2. Shawn owns 4 high value stamps, and Sean owns 11 high value stamps. How many more high value stamps does Sean own?"

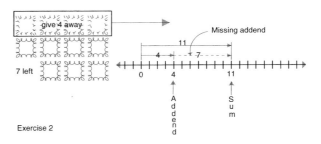

Exercise 2

3. Chris has 5 cards left but started with 17. How many are gone?

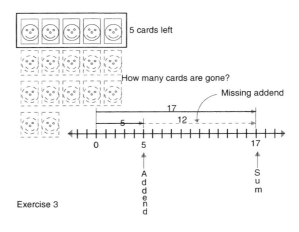

Exercise 3

4. Shawn scored 512 on a video game and Reggie scored 178 on the same game. How much higher was Shawn's score than Reggie's? Do this problem using each of the stages: concrete, denominate numbers, expanded notation, and standard algorithm. Write a concluding paragraph explaining how the different steps in the various stages are connected across the stages.

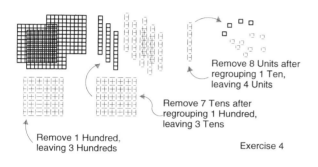

Remove 8 Units after regrouping 1 Ten, leaving 4 Units

Remove 7 Tens after regrouping 1 Hundred, leaving 3 Tens

Remove 1 Hundred, leaving 3 Hundreds

Exercise 4

4 Hundreds	10 Tens	12 Units	400	100	12	4	10	12
5̶ ̶H̶u̶n̶d̶r̶e̶d̶s̶	1̶ ̶T̶e̶n̶	2̶ ̶U̶n̶i̶t̶s̶	5̶0̶0̶ + 1̶0̶ + 2			5̶	1̶	2
− 1 Hundred	7 Tens	8 Units	− (100 + 70 + 8)			−1	7	8
3 Hundreds	3 Tens	4 Units	300 + 30 + 4			3	3	4

Answers will vary on written paragraph. Do the following subtraction problems using each of the following methods: borrow pay back, left to right, scratch, any column first and integer. Show your regroupings in each style in a manner that would show how you are doing your work.

5. 8314 − 2756

```
  13 11 14         13 11 14          13 11 14
8 3̶ 1̶ 4        8 3̶ 1̶ 4         8 3̶ 1̶ 4       8 3 1 4
3 8 6          −2 7 5 6          −2 7 5 6       −2 7 5 6
−2̶ 7̶ 5̶ 6       5 0 0 0           6̶ 6̶ 6̶ 8             − 2
5 5 5 8        6̶ 0̶0̶0̶           5 5 5            − 4 0
               6̶ 0̶ 0̶                             −6 0 0
               5 0 0                             6 0 0 0
               5̶ 0̶                                5 5 5 8
               4 0
               5 5 5 8
```

Note that the any column first method would look a lot like the left to right.

6. 703 − 164

```
  10 13          10 13            10 13
7 0̶ 3         7 0̶ 3          7 0̶ 3        7 0 3
2 7           −1 6 4          −1 6 4        −1 6 4
−1̶ 6̶ 4̶        6̶ 0̶0̶           6̶ 4̶ 9̶            − 1
5 3 9         5 0 0            5 3           −6 0
              4̶ 0̶                            6 0 0
              3 0                            5 3 9
              9
              5 3 9
```

Note that the any column first method would look a lot like the left to right.

7. How would a problem like 8152 − 1936 impact each of borrow pay back, left to right, scratch, any column first and integer subtraction?

Answers will vary. The process will be similar except that if there is a case where the digit in the sum is greater than the digit in the addend, no regrouping is required for that column.

Whole Number Multiplication

Use the partial product method of multiplication (in either the vertical or horizontal format) to find the products in the following exercises.

1. 23 × 47 = 💣

```
    23
×   47
    21    (7 × 3)
   140    (7 × 20)
   120    (40 × 3)
   800    (40 × 20)
  1081
```

2. 519 × 68 = 🗁

```
    519
×    68
     72    (8 × 9)
     80    (8 × 10)
   4000    (8 × 500)
    540    (60 × 9)
    600    (60 × 10)
  30000    (60 × 500)
  35292
```

3. 803 × 745 = ⌛

```
      803
  ×   734
       15      (5 × 3)
        0      (5 × 00)
     4000      (5 × 800)
      120      (40 × 3)
        0      (40 × 00)
    32000      (40 × 800)
     2100      (700 × 3)
        0      (700 × 00)
   560000      (700 × 800)
   598235
```

Use lattice, left to right, and the distributive property of multiplication over addition on the set of whole numbers methods to find the products in:

4. 23 × 47= ⌨

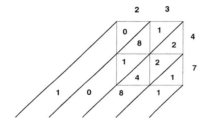

```
      23
  ×   47
     800      (40 × 20)
     120      (40 × 3)
     140      (7 × 20)
      21      (7 × 3)
    1081
```

(20 + 3)(40 + 7) = (20)(40) + (20)(7) + (3)(40) + (3)(7)
                 = 800 + 140 + 120 + 21
                 = 1081

5. 519 × 68 = 📫

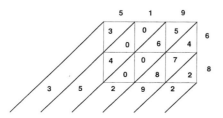

```
      519
  ×    68
    30000      (60 × 500)
      600      (60 × 10)
      540      (60 × 9)
     4000      (8 × 500)
       80      (8 × 10)
       72      (8 × 9)
    35292
```

(500 + 10 + 9)(60 + 8)

= (500)(60) + (500)(8) + (10)(60) + (10)(8) + (9)(60) + (9)(8)

= 30000 + 4000 + 600 + 80 + 540 + 72

= 35292

6. 803 × 745 = ✍

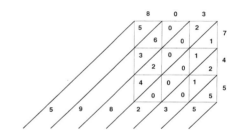

```
      803
  ×   745
    56000      (700 × 800)
        0      (700 × 00)
     2100      (700 × 3)
    32000      (40 × 800)
        0      (40 × 00)
      120      (40 × 3)
     4000      (5 × 800)
        0      (5 × 00)
       15      (5 × 3)
   598235
```

(800 + 0 + 3)(700 + 40 + 5)

= (800)(700) + (800)(40) + (800)(5) + (0)(700) + (0)(40) + (0)(5)
  + (3)(700) + (3)(40) + (3)(5)

= 560000 + 32000 + 4000 + 0 + 0 + 0 + 2100 + 120 + 15

= 598235

Use the Russian peasant method of multiplication to find the products in:

7. 23 × 47 = ✌

```
  23      47
  11      94
   5     188
   2     376
   1     752
        1081
```

8. $519 \times 68 = \text{♌}$

```
   519    68
  1038    34
  2076    17
  4152     8
  8304     4
 16608     2
 33216     1
 35292
```

9. $803 \times 745 = \text{♍}$

```
    803    745
   1606    372
   3212    186
   6424     93
  12848     46
  25696     23
  51392     11
 102784      5
 205568      2
 411136      1
 598235
```

Whole Number Division

1. $5184 \div 9 = 576$ Answers will vary

$5184 \div 9$ can be done as
$$500 \times 9 = 4500$$
$$50 \times 9 = 450$$
$$20 \times 9 = 4500$$
$$+6 \times 9 = 4500$$

2.
```
         58
    37)2146          Answers will vary
```

```
    37)2146
       1500    50 × 30    50
        350    50 × 7
        240     8 × 30     8       58 × 37 = 2146
         56     8 × 7
```

3. $\dfrac{2495618}{358} = ?$ Answers will vary

$$\frac{1800000}{300} = 6000 \quad \frac{270000}{300} = 900 \quad \frac{21000}{300} = 70 \quad \frac{300}{300} = 1$$

$$\frac{300000}{50} = 6000 \quad \frac{45000}{50} = 900 \quad \frac{3500}{50} = 70 \quad \frac{50}{50} = 1$$

$$\frac{48000}{8} = 6000 \quad \frac{7200}{8} = 900 \quad \frac{560}{8} = 70 \quad \frac{8}{8} = 1$$

$$1800000 + 300000 + 48000 + 270000 + 45000 + 7200 +$$
$$21000 + 3500 + 560 + 300 + 50 + 8 = 2495618$$

Therefore $\dfrac{2495618}{385} = 6971$

Equivalent Fractions and Multiplication of Fractions

1. Find an equivalent fraction to each of the following; be sure to show the steps that assure your result is correct.

Answers will vary. Some examples are:

a) $\dfrac{4}{5} = \dfrac{4 \times 2}{5 \times 2} = \dfrac{8}{10}$

b) $\dfrac{6}{18} = \dfrac{6 \times \frac{1}{3}}{18 \times \frac{1}{3}} = \dfrac{2}{6}$ or $\dfrac{1}{3}$

if all common factors are divided out

c) $\dfrac{17}{51} = \dfrac{17 \div 17}{51 \div 17} = \dfrac{1}{3}$

d) $\dfrac{7}{11} = \dfrac{7 \times 3}{11 \times 3} = \dfrac{21}{33}$

e) $\dfrac{24}{96} = \dfrac{24 \div 24}{96 \div 24} = \dfrac{1}{4}$

2. Convert the following mixed numbers to fractions. Please note we have not discussed any shortcuts you might have learned in the past, so the expectation is that you will not apply them at this point. You need to practice the skills of converting at a basic level so you will gain a full understanding of the shortcuts you might have learned previously.

a) $2\dfrac{5}{8} = 2 + \dfrac{5}{8}$

$\quad = \dfrac{16}{8} + \dfrac{5}{8}$

$\quad = \dfrac{16 + 5}{8}$

$\quad = \dfrac{21}{8}$

b) $3\dfrac{7}{9} = 3 + \dfrac{7}{9}$

$\quad = \dfrac{27}{9} + \dfrac{7}{9}$

$\quad = \dfrac{27 + 7}{9}$

$\quad = \dfrac{34}{9}$

c) $13\dfrac{5}{6} = 13 + \dfrac{5}{6}$

$\quad = \dfrac{78}{6} + \dfrac{5}{6}$ d) $4 = \dfrac{4}{1}$ or $\dfrac{12}{3}$, etc.

$\quad = \dfrac{78 + 5}{6}$

$\quad = \dfrac{83}{6}$

d) $97 \times \dfrac{42}{43} = \dfrac{97}{1} \times \dfrac{42}{43}$

$\qquad = \dfrac{97 \times 42}{43}$

$\qquad = \dfrac{4074}{43}$

$\qquad = 94\dfrac{32}{43}$

3. Convert the following improper fractions to mixed numbers. Once again, we ask that you practice the skills of converting at a basic level; leave the shortcuts for later.

a) $\dfrac{37}{5} = \dfrac{35 + 2}{5}$ b) $\dfrac{49}{9} = \dfrac{45 + 4}{9}$

$\quad = \dfrac{35}{5} + \dfrac{2}{5}$ $\quad = \dfrac{45}{9} + \dfrac{4}{9}$

$\quad = 7 + \dfrac{2}{5}$ $\quad = 5 + \dfrac{4}{9}$

$\quad = 7\dfrac{2}{5}$ $\quad = 5\dfrac{4}{9}$

c) $\dfrac{18}{7} = \dfrac{14 + 4}{7}$

$\quad = \dfrac{14}{7} + \dfrac{4}{7}$ d) $\dfrac{24}{6} = \dfrac{4}{1}$

$\quad = 2 + \dfrac{4}{7}$ $\qquad = 4$

$\quad = 2\dfrac{4}{7}$

4. Find the following products:

a) $9 \times \dfrac{1}{4} = \dfrac{9}{1} \times \dfrac{1}{4}$

$\qquad = \dfrac{9 \times 1}{1 \times 4}$

$\qquad = \dfrac{9}{4}$ (purposely not changed to mixed number)

b) $4 \times \dfrac{1}{9} = \dfrac{4}{1} \times \dfrac{1}{9}$ c) $6 \times \dfrac{4}{7} = \dfrac{6}{1} \times \dfrac{4}{7}$

$\qquad = \dfrac{4 \times 1}{1 \times 9}$ $\qquad = \dfrac{6 \times 4}{1 \times 7}$

$\qquad = \dfrac{4}{9}$ $\qquad = \dfrac{24}{7}$

$\qquad\qquad\qquad\quad = 3\dfrac{3}{7}$

5. Find the following products first by converting the mixed number to an improper fraction and then by using the distributive property of multiplication over addition on the set of rational numbers:

a) $4 \times 3\dfrac{1}{7} = 4 \times \dfrac{22}{7}$

$\qquad = \dfrac{88}{7}$

$4 \times 3\dfrac{1}{7} = 4\left(3 + \dfrac{1}{7}\right)$

$\qquad = 4(3) + 4\left(\dfrac{1}{7}\right)$

$\qquad = 12 + \dfrac{4}{7}$

$\qquad = 12\dfrac{4}{7}$

b) $6 \times 2\dfrac{5}{8} = 6 \times \dfrac{21}{8}$

$\qquad = \dfrac{126}{8}$

$\qquad = \dfrac{63}{4}$

$\qquad = 15\dfrac{3}{4}$

$6 \times 2\dfrac{5}{8} = 6\left(2 + \dfrac{5}{8}\right)$

$\qquad = 6(2) + 6\left(\dfrac{5}{8}\right)$

$\qquad = 12 + \dfrac{30}{8}$

$\qquad = 12 + 3\dfrac{6}{8}$

$\qquad = 12 + 3\dfrac{3}{4}$

$\qquad = 15\dfrac{3}{4}$

c) $8 \times 3\frac{7}{11} = 8 \times \frac{40}{11}$

$= \frac{320}{11}$

$8 \times 3\frac{7}{11} = 8\left(3 + \frac{7}{11}\right)$

$= 8(3) + 8\left(\frac{7}{11}\right)$

$= 24 + \frac{56}{11}$

$= 24 + 5\frac{1}{11}$

$= 29\frac{1}{11}$

$= 15\frac{3}{4}$

6. Find the following products:

a) $\frac{3}{7} \times \frac{5}{12} = \frac{3 \times 5}{7 \times 12}$

$= \frac{15}{84}$

b)

$$\frac{3}{7} \times \frac{8}{3} \times \frac{14}{64} = \frac{\cancel{3}^{1}}{\cancel{7}^{1}} \times \frac{\cancel{8}^{1}}{\cancel{3}^{1}} \times \frac{\cancel{14}^{\cancel{2}}}{\cancel{64}_{\cancel{8}_{4}}}$$

$= \frac{1}{4}$

c) Answers will vary.

7. Use both the partial product and distributive methods to complete the following exercises.

a) $4\frac{5}{9} \times 7\frac{11}{13}$

$\frac{6}{7} \times \frac{3}{4} = \frac{9}{14}$

$\frac{6}{7} \times 2 = \frac{12}{7}$

$5 \times \frac{3}{4} = \frac{15}{4}$

$5 \times 2 = 10$

$\frac{9}{14} + \frac{12}{7} + \frac{15}{4} + 10 = \frac{18}{28} + \frac{48}{28} + \frac{105}{28} + \frac{280}{28}$

$= \frac{18 + 48 + 105 + 280}{28}$

$= \frac{451}{28}$

$2\frac{3}{4} \times 5\frac{6}{7} = \left(2 + \frac{3}{4}\right)\left(5 + \frac{6}{7}\right)$

$= 2\left(5 + \frac{6}{7}\right) + \left(\frac{3}{4}\right)\left(5 + \frac{6}{7}\right)$

$= 2(5) + 2\left(\frac{6}{7}\right) + \left(\frac{3}{4}\right)(5) + \left(\frac{3}{4}\right)\left(\frac{6}{7}\right)$

$= \frac{9}{14} + \frac{12}{7} + \frac{15}{4} + 10$

$= \frac{18}{28} + \frac{48}{28} + \frac{105}{28} + \frac{280}{28}$

$= \frac{18 + 48 + 105 + 208}{28}$

$= \frac{451}{28}$

b) $4\frac{5}{9} \times 7\frac{11}{13} = \left(4 + \frac{5}{9}\right)\left(7 + \frac{11}{13}\right)$

$= 4\left(7 + \frac{11}{13}\right) + \left(\frac{5}{9}\right)\left(7 + \frac{11}{13}\right)$

$= 4(7) + 4\left(\frac{11}{13}\right) + \left(\frac{5}{9}\right)(7) + \left(\frac{5}{9}\right)\left(\frac{11}{13}\right)$

We leave the rest because it is all material that has been covered before.

$$
\begin{array}{r}
4 + \dfrac{5}{9} \\
\times \quad 7 + \dfrac{11}{13} \\
\hline
\dfrac{11}{13} \times \dfrac{5}{9} = \dfrac{55}{117} \\
\dfrac{11}{13} \times 4 = \dfrac{44}{13} \\
7 \times \dfrac{5}{9} = \dfrac{35}{9} \\
7 \times 4 = 28
\end{array}
$$

We leave the rest because it is all material that has been covered before.

Addition of Fractions

1. Find each of the following sums, showing the intermediate steps:

a) $\frac{5}{13} + \frac{7}{13} = ?$ $\frac{5}{13} + \frac{7}{13} = \frac{5+7}{13}$

$= \frac{12}{13}$

b) $2\frac{5}{17} + \frac{8}{17} = ?$

$2\frac{5}{17} + \frac{8}{17} = \left(2 + \frac{5}{17}\right) + \frac{8}{17}$

$= 2 + \left(\frac{5}{17} + \frac{8}{17}\right)$

$= 2 + \frac{5+8}{17}$

$= 2\frac{13}{17}$

c) $5\dfrac{11}{13} + 4\dfrac{5}{13} + 1\dfrac{7}{13} = ?$

$$5\dfrac{11}{13} + 4\dfrac{5}{13} + 1\dfrac{7}{13} = 5 + 4 + 1 + \dfrac{11}{13} + \dfrac{5}{13} + \dfrac{7}{13}$$

$$= 10 + \dfrac{11+5+7}{13}$$

$$= 10 + \dfrac{23}{13}$$

$$= 10 + 1\dfrac{10}{13}$$

$$= 11\dfrac{10}{13}$$

2. Do the following problems, showing the intermediate steps you made to get each sum:

a) $\dfrac{3}{19} + \dfrac{11}{57} = ?$ $\quad \dfrac{3}{19} + \dfrac{11}{57} = \dfrac{3 \times 3}{3 \times 19} + \dfrac{11}{57}$

$$= \dfrac{9}{57} + \dfrac{11}{57}$$

$$= \dfrac{9+11}{57}$$

$$= \dfrac{20}{57}$$

b) $5\dfrac{3}{11} + \dfrac{23}{88} = ?$ $5\dfrac{3}{11} + \dfrac{23}{88} = 5\dfrac{8 \times 3}{8 \times 11} + \dfrac{23}{88}$

$$= 5\dfrac{24}{88} + \dfrac{23}{88}$$

$$= 5 + \dfrac{24+23}{88}$$

$$= 5 + \dfrac{47}{88}$$

$$= 5\dfrac{47}{88}$$

c) $5\dfrac{3}{13} + \dfrac{63}{78} + 2\dfrac{25}{39} = ?$

$$5\dfrac{3}{13} + \dfrac{63}{78} + 2\dfrac{25}{39} = 5\dfrac{6 \times 3}{6 \times 13} + \dfrac{63}{78} + 2\dfrac{2 \times 25}{2 \times 39}$$

$$= 5\dfrac{18}{78} + \dfrac{63}{78} + 2\dfrac{50}{78}$$

$$= 5 + 2 + \dfrac{18+63+50}{78}$$

$$= 7 + \dfrac{131}{78}$$

$$= 7 + \dfrac{78+53}{78}$$

$$= 7 + \dfrac{78}{78} + \dfrac{53}{78}$$

$$= 7 + 1 + \dfrac{53}{78}$$

$$= 8\dfrac{53}{78}$$

3. Do the following problems, showing the intermediate steps you made to get each sum:

a) $\dfrac{4}{5} + \dfrac{8}{9} = ?$ $\quad \dfrac{4}{5} + \dfrac{8}{9} = \dfrac{4 \times 9}{5 \times 9} + \dfrac{8 \times 5}{9 \times 5}$

$$= \dfrac{36}{45} + \dfrac{40}{45}$$

$$= \dfrac{36+40}{45}$$

$$= \dfrac{76}{45}$$

$$= 1\dfrac{31}{45}$$

b) $2\dfrac{4}{5} + 3\dfrac{8}{9} = ?$ $\quad 2\dfrac{4}{5} + 3\dfrac{8}{9} = 2 + \dfrac{4 \times 9}{5 \times 9} + 3 + \dfrac{8 \times 5}{9 \times 5}$

$$= 2 + \dfrac{36}{45} + 3 + \dfrac{40}{45}$$

$$= 2 + 3 + \dfrac{36+40}{45}$$

$$= 5 + \dfrac{76}{45}$$

$$= 5 + 1\dfrac{31}{45}$$

$$= 6\dfrac{31}{45}$$

c) $2\dfrac{4}{7} + 9 + 3\dfrac{8}{11} + \dfrac{97}{154} + \dfrac{153}{154} = ?$

$$2\dfrac{4}{7} + 9 + 3\dfrac{8}{11} + \dfrac{97}{154} + \dfrac{153}{154}$$

$$= 2 + \dfrac{4 \times 22}{7 \times 22} + 9 + 3 + \dfrac{8 \times 14}{11 \times 14} + \dfrac{97}{154} + \dfrac{153}{154}$$

$$= 2 + \dfrac{88}{154} + 9 + 3 + \dfrac{112}{154} + \dfrac{97}{154} + \dfrac{153}{154}$$

$$= 2 + 9 + 3 + \dfrac{88+112+97+153}{154}$$

$$= 14 + \dfrac{450}{154}$$

$$= 14 + 2\dfrac{142}{154}$$

$$= 16\dfrac{142}{154}$$

$$= 16\dfrac{71}{77}$$

4. Do the following problems, showing the intermediate steps you made to get the sum:

a) $\dfrac{3}{8} + \dfrac{5}{12} = ?$ $\quad \dfrac{3}{8} + \dfrac{5}{12} = \dfrac{3 \times 3}{3 \times 8} + \dfrac{2 \times 5}{2 \times 12}$

$$= \dfrac{9}{24} + \dfrac{10}{24}$$

$$= \dfrac{19}{24}$$

b) $5\frac{3}{9} + 2\frac{11}{12} + 7\frac{14}{15} = ?$

$$5\frac{3}{9} + 2\frac{11}{12} + 7\frac{14}{15} = \frac{20 \times 3}{20 \times 9} + 2\frac{15 \times 11}{15 \times 12} + 7\frac{12 \times 14}{12 \times 15}$$

$$= 5\frac{60}{180} + 2\frac{165}{180} + 7\frac{168}{180}$$

$$= 14\frac{393}{180}$$

$$= 16\frac{33}{180}$$

$$= 16\frac{11}{60}$$

Subtraction of Fractions

1. Do each of these problems, showing basic intermediate steps:

a) $\frac{7}{9} - \frac{2}{9} = \frac{7-2}{9} = \frac{5}{9}$

b) $\frac{4}{5} - \frac{1}{5} = \frac{4-1}{5} = \frac{3}{5}$

c) $5\frac{3}{3} - 2 = \left(5 + \frac{3}{4}\right) - 2 = (5-2) + \frac{3}{4} = 3\frac{3}{4}$

d) $8\frac{9}{11} - 2\frac{6}{11} = \left(8 + \frac{9}{11}\right) - \left(2 + \frac{6}{11}\right)$

$$= 8 + \frac{9}{11} - 2 - \frac{6}{11} = (8-2) + \left(\frac{9}{11} - \frac{6}{11}\right) = 6\frac{3}{11}$$

e) $5\frac{15}{17} - 1\frac{6}{17} = \left(5 + \frac{15}{17}\right) - \left(1 + \frac{6}{17}\right)$

$$= (5-1) + \left(\frac{15}{17} - \frac{6}{17}\right) = 4\frac{9}{17}$$

2. Discuss what happens if a fraction subtraction problem involves two unit fractions with the same denominator.

The answer will always be zero because you would have $\dfrac{1-1}{\text{denominator}} = \dfrac{0}{\text{denominator}} = 0$.

3. Do each of these exercises, showing basic intermediate steps:

a) $\frac{7}{9} - \frac{2}{27} = \frac{21}{27} - \frac{2}{27} = \frac{21-2}{27} = \frac{19}{27}$

b) $\frac{4}{5} - \frac{7}{10} = \frac{8}{10} - \frac{7}{10} = \frac{8-7}{10} = \frac{1}{10}$

c) $8\frac{9}{72} - 2\frac{1}{18} = \left(8 + \frac{9}{72}\right) - \left(2 + \frac{4}{72}\right)$

$$= 8 + \frac{9}{72} - 2 - \frac{4}{11} = (8-2) + \left(\frac{9}{72} - \frac{4}{72}\right) = 6\frac{5}{72}$$

d) $5\frac{15}{17} - 1\frac{6}{153} = \left(5 + \frac{135}{153}\right) - \left(1 + \frac{6}{153}\right)$

$$= (5-1) + \left(\frac{135}{153} - \frac{6}{153}\right) = 4\frac{129}{153}$$

4. Discuss what happens if a fraction subtraction problem involves two unit fractions with related denominators.

Answers will vary. The smaller denominator should be listed first or the answer will be negative. Beyond that, the answer will be a unit fraction if the larger denominator is twice the smaller denominator. If the multiple of the larger denominator is more than twice the smaller denominator, then the missing addend will not be a unit fraction.

5. The examples we have shown in the text involved two fractions with relatively prime denominators. If the problem involved three (or more) fractions and the only common factor shared by the denominators is one, then how would you work the problem?

Answers will vary. The numerator and denominator of each fraction must be multiplied by each of the other denominators.

6. Do each of these problems, showing basic intermediate steps:

a) $\frac{5}{8} - \frac{3}{7} = \frac{5 \times 7}{8 \times 7} - \frac{3 \times 8}{7 \times 8}$

$$= \frac{35}{56} - \frac{24}{56}$$

$$= \frac{35-24}{56}$$

$$= \frac{11}{56}$$

b) $7\frac{8}{9} - 3\frac{1}{8} = 7\frac{8 \times 8}{9 \times 8} - 3\frac{1 \times 9}{8 \times 9}$

$$= 7\frac{64}{72} - 3\frac{9}{72}$$

$$= 7 - 3 + \frac{64}{72} - \frac{9}{72}$$

$$= 4\frac{64-9}{72}$$

$$= 4\frac{55}{72}$$

c) $15\dfrac{11}{13} - 2\dfrac{4}{11} = 15\dfrac{11 \times 11}{13 \times 11} - 2\dfrac{4 \times 13}{11 \times 13}$

$\qquad = 15 - 2 + \dfrac{121 - 52}{143}$

$\qquad = 13\dfrac{69}{143}$

d) $\dfrac{3}{4} + \dfrac{2}{3} - \dfrac{7}{11} = \dfrac{3 \times 3 \times 11}{4 \times 3 \times 11} + \dfrac{2 \times 4 \times 11}{3 \times 4 \times 11} - \dfrac{7 \times 4 \times 3}{11 \times 4 \times 3}$

$\qquad = \dfrac{3 \times 3 \times 11 + 2 \times 4 \times 11 - 7 \times 4 \times 3}{4 \times 3 \times 11}$

$\qquad = \dfrac{99 + 88 - 84}{132}$

$\qquad = \dfrac{103}{132}$

7. Do each of these problems, showing basic intermediate steps:

a) $\dfrac{5}{6} - \dfrac{5}{8} = \dfrac{5 \times 2 \times 2}{2 \times 2 \times 2 \times 3} - \dfrac{5 \times 3}{2 \times 2 \times 2 \times 3}$

$\qquad = \dfrac{20 - 15}{24}$

$\qquad = \dfrac{5}{24}$

b) $9\dfrac{1}{4} - 5\dfrac{1}{6} = 9\dfrac{1 \times 3}{4 \times 3} - 5\dfrac{1 \times 2}{6 \times 2}$

$\qquad = 9 - 5 + \dfrac{1 \times 3 - 1 \times 2}{4 \times 3}$

$\qquad = 4\dfrac{1}{12}$

c) $7\dfrac{13}{15} - 2\dfrac{7}{18} = 7\dfrac{13 \times 2 \times 3}{2 \times 3 \times 3 \times 5} - 2\dfrac{7 \times 5}{2 \times 3 \times 3 \times 5}$

$\qquad = 7 - 2 + \dfrac{78 - 35}{90}$

$\qquad = 5\dfrac{43}{90}$

8. Do each of these problems, showing basic intermediate steps:

a) $4 - \dfrac{5}{9}$ b) $6\dfrac{4}{7} - 1\dfrac{5}{7}$ c) $6\dfrac{1}{4} - 2\dfrac{2}{3}$

a) $4 - \dfrac{5}{9} = 3 + 1 - \dfrac{5}{9}$

$\qquad = 3 + \dfrac{9}{9} - \dfrac{5}{9}$

$\qquad = 3 + \dfrac{9 - 5}{9}$

$\qquad = 3\dfrac{4}{9}$

b) $6\dfrac{4}{7} - 1\dfrac{5}{7} = 5 + \dfrac{7}{7} + \dfrac{4}{7} - 1 - \dfrac{5}{7}$

$\qquad = 5 - 1 + \dfrac{11}{7} - \dfrac{5}{7}$

$\qquad = 4\dfrac{11 - 5}{7}$

$\qquad = 4\dfrac{6}{7}$

c) $6\dfrac{1}{4} - 2\dfrac{2}{3} = 6\dfrac{3}{12} - 2\dfrac{8}{12}$

$\qquad = 5 + \dfrac{12}{12} + \dfrac{3}{12} - 2 - \dfrac{8}{12}$

$\qquad = 5 - 2 + \dfrac{12 + 3 - 8}{12}$

$\qquad = 3\dfrac{7}{12}$

Division of Fractions

1. Do each of these problems, showing basic intermediate steps:

a) $6 \div \dfrac{1}{2} = 6 \times \dfrac{2}{1}$

$\qquad = 12$

b) $6 \div \dfrac{1}{3} = 6 \times \dfrac{3}{1}$

$\qquad = 18$

c) $8 \div \dfrac{1}{2} = 8 \times \dfrac{2}{1}$

$\qquad = 16$

d)

$\qquad 55 \div \dfrac{11}{28} = \dfrac{\overset{5}{\cancel{55}}}{1} \times \dfrac{28}{\underset{1}{\cancel{11}}}$

$\qquad = \dfrac{5 \times 28}{1 \times 1}$

$\qquad = 140$

e) $144 \div \dfrac{12}{7} = \dfrac{\overset{12}{\cancel{144}}}{1} \times \dfrac{7}{\underset{1}{\cancel{12}}}$

$\qquad = \dfrac{12 \times 7}{1 \times 1}$

$\qquad = 84$

2. We have shown the reasoning behind inverting the second fraction and following the rules for multiplication in division problems involving fractions. Do these exercises using the fraction over a fraction routine.

a) $\dfrac{2}{3} \div \dfrac{3}{4} = \dfrac{\dfrac{2}{3}}{\dfrac{3}{4}}$

$= \dfrac{\dfrac{2}{3} \times \dfrac{4}{3}}{\dfrac{3}{4} \times \dfrac{4}{3}}$

$= \dfrac{\dfrac{2}{3} \times \dfrac{4}{3}}{1}$

$= \dfrac{8}{9}$

b) $\dfrac{7}{9} \div \dfrac{11}{13} = \dfrac{\dfrac{7}{9}}{\dfrac{11}{13}}$

$= \dfrac{\dfrac{7}{9} \times \dfrac{13}{11}}{\dfrac{11}{13} \times \dfrac{13}{11}}$

$= \dfrac{\dfrac{7}{7} \times \dfrac{13}{11}}{1}$

$= \dfrac{91}{99}$

c) $\dfrac{8}{11} \div \dfrac{48}{55} = \dfrac{\dfrac{8}{11}}{\dfrac{48}{55}}$

$= \dfrac{\dfrac{8}{11} \times \dfrac{55}{48}}{\dfrac{48}{55} \times \dfrac{55}{48}}$

$= \dfrac{\dfrac{8}{11} \times \dfrac{55}{48}}{1}$

$= \dfrac{5}{6}$

3. Do each of these problems, showing basic intermediate steps:

a) $4\dfrac{7}{8} \div 2\dfrac{5}{6} = \dfrac{39}{8} + \dfrac{17}{6}$

$= \dfrac{39}{8} \times \dfrac{6}{17}$

$= \dfrac{39}{8} \times \dfrac{8}{17}$

$= \dfrac{39 \times 3}{4 \times 17}$

$= \dfrac{117}{68}$

$= 1\dfrac{49}{68}$

b) $11\dfrac{1}{2} \div 4\dfrac{2}{3} = \dfrac{23}{2} + \dfrac{14}{3}$

$= \dfrac{23}{2} \times \dfrac{3}{14}$

$= \dfrac{23}{2} \times \dfrac{3}{14}$

$= \dfrac{69}{28}$

$= 2\dfrac{13}{28}$

c) $4\dfrac{2}{3} \div 11\dfrac{1}{2} = \dfrac{14}{3} + \dfrac{23}{2}$

$= \dfrac{14}{3} \times \dfrac{2}{23}$

$= \dfrac{14 \times 2}{3 \times 23}$

$= \dfrac{28}{69}$

4. Use the least common multiple method to do the following problems:

a) $\dfrac{2}{3} \div \dfrac{3}{4} = \dfrac{8}{12} \div \dfrac{9}{12}$

$= \dfrac{9}{12} \overline{\smash{\big)}\dfrac{8}{12}}$

$= \dfrac{89}{1212}$

$= \dfrac{8 \div 9}{1}$

$= \dfrac{8}{9}$

b) $\dfrac{7}{9} \div \dfrac{11}{13} = \dfrac{91}{117} \div \dfrac{99}{117}$

$= \dfrac{99}{117} \overline{\smash{\big)}\dfrac{91}{117}}$

$= \dfrac{99 \div 99}{117 \div 117}$

$= \dfrac{91}{99}$

c) $\dfrac{8}{11} \div \dfrac{48}{55} = \dfrac{440}{605} \div \dfrac{528}{605}$

$= \dfrac{528}{605} \overline{\smash{\big)}\dfrac{440}{605}}$

$= \dfrac{440 \div 528}{605 \div 605}$

$= \dfrac{440}{528}$

$= \dfrac{5}{6}$

Addition of Decimals

1. Do the following problems showing any scratch work you generate:

a)
$$4.36$$
$$56.789$$
$$+321$$
$$\overline{382.149}$$

b)
$$0.3$$
$$21.4$$
$$367.963$$
$$+59.6921$$
$$\overline{449.3551}$$

c)
$$0.1$$
$$0.01$$
$$+0.001$$
$$\overline{0.111}$$

Subtraction of Decimals

1. Do each of these exercises using only pencil and paper:

a)
$$845$$
$$-270.156$$
$$\overline{574.844}$$

b)
$$23.01$$
$$-\ 2.3456$$
$$\overline{20.6644}$$

c)
$$8712$$
$$-\ \ \ 19.872$$
$$\overline{8692.428}$$

Multiplication of Decimals

1. Do each of the following problems to practice your multiplication skills when one or both of the factors involve decimals. Although we are proponents of calculator use, you should not use calculators here. You need to practice the skill and be sure you have a handle on decimal multiplication.

$0.3 \times 4.2 = 1.26$

$14.89 \times 0.005 = 0.07445$

$0.002 \times 0.0003 = 0.0000006$

$12.5 \times 4.2 = 52.5$ NOTE that the answer computes to be 52.50 but that last zero is generally not written.

Division of Decimals

1. Do these problems without a calculator. You should check your work by multiplying the factor times the missing factor.

a)
$$\begin{array}{r} 1.5 \\ 42\overline{)63.0} \\ 42 \\ \hline 21\ 0 \\ 21\ 0 \\ \hline 0 \end{array}$$

b)
$$\begin{array}{r} 1.5 \\ 12\overline{)18.0} \\ 12 \\ \hline 6\ 0 \\ 6\ 0 \\ \hline 0 \end{array}$$

c)
$$\begin{array}{r} 0.5 \\ 2\overline{)1.0} \\ 1\ 0 \\ \hline 0 \end{array}$$

d)
$$\begin{array}{r} 1.3\overline{3}33 \\ 3\overline{)4.0000} \\ 3 \\ \hline 1\ 0 \\ 9 \\ \hline 10 \\ 9 \\ \hline 10 \\ 9 \\ \hline 10 \\ 9 \end{array}$$

The decision in the last example on how far to go before you show the repeat is left you and your instructor.

2. Complete the following exercises being careful to align the decimal point in the missing factor:

a)
$$\begin{array}{r} 1.675 \\ 14\overline{)23.456} \\ 14 \\ \hline 94 \\ 84 \\ \hline 105 \\ 98 \\ \hline 76 \\ 70 \\ \hline 6 \ \ \text{etc.} \end{array}$$

b)
$$\begin{array}{r} 0.081 \\ 723\overline{)58.920} \\ 5784 \\ \hline 1080 \\ 723 \\ \hline 357 \ \ \text{etc.} \end{array}$$

c)
$$\begin{array}{r} 0.049 \\ 465\overline{)23.100} \\ 1860 \\ \hline 4500 \\ 4185 \\ \hline 315 \ \ \text{etc.} \end{array}$$

The degree of the precision of the answers is left to you and your instructor.

3. Tell the smallest power of 10 needed to make the factor a whole number:

a) $\left(\dfrac{23456}{1.4}\right)\left(\dfrac{10}{10}\right)$

b) $\left(\dfrac{5892}{7.23}\right)\left(\dfrac{100}{100}\right)$

c) $\left(\dfrac{231}{0.465}\right)\left(\dfrac{1000}{1000}\right)$

d) $\left(\dfrac{679}{3.54}\right)\left(\dfrac{100}{100}\right)$

4. Tell the smallest power of 10 needed to make the factor a whole number:

a) $1.4\overline{)234.56}$ (10)   b) $7.23\overline{)5892}$ (100)

c) $0.465\overline{)2.31}$ (1000)   d) $3.54\overline{)67.9}$ (100)

Addition of Integers

1. Do each of the following problems on a number line and record both the problem and the answer in a separate list. State a rule for adding integers when the addends have the same sign.

a) $^+3 + {}^+5 = {}^+8$ b) $^+7 + {}^+6 = {}^+13$

c) $^+4 + {}^+2 = {}^+6$ d) $^-3 + {}^-5 = {}^-8$

e) $^-7 + {}^-6 = {}^-13$ f) $^-4 + {}^-2 = {}^-6$

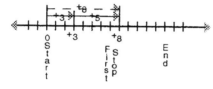

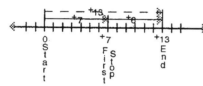

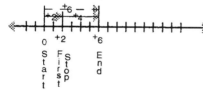

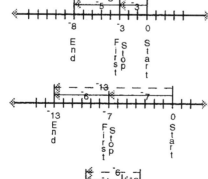

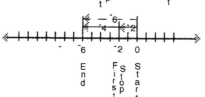

The conclusion is that adding like signed numbers is just like adding whole numbers without the signs and the answer has the common sign.

2. Do some integer addition problems on the number line to assure you can get the sums. Each of your problems should be similar to those in Figs. 2.56 and 2.57.

Answers will vary.

Subtraction of Integers

1. Do each of the following problems on a number line and record both the problem and the answer in a different location. State a rule for subtracting integers.

a) $^+3 - {}^+5 = ?$ b) $^+7 - {}^+6 = ?$

c) $^+4 - {}^+2 = ?$ d) $^-3 - {}^-5 = ?$

e) $^-7 - {}^-6 = ?$ f) $^-4 - {}^-2 = ?$

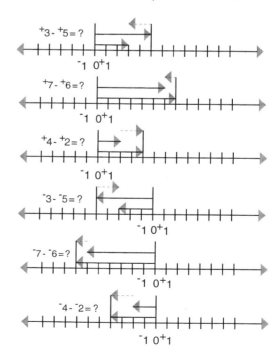

g) $^-3 - {}^+5 = ?$ h) $^-8 - {}^+2 = ?$

i) $^-10 - {}^+3 = ?$ j) $^+9 - {}^-3 = ?$

k) $^+7 - {}^-5 = ?$ l) $^+6 - {}^-1 = ?$

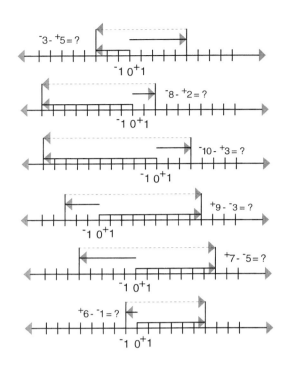

Multiplication of Integers

1. Now that all four types of multiplication problems involving integers have been considered, state two generalizations that deal with multiplying signed numbers:

If the two factors have the same sign, the product is positive.

If the two factors have different signs, the product will be negative.

2. Develop a generalization relating to multiplying more than two integers factors based on the number of negative factors that are involved.

If the number of negative factors in a multiplication problem is even, then the product is positive. If the number of negative factors in a multiplication problem is odd, then the product is negative.

3. State a generalization relating to multiplying two or more integers factors when one of them is zero.

If one factor is zero, then the product will be zero, no matter how many factors are involved.

Division of Integers

1. Considering problems only of the types $\dfrac{^{+}20}{^{+}4} = {^{+}5}$ $\dfrac{^{-}20}{^{-}4} = {^{+}5}$, for example (positive divided by positive and negative divided by negative), describe a generalization for working with dividing a product by a factor when their signs are the same.

Dividing with like signs gives a positive missing factor.

2. Considering problems only of the types $\dfrac{^{+}20}{^{-}4} = {^{-}5}$ $\dfrac{^{-}20}{^{+}4} = {^{-}5}$, for example (positive divided by negative and negative divided by positive), describe a generalization for working with dividing a product by a factor when their signs are not the same.

Dividing with unlike signs gives a negative missing factor.

Ratios and Proportions

1. Write ratios that compare the numbers of designs in Fig. 2.73.

a) Number of ⬡ to number of ♡

b) Number of ☀ to number of ◎

c) Number of ⬡ to total number of items

d) Number of figures that have only straight segments to number of figures that contain curves

a) $\dfrac{6}{4}$ b) $\dfrac{3}{6}$ c) $\dfrac{6}{19}$ d) $\dfrac{6}{13}$

2. The following ratios can be changed so that they have denominators that are powers of 10. Use the procedure shown in the examples to write these ratios as percentages.

a) Jose got 7 strikes out of his first 20 frames at the bowling tournament. What was his percentage of strikes during the first 20 frames?

$$\frac{7}{20} = \frac{7 \cdot (5)}{2^2 \cdot 5 \cdot (5)} = \frac{35}{2^2 \cdot 5^2} = \frac{35}{10^2} = \frac{35}{100}$$

Jose had 35% strikes in the first 20 frames of the bowling tournament.

b) Only 18 out of 250 people at the wedding selected chicken. What percent of the people at the wedding selected chicken?

$$\frac{18}{250} = \frac{18}{2 \cdot 5^3} = \frac{18 \cdot (2^2)}{2 \cdot 5^3 \cdot (2^2)} = \frac{18 \cdot 4}{2^3 \cdot 5^3} = \frac{72}{10^3} = \frac{72}{1000} = \frac{7.2}{100}$$

7.2% of the people at the wedding selected chicken.

c) For 135 of the 2500 cars that passed through the tollbooth on Tuesday, an error in the amount of the toll paid was indicated. What percentage of toll errors does this imply?

$$\frac{135}{2500} = \frac{135}{2^2 \cdot 5^4} = \frac{135 \cdot (2^2)}{2^2 \cdot 5^4 \cdot (2^2)} = \frac{135 \cdot 4}{2^4 \cdot 5^4} = \frac{540}{10^4} = \frac{540}{10000} = \frac{5.4}{100}$$

There was an error in 5.4% of the tolls on Tuesday.

3. The following ratios cannot be changed so that they have denominators that are powers of 10. Explain why this is true. Use your calculator to write these ratios as percentages. Round to the nearest tenth of a percent.

a) 19 of 23 students earned passing scores on the first exam. What percentage of the students earned passing scores?

23 is not a factor of a power of 10.
19 ÷ 23 □ 0.826

Approximately 82.6% of the students were passing after the first exam.

b) 11 of Kim's 18 matchbox cars represent American automobiles. What percentage of Kim's matchbox cars represents foreign automobiles?

18 is not a factor of a power of 10
7 ÷ 18 □ 0.389

Approximately 38.9% of Kim's cars represent foreign automobiles.

4. Write the two equivalent ratios that represent the quantities in the following statements. Use a letter to represent the missing quantity and set the ratios equal to one another and find the missing quantity by inspection.

a) I would like to make 3 identical shirts. My pattern for a single shirt requires 2 yards of fabric. How much fabric should I buy for my 3 shirts?

b) There are 4 tables and 16 chairs in our classroom. If we continue the same arrangement, then how many chairs would we need for 8 tables?

c) My small, 4-pound turkey requires 1 hour to roast. Assuming all other things are equal, how much time would be required to roast a 16-pound turkey?

$$\frac{3 \text{ skirts}}{y \text{ yards of fabric}} = \frac{1 \text{ skirt}}{2 \text{ yards of fabric}} \quad \text{or}$$

$$\frac{2 \text{ yards of fabric}}{1 \text{ skirt}} = \frac{y \text{ yards of fabric}}{3 \text{ skirts}}$$

a) $y = 6$

6 yards of fabric are needed for 3 skirts

$$\frac{4 \text{ tables}}{16 \text{ chairs}} = \frac{8 \text{ tables}}{c \text{ chairs}} \quad \text{or}$$

$$\frac{c \text{ chairs}}{8 \text{ tables}} = \frac{16 \text{ chairs}}{4 \text{ tables}}$$

b) $c = 32$

32 chairs are needed for 8 tables

$$\frac{4 \text{ pounds}}{1 \text{ hour}} = \frac{16 \text{ pounds}}{h \text{ hours}} \quad \text{or}$$

$$\frac{h \text{ hours}}{16 \text{ pounds}} = \frac{1 \text{ hour}}{4 \text{ pounds}}$$

c) h = 4

4 hours will be required to roast a 16-pound turkey

5. Use cross products to determine if each of the following is a true proportion.

a) $\dfrac{6}{17}$ ☐ = or ≠ $\dfrac{18}{51}$

6 · 51 = 306, 17 · 18 = 306, therefore, this is a true proportion.

b) $\dfrac{5}{31}$ ☐ = or ≠ $\dfrac{18}{111}$

5 · 111 = 555, 31 · 18 = 558, therefore, this proportion is not true.

c) $\dfrac{8}{19}$ ☐ = or ≠ $\dfrac{144}{342}$

8 · 342 = 2736, 19 · 144 = 2736, therefore, this is a true proportion.

6. Solve the following proportions (if necessary, round to the nearest tenth):

a) $\dfrac{14}{a} = \dfrac{5}{3}$

14 · 3 = a · 5
42 = 5a
$\dfrac{42}{5} = \dfrac{5a}{5}$
a = 8.4

b) $\dfrac{2}{7} = \dfrac{b}{147}$

2 · 147 = 7 · b
294 = 7b
$\dfrac{294}{7} = \dfrac{7b}{7}$
42 = b

c) $\dfrac{c}{135} = \dfrac{14}{27}$

c · 27 = 135 · 14
27c = 1890
$\dfrac{27c}{27} = \dfrac{1890}{27}$
c = 70

7. List at least four additional proportions for the triangles in Fig. 2.76.

$$\frac{13.3}{6} = \frac{24.6}{12}, \frac{10.75}{12.3} = \frac{21.5}{24.6}, \frac{12}{24.6} = \frac{6}{12.3}, \frac{12}{6} = \frac{24.6}{12.3}$$

8. Your recipe for Party Mix calls for 7 cups of wheat cereal, 2 cups of mixed nuts, 2 cups of pretzels, 1.5 sticks of butter, 1 tablespoon of special sauce, and seasoned salt to taste. You find that you have only 1.5 cups of mixed nuts. How much of each of the other ingredients do you use if you want to keep the recipe in proportion?

$$\frac{2}{7} = \frac{1.5}{w}$$

2w = 10.5
w = 5.25 cups of wheat cereal

$$\frac{2}{2} = \frac{1.5}{p}$$

p = 1.5 cups of pretzels

$$\frac{2}{1.5} = \frac{1.5}{b}$$

2b = 2.25
b ☐ 1.13 sticks of butter

$$\frac{2}{1} = \frac{1.5}{s}$$

2s = 1.5
s = 0.75 tablespoon of special sauce

**Seasoned salt will still be added "to taste"

9. For some incredibly interesting reason, you need to know the height of the telephone pole in front of your home. You know that you are 5.5 feet tall and that you cast a shadow that is 11 feet long. The telephone pole casts a shadow that is 26 feet long. How tall is the telephone pole?

$$\frac{5.5}{t} = \frac{11}{26}$$

$$143 = 11t$$

t = 13 feet is height of telephone pole

10. Trace the triangles in Fig. 2.76 and label them as follows. Smaller triangle—the shorter leg is 9 cm and the longer leg is 12 cm. Larger triangle—the hypotenuse is 37.5 cm and the shorter leg is 22.5 cm. What is the length of the hypotenuse of the smaller triangle?

One possible solution is:

$$\frac{9}{22.5} = \frac{h}{37.5}$$

$$337.5 = 22.5h$$

h = 15 cm is the length of the hypotenuse of the smaller triangle

11. As a teller in a bank that sales foreign currency, you are responsible for helping customers who are planning for trips abroad. The rates change very quickly, so you must calculate each transaction separately. A customer asks you how much it would cost to buy 200.00 Deutch Marks (DM). You check the rate and find that $1.00 is worth 1.32 DM. How much will it cost your customer to get the Deutch Marks he needs for his trip to Germany?

$$\frac{1}{1.32} = \frac{d}{200}$$

$$200 = 1.32d$$

d = 151.52 (Round up to $151.52)

3: ALGEBRA

1. Do this trick using a specific number and then using x for the number picked.

Pick a number.	7	x
Double it.	14	2x
Add 4.	18	2x + 4
Divide by 2.	9	x + 2
Subtract your original number.	2	2

What do you get? 2

If you begin the trick with a different number, will you still get that answer? Yes

2. Do the trick in Exercise 1 using a fraction. Is your answer still the same?

$$\frac{5}{7}$$

$$\frac{10}{7}$$

$$\frac{10}{7} + \frac{28}{7} = \frac{38}{7}$$

$$\frac{\frac{38}{7}}{2} = \frac{38}{14} \text{ or } \frac{19}{7}$$

$$\frac{19}{7} - \frac{5}{7} = \frac{14}{7} \text{ or } 2$$

Yes, the answer is still the same.

3. Do the trick in Exercise 1 using a negative number. Is your answer still the same?

−15

−30

−26

−13

−13 − (−15) = −13 + 15 or +2, which is 2. Yes, the answer is still the same.

4. Do this trick using a specific number and then using m for the number picked.

Pick a number.	71	m
Double it.	142	2m
Add 4.	146	2m + 4
Divide by 2.	73	m + 2
Subtract 2.	71	m

What do you get? I got the number I started with.

Will this always work? Yes.

Why or why not? The algebra shows why it will always work.

5. Do this trick using a specific number and then using p for the number picked.

Pick a number.

Triple it.

Add 12.

Divide by 3.

Subtract your original number.

$-\dfrac{5}{7}$ p

$-\dfrac{15}{7}$ 3p

$-\dfrac{15}{7}+\dfrac{84}{7}=\dfrac{69}{7}$ 3p + 12

$\dfrac{\dfrac{69}{7}}{3}=\dfrac{69}{21}$ or $\dfrac{23}{7}$ p + 4

$\dfrac{23}{7}-\left(-\dfrac{5}{7}\right)=\dfrac{23}{7}+\dfrac{5}{7}$ which is $\dfrac{28}{7}$ or 4 4

What do you get? 4.
Is this problem significantly different from the one given in Exercise 1? No. The numbers and variables are the same, but the algebra is similar and shows that you will always get your original number.

6. What are the next two lines in the pattern 1, 11, 21, 1112, 3112, 211213, 312213, 212223, ?, ?

The next term is 114213.
The term after that is 31121314.

7. What are the next two terms in the pattern 1, 11, 21, 1211, 111221, 312213, 1311221113, ?, ?

The next term is 111321223113.
The next term after that is 3113121122132113.

8. Make a model that shows how Gauss' trick applies to the triangular numbers.

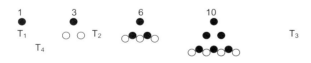

$T_1 = 1$ $T_2 = 1 + 2$ $T_3 = 1 + 2 + 3$ $T_4 = 1 + 2 + 3 + 4$

Thus, adding all of the counting numbers up to and including the number n can find any triangular number T_n.

9. Using the model of the rectangular numbers, write a generalizing statement about how to find any rectangular number, R_n.

$R_n = n(n + 1)$

10. Rewrite the rectangular model to show a relation between the rectangular numbers and the square numbers.

R_1 R_2 R_3 R_4 R_5

$R_n = n^2 + n$

11. Generalize the model you drew about the relation between rectangular and square numbers.

$T_n = \dfrac{n(n+1)}{2}$ and $R_n = n(n + 1)$, thus $T_n = \dfrac{R_n}{2}$.

12. How do the rectangular numbers relate to the triangular numbers?

A rectangular number is twice as much as a triangular number: $R_n = 2T_n$

13. Repeat traveled at a rate of 12 mph. Use the information you placed into the table at the beginning of this chapter.

a) Make a graph of Repeat's rate of change using the x axis for time and the y axis for distance traveled.

b) Find m for Repeat by counting $\dfrac{\text{rise}}{\text{run}}$ on the line segment.

$m = \dfrac{12}{1} = 12$

c) Use the two points from the table for how far Repeat had traveled at 2 hours and at 5 hours and find m algebraically. Does your answer here match your answer for Part b?

(2, 24) and (5, 60) $m = \dfrac{60 - 24}{5 - 2} = \dfrac{36}{3} = \dfrac{12}{1} = 12$ Yes!

14. In the word problem about renting a jackhammer, we found a cost pattern for each of the rental companies. For Rent It, the pattern was 20 + 3h ($20.00 plus $3.00 per hour) and for Get It Here, the pattern was 8h ($8.00 per hour).

a) Use the cost pattern for Rent It to write a cost equation for renting the equipment. State the rate of change and the y intercept.

C(h) = 20 + 3h or y = 3x + 20; m = 3; b = 20 or (0, 20)

b) Use the cost pattern for Get It Here to write a cost equation for renting the equipment. State the rate of change and the y intercept.

C(h) = 8h or y = 8x; m = 8; b = 0 or (0, 0)

c) At what point would the graphs of these two cost equations intersect?

(4, 32)

15. Peggy, a member of this book's dynamic author team, wants to paint her house a particular shade of blue such that the ratio of gallons of blue paint to white paint is 2:3.

a) How many gallons of blue paint and how many gallons of white paint will be needed to mix up 15 gallons?

	Gallons	Gallons	Gallons
Blue	2	4	6
White	3	6	9
Total	5	10	15

b) What is the algebraic solution for the slope of the ray that represents this color mixture no matter how many gallons of paint are needed?

$$m = \frac{6-2}{9-3} = \frac{4}{6} = \frac{2}{3}$$

c) If Peggy would like to make the trim of her house a darker shade of the same color, then how should she change the ratio of the paint mixture?
   Answers will vary: example—3 gallons of blue to 4 gallons of white
d) Using the trim mixture you decided on for Peggy, how many gallons of blue paint and how many gallons of white paint would be needed to make 3.5 gallons of paint?
   Answers will vary: example—

	Gallons	Gallons
Blue	3	1.5
White	4	2
Total	7	3.5

16. What is the 121st number in the following sequence: 4, 8, 12, . . . ?

$a_n = a_1 + (n - 1)d$
$a_{121} = 4 + (121 - 1)4$
$a_{121} = 4 + (120)4$
$a_{121} = 4 + 480$
$a_{121} = 484$

17. What is the 326th number in the following sequence: 9, 20, 31, . . . ?

$a_n = a_1 + (n - 1)d$
$a_{326} = 9 + (326 - 1)11$
$a_{326} = 9 + (325)11$
$a_{326} = 9 + 3575$
$a_{326} = 3584$

18. What is the sum of the first 84 even numbers: 2, 4, 6, . . . ?

$a_n = a_1 + (n - 1)d$
$a_{84} = 2 + (84 - 1)4$
$a_{84} = 2 + (83)4$
$a_{84} = 2 + 332$
$a_{84} = 334$
$S_n = \frac{n}{2}(a_1 + a_n)$
$S_{84} = \frac{84}{2}(2 + 334)$
$S_{84} = 42(336)$
$S_{84} = 14112$

19. What is the sum of the 9th through the 101st numbers in Question 16?

$a_n = a_1 + (n - 1)d$
$a_8 = 4 + (8 - 1)4$
$a_8 = 4 + (7)4$
$a_8 = 4 + 28$
$a_8 = 32$
$S_n = \frac{n}{2}(a_1 + a_n)$
$S_n = \frac{8}{2}(2 + 32)$
$S_8 = 4(34)$

$S_8 = 136$

$a_n = a_1 + (n - 1)d$

$a_{101} = 4 + (101 - 1)4$

$a_{101} = 4 + (100)4$

$a_{101} = 4 + 400$

$a_{101} = 404$

$S_n = a_1 + \dfrac{(n - 1)}{2}(a_2 + a_n)$

$S_{101} = 4 + \dfrac{(101 - 1)}{2}(8 + 404)$

$S_{101} = 4 + \dfrac{(100)}{2}(412)$

$S_{101} = 4 + 50(412)$

$S_{101} = 4 + 20600$

$S_{101} = 20604$

$S_{101} - S_8 = 20604 - 136$

$S_{101} - S_8 = 20468$

The sum of the 9th through the 101st numbers in the sequence 4, 8, 12, . . . is 20468.

20. What is the 15th number in the following sequence: 5, 10, 20, . . . ?

$a_n = a_1 r^{n-1}$

$a_{15} = 5 \cdot 2^{15-1}$

$a_{15} = 5 \cdot 2^{15-1}$

$a_{15} = 5 \cdot 2^{14}$

$a_{15} = 5 \cdot 16384$

$a_{15} = 81920$

21. What is the 19th number in the following sequence: 99, 33, 11, . . . ?

$a_n = a_1 r^{n-1}$

$a_{19} = 99 \cdot \left(\dfrac{1}{3}\right)^{19-1}$

$a_{19} = 99 \cdot \left(\dfrac{1}{3}\right)^{18}$

$a_{19} \approx 99 \cdot 0.000000002581$

$a_{19} \approx 0.000000256$

22. What is the sum of the first 20 numbers in the sequence: 5, 10, 20, . . . ?

$S_n = \dfrac{a_1(1 - r^n)}{(1 - r)}$

$S_{20} = \dfrac{5(1 - 2^{20})}{(1 - 2)}$

$S_{20} = \dfrac{5(1 - 1048576)}{(-1)}$

$S_{20} = \dfrac{5(-1048575)}{(-1)}$

$S_{20} = 5242875$

23. What is the sum of the first 500 numbers in the sequence: 99, 33, 11, . . . ?

$S_n = \dfrac{a_1(1 - r^n)}{(1 - r)}$

$S_{500} = \dfrac{99\left(1 - \left(\dfrac{1}{3}\right)^{500}\right)}{\left(1 - \dfrac{1}{3}\right)}$

$S_{500} \approx \dfrac{99(1 - 0)}{\left(\dfrac{2}{3}\right)}$

$S_{500} \approx 148.5$

GEOMETRY SOLUTION MANUAL

1. For each of the following, provide a labeled sketch and explain in your own words:

a) Point Q
b) Line segment ST
c) Line k
d) Plane R
e) Ray UV
f) Vector **u** of length 3 and heading to the right
g) Which of these can be measured?

a) °Q This is a dot that marks the location in space of point Q.

b) S —— T This is the straight array of points from S to T.

c) ←————— r —————→ This is a straight array of points that has no endpoint.

d) This represents a flat surface that has no edge in any direction.

e) This is the ray that starts at point U and goes on forever in the direction of point V.

f) This is the vector AB, which starts at 0 and goes to 1 on the number line.

0   1

g) Only line segment ST and vector AB can be measured.

2. Answer each of the following questions and provide a sketch:

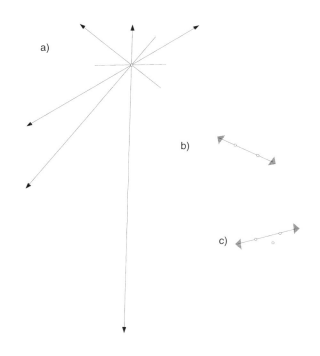

a) How many different lines could you sketch through a single point?

b) How many different lines could you sketch through two points?

c) Is it always possible to sketch one line through three points?

a) You can sketch many (an infinite number) of lines, segments, or rays through one point.

b) You can sketch only one distinct line or segment given two given points. However, two distinct rays can be defined (each beginning at one of the points and going through the other point).

c) Unless three points line up in a straight array, a line cannot be sketched that includes all three.

3. Use a straight edge to sketch an angle. Label a few interior points, exterior points, and points on your angle (remember to use printed capital letters when you label points). Shade the part of the interior that is within the rays you drew. If you continued the rays, would this interior shading continue to expand?

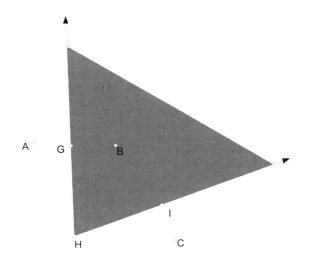

Points G, H, and I are on the angle. Points A and C are exterior points. Point B is an interior point. If the shaded area were extended, it would get wider and wider and extend infinitely, like a wedge of a plane.

4. Given that $\overline{HL} \perp \overline{JK}$, name every angle in Figs. 4.2–4.11; then identify each angle as right, acute, obtuse, or straight. (There are at least 10 angles in the figure.)

Right angles: ∠JML, ∠KML, ∠HMK, ∠HMJ
Acute angles: ∠HMI, ∠IMJ
Obtuse angles: ∠IMK, ∠IML
Straight angles: ∠HML, ∠JMK

5. Explain why there is a tiny box drawn at the intersection labeled with an M in Fig. 4.11.

The tiny box means that $\overline{HL} \perp \overline{JK}$ (Line Segment HL is perpendicular to Line Segment JK), so that ∠HMK and three of the other angles, ∠JML, ∠KML, and ∠HMJ are right angles.

6. Explain why we need to use three letters to identify any angle in Fig. 4.11.

We use three letters to make sure we identify the correct angle. If we say ∠M, we could

mean any one of the 10 angles in Fig. 4.11, but if we identify a point on each leg of an angle, as well as the vertex, there will be no doubt about which angle is being named.

7. In Fig. 4.11, we say that ∠HMI and ∠HMK are "adjacent angles." Write a definition of adjacent angles.

The two angles, ∠HMI and ∠IMK, are adjacent because they share a vertex and one leg, Ray MI, and are side by side (not overlapping). Two angles are adjacent if they share a vertex and one leg without overlapping.

8. Write an informal definition for the term *complementary angles*.

Two angles are complementary angles if they can be combined (without overlapping) to form a right angle.
Another way to look at this is to consider their measures, because a right angle has a measure of 90°.
m∠JMI = 47°, m∠HMI = 43° The sum of their measures is 90°.
Two angles are complementary angles if their measures add up to 90°.

9. Write an informal definition for the term *supplementary angles*.

Two angles are supplementary angles if they can be combined (without overlapping) to form a straight angle.
Another way to look at this is to consider the angle measures, because a straight angle has a measure of 180°.
m∠JMI = 47° and m∠KMI= 133° The sum of their measures is 180°.
Two angles are supplementary angles if their measures add up to 180°.

10. Do you think it is possible for two angles to be complementary or supplementary without being adjacent? If your answer is yes, then provide sketches that indicate your thinking.

The requirement is that the angles be combined to form a right angle or a straight angle.

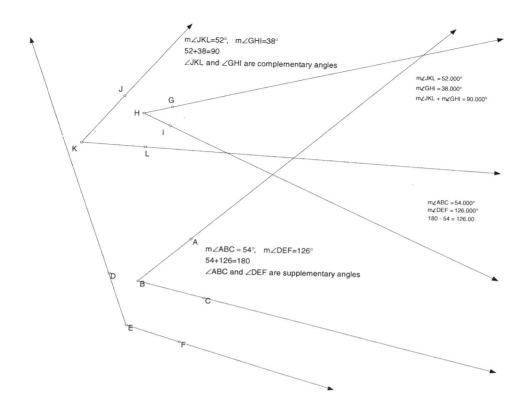

m∠JKL=52°, m∠GHI=38°
52+38=90
∠JKL and ∠GHI are complementary angles

m∠JKL = 52.000°
m∠GHI = 38.000°
m∠JKL + m∠GHI = 90.000°

m∠ABC =54.000°
m∠DEF = 126.000°
180 - 54 = 126.00

m∠ABC = 54°, m∠DEF=126°
54+126=180
∠ABC and ∠DEF are supplementary angles

You could cut out two angles that aren't adjacent and rearrange them to form the required angle. The definitions could mention the sums of the measures; neither would require that the angles be adjacent.

11. Explain why Table 4.1 begins with a polygon of three sides.

Because polygons are made up of line segments, it takes at least three sides to make a figure that will close.

12. There are several common polygons, called *quadrilaterals*, that have four sides. Use the diagram of the quadrilateral family in Fig. 4.14 to answer the following questions:

a) What are the similarities and differences among the special quadrilaterals in Fig. 4.14?
b) What does it mean if there is not an arrow connecting two quadrilaterals?
c) Is every square a rectangle?
d) Is every rectangle a square?
e) Where does a four-sided figure shaped like a child's kite fit in this diagram?

a) The general quadrilateral doesn't have anything special. It just has four sides and four angles. The sides may or may not be the same length; the angles may or may not be of any specific measure.

All of the special quadrilaterals shown in the diagram are similar because they all have four sides and at least one pair of parallel sides.

The family tree is built on differences as much as similarities. The trapezoid has only one pair of parallel sides, whereas the rest have two pairs of parallel sides. The parallelograms get more and more special as you move down the chart. The parallelogram has two pairs of congruent, parallel sides. The rhombus has two pairs of parallel sides, but also has all sides congruent. The rectangle has two pairs of congruent, parallel sides, but also has right angles. The square has two pairs of parallel sides, all sides congruent, and right angles.

b) The arrows connect the quadrilaterals that have similarities. If there is no arrow connecting two quadrilaterals, then there is at least one attribute that is not shared.

c) A square has all the attributes of a rectangle (two pairs of congruent, parallel sides, and right angles), so it is a rectangle.

d) A rectangle that has all sides congruent is a square. Some rectangles are not squares because they have different lengths for their height and width.

e) In Fig. 4.14, a child's kite might be a rhombus if all four sides are the same length. However, such a kite would be difficult to fly. Start a new branch for quadrilaterals with adjacent sides congruent in pairs, as the following figure.

13. Use a piece of nonelastic string (thread, dental floss, etc.) to form a loop. Use your closed loop to model the polygons in Table 4.1. What do all your models have in common? How do your models differ as you add sides to create new polygons?

The models all have the same perimeter, because the string has a fixed length. The lengths of the sides change, growing shorter as more and more sides are added. The angles also change, growing larger as more and more sides are added. Because the sketches in the figure represent regular polygons, the areas of the enclosed regions increase as sides are added.

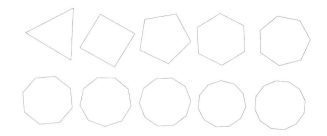

14. Most of our sketches were created using Geometer's Sketchpad®. You may want to use this or another dynamic software application as you complete this exercise. You may, of course, complete the sketches using a straightedge and protractor. Draw and label polygons with the given characteristics. Name the polygons (a) based on the letters at their vertices, and (b) based on their characteristics (Choose from these terms, using each term only once: acute triangle, equilateral triangle, isosceles triangle, obtuse triangle, parallelogram, quadrilateral, rectangle, rhombus, right triangle, scalene triangle, and trapezoid.):

a) Three sides with as many right angles as possible.

b) Three sides with as many obtuse angles as possible.

c) Three sides with as many acute angles as possible.

d) Three sides with no sides the same length.

e) Three sides with two sides the same length.

f) Three sides with all three sides the same length.

g) Four sides with no sides the same length.

h) Four sides with two opposite sides parallel and the other two opposite sides not parallel.

i) Four sides with as many right angles as possible.

j) Four sides with all sides the same length and as many obtuse angles as possible.

k) Four sides with opposite sides parallel and as many acute angles as possible.

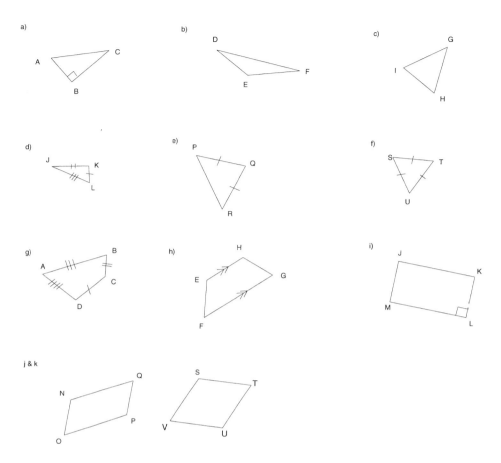

a) ⊔ CBA is a **right triangle**; it has exactly one right angle (∠ABC).

b) ⊔ FED is an **obtuse triangle**; it has exactly one obtuse angle (∠DEF).

c) ⊔ IHG is an **acute triangle**; all three angles are less than 90°.

d) ⊔ JKL is a **scalene triangle**; it has no sides the same length. We indicate that the sides are not the same length by placing a single mark on the shortest, two marks on the next longer, and three marks on the longest.

e) ⊔ RQP is an **isosceles triangle**; it has at least two sides the same length (all three could be the same length). Congruent sides, PQ and RQ, are indicated because they each have a single mark.

f) ⊔ STU is an **equilateral triangle**; all three sides are congruent. The congruent sides are indicated because they all have the same number of marks.

g) General **quadrilateral** ADCB has no sides the same length, as indicated by the

marks. This time the number of marks does not indicate relative length, only that no two sides are the same length.

h) **Trapezoid** EFGH is a quadrilateral with two opposite sides parallel (as indicated by the double arrowheads on sides EH and FG) and the other two opposite sides not parallel.

i) A parallelogram that is a **rectangle** (or a square) has four right angles (it is only necessary to mark one of them).

j & k) A general **parallelogram** (or a **rhombus**) has four sides with opposite sides parallel and as many acute angles as possible. Parallelogram ONQP has two (opposite) acute angles, ∠O and ∠Q, and two (opposite) obtuse angles, ∠P and ∠N. Although Rhombus STUV has all four sides the same length, it has two (opposite) acute angles ∠T and ∠V, and two (opposite) obtuse angles ∠U and ∠S.

15. Write an informal definition for each of the following terms:

a) Side of a polygon—How many sides does a 12-gon have?

b) Vertices of a polygon—How many vertices does a 7-gon have?

c) Diagonal of a polygon—How many diagonals does a 5-gon have?

d) Altitude of a polygon—How many altitudes does a 3-gon have?

a) A **side of a polygon** is a straight line segment. The sides of a polygon are joined by their endpoints to create a region on a plane. Polygons can have three or more sides. A 12-gon has 12 sides.

b) The **vertices of a polygon** are the corners where the sides are joined at their endpoints. Polygons have the same number of vertices as sides. A 7-gon has 7 vertices.

c) The **diagonal of a polygon** is an auxiliary line segment that joins nonconsecutive vertices. The number of diagonals in a polygon is determined by the number of vertices it has. In a pentagon, there are five diagonals, representing two connections across the interior from each vertex, as shown in the figure.

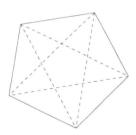

d) The **altitude of a polygon** is a line segment that starts at a vertex and ends perpendicular to a side. It is the height of the polygon. The number of altitudes is determined by the number of vertices a polygon has. In a triangle, an altitude can be drawn from each of the three vertices, as shown in the figure.

16. Use the information in Fig. 4.18 and Fig. 4.19 to write your own informal definitions for the following terms:

a) Center
b) Chord
c) Circle
d) Circumference

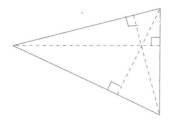

e) Diameter
f) Radius
g) Sector
h) Segment

a) The center of a circle is a given point from which all the points on the circle are the same distance.

b) A chord of a circle is a line segment that connects two points on the circle.

c) A circle is a given point, called the center, and a set of points that are equidistant from the center. It creates a region in the plane and divides the plane into three parts: the points inside the circle, the points outside the circle, and the points on the circle.

e) A diameter of a circle is a chord that goes through the center of the circle. It is the longest possible chord.

f) A radius is a line segment that connects the center and a point on the circle. All the radii of a circle are the same length.

g) A sector of a circle is a pie wedge region defined by two radii and an arc of the circle.

h) A segment of a circle is a region defined by a chord and an arc of the circle.

17. Use a straightedge and a sharp pencil to score a line segment on your paper and label the endpoints A and B. Fold the paper so that Points A and B coincide; crease the paper along the fold. What geometric figure have you constructed? Place a few points at random positions on the fold line and label them C, D, E, and F (be sure that one of the points is at the intersection of the fold with the original segment from A to B). From each of these points, one by one, compare the distance to A with the distance to B. What might you conjecture based on this construction?

When the segment is created so that Point A and Point B coincide, the resulting crease is the perpendicular bisector of Segment AB. From a point on the perpendicular bisector, the distance is the same to each of the endpoints of the segment. The point where the perpendicular bisector intersects the segment is the midpoint of the segment.

CA = 4.397 cm   DA = 3.363 cm   EA = 4.056 cm   FA = 3.066 cm
CB = 4.397 cm   DB = 3.363 cm   EB = 4.056 cm   FB = 3.066 cm

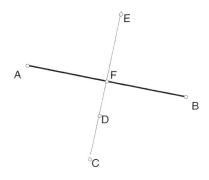

18. Start on a new piece of paper with a line segment from A to B scored. Place a point, C, on the segment, not very near the center. Fold the paper through Point C so that the parts of the line segment on either side of Point C coincide; crease the paper on this fold. How does this construction compare to the construction in Exercise 17? How does it differ?

The crease is perpendicular to the segment, but the point of intersection is not the midpoint of the segment because it was placed away from the center of the segment.

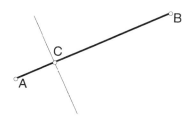

19. Start on a new piece of paper with a line segment from A to B scored. Place a point C somewhere off the line segment. Fold the paper through point C so that the parts of the line segment on either side of point C coincide; crease along the fold. How does this

construction compare to the constructions in Exercises 17 and 18? How does it differ?

The crease is perpendicular to the segment, but the point of intersection is not the midpoint of the segment because it was placed away from the center of the segment.

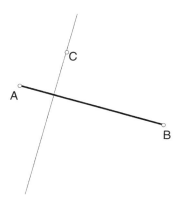

20. Start on a new piece of paper with a line segment from A to B scored. Place two points, C and D, on the segment. Using first C and then D, fold through the point so that the parts of the line segment on either side of the point coincide; crease along the fold. How does each of these two creases meet the line segment from A to B? What conjecture can you make about these two creases?

Each of the creases is perpendicular to the line segment. The two creases are parallel to one another.

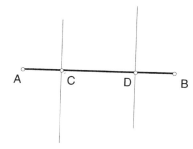

21. On a new piece of paper, score an angle on your paper; label the Vertex B and the Rays *t* and *s*. Fold the paper through Point B so that Rays *t* and *s* coincide; crease the paper along this fold. What construction have you completed? (If you used an acute angle, try this again with an obtuse angle—if you used an obtuse angle first, then try it again with an acute angle and a right angle.)

The crease divides the angle into two equal size angles. It is the angle bisector of the angle whether the angle is acute, right, or obtuse.

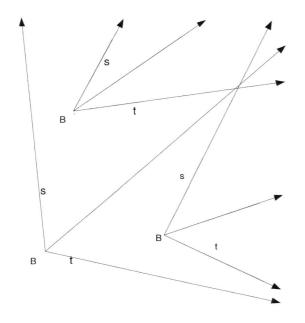

22. Using only a compass and straightedge, construct a triangle and the altitude to one side of the triangle. For which of the paper folding constructions is this an application? (If you wish, you may complete this construction using paper folding or Geometer's Sketchpad® or other dynamic software.)

The altitude of a triangle is an application of constructing a perpendicular to a segment from a point not on the segment.

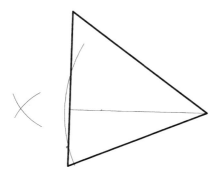

23. All of the figures in this discussion were sketched as if we were viewing them from above (indicated by the segments or curves that are dashed). Sketch each figure as if you were looking at it from below.

Changing only the perspective from which the objects are viewed, the sketches would appear as shown in the figure.

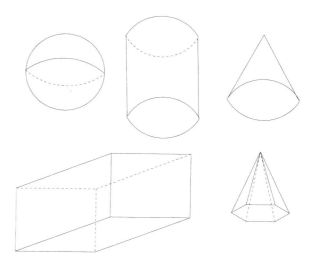

24. Consider the following capital letters of our alphabet:

A B C D E F G H I J K L M N O P Q R S T U V W X Y Z

a) Determine which have reflectional symmetry about a vertical mirror.
b) Determine which have reflectional symmetry about a horizontal mirror.
c) Determine which have rotational symmetry.
d) Do any of the letters have more than one type of symmetry?
e) Do any letters have all three types of symmetry?
f) Do any have no symmetry?

a) A, H, I, M, O, T, U, V, W, X, Y
b) B, C, D, E, H, I, O, X
c) H, I, O, S, X, Z
d) Both vertical and horizontal mirror: H, I, O, X
e) Mirror and rotational: H, I, O, X
f) No symmetry: F, G, J, K, L, P, Q, R

5: MEASUREMENT

1. Make a list of all the measurement words you can think of in 2 minutes. Share your list with classmates.

A few words to get your list started are amplitude, area, bushel, calendar, capacity, centimeter, circumference, cubic, cup, degrees, diameter, digit, dimensions, distance, estimation, fat-free, fathom, foot, furlong, gallon, hand, height, inch, length, light year, linear, liter, meter, mile, millimeter, nautical mile, palm, peck, perimeter, pint, quart, radians, radius, rod, ruler, scale drawing, seriation, span, surveying, tape measure, temperature, tiling, time, volume, weight, width, and yard . . .

2. Make a list of all the dichotomous measurement words you can think of in two minutes. Compare your list with those of your classmates.

A few pairs of words to get your list started are shorter–longer, littler–bigger, smaller–larger, shorter–taller, less–more, few–many, fewer–more, lighter–heavier, shallower–deeper, lower–higher, and narrower–wider . . .

3. Find a subtle example of confusing dichotomous terminology using the terms *larger* and *smaller*.

Consider the books that are usually found in an elementary classroom. Could a "large" book have fewer words than a "small" book?

4. When can the "smallest" be larger than even the "biggest"? When can the "biggest" be smaller than even the "smallest"?

The smallest second-grade student might be just a bit larger than the largest first-grade student, but the biggest child in kindergarten might be a great deal smaller than the smallest child in sixth grade.

5. When you say that a beach ball is "bigger" than a bowling ball, what attributes are you ignoring?

Mass, density, or weight might be ignored.

6. What attributes, other than the number of square yards required, influence the cost of carpeting?

Thickness, height of pile, or weight of material might influence the cost of carpet.

7. Attribute Blocks™ help children learn the terminology and concepts of "differences." The 60-piece set includes squares, rectangles, circles, triangles, and hexagons, in two sizes, three colors, and two thicknesses. List at least 10 different ways by which Attribute Blocks™ could be sorted.

A few sorting criteria to get your list started are color; size; shape; thickness; color and size; color and shape; color and thickness; size and shape; size and thickness; shape and thickness; color, size, and shape . . .

8. Measure the height of your coffee cup using anything except a ruler. Would you want to use a new pencil as your unit?

My coffee mug is approximately as tall as 3.5 times the diameter of a quarter. Few coffee mugs are as tall as a new pencil.

9. Measure the length of a room in paces. (A pace is two steps or about 5 feet. The Romans figured that 1000 paces was a mile.) Would it have made sense to use a new pencil for this measurement?

ANSWERS WILL VARY. It would take too long (and return meaningless data) to measure a room in new pencils.

10. Trace your hand and wrist. How many measurements can you discuss about your tracing? Measure in inches, then in centimeters. Which was easier? What is the finest degree of precision you can reach with your ruler?

ANSWERS WILL VARY.

11. Measure the line segments in Fig. 5.4 to the finest degree of precision available to you in the customary system and the metric system. Measure the distances AB, AC, AD, AE, BC, BD, BE, CD, CE, and DE.

AB $\square \frac{13}{32}$ in $\square$ 1 cm, AC $\square 2\frac{1}{32}$ in $\square$ 5.15 cm,

AD $\square 3\frac{11}{16}$ in $\square$ 9.35 cm

AE $\square 5\frac{3}{8}$ in $\square$ 13.65 cm, BC $\square 1\frac{5}{8}$ in $\square$ 4.1 cm,

BD $\square 3\frac{9}{32}$ in $\square$ 8.3 cm,

BE $\square 4\frac{31}{32}$ in $\square$ 12.6 cm, CD $\square 1\frac{5}{8}$ in $\square$ 4.1 cm,

CE $\square 3\frac{5}{16}$ in $\square$ 8.4 cm,

DE $\square 1\frac{11}{16}$ in $\square$ 4.3 cm

12. What is the total length of a corner shelf that is 5 yd 1 ft 9 in along one wall and 4 yd 2 ft 7 in along the other wall? Be careful as you regroup the measures in your solution.

    5 yds 1 ft 9 in
+ 4 yds 2 ft 7 in
    9 yds 3 ft 16 in or 10 yds 1 ft 4 in

13. What is the total length of a corner shelf that is 5m 10 cm 5 mm along one wall and 4 m 44 cm 5 mm along the other wall?

    5.105 m
+ 4.445 m
    9.550 m or 9 m 55 cm

14. Use a piece of string to measure the distance an ant would walk around the outer edge of the leaf in Fig. 5.5. Compare your string measure to a ruler to find the actual distance.

ANSWERS WILL VARY.

15. Make a set of unit square tiles for measuring area using any unit you like. Find an everyday item with a flat surface and estimate the area of the flat surface by tiling. You may need to use partial tiles. How can you make your estimate as "good" as possible?

ANSWERS WILL VARY.

16. Create a one-foot square using 144 square inch tiles. Create a one-yard square using 9 square foot tiles.

You will need 144 one-inch squares for a one-foot square. You will need 9 one-foot squares for a one-yard square.

17. Find the perimeter of each region in Fig. 5.7 using your string and a centimeter ruler; then find the area of each by counting and estimating the number of squares covered by each.

Rectangle: P = 16 units; A = 15 square units

Parallelogram: P $\square$ 19 units; A = 18 square units

Trapezoid: P $\square$ 14 units; A = 9 square units

Triangle: P $\square$ 11 units; A = 7.5 square units

Circle: C = 6 π $\square$ 18.8 units; A = 9 π $\square$ 28.3 square units

Square: P = 16 units; A = 16 square units

18. At some point, we will put away our string and grid paper and begin to use the concepts of perimeter and area abstractly. From your previous experience with algorithms, identify these common formulas and tell the meaning of each letter and symbol.

a) $A = l \cdot w$ Area equals length times width—Area of a rectangle or square

b) $P = 2l + 2w$ Perimeter equals twice the length plus twice the width—Perimeter of any parallelogram

c) $A = s^2$ Area equals length of side squared—Area of a square

d) $P = 4s$ Perimeter equals four times the length of side—Perimeter of a square

e) $A = \frac{1}{2}b \cdot h$ Area equals one half of the length of the base times the length of the height (altitude)—Area of a triangle

f) $A = \frac{1}{2}h(b_1 + b_2)$ Area equals one half of the height (altitude) times the sum of the lengths of the bases—Area of a trapezoid (Special Note: This formula can be used to find the area of any regular polygon.)

g) P = ns Perimeter equals number of sides times the length of a side—Perimeter of a regular polygon

h) A = $\frac{1}{2}$ans Area equals half of the apothem (a line segment from the center of the polygon perpendicular to a side) times the number of sides times the length of a side—Area of a regular polygon

i) A = πr^2 Area equals πr times the radius squared—Area of a circle

j) C = $2\pi r$ Circumference equals two times π times the radius—Circumference (perimeter) of a circle

19. Use the appropriate algorithms in Exercise 18 to check your measures and estimates in Exercise 17.

See answers for Exercise 17.

20. Which algorithms in Exercise 18 were not helpful in completing Exercise 17?

There were no figures in Exercise 17 that required the algorithms (g) and (h).

21. Why is there no algorithm in Exercise 18 for finding the perimeter of the trapezoid or the triangle? Do you think perimeter algorithms are needed?

ANSWERS WILL VARY. All that is needed for perimeter is to add the measures for all sides of the figure. Perhaps a generic formula for perimeter is P = da (distance around).

22. Use the formula, A = $\frac{1}{2}$ans, to find the area of a region defined by a regular octagon with sides of length 4 cm and an apothem of length 4.828 cm.

A = $\frac{1}{2}$ · 4.828 · 8 · 2

A = 77.248 square centimeters

23. Build a cube using 27 unit cubes. Use any unit cube, even a sugar cube.

a) What are the linear measurements associated with this cube?

The cube will be three units in height, width, and depth.

b) What are the area measurements associated with this cube?

The area of each face will be 9 square units. Because there are six faces, the total surface area will be 54 square units.

24. Use 24 cubes to answer the following:

a) How many different rectangular prisms can you form using the 24 unit cubes?

1 × 1 × 24; 1 × 2 × 12; 1 × 3 × 8; 1 × 4 × 6; 2 × 2 × 6; 2 × 3 × 4

b) Do all of the prisms have the same volume?
All have the same volume, 24 cubic units.

c) Use your prisms to justify the volume formula, V = lwh, for rectangular prisms.
Each of the products in Part 1 is 24.

d) Add the areas of the six faces to determine the total surface area for each of your prisms. Do they all have the same surface area?

The sum of the areas of the faces of the 1 × 1 × 24 is 24 + 24 + 24 + 24 + 1 + 1 = 98 square units. The sum of the areas of the faces of the 1 × 2 × 12 is 12 + 12 + 24 + 24 + 2 + 2 = 76 square units. This is sufficient to say that the prisms do not all have the same surface area.

25. Consider a solid cube that is 6 unit cubes in height, width, and depth. If you paint the six faces of this large cube, each unit cube may have zero, one, two, or three painted faces, depending on its location in the cube.

a) How many of the unit cubes will have paint on at least one face?

152 unit cubes will have paint on at least one face.

b) How many of the unit cubes will have only one face painted?

96 will have one face painted.

c) How many of the unit cubes will have two faces painted?

48 will have two faces painted.

d) How many of the unit cubes will have three faces painted?

8 will have three faces painted.

e) How many of the unit cubes will have 4, 5, or 6 faces painted?

None will have 4, 5, or 6 faces painted.

f) How many of the unit cubes will have no faces painted?

64 will have no faces painted.

26. The formula for the volume of a right circular cylinder is $V = \pi r^2 h$, or the area of the circular top face times the height. Use the information in Fig. 5.20 to find the volume of the cylinder.

$V = \pi \cdot 5^2 \cdot 18$

$V = 450\pi \;\square\; 1313$ cubic centimeters

27. The formula for the volume of a right circular cone is $V = \dfrac{1}{3}\pi r^2 h$. Use the information in Fig. 5.21 to find the volume of the cone.

$V = \dfrac{1}{3} \cdot \pi \cdot 7^2 \cdot 9.5$

$V = 155.1\overline{6}\pi \;\square\; 487.2$ cubic centimeters

28. How do the volume formulas in Exercises 26 and 27 compare?

If a cylinder and a cone have identical bases and heights, then the cylinder will have three times the volume of the cone.

29. To find the volume of a regular right polygonal prism, find the area of the top face and multiply by the height. For this exercise, use the formula $V = \dfrac{1}{2}asnh$ to find the volume of the right hexagonal prism in Fig. 5.22.

$V = \dfrac{1}{2} \cdot 4.3 \cdot 5 \cdot 6 \cdot 24$

$V = 1548$ cubic units

30. The volume of a pyramid also depends on the number of edges on the base. Use $V = \dfrac{1}{3}s^2h$ and the information in Fig. 5.23 to find the volume of the right square pyramid.

$V = \dfrac{1}{3} \cdot 9 \cdot 18.2$

$V = 54.6$ cubic centimeters

31. Name everyday items that you could use to approximate each of the following: 1 gm, 1 kg, 1 oz, 1 lb, 1 T

ANSWERS WILL VARY. Examples: paperclip, two pounds of coffee, a McDonald toy, box of powdered sugar, half a car

32. What is the sum of 8 T 1700 lb 13 oz and 5 T 980 lb 6 oz?

8 Tons	1700 pounds	13 ounces
+ 5 Tons	980 pounds	6 ounces
13 Tons	~~2680 pounds~~	~~19 ounces~~
	~~1 Ton~~ 680 pounds	~~1 pound~~ 3 ounces
14 Tons	681 pounds	3 ounces

33. Explain why you would know that a clock with one hand pointed directly at the 9 and the other hand pointed directly at the 3 was broken.

The tip of the shorter "hour" hand moves slowly from one number to the next in one hour, whereas the tip of the longer "minute" moves all the way around the clock face in one hour. If it is 9:15, then the tip of the shorter hand should be one fourth of the way from the 9 to the 10. If it is 15 minutes until 3, the tip of the shorter hand should be three quarters of the way from the 2 to the 3.

34. What other measure uses base 60? Is there a connection between these two measures?

Angles are measured in degrees, minutes, and seconds. There are 60 seconds in a minute, 60 minutes in a degree, and 360 degrees in a revolution. The measures used for time and rotations both stem from earth measures.

35. Use denominate numbers to determine how much time elapses between 9:24:13 AM and 1:15:08 PM? (Don't forget that, on the 24-hour clock, you can use 13:00 for 1:00 PM.)

```
   12      74
        14        68
  13 hours  15 minutes   8 seconds
 − 9 hours  24 minutes  13 seconds
  ─────────────────────────────────
   3 hours  50 minutes  55 seconds
```

36. List as many different ways as you can think of to use U.S. coins to make a dollar.

A few of the combinations are 100 pennies; 95 pennies and 1 nickel; 90 pennies and two nickels; 90 pennies and one dime; 85 pennies and three nickels; 85 pennies, one dime and one nickel; . . .

37. How much change should you receive if you have a $10 bill and the amount you must pay is $4.15? How many different ways might you receive the change? (Please re-

$$\frac{30\ mi}{1\ hr}\left|\frac{5280\ ft}{1\ mi}\right|\frac{1\ hr}{60\ min}\left|\frac{1\ min}{60\ sec}\right.$$

$$=\frac{158400\ ft}{3600\ sec}=\frac{44\ ft}{1\ sec}$$

member that 585 pennies might not be reasonable, but is possible.)

One way is 1 $5 bill, 1 half dollar, 1 quarter, 1 dime, and 1 nickel

38. Using Fig. 5.25, find the boiling point and the freezing point of water at sea level in degrees Fahrenheit and degrees Celsius.

212°F, 100°C is the boiling point of water; 32°F, 0°C is the melting point of ice;

39. Using Fig. 5.25, determine the comfort range for humans in degrees Fahrenheit and degrees Celsius.

Answers will vary around 72°F, 20°C

40. How many degrees are in one full rotation?

360°

41. Do the lengths of the legs of an angle have any meaning in degree measure?

No. The degree measure of an angle is a measure of rotation.

42. Is there a special name for an angle of 180°?

Straight angle

43. Identify each named angle in Fig. 5.27 as "less than," "exactly," or "greater than" 90°, then measure the angles using a protractor.

Angles HGI and ABC are acute

m∠HGI = 52°

m∠ABC = 35°

Angle KJL is a right angle

m∠KJL = 90°

Angles EDF and NMO are obtuse

m∠EDF = 107°

m∠NMO = 124°

44. Given that Angle 1 measures 48°, Angle 10 measures 90°, Angle 20 measures 115°, and Line m is parallel to Line n, use your knowledge of perpendicular lines, parallel lines, supplementary angles, complementary angles, and triangles to determine the measure of each angle in Fig. 5.30.

m∠1 = 48°; m∠2 = 42°; m∠4 = 48°; m∠5 = 42°; m∠3 = 90°; m∠6 = 90°; m∠7 = 90°; m∠8 = 90°; m∠9 = 90°; m∠10 = 90°; m∠11 = 42°; m∠20 = 115°; m∠18 = 115°; m∠17 = 65°; m∠19 = 65°; m∠13 = 65°; m∠14 = 42°; m∠16 = 65°; m∠12 = 73°; m∠15 = 73°

45. Find and confirm five or six more Pythagorean Triples.

5, 12, 13; 7, 24, 25; 5n, 12n, 13n; 7n, 24n, 25n; 3n; 4n; 5n

46. How are the two formats demonstrated the same? How do they differ?

They are the same because both involve multiplying and simplifying fractions. They are different because the first explicitly shows the multiplication and the second implies it.

47. How did the units go from feet per sec-

$$\frac{14\ \text{ft}}{0.2\ \text{sec}} \bigg| \frac{1\ \text{mi}}{5280\ \text{ft}} \bigg| \frac{60\ \text{sec}}{1\ \text{min}} \bigg| \frac{60\ \text{min}}{1\text{hr}}$$

$$= \frac{50400\ \text{mi}}{1056\ \text{hr}} = \frac{47.7\ \text{mi}}{1\ \text{hr}}$$

ond in the first column to miles per hour in the last column?

The units changed because the fractions were simplified:
The ft in the numerator of the first fraction was divided out by the ft in the denominator of the second fraction; the sec in the numerator of the third fraction was divided out by the sec in the denominator of the first fraction; the min in the numerator of the fourth fraction was divided out by the min in the denominator of the third fraction. This simplification process left only mi in the numerator and hr in the denominator.

48. If it is reported that a matchbox car had an average speed of 30 mph, how many feet did it travel in 1 second?

6: DATA ANALYSIS AND PROBABILITY

Data Collection and Representations

1. Gather three types of data about your classmates, for example: How many of your classmates are wearing glasses? How many of your classmates are wearing shoes?

Answers will vary. Example: 15 people wore glasses and 15 did not; 20 are women and 10 are men; 30 people wore shoes.

2. Gather three types of data about the room or building in which you are taking this class, for example: How many desks/tables are in the room? How many ceiling tiles are there?

Answers will vary. Example: 30 desks; 3 white boards; 8 banks of fluorescent lights.

3. Gather three types of data about the environment in which you currently live (dorm, house, apartment, etc.), for example: How many books? How many chairs?

Answers will vary. Example: 3 cats; 9 chairs; 1 TV.

4. Using proportional reasoning, what percentage of the people in your class: wear glasses; are male; wear shoes; have cats; have dogs; have 3 keys?

Answers will vary. Example:

5. Construct circle graphs to represent the data you collected about eyeglasses, shoes,

Category	Observations	Percentage
Glasses: Yes	15	50%
Gender: Male	10	33.33%
Shoes: Yes	30	100%
Pets: Cat	12	40%
Pets: Dog	9	30%
Keys: 3	8	26.67%

and pets.

Answers will vary. Example:

50%
Wear Glasses

100%
Wear Shoes

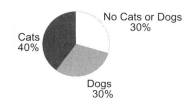

No Cats or Dogs
30%

Cats
40%

Dogs
30%

6. Construct a line graph to represent the number of keys each person in the class reported.

Answers will vary. Example:

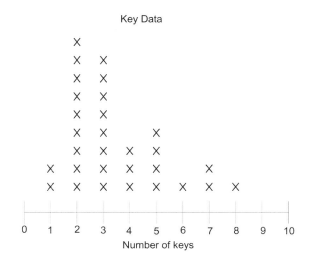

7. Construct a bar graph to represent the number of keys each person in the class reported.

Answers will vary. Example:

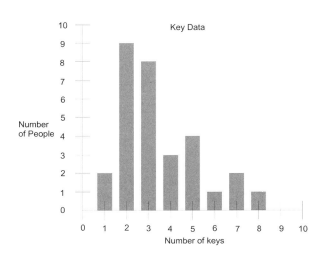

8. Construct a line graph from the data you collected about how many keys your classmates had with them.

Answers will vary. Example:

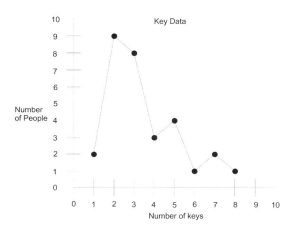

9. Construct a horizontal histogram for the data you collected about eyeglasses, gender, shoes, and pets.

Answers will vary. Example:

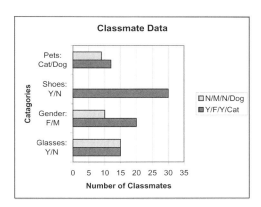

10. Construct a frequency polygon for the data you collected about eyeglasses, gender, shoes, and pets.

Answers will vary. Example:

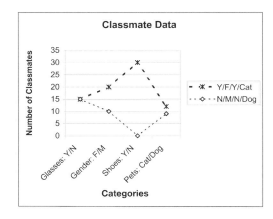

11. Construct a table for your key data with equal classes and tabulate the frequency of each.

Answers will vary. Example:

Key Data

Class	Frequency
1-3	19
4-6	8
7-9	3

From the table construct a frequency polygon for the key data.

Answers will vary. Example:
Re-poll your classmates and keep track of the model year of each person's car along with how many keys they each have. Place the data into an appropriate table and do the exercises that follow.

12. Construct a scatter plot for your data using car year versus keys.

Answers will vary. Example:

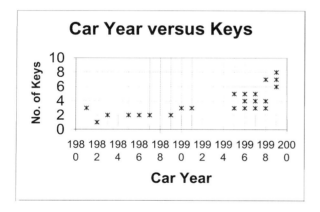

13. What, if any, relation do you see between the model years of your classmates' cars and the number of keys they had?

Answers will vary. The most likely response is, "No relation is seen between my classmates cars and the number of keys."

14. How would a scatter plot look if there were a positive relation between the model

years of your classmates' cars and the number of keys they had?

A scatter plot with a perfect positive relation would show that for each new model year, they would gain another key, with all classmates with the same age of car having exactly the same number of keys. The older their cars, the fewer keys they had.

15. How would a scatter plot look if there were a negative relation between the model years of your classmates' cars and the number of keys they had?

A scatter plot that showed a negative relation between the ages of my classmate's cars and their number of keys would have points that started in the top left of the plot with points gradually shifting down and to the right. The newer their cars, the fewer keys they had.

Data Analysis and Statistics

1. Find the mean, median, mode, and range of the key data you collected from your classmates.

Answers will vary. See data in the Line Plot section

Mean = 3.467
Median = 3
Mode = 2
Range = 7

2. Find the mean, median, mode, and range of the rainbow centimeter cube data.

Answers will vary. See data in Table 6.5

Mean = 30
Median = 28.5
Mode = 25 and 40
Range = 22

Use the first 10 key data points reported by your classmates to answer the following:

3. Find the variance of the sample using both formulas. Calculate each by hand and then verify your results using a software application.

Answers will vary. An example follows:

First 10 data points from key data:

1	3	5	7	1
2	2	2	3	3

Keys	$x_i - \bar{x}$	$(x_i - \bar{x})^2$	x_i^2
1	-1.9	3.61	1
3	0.1	0.01	9
5	2.1	4.41	25
7	4.1	16.81	49
1	-1.9	3.61	1
2	-0.9	0.81	4
2	-0.9	0.81	4
2	-0.9	0.81	4
3	0.1	0.01	9
3	0.1	0.01	9
Sum = 29	0	30.9	115
Mean = 2.9	Variance =	3.09	

$$s^2 = \frac{\sum_{i=1}^{n} x_i^2 - n\bar{x}^2}{n} = \frac{115 - 10 \cdot 2.9^2}{10}$$

$$= \frac{115 - 84.1}{10} = \frac{30.9}{10} = 3.09$$

4. Find the standard deviation for this sample of your data.

Answers will vary. An example follows:

$$s = \sqrt{s^2} = \sqrt{3.09} = 176$$

5. Look back at your full data set for the key data. Are there any outliers based on the standard deviation of the sample?

Answers will vary. An example follows:

Mean = 2.9; s = 1.76; ±2s = [−0.62, 6.42]

Yes, 7 keys would be considered an outlier, as it is greater than 2 standard deviations away from the mean.

6. Does this sample accurately represent the whole class? Why or why not?

Answers will vary.
No, the mean for the whole sample was 3.47 keys per person, whereas the mean for the sample was only 2.9 keys per person. There would have been less than 95% (only 27 keys or 90% of the keys) of the whole data set within (2s of the mean (2.9 keys).

Use your key data for the following problems:

7. Find the first, second, and third quartiles.

Answers will vary. An example is: $Q_1 = 2$; $Q_2 = 3$; $Q_3 = 5$.

8. Find the IQR.

Answers will vary. An example is:
$Q_3 - Q_1 = 5 - 2 = 3$.

9. Create a box and whisker plot.

Answers will vary. An example is:

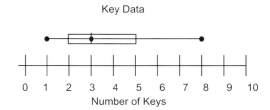

Key Data

Number of Keys

10. Determine the expected range using the IQR and identify any outliers.

Answers will vary.
An example is:
$Q_1 - 1.5(IQR) = 3 - 1.5(3) = 3 - 4.5 = -1.5$
$Q_3 + 1.5(IQR) = 5 + 1.5(3) = 5 + 4.5 = 9.5$
The expected range is [−1.5, 9.5]
There are no outliers present.

Counting and Probability

1. $3! = 6$ 2. $8! = 40320$ 3. $0! = 1$
4. $\dfrac{12!}{6!} = 665280$ 5. $\dfrac{7!}{5!} = 42$ 6. $\dfrac{11!}{4!} = 1663200$
7. $\dfrac{9!}{3!6!} = 84$ 8. $\dfrac{13!}{7!5!} = 10296$ 9. $\dfrac{15!}{9!11!} = \dfrac{13}{144}$

10. Suppose the rainbow colors could come in any order. How many different patterns of colors of the rainbow (ROYGBIV) could there be?

　　a) Permutation: $P(n, n) = n!$
　　b) The question wants to know how many different patterns or arrangements of the rainbow colors there are. Order is important.
　　c) $P(7, 7) = 7! = 5040$

11. A certain guitar has 12 strings. How many different orders can a guitarist pluck any 5 strings on this guitar?

　　a) Permutation: $P(n, r) = \dfrac{n!}{(n - r)!}$
　　b) Looking for different orders of strings to be plucked. Order is important.
　　c) $P(12, 5) = \dfrac{12!}{(12 - 5)!} = \dfrac{12!}{7!} = 95040$

12. How many different pairs of colors can be made using colors of the rainbow (ROYGBIV)? (We understand that you would not wear or be seen in some of these combinations, but we do want you to consider and count them all.)

　　a) Combination: $C(n, r) = \dfrac{n!}{r!(n - r)!}$
　　b) Looking for different pairs of colors. Order is not important.
　　c) $C(7, 2) = \dfrac{7!}{2!(7 - 2)!} = \dfrac{7!}{2!\,5!} = \dfrac{7 \cdot 6 \cdot 5!}{2!\,5!}$
　　$= \dfrac{7 \cdot 6}{2!} = \dfrac{7 \cdot 6}{2} = \dfrac{7 \cdot 3}{1} = 7 \cdot 3 = 21$

13. What is the cardinality of the sample space for each of the following?

　　a) an experiment tossing 5 coins　$2^5 = 32$
　　b) an experiment rolling 3 dice　$6^3 = 216$

14. What is the probability of obtaining the following outcomes from the experiments in Exercise 13?

　　a) HHTHT　$P(HHTHT) = 0.5^5 = 0.03125 = \dfrac{1}{32}$
　　b) 352　$P(352) = \dfrac{1}{6} \times \dfrac{1}{6} \times \dfrac{1}{6} = \dfrac{1}{216} = 0.0046$

15. There are R = 3 marbles, O = 4 marbles, Y = 4 marbles, G = 2 marbles, B = 1, I = 3 marbles, and V = 3 marbles in a bag. What is the probability of drawing BORG from the given bag of rainbow marbles when there is replacement?

$$P(BORG) = \dfrac{1}{20} \times \dfrac{1}{5} \times \dfrac{3}{20} \times \dfrac{1}{10} = \dfrac{3}{20000} = 0.00015$$

16. What is the probability of drawing BORG from the given bag of rainbow marbles when there is no replacement? There are R = 3 marbles, O = 4 marbles, Y = 4 marbles, G = 2 marbles, B = 1, I = 3 marbles, and V = 3 marbles in the bag.

$$P(BORG) = \dfrac{1}{20} \times \dfrac{4}{1} \times \dfrac{1}{6} \times \dfrac{2}{17} - \dfrac{1}{4845} = 0.000206$$

17. What is the probability of drawing an AD through 10D, any J, or a 3S from a fair standard deck of 52 playing cards when there is no replacement and five cards are drawn? Consider that each draw was a success.

$P_1(AD - 10D, \text{ any } J, 3S)$
$= \dfrac{15}{25}$, $P_2(AD - 10D, \text{ any } J, 3S) = \dfrac{14}{51}$,

$P_3(AD - 10D, \text{ any } J, 3S) = \dfrac{13}{50}$

$P(AD - 10D, \text{ any } J, 3S)$
$= \dfrac{15}{52} \times \dfrac{14}{51} \times \dfrac{13}{50} = \dfrac{2730}{132600} = \dfrac{7}{340} \approx 0.021$

18. What is the probability of drawing a 10H card, given that a red card was drawn?

$P(10H|red) = 1{:}26$

19. What is the probability of rolling a 2 on either of two dice, given that the sum of the dice is 7?

P(2|sum = 7) = 2:6 or 1:3

20. What is the probability of drawing a red K card, given that a black card was drawn?

P(red K |black) = 0:26 or 0

21. Drawing a black card from a fair standard deck of 52 playing cards?

a) m = 26; m′ = 26; 26:26 = 1:1 (we call 1:1 even odds)
b) m′ = 26; m = 26; 26:26 = 1:1
c) m = 26; n = 52; P(m) = 26:52 = 1:2
d) m′ = 26; n = 52; P(m′) = 26:52 = 1:2

22. Flipping two coins and obtaining HT?

a) m = 1; m′ = 3; 1:3
b) m′ = 3; m = 1; 3:1
c) m = 1; n = 4; P(m) = 1:4
d) m′ = 3; n = 4; P(m′) = 3:4

23. Drawing BORG from the given bag of marbles when there is replacement?

There are R = 3 marbles, O = 4 marbles, Y = 4 marbles, G = 2 marbles, B = 1, I = 3 marbles, and V = 3 marbles in the bag.

a) m = 3; m′ = 19997; 3:19997 (use the answer from 14. C. and m′ = n − m)
b) m′ = 19997; m = 3; 19997:3 (use the answer from 14. C. and m′ = n − m)
c) P(m) = 3:20000 (we knew this from Exercise 14. C.)
d) m′ = 19997; n = 20000; P(m′) = 19997:20000 (use the answer from Exercise 14. C. and m′ = n − m)

7: PROBLEM SOLVING

Riddle Me This

#1: List the numbers 1 through 20:

1, 2, 3, 4, 5, 6, 7, 8, 9, 10, 11, 12, 13, 14, 15, 16, 17, 18, 19, 20

Cross out one (remember one is not prime) and all the prime numbers

~~1~~, ~~2~~, ~~3~~, 4, ~~5~~, 6, ~~7~~, 8, 9, 10, ~~11~~, 12, ~~13~~, 14, 15, 16, ~~17~~, 18, ~~19~~, 20

Cross out all the numbers that can't easily be written as a power of another number

4, 6, 8, 9, ~~10~~, ~~12~~, ~~14~~, ~~15~~, 16, ~~18~~, ~~20~~

Show the remaining numbers using exponents

$4 = 2^2$ $8 = 2^3$ $9 = 3^2$ $16 = 4^2$

We eliminate 4 because the power (2) is equal to the base (2)

We see that $2^3 \neq 3^2$, eliminating both 8 and 9

We know that $4^2 = 16$, we test $2^4 = 2 \times 2 \times 2 \times 2 = 16$, so the solution to the riddle is 16. $16 = 4^2 = 2^4$

#2: Make a list with one column for the number of teams, one for the number of games, and one for the number of winners. It was single elimination with no ties allowed, so only the winning team of any contest gets to move on:

Number of Teams	Number of Games	Number of Winners
128	64	64
64	32	32
32	16	16
16	8	8
8	4	4
4	2	2
2	1	1
Total	127	

If 128 teams played in a single elimination tournament, then a total of 127 games would be played. Another way of looking at it would be to say that, if the tournament is single elimination, then all teams except the champion lost, so out of all 128 teams, 127 lost. A loss occurs each time a game is played. Thus, 127 games were played.

#3: **Original question**—If the length of the Loch Ness monster is 20 meters long plus half of its own length, how long is Nessie?

Rewrite and translate—How long is Nessie if the length is 20 meters plus half of its own length?

How long is Nessie

L = Nessie's length

if the length is 20 meters plus half its own length?

$$L = 20 \text{ meters} + \frac{L}{2}$$

$L = 20 \text{ m} + \frac{L}{2}$, combine like terms by subtracting $\frac{L}{2}$ from both sides of the equation, then

$\frac{L}{2} = 20 \text{ m}$, multiply both sides of the equation by 2, then

L = 40 m

Nessie the Lock Ness monster is 40 meters long if the length of the Loch Ness monster is 20 meters long plus half of its own length.

#4: 642 digits were written

642 − 9 = 633	(first 9 pages took nine digits)
633 − 180 = 453	(the next 90 pages used 2 digits each)
$\frac{453}{3} = 151$	(each new page will have 3 digits each)

9 pages + 90 pages + 151 pages = 250 pages

#5: **Using reasoning**: If every dollar weighs a gram, then $1,000,000 weighs 1,000,000 grams. There are 1000 grams in a kilogram, thus there are 1000 kilograms in 1,000,000 grams. You can either recall or look up that one kilogram is about 2.2 pounds. Then 1000 kilograms is approximately equivalent to 2200 pounds or about one ton. You should advise the producer that no ordinary person would be able to pick up $1,000,000 in $1 bills because they would weigh about one ton!

Collection of problems:

1. Take an ordinary sheet of paper and fold it in half. Fold it in half a second time. Fold it in half a third time. If you could continue folding it in half 50 times, how high would the stack of paper be?

0.375 in. ≈ 87 pages then 1 page ≈ 0.00431 in.

$2^{50} = 1.126 \times 10^{15}$

$0.00431(1.126 \times 10^{15}) = 5.43186 \times 10^{12}$ in. or 85,730,114 miles

2. A farmer had 26 cows. All but 9 died. How many lived?

17 cows died and 9 cows lived

3. A uniform log can be cut into three pieces in 12 seconds. Assuming the same rate of cutting, how long will it take for a similar log to be cut into four pieces?

2 cuts divide the log into 3 pieces; then 3 cuts divide the log into four pieces

2 cuts take 12 seconds; then 3 cuts will take 18 seconds. Another way of looking at this is to make one cut parallel to the long sides of the log and then a second cut perpendicular to it. That will give 4 pieces. Granted, the length of the log could be such that the time required would differ, but you have to admit that this is a pretty creative solution, and it was proposed by a third grader.

4. How many different ways can you add four odd counting numbers to get a sum of 10?

{1, 1, 1, 7}, {3, 3, 3, 1}, and {1, 1, 3, 5} are the sets of four odd counting numbers that total 20.

{1, 1, 1, 7}—1 + 1 + 1 + 7, 1 + 1 + 7 + 1, 1 + 7 + 1 + 1, 7 + 1 + 1 + 1

{3, 3, 3, 1}—3 + 3 + 3 + 1, 3 + 3 + 1 + 3, 3 + 1 + 3 + 3, 1 + 3 + 3 + 3

{1, 1, 3, 5}—1 + 1 + 3 + 5, 1 + 3 + 1 + 5, 3 + 1 + 1 + 5, 1 + 1 + 5 + 3, 1 + 5 + 1 + 3, 5 + 1 + 1 + 3, 5 + 3 + 1 + 1, 5 + 1 + 3 + 1, 1 + 5 + 3 + 1, 3 + 1 + 5 + 1, 3 + 5 + 1 + 1, 1 + 3 + 5 + 1

5. What is the sum of the first 100 consecutive counting numbers?

100 + 1 = 101; 99 + 2 = 101; 98 + 3 = 101; etc. down to 50 + 51 = 101

50 × 101 = 5050 OR

$$\begin{array}{r} 1 + 2 + 3 + \ldots + 98 + 99 + 100 \\ \underline{100 + 99 + 98 + \ldots + 3 + 2 + 1} \\ 101 + 101 + 101 + \ldots + 101 + 101 + 101 \end{array}$$

This gives 100 pairs of addends, each with a sum of 101, for a total of 10100. That is twice as much as needed, because each number is used twice. Divide by two, getting 5050.

6. How many cubic inches of dirt are there in a hole that is 1 foot deep, 2 feet wide, and 6 feet long?

The hole is 12 in × 24 in × 72 in; there are 0 cubic inches of dirt in it or it wouldn't be a hole.

7. How many squares are there in a 5 by 5 square grid?

1—5 × 5 square; 4—4 × 4 squares; 9—3 × 3 squares; 16—2 × 2 squares; 25—1 × 1 squares

1 + 4 + 9 + 16 + 25 = 55

8. A little green frog is sitting at the bottom of the stairs. She wants to get to the 10th step, so she leaps up 2 steps and then slides back 1. How many leaps will she have to take if she follows this pattern until she reaches the 10th step?

9 leaps. Ground **to 2** to 1 **to 3** to 2 **to 4** to 3 **to 5** to 4 **to 6** to 5 **to 7** to 6 **to 8** to 7 **to 9** to 8 **to 10**. The **bold** indicates leaps up.

9. If there are 7 months that have 31 days in them and 11 months that have 30 days in them, then how many months have 28 days in them?

All of the months have 28 days.

10. There are exactly 11 people in a room and each person shakes hands with every other person in the room. When A shakes with B, B is also shaking with A; that counts as ONE handshake. How many handshakes will there be when everyone is finished?

A B C D E F G H I J K people in the room
AB AC AD AE AF AG AH AI AJ AK
BC BD BE BF BG BH BI BJ BK
CD CE CF CG CH CI CJ CK
DE DF DG DH DI DJ DK
EF EG EH EI EJ EK
FG FH FI FJ FK
GH GI GJ GK
HI HJ HK
IJ IK
JK
10 + 9 + 8 + 7 + 6 + 5 + 4 + 3 + 2 + 1 = 55

11. TTTTTTT9 What number does this represent?

sevenT-nine

12. There are 9 stalls in a barn. Each stall fits only 1 horse. If there are 10 horses and only 9 stalls, how can all the horses fit into the 9 stalls without placing more than one horse in each stall?

NINESTALLS = 10 letters; one on each stall for each horse

13. You are given 5 beans and 4 bowls. Place an odd number of beans in each bowl. Use all beans.

Visualize 4 bowls arranged from smallest to largest and stack the bowls one inside the other. You could place all 5 beans in the smallest bowl and be done. There are other solutions.

14. You are to take a pill every half hour. You have 18 pills to take. How long will you be taking pills?

3 are taken the first hour, then 2 each hour after—8.5 hours

15. If you got a 40% discount on a $150.00 pair of sport shoes and 20% off a

$200 set of roller blades, what was the percent discount on the total purchase (assuming no taxes are involved)?

$$\frac{100}{350} = 28.57\%$$

16. Where should the Z be placed and why?

```
A        E F  H I   K L M N            T   V W X Y
  B C D      G    J          O P Q R S  U
```

Z goes in the top because it doesn't have any curved parts.

17. Estimate how old will you be in years if you live 1,000,000 hours?

$$\frac{1000000}{(24)(365.25)} \approx 114.39 \text{ years}$$

18. A child has $3.15 in U.S. coins, but only has dimes and quarters. There are more quarters than dimes. How many of each coin does the child have?

$3.15 − $0.10 = $3.05

$3.05 − $0.10 = $2.95

$2.95 − $0.10 = $2.85

$2.85 − $0.10 = $2.75 −−$2.75 is a multiple of 25 so 11 quarters and 4 dimes is a solution. Continuing this thinking, $2.25 is the next possible answer for quarters but that is 9 quarters and that demands 9 dimes.

19. There are three children in a family. The oldest is 15. The average of their ages is 11. The median age is 10. How old is the youngest child?

8, 10, and 15 are the ages. You are given 2 of the ages. One of them is directly shown as 15. Median, because there are 3 kids, must be the middle age. So, 10 + 15 + n must equal 33, if the average is 11. 33 − (10 + 15) = 8.

20. A famous mathematician was born on March 14, which could be written 3.14. This date is the start of a representation for pi. It is interesting that this mathematician was born on "pi day." Give his name.

Albert Einstein

8: REASONING AND PROOF

1. Using p, q, r, and the truth table in Table 8.3, determine if the associative property is true for conjunctions. In other words does the following statement hold: $p \wedge (q \wedge r) = (p \wedge q) \wedge r$. (Hint: You will need columns for both $q \wedge r$ and $p \wedge q$.)

The associative property holds for "and" statements.

p	q	r	q∧r	p∧q	p∧(q∧r)	(p∧q)∧r
T	T	T	T	T	T	T
T	T	F	F	T	F	F
T	F	T	F	F	F	F
T	F	F	F	F	F	F
F	T	T	T	F	F	F
F	T	F	F	F	F	F
F	F	T	F	F	F	F
F	F	F	F	F	F	F

2. Using what you have learned about probability, what is the probability of getting:

a) a true "and" statement (p∧q) with two variables?
b) a true "and" statement with three variables?
c) a false "and" statement with two variables?
d) a false "and" statement with three variables?

a) P(p∧q = T) = 1:4 or 0.25 or 25%
b) P(p∧(q∧r) = T) = 1:8 or 0.125 or 12.5%
c) P(p∧q = F) = 3:4 or 0.75 or 75%
d) P(p∧(q∧r) = F) = 7:8 or 0.875 or 87.5%

3. Experiment with the different types of logical expressions that have been discussed. Find at least two different tautologies that have not already been discussed. Make a truth table for each to prove it is a tautology.

Answers will vary.
Informally prove or disprove the following statements:

4. The operation of addition is closed on the set of whole numbers.

Answers will vary. 1 + 1 = 2; 1 + 2 =3; 1 + 3 =4; . . .

5. The operation of addition is closed on the set of digits.

Answers will vary.

Suppose the operation of addition is closed on the set of digits. Arbitrarily choose 5 and 6 as addends. But, we know that 5 + 6 = 11, which is not a digit, a contradiction. Thus, the operation of addition is not closed on the set of digits. QED

6. Make up a 5 by 5 addition table like the one show in Fig. 8.2 (be sure the addends are hidden) and give it to someone who is not in this class to do, following the directions given for Fig. 8.2. Record their reaction to the trick.

Answers will vary.

9: COMMUNICATION

1. Write a paragraph explaining how you would add 842 + 136. Put the paragraph aside and don't look at it for 24 hours. Is your paragraph organized and coherent? Does it concisely explain what you did and why you did it?

Answers will vary.

2. Exchange paragraphs with a classmate. Do you understand that person's explanation? Ask questions that might help the person clarify their explanation.

Answers will vary.

3. Compare the two paragraphs, identifying the strong points of each. Reason together logically about disputed points.

Answers will vary.

4. Using the strong points of each, collaborate to write a paragraph that is better than either of you wrote alone. Ask someone who is not in your class to use the paragraph to complete the addition problem.

Answers will vary.